WHY TRUMAN DROPPED THE ATOMIC BOMB ON JAPAN

WHY TRUMAN DROPPED THE ATOMIC BOMB ON JAPAN

CODE-NAME DOWNFALL: THE SECRET PLAN TO INVADE JAPAN

With a New Afterword by the Authors on
"THE PLAN TO POISON JAPAN"

BY

THOMAS B. ALLEN & NORMAN POLMAR

Ross & Perry, Inc.
Washington, D.C.

Ross & Perry, Inc. Publishers
216 G Street, N.E.
Washington, D.C. 20002
Telephone (202) 675-8300
Facsimile (202) 675-8400
info@RossPerry.com
http://www.RossPerry.com

Library of Congress Control Number: 2001096253
ISBN 1-931839-38-7

Image on cover provided by www.nv.doe.gov

⊗ The paper used in this publication meets the requirements for permanence established by
the American National Standard for Information Sciences "Permanence of Paper for Printed
Library Materials" (ANSI Z39.48-1984).

**Originally Published by Simon & Schuster as Code-Name Downfall: The Secret Plan to
Invade Japan—and Why Truman Dropped the Bomb.**

Original Library of Congress Cataloging-in-Publication Data

Allen, Thomas B.
    Code Name downfall: The Secret Plan to Invade Japan and Why Truman dropped the
Bomb / Thomas B. Allen and Norman Polmar.

    P. CM.
    Includes Bibliographical References and Index.
    1. World War, 1939–1945—United States. 2. World War, 1939–1945—Japan.
3. Strategy. 4. Atomic Bomb. I. Polmar, Norman. II. Title.

D769.2.A48   1995
940.54'4973—DC20   95-10418

ALSO BY THOMAS B. ALLEN AND NORMAN POLMAR

CNN: War in the Gulf

World War II: America at War 1941–1945

Merchants of Treason

Rickover: Controversy and Genius

Ship of Gold *(a novel)*

Dedicated to the
memory of

ROGER PINEAU and
JOHN A. WAMSLEY,

naval officers,
intelligence specialists,
historians, and friends

CONTENTS

PROLOGUE

THE MEN FROM SHANGRI-LA

A U.S. Army B-25B bomber taking off
from the carrier *Hornet* in April 1942
for the first aerial attack against
Japanese cities in the Pacific War.

The United States was plunged into despair on Sunday, December 7, 1941, when Japanese carrier-based aircraft struck the U.S. Pacific Fleet at anchor in Pearl Harbor. Within minutes seven battleships were sunk or heavily damaged, 188 Army and Navy aircraft were destroyed or damaged, and 2,403 Americans were dead. The Japanese attack force escaped unscathed except for the loss of 30 carrier planes and five two-man midget submarines.

Hours later the U.S. Army aircraft in the Philippines were virtually wiped out in another surprise attack that caught the planes on the ground. Japanese troop landings in the Philippines, then an American commonwealth, followed rapidly. Soon the American and Filipino troops on the main island of Luzon were forced down onto the Bataan peninsula, their backs to Manila Bay.

Three days after Pearl Harbor, Japanese land-based naval aircraft sank the British battleship *Prince of Wales* and the battle cruiser *Repulse* off the coast of Malaya. They had been attempting to prevent the Japanese landings on the rubber-rich Malay Peninsula. The Japanese swiftly took the peninsula and Singapore, the fortress-port that was Britain's prize possession in the Far East. Japanese forces had already attacked Wake Island and Guam, both of which flew the American flag. These were quickly taken, as were New Britain, portions of New Guinea, the Admiralty Islands, the Gilbert Islands, and the oil-rich Dutch East Indies (now Indonesia).

The Japanese strategy was self-evident and supremely successful. Beyond capturing the riches of Southeast Asia, they now stood astride every area that would have left the home islands vulnerable to attack from land, sea, or air.

U.S. plans for a retaliatory attack on Japan were conceived in desperation. A month after the Pearl Harbor disaster, at a White House meeting on January 4, 1942, President Roosevelt asked his senior military leaders to find a way to strike back at Japan. At this grim point in the Pacific War, he believed that an air attack against Japan was the best way to bolster American morale.

Realistically, little could be done. Proposals included sending Army planes to bomb Japan from bases in the Aleutian Islands, Soviet Siberia, and China. But the Aleutians were too far from the main Japanese island of Honshu. The Soviet Union and Japan were not at war. Transporting bombs and fuel to bases in China was extremely difficult, and Japanese air and ground forces could easily thwart such a venture.

Roosevelt was particularly taken with the idea of bombing from bases in China. Lieutenant General H.H. Arnold, the Chief of the Army Air Forces, responded that he was studying such a bombing mission against Japan. Preliminary plans were being developed calling for the bombers to fly to advanced bases in China, land under cover of darkness, refuel, and fly on to bomb Japan. But, added Arnold, it would take "a few months" to get the gasoline and fields available for the bombers.

This left only one other option: to bomb Japan with Navy carrier-based planes. But their striking range was short, only some 200 miles if they were to return to their carriers. At that distance the Navy's few carriers would be at high risk from longer-range Japanese bombers flying from land bases. As early as January 4, the question of flying the Army's twin-engine B-18 Bolo bombers from Navy carriers was discussed at a White House meeting of Roosevelt, British Prime Minister Winston Churchill, and their military leaders. It was part of a proposal of Roosevelt and Churchill to invade French North Africa, but no one knew if such an air operation was possible.

The problem seemed unsolvable until an idea came to Captain Francis S. Low, the operations officer on the staff of Admiral Ernest J. King, the Commander in Chief U.S. Fleet. Low told King that when he was taking off from Norfolk, Virginia, on a flight back to Washington, he had noticed the outline of a carrier flight deck painted on the runway of the naval airfield used to train Navy pilots. "I saw some Army twin-engine planes making bombing passes at this simulated carrier deck. I thought if the Army had some twin-engine bombers with a range greater than our [carrier planes], it seems to me a few of them could be loaded on a carrier and used to bomb Japan."

After listening to Low, a submarine specialist, King, who had been both an aviation and submarine officer, leaned back and thought a moment. Then he said, "You may have something there, Low. Talk to Duncan about it in the morning. And don't tell anyone else about this."

Thus, the plan was born for the first direct attack against Japan. It was the evening of January 10, 1942, on board King's flagship *Vixen,* a former German yacht moored at the Washington Navy Yard. The next morning, Low met with Captain Donald B. Duncan, a pilot, who was King's air operations officer. Duncan told Low that it was impossible for an Army twin-engine bomber to land on a carrier. If it could be lifted on by crane, a fully armed plane might be able to take off, but it would have to fly back to a land base.

Despite the many provisos, Duncan was intrigued by the possibilities of a carrier-based raid on Japan, and for the next few days he read Army technical manuals on twin-engine aircraft, checked carrier specifications, and prepared a 30-page handwritten memo, a brilliant analytical paper. It concluded that such an operation was possible, although fraught with problems and risks. Duncan and Low then went to Admiral King and briefed him on their progress. After hearing them out, King told them, "Go see General Arnold about it, and if he agrees with you, ask him to get in touch with me. And don't you two mention this to another soul!"

On January 17, Low and Duncan outlined the idea to General Arnold, who immediately agreed to the proposal. Arnold, one of the first pilots in what would become the U.S. Army Air Forces, had got his wings in 1911 after being personally instructed by one of the Wright brothers. He had been an early disciple of General William (Billy) Mitchell, who had advocated an independent air force. But while Mitchell was being punished for his insubordination, Arnold had managed to avoid trouble and by 1938 was a major general and Chief of the Air Corps. His geniality had won him the nickname "Hap," and his political shrewdness had won him friends in Congress. After the creation of the Army Air Forces in 1941, Arnold had begun overseeing a quiet evolution toward an independent service. Now, when the Navy needed cooperation, he saw the advantage of giving it.

Much had to be done. Duncan and Low proposed a test takeoff of twin-engine B-25 Mitchell bombers from the aircraft carrier *Hornet,* then at Norfolk, Virginia. Arnold assigned three B-25s to try some short-field takeoffs, and on February 2 two of them were lifted aboard the *Hornet* by crane and spotted, one forward and one aft, as if they were two of 15 planes tightly arranged on the flight deck. The carrier steamed out into the Atlantic, and the Army pilots easily took off. But there was a great difference between flying off two bombers, with little fuel and no bombs, and perhaps a dozen or more fully loaded planes in the rough seas of the North Pacific.

Meanwhile, Arnold had assigned Lieutenant Colonel James H. Doolittle to assemble the pilots and planes for the raid, modify the planes with extra gas tanks and other features, and start a training program—all quickly and with the utmost secrecy. A handsome and charismatic man, Doolittle had grown up in Los Angeles, gaining renown as a street fighter. After at least one arrest for brawling, "Jimmy" had turned to amateur boxing and become the flyweight (105-pound) amateur champion of the West Coast. He went on to college, but dropped out in 1917 to enlist in the aviation section of the Army. He learned to fly with the same sure, tough instincts he had shown as a boxer.

After World War I, Doolittle remained in the Army, flying on a stunt team, winning air races, setting speed and distance records, and attending the Massachusetts Institute of Technology, where he received one of the first doctorates in aeronautics. He resigned his Army commission in 1930 because of what he called his advanced age. He was 34. He remained in the Officer Reserve Corps, often testing planes for the Army while also flying in races. He won the coveted Thompson Trophy at the National Air Races in Cleveland, setting a world record of 296 miles per hour in an erratic aircraft called the "flying death trap."

Returning to active duty in the Air Corps in 1940, Doolittle initially worked with industry executives on aircraft-engine production and in the fall of 1941 made a survey of British aircraft production. His next assignment put him at the controls of the new, twin-engine B-26 Marauder bomber, which pilots were calling a "widow maker" because several had crashed. Its 100-mile-per-hour landing speed and stubby wings made it tricky to handle. Arnold gave Doolittle the job of proving that the B-26 was a safe and effective aircraft. He tamed the Marauder and convinced pilots that all they needed to do was to learn how to fly it properly.

Doolittle now began one of the most intense training programs in aviation history. Lieutenant Henry L. (Hank) Miller, a Navy carrier pilot, was assigned to him to teach the Army pilots how to take off with a run of only 350 feet—about a quarter of what the Army pilots were used to when they took off bomb-laden B-25s. Meanwhile, the carrier *Hornet* raced south from Norfolk, through the Panama Canal, and up to San Francisco. At Pearl Harbor, Vice Admiral William F. Halsey, the Navy's senior carrier force commander, and Admiral Chester W. Nimitz, the Pacific Fleet commander, worked out details of the raid. The *Hornet* would carry the Army bombers, while Halsey, aboard the carrier *Enterprise,* would provide cover for the task force, which would also include four cruisers, eight destroyers, and two oilers.

There was not enough time to fully train the B-25 crews, and their new, extensively modified B-25B bombers still had "bugs." The additional fuel tanks being installed leaked, and the electrically operated twin .50-caliber gun turrets atop the fuselage were not working properly. The turret problems and an ammunition shortage prevented any of the gunners from firing on a moving target from a B-25 in flight. But the mission was urgent. The Japanese continued to win victory after victory in the South Pacific, and President Roosevelt was growing impatient. So fast were developments taking place—and so secret were the preparations—that until 24 hours before the raid, only seven people knew the *complete* plan to attack Tokyo—King, Nimitz, Arnold, Halsey, Low, Duncan, and Doolittle. Only as the *Hornet* was nearing the takeoff point did King go to the White House and give details about the raid to President Roosevelt.

An old man at 45 by Army Air Forces standards, and never having flown in combat, Doolittle knew he would have to do some fast talking to get Arnold to let him lead the strike. Arnold at first did refuse, but Doolittle was able to outmaneuver his chief and won approval to lead the strike.

Doolittle's bombers flew from their training site, Eglin Field in Florida, to McClellan Field in Sacramento, California. After a final series of checks, the B-25s then flew to Alameda Naval Air Station near San Francisco. There 16 of the twin-engine bombers were loaded by crane onto the deck of the *Hornet*—the maximum number that Doolittle and the Navy felt could be safely flown off. Doolittle met secretly with Halsey in San Francisco to go over the final steps of the plan, and on April 2 the *Hornet* steamed out of

San Francisco Bay in daylight with 16 Army bombers conspicuously on her flight deck. With crews filled with new recruits, the task group commander could not risk sailing the ships out of the harbor at night. The rumor went around that the ship was going up to Alaska to deliver the bombers there. Many, on the shore and in the ships of the task group, guessed correctly that Tokyo was the real target.

West of Hawaii, the *Enterprise* and *Hornet* task groups rendezvoused on April 13, and the 16 ships set course for Japan with fighters and scout bombers from the *Enterprise,* Halsey's flagship, flying protective cover. If the force was detected by the Japanese within one-way bomber range of Hawaii, the B-25s would take off and fly there to free the *Hornet*'s flight deck to launch her own Navy fighters and attack planes, which were stowed on the hangar deck. If the ships were detected beyond range of Hawaii, the B-25s would simply be pushed into the sea so that the *Hornet*'s own planes could take off.

The attack plan was to launch the bombers when the carriers were about 450 miles from the Japanese coast. Doolittle was to take off at dusk on April 19, with the other planes following and homing in on the fires started by his bombs. The planes were then to fly on to bases in China that would be, it was hoped, ready for them with radio homing beacons and fuel. The raiders would then become part of the U.S. Army forces that were being assembled there to help Nationalist leader Chiang Kai-shek.

If forced down before reaching those airfields, each pilot was to decide for himself what to do and what to tell his crew to do. "I don't intend to be taken prisoner," Doolittle told his fliers. "I'm 45 years old and have lived a full life. If my plane is crippled beyond any possibility of fighting or escaping, I'm going to have my crew bail out and then I'm going to dive my B-25 into the best military target I can find. You fellows are all younger and have a long life ahead of you. I don't expect any of the rest of you to do what I intend to do."

The planes were loaded with bombs and ammunition, fueled, and spotted on the *Hornet*'s deck for takeoff when, at 3:15 A.M. on April 18, the plans went awry. The carrier *Enterprise* flashed a message to the other ships in the task force: TWO ENEMY SURFACE CRAFT SPOTTED. In the predawn darkness the carrier's radar had detected, only ten miles away, the large fishing boats being used by the Japanese as pickets to warn of approaching ships. The U.S. force rapidly changed course, but soon other fishing craft were sighted. Three hours later, one of the patrolling *Enterprise* SBD Dauntless dive bombers spotted a patrol vessel, and the pilot was certain that he had been seen by the Japanese.

More small craft were sighted as the American ships steamed westward at 22 knots. The cruiser *Nashville* was ordered to open fire and sink one that was approaching the task force. The picket craft had sent off radio messages to Japan, but the Japanese were already alerted to the American carrier force

Lieutenant Colonel Jimmy Doolittle fastens medals previously given to U.S. Navy personnel by Japan to the tail fins of a bomb for return to Japan "with interest."

steaming westward, apparently from analyses of U.S. radio communications. The Japanese believed, however, that the carriers would attack with standard naval aircraft and would have to approach much closer before launching an air strike.

Halsey gave the order to go, sent by flashing light from the *Enterprise* to the *Hornet:* LAUNCH PLANES. TO COL DOOLITTLE AND GALLANT COMMAND GOOD LUCK AND GOD BLESS YOU—HALSEY. At 8:20 A.M., as heavy seas made the carrier's 800-foot flight deck rise and fall, Doolittle took off the lead bomber. The *Hornet* was some 770 miles east of Japan. In just over an hour all 16 of the heavily laden planes took off, each flown by a crew of five and carrying one ton of bombs. Racing westward toward Japan, they kept low over the water, hoping to avoid detection by Japanese radar.

Thirteen planes struck Tokyo beginning at 12:15 P.M. The other planes hit Kobe, Nagoya, and Yokohama, all with little opposition. The pilots were briefed to hit military and industrial targets, but in their low-level attacks some bombs went astray, striking residential areas. (The pilots had specific orders not to bomb the Imperial Palace, a target suggested by several of them.) The bombers arrived immediately after a scheduled air-raid drill, and most people in Tokyo who saw the bombers and the sparse anti-aircraft fire thought they were part of the exercise. When the smoke cleared, the bomb damage was minimal.

One B-25 was hit by anti-aircraft fire, but not one was shot down. However, because of bad weather and the longer-than-expected flight, 15 of the planes crashed in China. One landed at a Soviet base at Primorsky in Siberia, 40 miles north of Vladivostok. Of the 75 fliers whose planes crashed in China, three died accidentally, and eight fell into Japanese hands. The five-man crew that landed in the Soviet Union was interned for 14 months and then released, with the U.S. government being billed for their food. The Soviets did not return the B-25.

After parachuting from his plane over China at night and being "captured" by Chinese soldiers, Doolittle was distraught. He had lost his plane and— he guessed—most of the others. Sitting in the darkness and rain that night, exhausted and frustrated, he later recalled, ". . . I was sure that when the outcome of this mission was known back home, either I would be court-martialed or the military powers would see to it that I would sit out the war flying a desk. I had never felt lower in my life."

The Japanese military leadership was shocked and angered by the attack. They had failed to defend the homeland and the Emperor. Air and naval searches sought out the U.S. carriers, and three Japanese carriers north of Formosa changed course to the northeast and increased speed in an effort to catch the Halsey task force. Halsey—for the only time in his career—beat a hasty retreat and escaped his pursuers.

The eight fliers captured by the Japanese were interrogated in China, taken to Tokyo, and after torture and show trials, all were sentenced to death. The eight condemned men were then flown back to China. On October 15 three of them were shot by a firing squad in a graveyard outside Shanghai. A fourth American died of beriberi and malnutrition after a year of solitary confinement. The four others, their sentences commuted to life imprisonment, were repeatedly beaten and tortured. According to Doolittle, they were "never to be released, even when the war ended; presumably, they were to be hidden so the sentence could be carried out, no matter which side won." The four men did survive 40 months of solitary confinement and near-starvation. They were liberated when American troops opened the gates of their Chinese prison in August 1945.

To retaliate for the raid on their sacred capital, the outraged Japanese military leaders ordered troops to scour the areas in China where the planes had crash-landed. Japanese troops attacked Chinese airfields to prevent additional raids; they pillaged and torched villages suspected of aiding the American fliers. A bishop told what happened to a man who had helped one of the pilots: He was wrapped in blankets, oil was poured on him, and his wife was ordered to set him afire. The American air commander in China, Brigadier General Claire L. Chennault, estimated that 250,000 Chinese paid with their lives during the three-month Japanese campaign of retaliation for the American raid.

Doolittle and, eventually, 63 other fliers who came down in China made their way back to the United States. Contrary to his expectations, Doolittle was hailed as a hero. He was awarded the Medal of Honor by President Roosevelt and promoted to brigadier general, skipping the rank of colonel. When asked where the bombers came from, President Roosevelt laughed and replied, "Shangri-La," referring to the mythical Asian kingdom in James Hilton's popular novel *Lost Horizon.* (The U.S. Navy promptly named an aircraft carrier under construction the *Shangri-La.*)

The "Tokyo raiders" had accomplished their daring mission. Although the B-25s never reached the struggling U.S. forces in China and the damage to their targets was insignificant, Doolittle and his raiders had given American morale a much-needed boost.

It would be more than two years before another bomb would fall on Japan and several months after that before another would strike the capital of Tokyo. Still, the Doolittle raid was the first step on the long and bloody road of retribution for the Japanese attack on Pearl Harbor. And as the Pacific War raged on, both American and Japanese leaders would wonder if that road would ultimately lead to the shores of Japan itself. The Doolittle raid had proved that the home islands were indeed vulnerable to air and sea attack. But the question remained: Would the United States have to invade Japan?

CHAPTER 1

WAR PLAN ORANGE

U.S. Marines, wearing neckties and accompanied by their mascot, stage a mock amphibious landing in 1937. Real island assaults would be bloody and bitterly fought battles.

Officers at the U.S. Naval War College in Newport, Rhode Island, had begun to work on plans for a possible campaign against the Empire of Japan as early as 1897. Only half a century earlier, it had taken a show of force to compel the reclusive Japanese to open their doors to world commerce. And now so exuberantly were the Japanese adapting to Western imperialistic and militaristic ways that force might be necessary to subdue them.

The first American thought about an actual invasion of Japan came soon after 1900, when U.S. Navy planners began to write the initial version of War Plan Orange, a secret strategy for fighting Japan. The term "Orange," in a scheme adopted by U.S. Army and Navy planning officers, indicated Japan in planning documents, avoiding the political problem of specifically calling Japan a potential enemy. In the nation-color scheme, blue was used for the United States, red for Great Britain, and black for Germany.

Early in the century events were creating an environment in which some U.S. military leaders believed that a war with Japan was inevitable. In 1898 the United States had taken the Philippine Islands and Guam away from Spain, establishing the United States as a power in the western Pacific in competition with Japan. In 1904–1905 the Japanese had inflicted a humiliating military defeat upon Russia, marking the first time in modern history that an Asian power had overcome a European nation and paving the way for further Japanese expansion. Strong anti-Oriental feeling in California erupted in rioting in 1906–1907. Just the year before, President Theodore Roosevelt had intervened in the Russo-Japanese War to bring the two nations to the negotiating table in Portsmouth, New Hampshire. Now the violence in California led Roosevelt to inquire if the Navy had a plan for fighting a war against Japan. He was quickly briefed on War Plan Orange.

The general scheme of the early versions of War Plan Orange was modified over the years, but all basically called for the rapid transfer of U.S. warships in the Atlantic to the Pacific (sailing around South America until the Panama Canal was completed in 1914). The fleet would then embark Army troops and Marines at San Francisco and steam westward. Stops for coal would be made at Hawaii (where there was not yet a naval base), Midway, and then Guam. While the Japanese could be expected to assault the northern Philippines, it was hoped that Manila harbor could be defended or at least denied to the Japanese, forcing them to support their fleet from more distant bases.

The Army and Navy planners disagreed over the question of where to establish an advance naval base in the Pacific. The Army wanted Luzon, but the Navy wanted and got Hawaii in 1908. Another argument arose over a secondary base in the Philippines. This time the Army got its choice, Manila Bay. But that base, at Cavite on the western side of the bay, was never developed enough to maintain a major fleet.

While refined versions of War Plan Orange were produced every couple of years, certain basics remained. If Manila was denied to American forces, a base would be established at Dumanquilas Bay on the Philippine island of Mindanao, using prefabricated dry docks and barges towed from the United States. Then, with the fleet replenished and rehabilitated at its Philippine base, it would sortie forth to do battle with the Imperial Japanese Navy somewhere between the Philippines and the Japanese home islands. It would be the all-out, decisive naval battle that had been called for ever since publication in 1890 of *The Influence of Sea Power upon History* by Captain Alfred Thayer Mahan, the world's most celebrated naval strategist. Mahan's theories—centered on a decisive naval battle between battleship-led fleets—had considerable influence on world leaders. His enthusiastic readers included Theodore Roosevelt and senior American and Japanese naval leaders.

The American fleet would inevitably triumph in the battleship-versus-battleship contest, at least in the eyes of U.S. naval planners. The fleet would then blockade the Japanese home islands, cutting off trade with China and the East Indies, forcing negotiations that would favor the United States. While these early Orange war plans did not provide for an invasion of the Japanese home islands, certainly the issue was raised in discussions at the Naval War College and by the Navy's General Board, composed of admirals who served as the principal advisers to the Secretary of the Navy.

The alarming buildup of the Japanese Navy fueled American fears of war with Japan. But the planning for a Pacific campaign became more difficult after the Washington Treaty of 1922, which limited U.S. and Japanese base fortifications in the Pacific and established a U.S.-Japanese ratio of capital ships of 5:3, respectively. (Capital ships were battleships and battle cruisers. The ratio was also established for aircraft carriers, with the subsequent London Treaty of 1930 additionally providing limitations on smaller warships.) While the U.S. Navy would still have a superiority, many planners now considered the ratio too close for assured victory in a battle so far from major American bases on the West Coast and so close to the Japanese home islands. The Japanese, of course, resented the restrictions, which added to the growing enmity that would in fact, not just in theory, lead to war with America.

• • •

In the 1920s, land-based aircraft became a factor in American strategic planning. Japanese planes flying from northern Luzon in the Philippines, from the Marianas (including Guam, which was expected to be quickly captured by the Japanese), and from other islands could bomb the American fleet as it steamed westward. Thus, the Orange plans were revised to encompass the capture of islands in the Caroline and Marshall groups to prevent their use by the Japanese as air bases.

The capture of these islands would be difficult, if not impossible. In 1930 the Army had only 145,000 troops, and the Marine Corps numbered some 20,000. General Douglas MacArthur, the Chief of Staff of the Army in 1930, would later recall:

> ... my complete disagreement with the Orange Plan when I became Chief of Staff but I realized at once that I would be wasting my time in trying to educate others to my own point of view. I, therefore, short-circuted [sic] by seeing the President [Herbert Hoover] personally and telling him that if mobilization became necessary during my tenure of office that my first step would be to send two divisions from the Atlantic coast to reinforce the Philippines; two divisions from the Gulf of Mexico to reinforce Panama, and two divisions from the Pacific coast to reinforce Hawaii, and that I intended to defend every inch of those possessions and defend them successfully. This being the case, the Orange Plan was a completely useless document. The President agreed with me entirely.

While completely ignoring War Plan Orange, MacArthur also ignored the ability of the Japanese to interfere with the transfer of two American divisions to the Philippines and the possible need to assault their positions in the Marianas and other Pacific areas to gain safe passage for his transports. Indeed, even if the U.S. Fleet's movement westward was successful and the battleship-versus-battleship shoot-out ended in an American victory, how long would it take the proposed blockade to force Japanese capitulation or negotiation? Would a troop landing in Japan be necessary? Could China or even the Soviet Union be enticed into joining the campaign against Japan? All of these issues were considered by the planners.

Further complicating War Plan Orange's assumptions was that American amphibious doctrine and equipment at the time were primitive. The Marine Corps had not made a major amphibious assault since the American Civil War. Even so, with the end of World War I the Marine Corps had immediately begun planning for landing operations in the Pacific, in accord with War Plan Orange. At Marine Corps headquarters in Washington, D.C., a planning division was set up to prepare plans and exercises for assaults on Japanese-held islands. Lieutenant Colonel Earl H. (Pete) Ellis was among the officers assigned to this division.

Pete Ellis, growing up in Kansas, had dreamed of seeing the world and joined the Marines shortly after the Spanish-American War ended. His analytic, questioning mind was not exactly what the Marines were looking for in their officers in those pre–World War I days. Flunking or errant midshipmen at the U.S. Naval Academy, their Navy careers seemingly doomed, were often offered Marine commissions. Ellis was an exception. When he was working on plans for a mock assault on a Caribbean island in 1914, he was taken under the wing of Lieutenant Colonel John A. Lejeune, who appreciated brilliance in his officers. When Lejeune graduated from the academy, he had been told he was too bright to be a Marine; he had to resort to congressional intervention to get his Marine commission.

While a student at the Naval War College in 1912–1913, Ellis became obsessed with the belief that Japan was a future enemy and concentrated his efforts on planning for amphibious assaults in the Pacific. In 1915 he gave a series of highly classified lectures on how American troops could seize outlying naval bases in a war with Japan. Ellis put aside his interests in the Pacific when America entered World War I in 1917, serving during the war as aide to the Commandant of the Marine Corps and then as adjutant of the 4th Marine Brigade during its hard fighting in France.

After the war, Ellis returned to his contemplation of an island campaign against Japan, with the vigorous support of Lejeune, who became Commandant of the Marine Corps in 1920. Lejeune believed that the "true mission" of the Marines was defending and assaulting island bases, and that in the next war Marines "would be the first to set foot on hostile soil in order to seize, fortify, and hold a port from which, as a base, the Army would prosecute the campaign."

Ellis, his desk piled high with maps and planning documents, worked solitarily and silently, like a meditative monk, on Operation Plan 712, which was at least partially inspired by War Plan Orange. In 1921 he completed his opus, a 50,000-word plan for a Marine advance across the Pacific, which began, "In order to impose our will upon Japan, it will be necessary for us to project our fleet and land forces across the Pacific and wage war in Japanese waters." His assault targets included the Marshall, Caroline, Palau, and Ryukyu Islands (including Okinawa)—all of which would become sites of World War II amphibious assaults. He listed specific atolls to be captured as well as the troops and weapons needed. He also described reef-crossing vehicles and the tactics to be used. His prophetic conclusion:

> To effect such a landing under the sea and shore conditions obtaining and in the face of enemy resistance requires careful training and preparation. . . . It is not enough that the troops be skilled infantry men and jungle men or artillery men of high morale; they must be skilled water men and jungle men who know it can be done—Marines with Marine training.

As early as 1921, Marine Lieutenant Colonel Pete Ellis had mapped out an amphibious campaign for a war in the Pacific against Japan. When that war finally came, American forces were ill prepared to fight it.

In May 1921, Lejeune arranged for Ellis to get extended leave and to make, in the guise of a businessman, an extensive tour of the western Pacific, beginning with Australia, Samoa, the Philippines, and possibly Fiji. Ellis was not a good spy. He became increasingly neurotic, and at several stops he was ill and often drunk. When he reached Yokohama, Japan, in July 1922, he again became ill and was admitted to the U.S. naval hospital and diagnosed as suffering from alcoholism. In and out of the hospital several times, he discharged himself on October 6.

A short time later, he sailed for the Japanese-held island of Saipan and then went on to the Caroline and Marshall Islands, also under Japanese control. Everywhere he went he charted the islands and reefs and listed other items of potential interest for amphibious operations. His presence did not go unnoticed. Throughout his travels Ellis was carefully watched by the Japanese, but he managed to slip a packet of information to at least one businessman, asking that it be mailed for him in the United States.

Ellis was hospitalized again for two weeks on Jaluit in the Marshalls. Then, back in the Carolines, on Koror in the Palau group, he moved in with the native royalty, who had befriended him, and was provided with a wife, Metauie, a beautiful woman 25 years his junior. His behavior grew ever more erratic. He continued to drink heavily, mainly beer and sake. He would sometimes rant and rave and once pranced around "like a soldier and punched his arm through the wall," according to an eyewitness.

Finally, in May 1923, he became violently ill and confided to his wife and their houseboys that he "was an American spy sent by higher authority from New York." He still drank when he could manage it and refused to take medicine that was prescribed for him. He died on May 12 and was buried on Koror. His belongings, including maps and notes and—reportedly—a confidential code book, were confiscated by the Japanese.

When the U.S. government was informed of Ellis's death, an attempt was made to have a U.S. Navy ship call at the island for his remains, but the Japanese refused permission. Rather, a U.S. Navy chief pharmacist was allowed to travel, on a Japanese ship, to Koror, where Ellis's remains were exhumed, photographed, and cremated. They were then returned to Japan with Chief Pharmacist Lawrence Zembsch.

Obviously, the Japanese had a keen interest in Ellis's mission. But he could have garnered no information about defenses and fortifications in the Caroline and Marshall Islands. The Japanese did not fortify those islands until the 1930s.

Ellis's 1921 plan for future amphibious assaults and his few notes from the Japanese-held islands he visited meant little to the U.S. Marine Corps at the time simply because it lacked the strength, structure, doctrine, tactics, and equipment to undertake such operations. While landings were envisioned on various Pacific islands and even in the Philippines after those islands were conquered by the Japanese in some future war, no invasion of

Japan was formally contemplated. Rather, as the 1929 version of War Plan Orange stated, the overall concept was

> An offensive war of long duration, primarily naval throughout, unless large army forces are employed in major land operations in the western Pacific, directed toward the isolation and exhaustion of Orange through control of her vital sea communications and through offensive operations against her armed forces and her economic life.

The term "long duration," however, was of concern to many naval planners, who wondered if the American people would support a prolonged Pacific conflict. They postulated that Japanese raids on Hawaii (not yet a fleet base) or even on West Coast cities would certainly enrage Americans, but would Japan be so obliging? An attack on the Philippines, which many Americans were ready to relinquish, would not have the same impact on American resolve to fight a long-term Pacific war.

The obvious difficulties of a westward sortie across the Pacific led to development of the "Through Ticket to Manila" option, a variation of War Plan Orange that provided for a rapid thrust—with refuelings at sea—from Hawaii straight to Manila to relieve the small American garrison presumed to be holding out in the Philippines after a Japanese invasion. The 5,000 nautical miles would be traversed by more than 300 warships and some 240 transports and auxiliary ships carrying 72,000 troops; their average speed was to be 10½ knots—a 20-day voyage if the ships sailed continuously in a straight line. The distances the Japanese Fleet would have to sail from its bases on Formosa and in the home islands to intercept such an armada were less than 600 nautical miles.

The unreality of this kind of planning was not lost on senior Army or Navy officers who were less politically oriented and less bombastic than MacArthur. In 1933 the commander of the island fortress of Corregidor in the mouth of Manila Bay, Brigadier General Stanley D. Embick, called the plan to dispatch a fleet to the Philippines "literally an act of madness." He maintained that unless the American people were willing to bear the cost of greatly increasing the defenses of the Philippines—this in the midst of the Great Depression—the only correct course would be to withdraw behind the natural "strategic peacetime frontier in the Pacific," the line that ran through Alaska-Oahu-Panama, the "strategic triangle" that had first priority for the Army's defenses in the Pacific.

Embick's protests against War Plan Orange would be echoed almost a decade later, in 1940, by Admiral James O. Richardson, Commander in Chief of the U.S. Fleet, who would have been responsible for carrying out the plan. He wrote:

In the twenty-year period between the end of World War I and the time I was designated to command the Battle Force of the United States Fleet [June 1939], our War Plans, insofar as they related to the Navy and to war with Japan, *had never been feasible War Plans*. I state this as a fact, because I believe it to be such.

One reason that War Plan Orange was becoming increasingly impractical was the unwelcome intrusion of aircraft on traditional strategy. As early as 1921, American air-power advocate Billy Mitchell had conducted a test that had "proven"—at least to his own satisfaction—that land-based bombers could find and sink enemy ships at sea. The target ships in his test were near the coast in a known area, at anchor or under radio control, without crews to man anti-aircraft guns or perform damage control. But farsighted naval and aviation officers realized that it would only be a matter of time before improvements in aviation would truly put warships at risk to aerial attack.

An American thrust into the western Pacific and a blockade of Japan became even less plausible in the 1930s when Japan seized and occupied much of the coastal area of China. And the world of War Plan Orange had drastically changed by June 1940, when, with the fall of France, Japan, a partner of Germany's, took over French bases in Indochina (now Vietnam). With Japanese bases already established on Formosa as well as on Tinian and Saipan in the Marianas, the Philippines could be easily isolated if an American fleet tried to rescue or reinforce the garrison.

A small effort was begun secretly by the United States in the fall of 1938 to prepare defenses for islands that could provide airfields for use as steppingstones from Hawaii to the Philippines and Australia. The fortification of islands between Hawaii and the Philippines had been forbidden by the Washington Treaty of 1922. But in September 1938 the Commandant of the Marine Corps asked the Chief of Naval Operations for permission to send a Marine officer to Midway, Wake, and Johnston Islands "on a secret mission, for the purpose of definitely locating the positions of defensive weapons and obtaining other necessary information for the preparation of plans for executing the O-1 Plan, Orange."

The secret survey was carried out, and plans were drawn up for the rapid arming of those islands with anti-aircraft and coastal-defense guns as well as aircraft to defend them against Japanese assaults. Still, these were defensive measures. Offensive tactics in the event of war with Japan remained in the area of pure speculation.

In May 1939, as war neared in Europe, the U.S. Navy and Army agreed to develop a series of plans for multinational conflicts between the Axis— Japan, Italy, and Germany—and the United States, either alone or in a coalition with various allies. Thus were born the Rainbow plans, so called for their multicolor participants. Rainbow marked the end of the long-lived but largely impotent Orange plans.

For the next 18 months Army and Navy planners prepared a series of Rainbow plans. Plans No. 1 and No. 4 were intended to appease the Army's desire to defend the Western Hemisphere and waters out to a distance of 2,000 miles from U.S. shores. The Navy's desire for offensive operations against Japan was addressed in plans No. 2 and No. 3. But offensive operations would be feasible, according to the joint planners, only in collaboration with Britain, France, or the Netherlands, all of which had colonial interests in Asia.

Rainbow Plan No. 5, which made the defeat of Germany as America's first priority, was not addressed until 1941. And by that time, the Nazi victories in Europe in 1939–1940, coupled with the questionable survival of Great Britain against the Nazi aerial onslaught that followed, had led President Roosevelt to enter the Battle of the Atlantic without a formal declaration of war. American planes and warships began a "neutrality patrol" in the North Atlantic, which greatly helped the hard-pressed British in the battle against German U-boats. Also in 1940, at Roosevelt's direction, the Navy began shifting warships and patrol planes from the Pacific to the Atlantic to enforce the neutrality patrol. And Marines stationed on the coral atolls in the Pacific were transferred to garrison duty in Iceland in order to release British troops from occupation duties there.

At the same time—in May 1940—Roosevelt also ordered most of the U.S. Fleet to move from its base at San Pedro, California, to Pearl Harbor in the mid-Pacific to deter further Japanese aggression. Germany's defeat of France and the Netherlands left French Indochina and the Dutch East Indies vulnerable to takeover by the Japanese. British Malaya was also vulnerable because Britain had to concentrate its military forces on fighting Germany and Italy in the European-Atlantic-Mediterranean sphere of the war. It was no secret that Japan, coveting the oil, rubber, and minerals of the Pacific colonies, saw them as part of an eventual overseas empire that it called the Greater East Asia Co-Prosperity Sphere.

Roosevelt's shift of the fleet to Pearl Harbor, which harked back to War Plan Orange, was done over the protests of the fleet commander, Admiral Richardson, who argued that the fleet lacked support at Pearl Harbor and was vulnerable to attack, especially since large numbers of his ships, planes, and men were being transferred to the Atlantic. Richardson made two trips to Washington, in July and again in October 1940, to protest the basing policy. In July he met with Secretary of State Cordell Hull and Under Secretary Sumner Wells:

I fully stated my views that (a) our ORANGE War Plan was useless, and that (b) the timetable therein was silly and could not be carried into execution because of the lack of men, matériel, a fleet train [auxiliary ships], training for large overseas operation, and adequate information of the enemy-held Western Pacific islands. I considered the ORANGE War Plan useful only to fulfill the law that we must have a plan and to serve as a basis upon which to build a Navy.

On his October 1940 trip to Washington, Richardson met with Roosevelt and voiced his opposition to keeping the fleet in Hawaii. The President, Richardson later recalled, said: "Despite what you believe, I know that the presence of the fleet in the Hawaiian area has had, and is now having, a restraining influence of the actions of Japan."

"Mr. President," Richardson replied, "I still do not believe it, and I know that our fleet is disadvantageously disposed for preparing for or initiating war operations."

Secretary of the Navy Frank Knox later told Richardson, "You hurt the President's feelings by what you said to him." Richardson was relieved as U.S. Fleet commander by Admiral Husband E. Kimmel in February 1941, the movement of naval forces from the Pacific to the Atlantic continued, and the Pacific Fleet remained at Pearl Harbor.

In May 1941, Rainbow War Plan No. 5 was completed, putting forth a U.S. offensive strategy in the Pacific while also fighting a war against Germany. The plan provided for 23,000 troops to embark in transports at Seattle, Washington, for transit to Alaska and another 23,000 to board transports in San Francisco for transit to Hawaii. While the plan did not say specifically what these troops would do (and there was already an Army division stationed in Hawaii), it did list the U.S. possessions in the Pacific that were to be defended—Midway, Johnston, Palmyra, Samoa, and Guam as well as the Philippines. The Army agreed to prepare Midway and Wake atolls for B-17 Flying Fortress bombers to refuel. (The atolls were already steppingstones for commercial aircraft flying from Hawaii to the Far East.)

Modifications were rapidly issued to Rainbow War Plan No. 5, which, at last, seemed to anticipate the realities of a war with Japan. The Army was directed to "support the Navy in the capture and establishment of control over the Caroline and Marshall Islands by air operations within tactical operating radius of Army and Navy air bases equipped for effective operations by the Army Air Forces." But this emphasis on a Pacific campaign was limited from a political as well as a military perspective. In August 1941, President Roosevelt and Winston Churchill (who had become Britain's prime minister in May 1940) met secretly at Placentia Bay, Newfoundland, and agreed that upon U.S. entry into the war Anglo-American forces would pursue a "Germany-first" strategy. The planned capture of Pacific islands and the recapture of the Philippine Islands, in the event of war with Japan, would have to wait until an Anglo-American coalition defeated Hitler.

• • •

Despite the disenchantment of the leaders of the U.S. Army and Navy with War Plan Orange, the diminutive U.S. Marine Corps continued planning— and developing the equipment and tactics—for amphibious assaults in the Pacific.

Amphibious landings, the most complex of all military operations, had to surmount the difficult transition from sea to land, and they involved the use of naval and ground forces as well as—since the 1930s—air forces. Because landing ships must enter defended, restricted waters, they are highly vulnerable to hostile attack. And the landing troops must reach the beach without the support of their own heavy weapons. Thus, the potential for large-scale disaster in amphibious landings is always present. This was tragically demonstrated in the 1915 landings by British and French forces at Gallipoli, the southern entrance to the Turkish Straits. That debacle, which cost the Allies more than 25,000 men killed and another 88,000 wounded, convinced many military and political leaders that amphibious assaults against defended positions were impossible.

But neither the U.S. Marines nor the Japanese Army and Navy drew that lesson from Gallipoli. Rather, they concluded that specific training and techniques and specialized ships and landing craft would be needed for successful assaults. U.S. Marines had made no amphibious landings during World War I, when the equivalent of a Marine division had fought in France. But at the end of the war, the Marine Corps, in accord with War Plan Orange, began planning for landing operations against Japanese-held islands in the Pacific. Building on the writings of Pete Ellis, during the 1920s and 1930s the Marine Corps carried out numerous landing exercises, sometimes with Army troops, to develop amphibious tactics. The Fleet Marine Force was established in 1933 to make landing forces an integral part of the U.S. Fleet.

Initially, a ship's small, steam-powered boats were used to land troops in the surf during these exercises. Obviously, new and better methods of getting troops—and possibly their vehicles—ashore were vital if landings were to be effective on hostile beaches swept by enemy fire. That was why the Marines enthusiastically supported Andrew Jackson Higgins, who had a genius for designing small boats. He had built one he named *Eureka* for oilmen to use in the Louisiana bayous. The wooden boat had a shallow draft and could pull up onto bayou banks and back off with no trouble. When the Marines tested his boat in the summer of 1936, they wanted it. They still wanted it in 1939, when, following an exercise, an enthusiastic Marine wrote, "The Higgins boat gave the best performance under all conditions. It has more speed, more maneuverability, handles easier, and lands troops higher on the beach" than another craft evaluated.

But the Navy's Bureau of Ships opposed Higgins, a gruff, outspoken man who drank a bottle of whiskey a day and who told his prospective customers in the bureau that the "Navy doesn't know one damn thing about small boats." The bureau had a design of its own and stuck with it. Bureau officers simply disliked Higgins. He was an outsider, a man from the swamps of Louisiana who built wooden boats and did not have the old Navy connections of his East Coast rivals.

But the bureau eventually gave up, and the Higgins design won. Word spread about the bureau's opposition to Higgins, and in 1942, when the United States and Japan were finally at war, the U.S. Senate War Investigating Committee, chaired by the indomitable Harry S. Truman, observed that "the Bureau of Ships, for reasons known only to itself, stubbornly persisted for over five years in clinging to an unseaworthy tank lighter design of its own. . . . The Bureau's action has caused not only a waste of time but has caused the needless expenditure of over $7,000,000 for a total of 225 Bureau lighters which do not meet the needs of the Armed Forces."

Higgins set up landing-craft production lines, some of them under canvas. He hired 30,000 men and women, and his integrated employees formed the first such black-and-white workforce ever seen in New Orleans. They would produce more than 20,000 boats during the war. In the rest rooms of his factories he put pictures of Hitler, Mussolini, and Tojo sitting on toilets. "Come on in, brother," said the captions. "Take it easy. Every minute you loaf here helps us plenty."

The Higgins boat—dubbed LCP(L) for Landing Craft Personnel (Large)— would become the standard U.S. and British landing craft in World War II. It was a spoon-bowed craft, just under 37 feet in length and powered by a gasoline engine that could drive it 8 to 11 knots while fully loaded and carry 36 troops or four tons of cargo. When Higgins was shown a photo of a Japanese landing craft with bow ramp in April 1941, he quickly evolved the modified LCP(R)—for ramp—which could land small vehicles on the beach and easily be carried in davits of cargo ships and transports. The LCP series led to the improved Landing Craft Vehicle and Personnel (LCVP), of which thousands would be built. Marine Lieutenant General Holland M. Smith wrote that this craft ". . . did more to win the war in the Pacific than any other single piece of equipment." General Dwight D. Eisenhower called Higgins "the man who won the war for us."

Simultaneously, the U.S. Marines sponsored the development of amphibious tractors that would eventually succeed conventional landing craft in wartime assaults—the Landing Vehicle Tracked (LVT). In the 1930s, Donald Roebling had developed a tracked amphibious vehicle for rescue work in the Everglades. It could move through water and on land with equal ease. A photo of the Roebling craft in Life magazine on October 4, 1937, caught the eye of an admiral, who passed it on to the general commanding the Atlantic Fleet Marine Force. After looking at the swamp vehicle, the Marines tested pilot models of a military version and in 1940 obtained funds to produce the first "Alligators" of the LVT-1 model, which began coming off the assembly line in July 1941. Its Mercury V-8 gasoline engine provided a speed of 25 miles per hour on land and ten in the water. It could carry 24 troops or more than two tons of cargo. Most important, an Alligator could climb over reefs and traverse surf to deliver Marines up onto the beach.

Improved amphibious tractors, or "amtracs," were rapidly developed. While most LVTs had one or more machine guns, in 1940 the Marines installed a gun turret in place of the cargo compartment to produce an amphibious tank that could accompany the personnel carriers onto the beach, providing fire support after naval bombardments were lifted. This LVT(A)—the A for armored—initially carried a 37-mm gun. The later LVT(A)-4 would have a 75-mm howitzer. The Marine Corps would procure 18,620 LVTs of various models during World War II.

Many specialized ships were also developed for carrying troops and weapons to the landing area. The most celebrated was the Landing Ship, Tank (LST), which, in many respects, would become the most important ship of World War II. Winston Churchill would later write of the problems in planning the great Allied invasions of Europe:

> The whole of this difficult [strategy] question only arises out of the absurd shortage of the L.S.T.s. How it is that the plans of two great empires like Britain and the United States should be so much hamstrung and limited by a hundred or two of the particular vessels will never be understood by history.

The first LSTs were shallow-draft tankers that the British converted to tank carriers. Because British shipyards were giving priority to producing anti-submarine escort ships and merchant ships, there were no facilities available to build LSTs. They took their plans to the United States in November 1941, and within a few days, John Niedermair of the U.S. Navy's Bureau of Ships "sketched out . . . the basic design for the more than 1,000 LST's which would be built during World War II."

The *LST 1* was laid down in July 1942 and completed five months later; other LSTs took less time to build, and 1,050 were completed by June 1945, providing the U.S. and British navies with an invaluable amphibious tool. The American-built LST was 328 feet long, with a broad beam of 50 feet. (A war-built destroyer was 376 feet long, with a beam of only 39⅔ feet.) The LST could carry up to 18 of the 33-ton Sherman tanks or an equivalent in amphibious tractors or trucks and cargo. Vehicles could be parked on the upper (main) deck or lower (tank) deck, which were connected by ramp in the early ships and by an elevator in the later ones. The vehicles were unloaded through bow doors. In addition to a crew of some 210 officers and enlisted men, the LSTs could accommodate 160 troops. Flat-bottomed and likely to roll in any seaway, the LSTs were nicknamed "Large Slow Targets," although their casualty rate in the war would be remarkably low.

Landing ships and craft of all sizes would become the sine qua non of the amphibious landings that were the basis of Allied strategy to defeat Germany and Japan. Army Chief of Staff George C. Marshall would later remark, "Prior to the present war I never heard of any landing craft except a rubber boat. Now I think of little else." The new generation of landing ships and craft would make the amphibious assaults envisioned by Pete Ellis and Rainbow Plan No. 5 feasible in the event of war with Japan, presuming, of course, they could be transported safely to their island targets and not blown out of the water during the perilous transit from ship to shore.

Following the fall of France in June 1940, Japan began making demands that France, which had fewer than 13,000 troops in all of Indochina, had to accept. Ignoring protests from the United States and Britain, Japan moved to fulfill a strategic need, cutting off supplies reaching Nationalist troops in China via a railroad from the Indochinese port city of Haiphong. Japanese forces, while using French airfields, railways, and ports at Saigon and Cam-ranh Bay, allowed the French to continue administering Indochina.

In July 1941 the military-dominated Japanese Cabinet directed a takeover of the rest of Indochina. President Roosevelt responded by freezing all Japanese assets in the United States and cutting off oil exports to Japan. Premier Fumimaro Konoye tried to work out a diplomatic solution to the crisis, but the military leadership favored a tougher stand and at a conference in October 1941 urged that the nation "get ready for war."

Konoye resigned and was replaced by the Minister of War, General Hideki Tojo. Tojo had gained prominence as commander of the military police in Japanese-controlled Manchuria. He later became chief of staff of the Army forces there. An advocate of military control of the Japanese government, he became vice minister of war in 1938 and war minister in 1940—by far the most powerful member of the Cabinet.

A career Army officer, Tojo, in October 1941, simultaneously was appointed premier and promoted to full general by Emperor Hirohito. He was undoubtedly more soldier than statesman, and he oversaw a nation mobilizing for war. Gasoline was rationed, prices fixed, newspapers censored, and secret police were enforcing a law against "dangerous thoughts." Traditional military conscription was augmented by the drafting of workers for defense industries and mines. If the Japanese people "merge into one in iron solidarity," Tojo said after his appointment, "nothing can stop us. . . . Wars can be fought with ease."

With the military primed for war, Tojo reiterated Japanese demands: The United States must end aid to China, accept the Japanese seizure of Indochina, resume normal trade, and not reinforce U.S. bases in the Far East. He publicly maintained that the demands were not negotiable and set a deadline for American acceptance. Unaware that U.S. code breakers were reading Japanese diplomatic codes, he told the Japanese Ambassador to the United States, Kichisaburo Nomura, that negotiations were still possible.

Talks began between Secretary of State Cordell Hull and Nomura, aided by special envoy Saburo Kurusu, but the two nations were at an impasse. On November 26, Hull once more stated the U.S. position, which centered on Japanese withdrawal from China and Indochina. Tojo saw Hull's statement as an "ultimatum" and cocked the gun of war. The Japanese Navy's leadership had opposed war with the United States. The senior naval officers knew that Japan's resources were severely limited, especially oil. It was a long way from the oil fields in the Dutch East Indies—if they could be captured—and shipping routes would be vulnerable to enemy attacks. Senior naval officers understood the industrial potential of the United States. However, intimidated by Army officers and even by younger naval officers, they did not oppose Tojo and those who favored war.

Of all Japanese military leaders, Admiral Isoruku Yamamoto, Commander in Chief of the Japanese Combined Fleet, was perhaps the most aware of the quality and the industrial capacity of the enemy he would face if Japan went to war with the United States. He had been a member of the advisory team that accompanied Navy Minister Tomasaburo Kato to the 1921–1922 naval conference in Washington, D.C. He had also studied English at Harvard University and later served as Japanese naval attaché in Washington. As a result of his firsthand exposure to the U.S. potential for war, Yamamoto remained a part of the "Treaty Faction" throughout the 1920s and 1930s, believing that Japan could never match the United States in resources and that it was perilous to underestimate the American willingness to do battle, as many of his peers were prone to do.

But in January 1941, with Japan unalterably committed to a war with the United States, Yamamoto, a fervent gambler, heeded his instinct for high-stakes moves and conceived the idea of a preemptive attack on the U.S. Fleet at Pearl Harbor. He believed that the attack would be made 30 minutes to one hour *after* the declaration of war against the United States.

Yamamoto studied the successful November 1940 attack, by a single British carrier with 21 Swordfish torpedo planes, that smashed the Italian fleet in harbor at Taranto. He then convened a small, select group of naval aviation officers to plan the attack on Pearl Harbor and organized the massive strike force that would carry out the attack. Yamamoto believed that if he could destroy the U.S. Fleet's battleships and aircraft carriers, there would be no interference with Japanese offensive actions in the Pacific for six months.

The carrier pilots of the strike force trained intensively, attacking simulated targets in Kagoshima Bay on the southern Japanese island of Kyushu, which resembled Pearl Harbor. In mid-November the aircraft carriers secretly departed port, as did the other ships of the "Operation Hawaii" strike force. They converged at Hitokappu Bay on the island of Etorofu in the bleak Kuril Islands, north of Japan's home islands. There were six large carriers with almost 400 aircraft on their decks, two battleships, three cruisers, nine destroyers, three large (fleet) submarines, and eight oilers for refueling the warships in the carrier strike force.

On November 26, with radio transmitters sealed to ensure radio silence, the strike force headed east on the first leg of the voyage. The course, roughly along latitude 43 degrees north, took the force far from the usual shipping lanes, through high seas that swept several sailors overboard as the ships steamed eastward. In addition to the three submarines that proceeded the striking force, 27 other fleet submarines headed for Oahu to torpedo any U.S. warships that managed to escape from the aerial onslaught on Pearl Harbor. Five of these submarines carried two-man midget submarines to slip into the harbor before the air attack and add to the devastation.

On December 2 (Tokyo time), Yamamoto sent the strike force a message: "CLIMB MOUNT NITTAKA 1208." The message, naming Japan's highest mountain (on Formosa, then part of Japan), authorized the attack and ordered its date: December 8. At Pearl Harbor that date would be Sunday, December 7, 1941.

On December 5, during a Cabinet meeting in the White House, Navy Secretary Frank Knox told President Roosevelt, "Well, we have very secret information that mustn't go outside this room that the Japanese fleet is out. They're out of harbor. They're out at sea. . . . Every indication is that they are going south, Mr. President. That's the obvious direction."

"But," Roosevelt said, "it's not absolutely certain that they're not going north. You haven't got information with regard to direction."

"That's right, we haven't, but we must conclude that they are going south. It is so unlikely that they would go north."

South—the expected direction—was toward the riches of Malaya and the Dutch East Indies. North was toward Hawaii via the great-circle sailing route.

Meanwhile, Army and Navy code breakers in Washington were deciphering a 14-part message from Tokyo to the Japanese Embassy on Massachusetts Avenue. Sent in the Purple, or diplomatic, code, which Americans had been deciphering with some regularity since 1921, the last part of the message, not transmitted until the morning of December 7 (Washington time), was to be delivered to Secretary of State Hull at precisely 1 P.M., 20 minutes before the scheduled time of the attack on Pearl Harbor—7:50 in the morning. But because of delays by the Japanese Embassy staff in deciphering the last part of the message, the meeting with Hull was postponed until 2 P.M., and the Japanese emissaries were finally able to present the document to Hull at 2:20 P.M.—or 9:10 on Sunday morning in Pearl Harbor.

The Japanese strike force was on time. A little man than an hour before the deadline for delivery of the last part of the message that meant war between Japan and the United States, the six aircraft carriers, now 230 miles north of Oahu, turned into the wind, and green lights on their darkened flight decks signaled the start of the launch. The bomb- and torpedo-laden bombers and Zero fighters sped down the flight decks and into the brightening sky. The first wave consisted of 43 Zero fighters and 140 dive, torpedo, and level bombers—183 aircraft to fall upon the sleeping U.S. Fleet in Pearl Harbor on a Sunday morning.

At 7:55 A.M. the first bombs struck the naval air station on Ford Island in the center of Pearl Harbor. Torpedoes as well as bombs rained down on the warships. Zero fighters and Val dive bombers struck the several Army and Navy airfields on Oahu, destroying aircraft that had been parked wingtip to wingtip so that they could be more easily guarded against sabotage. The Army barracks at Hickham Field, adjacent to Pearl Harbor, were bombed and strafed.

But the most significant—and devastating—damage was done to "Battleship Row," the line of seven American dreadnoughts in berths along the eastern side of Ford Island: the battleship *California,* in the southernmost berth; the *Oklahoma,* moored outboard of the *Maryland;* the *West Virginia,* moored outboard of the *Tennessee;* the *Arizona* with the repair ship *Vestal,* moored outboard; and the *Nevada,* alone in the northernmost berth. (The eighth battleship at Pearl Harbor was the fleet flagship *Pennsylvania,* in dry dock at the adjacent navy yard.) Eighty-four other Navy ships were moored in the harbor, and two more were patrolling just outside the narrow entrance.

Bombs and torpedoes smashed into the battleships, and one by one they sank at their berths. The *Oklahoma,* struck by five torpedoes, rolled over, her masts digging into the harbor's mud bottom, hundreds of men trapped within her hull. One battleship, the *Nevada,* got under way during the attack, and as she slowly turned toward the harbor's entrance, Japanese planes pounced on her, hoping to block the channel. Badly battered, she was intentionally run aground to prevent her sinking.

A bomb stabbed the *Arizona,* passing into her forward magazines before exploding. Hundreds of 14-inch shells and thousands of bags of gunpowder—several hundred tons of high explosives—detonated. In that instant blast of flame more than 1,000 men died. The ship quickly settled to the shallow bottom of the harbor, a twisted, burning wreck.

More Japanese planes appeared over Oahu, the second wave of 37 Zeros and 132 dive and level bombers. More ships were struck and sunk. And when the last of the attackers flew away to return to their carriers, Pearl Harbor was shrouded in smoke, and several airfields had been devastated. The U.S. Fleet was crippled except for the fleet's three carriers, which had been absent from Pearl Harbor during the attack. There were 2,403 Americans dead, dying, or, trapped in ships, suffocating. Another 1,178 were wounded.

After attacking Pearl Harbor, the Japanese struck Singapore, the Philippines, Guam, and Wake. Although General MacArthur had nine hours of warning, the Japanese bombers caught most of his aircraft on the ground.

One hour and 20 minutes before the Pearl Harbor attack, the Japanese made amphibious landings in northern Malaya and began the march on Singapore. Troops also landed on the southern tip of Burma.

By the spring of 1942, Japan would control the entire western Pacific, along with the Philippines, Indochina, Malaya, Burma, and much of the coastal areas of China. The conquering soldiers carried with them a little book, *Read This Alone—And the War Can Be Won*, which told them they were liberating a "treasure-house of the Far East, seized by the British, the Americans, the French and the Dutch." Unlike the lands of the treasure-house, said the book, "our land has never once, to this day, experienced invasion and occupation by a foreign power. The other peoples of the Far East look with envy upon Japan. . . ."

In the 44 months of war that began on December 7—"a date which will live in infamy," said President Roosevelt—the goal of the United States would become the complete defeat of Japan. But how was that to be accomplished and at what cost in American lives? For those who had labored over war plans, the swift Japanese conquests seemed to mock their work. They had presumed U.S. naval superiority; much of the Pacific Fleet lay in ruin. They had presumed that American-held island bases would provide steppingstones across the vast Pacific to the shores of Japan; now the Japanese held them. The linchpins of American strategy against Japan—naval blockade and aerial bombardment—could not be carried out until the home islands were within range of ships and planes that were yet to be built. The visionary planners had been right about an eventual American-Japanese conflict. They had been wrong in assuming that victory would be swift and easy.

CHAPTER 2

THE BLOODY ROAD TO JAPAN

The assault on Tarawa in the Gilbert Islands in November 1943 was a harbinger of the high cost of amphibious warfare. Almost a thousand Marines died in just three days.

Admiral Chester W. Nimitz, a soft-spoken Texan, was far from the Pacific when the Japanese attacked Pearl Harbor. He was a Washington naval bureaucrat, the chief of the Navy's Bureau of Navigation, which oversaw personnel matters.

On the days that followed the attack, Nimitz worked around the clock. Among his tasks were grim new ones—compiling casualty lists, replacing the dead and wounded. Then, on December 16, Secretary of the Navy Frank Knox, just back from an inspection of the disaster at Pearl Harbor, called Nimitz to his office. The day before and again that morning, Knox had conferred with President Roosevelt about relieving Admiral Husband E. Kimmel, the fleet commander at Pearl Harbor.

Nimitz walked wearily down to the secretary's office in the Main Navy Building, a World War I "temporary" structure on Constitution Avenue. Knox, seated at his desk and obviously excited, did not ask Nimitz to sit down. He blurted out, "How soon can you be ready to travel?"

Nimitz, his nerves on edge from fatigue, answered a little crossly: "It depends on where I'm going and how long I'll be away."

"You're going to take command of the Pacific Fleet, and I think you will be gone for a long time," replied Knox.

On the afternoon of December 19, Nimitz and his aide departed Washington by train for the West Coast. They wore civilian clothes and traveled under assumed names. The aide, Lieutenant (junior grade) H. Arthur Lamar, carried a canvas sack, given to him by the Chief of Naval Operations, who said, "Don't let this out of your possession, and don't open it until you are well along the way outside of Chicago. Then show Admiral Nimitz what's inside." Another admiral had given Lamar two quarts of Old Granddad and said, "Every night, before dinner, make sure the admiral gets two good slugs, because he's got to get some rest."

In Chicago, between trains, Nimitz took a taxi to the Navy pier for a much-needed haircut and a quick visit to the reserve midshipman's school. He learned by radio that Wake Island was still holding out against a Japanese onslaught. He and Lamar then boarded the Santa Fe Superchief for California. On that train, Lamar opened the sack. Until then Nimitz did not know the full extent of the damage to the fleet he was to command. The sack contained vivid photographs of the disaster. Nimitz looked them over and, thinking of his old friend Kimmel, said, "It could have happened to me."

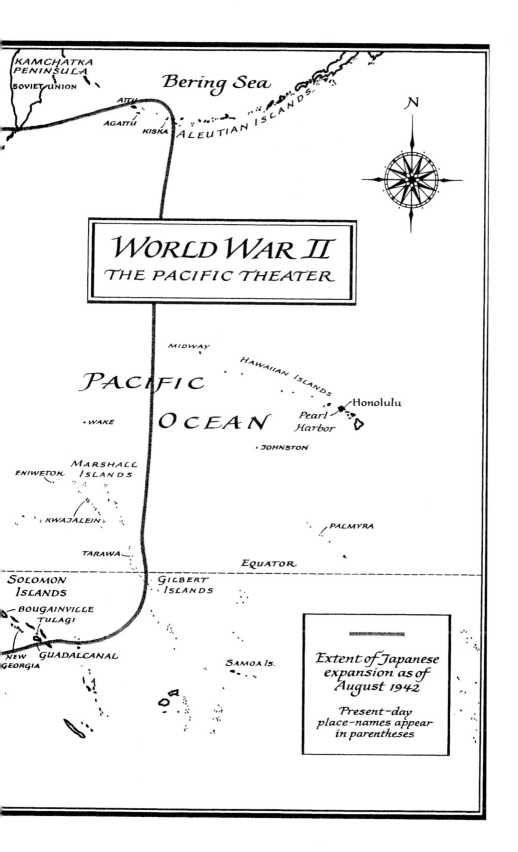

From California Nimitz flew on to Hawaii, where he met with Kimmel, who had been temporarily relieved of command by Vice Admiral W.S. Pye on December 17. Kimmel told Nimitz that while he was standing at his office window on the morning of December 7, watching his fleet being destroyed, a spent .50-caliber bullet had broken the window and hit his chest. "Too bad it didn't kill me," Kimmel said. Nimitz comforted his friend and later sat down with him for a game of cribbage.

Nimitz took command of the Pacific Fleet on December 31, when his four-star flag was hoisted aboard the submarine *Grayling,* the only warship readily available, he said, amid the wreckage of Pearl Harbor. Kimmel's staff officers assumed that they were wreckage, too, but Nimitz kept virtually all of them. It was sensible as well as a sensitive act because it preserved their experience as well as instantly raising morale.

Meanwhile, the Japanese were engulfing the western Pacific, with little opposition from Allied warships, just as Admiral Yamamoto had planned. Among their many targets was New Guinea, one of the world's largest islands, separated from Australia to the south by the Torres Strait. It was a necessary steppingstone for Japanese plans to occupy or at least neutralize the northern coast of Australia. When the war began, the western half of New Guinea was a Dutch colony and largely unexplored; the eastern half, which included Papua, was under British-Australian administration.

Japanese troops landed without opposition on the northern coast of New Guinea in early March 1942. The small Australian garrison had withdrawn. But the Australians knew they had to hold Port Moresby, capital of Papua, on the southeastern coast because if the Japanese captured the port and airfields, their bombers could attack Australia, and Port Moresby's harbor would be a staging area for assault ships for an invasion.

The Japanese planned a major assault against Port Moresby—designated Operation MO (for *Moresby*)—with 70 ships involved. The assault and support force included a small carrier, while two large carriers and their escorts were to provide protective cover in the unlikely event that U.S. naval forces interfered. But Admiral Nimitz knew in advance of the Japanese plans through the efforts of his code breakers, who, by the spring of 1942, were able to systematically read some Japanese naval communications. As the Japanese ships steamed toward Port Moresby, Nimitz positioned two U.S. carriers and their cruiser-destroyer escorts in the Coral Sea to intercept them.

The ensuing Battle of the Coral Sea, on May 7–8, 1942, was the first naval battle in history fought entirely by aircraft; the opposing ships never sighted the enemy. The Japanese light carrier *Shoho* was sunk, and one of the larger flattops, the *Shokaku,* was damaged. The U.S. Navy lost the carrier *Lexington* —at the time one of the two largest aircraft carriers in the world—as well as an oiler and a destroyer. The sinking of the "Lex" was far more significant than the Japanese loss of the light carrier *Shoho*. However, the Japanese suffered another loss: many irreplaceable carrier pilots. The large *Shokaku* had to enter a shipyard and would not be available for operations for a month, and the *Zuikaku* required time to rehabilitate her air group. Most important, the Japanese assault force heading toward Port Moresby was turned back. It was by no means the decisive naval encounter envisioned by the Orange war plans, but it was the first Japanese setback of the war.

Port Moresby was only one target of the advancing Japanese octopus. Another arm subsequently sought to capture the U.S. atoll outpost of Midway, 1,100 miles northwest of Pearl Harbor. For this assault, planned for early June 1942, the Japanese assembled the largest fleet yet seen in the war. The main force consisted of seven battleships and four fleet carriers, with several smaller carriers distributed among the Japanese task forces.

Again warned by U.S. code breakers, Admiral Nimitz secretly deployed three carriers to the area. In the carrier-versus-carrier battle on June 4, the Japanese lost all four fleet carriers and most of their pilots as well as aircraft, plus a heavy cruiser. The U.S. Navy lost one carrier, the *Yorktown,* which had been previously damaged in the Coral Sea. Midway was an overwhelming American tactical victory as well as a strategic victory, for again a Japanese invasion force was turned away.

With the victory at Midway, the United States suddenly had the Japanese off balance, and major U.S. naval forces were now available for offensive operations in the Pacific, including the 1st Marine Division. But American forces were still on the defensive, and more had to be done to stop the Japanese, especially since their next major operation would almost certainly be another thrust to take Port Moresby and then an assault against the northern coast of Australia.

The Battle of the Coral Sea had temporarily postponed the Japanese plans (although several cities on the Australian north coast were bombed by Japanese aircraft). The Japanese now moved toward the Solomon Islands as a prelude to a renewed assault on Port Moresby. Tulagi, the capital of the British Solomon Islands government, was invaded and the town captured in May 1942. Since most of the defense forces had been evacuated, the Japanese troops of the 3rd Kure Special Naval Landing Force, and the accompanying contingent of laborers, found little opposition when they landed.

The Japanese immediately set to work building a seaplane base at Tulagi and sent survey teams across the Sealark Channel to the jungle-covered island of Guadalcanal. The surveys were completed in June, and by July work was begun on an airstrip. The Japanese effort was observed by Australian coast watchers. Courageous men under Commander Eric Feldt, they led solitary and incredibly dangerous lives to monitor Japanese activities and radio the information from behind enemy lines.

One coast watcher reported that 3,000 Japanese were at work building the airfield on Guadalcanal. This report, along with other intelligence, convinced Allied planners that a counterattack had to be launched to deny the

Japanese the airfield. As early as February 1942, Admiral Ernest J. King, the Commander in Chief U.S. Fleet, had told General George C. Marshall, the Army Chief of Staff, that it would be necessary to invade the Solomons, not only to protect Australia but also to provide airfields for offensive bombing attacks against the major Japanese naval base at Rabaul on northern New Britain. The American assault on Guadalcanal would be the first American amphibious landing in World War II and the first offensive action in the Pacific War.

Decisions concerning U.S. offensive operations in the Solomons—and indeed in the entire course of the Pacific War—emerged from a complex command structure. President Roosevelt and Prime Minister Churchill were not only national leaders but actively participated in the direction of the war. The principal military advisers of each of these men were their chiefs of staff—the military heads of their army, navy, and air force. The Combined Chiefs of Staff, the service chiefs of both countries, met periodically, were in daily communication, and sponsored several joint planning committees.

The U.S. Joint Chiefs of Staff (JCS) was established on February 9, 1942, as a counterpart to the British chiefs of staff. The JCS consisted of the heads of the Army, Navy, and Army Air Forces and, from June 1942, was chaired by Admiral William D. Leahy, chief of staff to the President. The JCS decided the strategy for American military forces. Under their direction, area commanders in chiefs directed all U.S. forces in their respective areas (regardless of service) as well as Allied forces that could be made available.

For most of the war the Joint Chiefs would consist of General Marshall, Admiral King, and General H.H. Arnold. If there was anything that bound them together, it was their ability to focus on the war. They sometimes opposed Roosevelt's decisions, particularly his prewar machinations to evade neutrality laws. But, unlike General Douglas MacArthur, they never advertised disagreement or discontent. And they managed to keep their considerable egos from colliding while they went about the business of fighting a war.

Marshall had been appointed Army Chief of Staff in September 1939, when the Germans marched into Poland to ignite World War II in Europe. He had based a solid career on his excellent staff work at headquarters of the U.S. expeditionary force in France in World War I. When he began building an Army for the next war, he turned to old friends and was often disappointed. One, selected for an overseas assignment, begged off, saying he could not leave because his furniture was not packed and his wife was away. "My God, man, we are at war, and you are a general," Marshall told him. The man said he was sorry. "I'm sorry, too," Marshall said, "but you will be retired tomorrow."

In a black notebook that he kept in a desk drawer, Marshall listed the names of officers he personally knew. When he was mulling over an assign-ment or a promotion, he looked in the book, sometimes drawing a line through a name, sometimes adding a name. "I was accused of getting rid of all the brains of the Army," he once said. "I couldn't reply that I was eliminat-ing considerable arteriosclerosis."

Marshall had wanted Admiral Leahy to be a "Chief of Staff of the military services." But Roosevelt insisted that he, as Commander in Chief, was also *the* Chief of Staff. "I explained to him in great frankness," Marshall recalled, that one man could not be President and head of all the military services—not even a man with "the powers of Superman." Although Roosevelt did not like the idea that he was not Superman, he did name Leahy to serve as chairman of the JCS.

Leahy acted as an interlocutor between the Joint Chiefs and the President. "I was a legman," he once explained, gathering information for the President from his other military advisers. When he gave Roosevelt a JCS view contrary to the President's, Roosevelt would tell him, "I am a pig-headed Dutchman, Bill, and I have made up my mind about this. We are going ahead with this, and you can't change my mind." As Marshall put it, Leahy "became more the Chief of Staff of the President and less the chairman of the Chiefs of Staff."

Marshall's most troublesome relationship was with Admiral King, a tall, arrogant man who rarely displayed any patience. King had long been in line for the highest Navy post, Chief of Naval Operations. Stiff-necked and easily infuriated, he would not curry favors. "He is the most even-tempered man in the Navy," one of his daughters once said. "He's always in a rage." In December 1940 he was given command of the Atlantic Squadron, which Roosevelt upgraded to fleet status two months later to wage his undeclared war against German U-boats. With the fleet status, King received four-star rank. His fortune in being Commander in Chief of the Atlantic Fleet and not Chief of Naval Operations in Washington at the time of the attack on Pearl Harbor, coupled with Roosevelt's high opinion of his abilities, led to his appointment as Commander in Chief U.S. Fleet after Pearl Harbor. In the Navy's custom of creating speakable abbreviations, his command was known as CinCUS (pronounced *Sinkus*). He did not like the sound of that and changed his title to CominCh *(Cominch)*. As CominCh, King virtually ran naval operations, while Admiral Stark, with the title of Chief of Naval Opera-tions, watched over logistics. In March 1942, Roosevelt gave King the addi-tional position of Chief of Naval Operations. When a friend who knew King's temperament asked in amazement how he had managed to get the job, legend says King replied, "When they get in trouble, they send for the sons of bitches."

Soon after becoming Chief of Naval Operations, King called on Marshall and, deciding he had been kept waiting too long, stalked out of the general's office. Marshall hurried to King's office and tried to explain that other busi-ness, not discourtesy, had delayed their meeting. "We can't afford to fight,"

Marshall said. "So we ought to find a way to get along together." King did not reply for a while. Then, grudgingly, he said, "We will see if we get along, and I think we can."

They did get along, and part of the reason was that King, who watched closely over the Pacific War, knew that if he were going to have an Army ally, Marshall would be much better to deal with than the senior Army officer in the Pacific, Douglas MacArthur. King worried about the Pacific because he did not entirely accept Nimitz's strategic judgment, perhaps because he did not trust a man so kind and courteous.

Lieutenant General Hap Arnold was often the odd man out in the Joint Chiefs of Staff. He was given a seat on the JCS only because Britain's Royal Air Force was a separate service and the Americans needed an "opposite number" when they met with the British. The Army Air Forces were a part of the Army; Marshall, as Army Chief of Staff, was Arnold's superior. But he gave Arnold a considerable degree of independence in running Army aviation.

In November 1938, President Roosevelt had ordered 10,000 aircraft a year for what was then the small, struggling Air Corps. In May 1940 he asked for 50,000 planes a year. "In forty-five minutes," Arnold later said, "I was given $1,500,000,000 and told to get an air force." He did, and on June 21, 1941, the War Department recognized it by creating the Army Air Forces, with Arnold as its chief.

Marshall and Arnold had met in the Philippines in 1914, when Marshall was a first lieutenant and Arnold, although certified as an Army pilot, was posted as an infantry officer. Seeing Marshall's brilliance as a planner of an exercise, Arnold told his wife he had just met a future Army Chief of Staff. Arnold's admiration endured. When they served together as Joint Chiefs, Marshall later said, "Arnold's disposition to cooperate with me was a very wonderful thing."

Arnold, however, brooded over what he saw as a misuse of air power. He confided to his diary that the Navy, to keep its warships out of harm's way, was using "subterfuge and cunning" in a plot "to run a land war relying upon the Army, Air and Marines to put it across." Just as King saw the Pacific as his main theater, Arnold saw Europe—"to demonstrate we can do things against Goering"—as the most important place for his air forces to prosper. But gradually, under subordinate officers with a brilliance that Arnold enviously lacked, the Army Air Forces would achieve major roles in both Europe and the Pacific.

In early March 1942, Prime Minister Churchill and President Roosevelt decided to set up a new command structure for the Pacific. There had been the so-called ABDA Command, for American, British, Dutch, and Australian forces, established on January 15, 1942. But little more than a month later—

on February 25—the command was dissolved, and the hopeless defense of Java was left to Dutch forces. Subsequently, Churchill and Roosevelt agreed that operational responsibility for the Pacific area would rest with the United States—which would have most of the combat forces in the region—with operational decisions made by the U.S. Joint Chiefs of Staff, advised by representatives from other Allied nations.

An American would thus be the principal commander in the Pacific. But the key question was which American would hold that position. The obvious choice was MacArthur, a national hero for his stand against the Japanese invaders in the Philippines. Equally important, MacArthur was in Australia and hence in the war zone. But, from the Navy's viewpoint, he could not be put in command of naval forces in the Pacific. The Joint Chiefs accordingly set up two commands that would function under the Joint Chiefs of Staff. Two theater commanders were appointed in March 1942 to direct the Pacific campaigns: General MacArthur was named Commander in Chief Southwest Pacific Area, and Admiral Nimitz was named Commander in Chief Pacific Ocean Areas.

MacArthur's life and career were a parade of superlatives. He had garnered virtually every possible award at West Point and had graduated first in his 1903 class of 94 cadets, with a record that was surpassed by only two other graduates, one in 1884 and one in 1829—the latter, Robert E. Lee, the leading Confederate general of the American Civil War. During World War I combat in France, while commanding the 42nd (Rainbow) Division, MacArthur won several decorations for valor and became the youngest brigadier general in the U.S. Army. He was one of the few men ever to be twice nominated for the Medal of Honor, which was finally awarded in March 1942 after his escape from the Philippines—which had been ordered by President Roosevelt.

In 1930, MacArthur became the Chief of Staff of the Army, a position he held until 1934, after which he was appointed head of the Philippine Army by President Manuel Quezon, averting an anti-climactic retirement. For his new role MacArthur chose the title of Field Marshal.

MacArthur was recalled to active U.S. service on July 27, 1941, and named commanding general of U.S. Army Forces (including air forces) in the Far East. By then, with war against Japan becoming likely, MacArthur was convinced that he could repel a Japanese invasion of the Philippines. This conviction, expressed with MacArthur's usual vigor, overturned a central assumption of the U.S. war plans and led directly to the stubborn, ultimately futile stands against Japanese invaders on Bataan and Corregidor in 1942.

MacArthur's relationship with Quezon produced two odd episodes that did not become known until long after he was being hailed as a hero. On January 3, 1942, in a secret order, Quezon gave $500,000 in Philippine funds to MacArthur (and $140,000 to members of his staff), placing the funds on deposit in the United States. Under Army regulations, MacArthur should not have accepted the money, but he may have interpreted it as payment for his previous service as Field Marshal MacArthur.

MacArthur also supported Quezon in early 1942 when he began to think about negotiating a separate peace with Japan. Quezon notified Roosevelt about his plans, and MacArthur said the idea might be the "best possible solution of what is about to be a disastrous debacle." The proposal shocked and outraged Roosevelt, who ordered MacArthur to get Quezon and himself out of the Philippines. Quezon was evacuated by a U.S. submarine. MacArthur said he and his family would "share the fate of the garrison," but ultimately he did leave and took command of the few U.S. troops in Australia.

Roosevelt disliked MacArthur's arrogant behavior, although he made no public move against him. In the spring of 1942, Congressman Lyndon B. Johnson, a lieutenant commander in the Naval Reserve, was a member of a survey team sent by Roosevelt to the Southwest Pacific. Johnson later claimed that Roosevelt also told him to "look into charges against General MacArthur," but nothing came of the Johnson report.

In contrast to MacArthur, Admiral Nimitz commanded the immense U.S. effort in the Pacific with little self-promotion but great confidence, based on a career in which he had shown a flexibility of mind and a firmness of character. His interests before World War II ranged from submarines (he was the Navy's expert on diesel engines) to naval aviation. His commands included a submarine, a heavy cruiser, a cruiser division, and a battleship division. Now, as Commander in Chief Pacific Ocean Areas, Nimitz would rely heavily on his subordinate commanders and staff, much more so than MacArthur, who left little initiative to his subordinates.

MacArthur's Southwest Pacific Area included Australia and the Philippines —and all waters between them—as well as New Guinea and the Bismarck and Solomon Islands; Nimitz had the vast Pacific regions to the east, including the Japanese home islands. Both men were given command of all U.S. and Allied forces in their respective areas, with Nimitz also remaining the commander of the Pacific Fleet.

Soon after arriving in Australia, MacArthur proposed—some would say demanded—that an immediate offensive be launched from Australia against the Japanese, with the first target to be Rabaul, on New Britain, an Australian-mandated island. It was a bold wish. Rabaul had been captured by the Japanese in January 1942 and turned into a stronghold. There were five airfields on the island, which, combined with the large sheltered harbor, led some Allied planners to call Rabaul the "Gibraltar of the Pacific."

The small number of U.S. and Australian troops and aircraft available to MacArthur could not undertake so ambitious an operation as an assault on Rabaul. They lacked amphibious training, and there was a shortage of suitable ships and landing craft. The only U.S. troops in the Pacific capable of making an assault landing at the time were the men of the 1st Marine Division, and they belonged to the Pacific Fleet—Admiral Nimitz's command. Also, aircraft carriers would be needed to support any offensive operation in the area. The Navy, with only three carriers and a correspondingly small number of aircraft, was not anxious to place its Marines or carriers under the control of an Army general.

MacArthur's plan to attack Rabaul was stillborn when Admiral King directed Nimitz to begin planning an invasion of Guadalcanal. The previously obscure Japanese-occupied island in the Solomon Islands chain, lying to the east of New Guinea, had not been a target of either American or Japanese planners when the war began.

Guadalcanal lay in the Southwest Pacific and was technically under MacArthur's jurisdiction. The line between the two theaters was the 160th degree of east longitude. After vigorous debate, King and Marshall changed the boundary to the 159th degree to put Guadalcanal under Nimitz's command because his Navy and Marine units were to be used in the assault against the island. A tacit agreement was reached that after the initial, primary invasion was satisfactorily completed by the Navy-Marine team, the Army (under MacArthur) would take over the Guadalcanal operation and begin a drive northward toward the Philippines, in accord with a modified approach to the War Plan Orange objective—and MacArthur's insistence that the Philippines be recaptured.

The assault force for Operation Watchtower—the invasion of Guadalcanal —included 24 transports and cargo ships carrying some 19,000 Marines, screened by 54 warships, including three aircraft carriers. The U.S. warships, transports, and cargo ships evaded Japanese detection en route to Guadalcanal. Bad weather had kept Japanese scouting planes grounded, and raids by U.S. Army B-17 Flying Fortress bombers, beginning on July 31, had apparently given the Japanese little cause for concern.

A company from the 2nd Marine Regiment waded ashore on Florida Island, just beyond Tulagi, to the north of Guadalcanal, at 7:40 A.M. on August 7, 1942. Minutes later, Marines landed on adjacent Gavutu Island and Guadalcanal. The landings completely surprised the Japanese, and no immediate opposition was encountered.

At 8 A.M. the 1st Marine Raider Battalion stormed onto Tulagi, again meeting no defenses, luckily, since their landing craft hung up on an uncharted reef and the troops waded ashore from distances of 30 to 100 yards out. The Japanese force on Tulagi, earlier estimated to be around 8,000, was, in reality, closer to 500 troops. After some delay they regrouped and defended the island, almost to the last man. The Raiders and reinforcing 2nd Battalion, 5th Marines, fought through the night against Japanese counterattacks, a frightening foretaste of things to come. By the afternoon of August 8, Tulagi was controlled by Marines.

The Marines who landed on Guadalcanal at 9:10 A.M. on August 7 waded through the surf and walked ashore. There had been a prelanding bombardment by American cruisers and destroyers, and here, too, the Japanese were caught by complete surprise. No Japanese were sighted even after the Marines left the beach to push inland toward the steaming jungle. Finding no one to fight, they turned their attention to bringing supplies ashore through the night.

During the first 24 hours of the landing 11,145 Marines came ashore on Guadalcanal; 6,805 more landed on adjacent Tulagi and Gavutu-Tanambogo. When the Japanese finally woke up to the fact that there was a full-scale invasion under way, the area headquarters at Rabaul, some 600 miles northwest of Guadalcanal, mounted an immediate air strike against the invasion force.

Twenty-seven Betty bombers—twin-engine Mitsubishi G4M aircraft—with an escort of 18 Zero fighters, flew over coast watcher Paul Mason's position at 11 A.M. on August 8. Mason radioed his sighting, and Rear Admiral Richmond Kelly Turner, commander of the landing forces, ordered the landing craft away from the beach and got the assault fleet under way. The Bettys, armed for a strike against New Guinea, were unable to change their bombs for torpedoes, a more appropriate weapon for attacking ships. The bombers found their moving targets difficult to hit with bombs, and no damage was inflicted on the ships. Two Bettys were shot down. A later strike by Japanese dive bombers also failed; three were shot down, and six more of the single-engine planes were lost at sea en route back to Rabaul. By then the Marines were headed inland toward their main objective, the unfinished airfield, to which the Japanese had retreated when they belatedly realized the strength of the U.S. landing. The period of relative calm on Guadalcanal was about to end.

On August 8–9 a nighttime naval battle—called the Battle of Savo Island—ended in a tactical victory for the Japanese as their cruisers and destroyers made a successful night attack against an Allied cruiser-destroyer force, sinking three U.S. cruisers and one Australian cruiser. Other U.S. ships were damaged or disabled, and the U.S. carrier force was withdrawn in fear of more Japanese attacks, leaving the troops ashore on their own. The Japanese ships suffered minor damage and withdrew before attacking the vulnerable troopships standing off Guadalcanal.

Over the next two months, the Guadalcanal assault developed into a land campaign supported by ships and aircraft that engaged in major naval and air battles with the Japanese. In October 1942 the U.S. Army's Americal Division began landing on Guadalcanal to reinforce the tired and bloodied Marines. By mid-October there were 23,000 U.S. Marines and soldiers on Guadalcanal to face some 20,000 surviving Japanese troops.

The amphibious phase of the battle had done what it was supposed to: get the men and their weapons ashore. And it was a total success, in part because it caught the Japanese by surprise. But the Japanese did not give up

Guadalcanal without a fight. They even mounted their own limited amphibious landings behind Marine lines to counterattack the U.S. invaders. They conducted supply operations through night runs down "The Slot," the passage between the main islands of the Solomons. The troops and supplies sent down The Slot by the "Tokyo Express" at one time seriously threatened the American hold on Guadalcanal. In six major naval engagements around the island within a space of four months, the U.S. Navy lost two aircraft carriers as well as several other warships.

On December 31, 1942, when Japanese military leaders finally realized that Guadalcanal had been lost, Emperor Hirohito gave his permission to evacuate. The Japanese conducted a massive, largely successful operation to withdraw their surviving troops from the island, beginning on the night of February 1–2 and concluding on February 7–8. Under the cover of ably handled destroyers, the Japanese made an "amphibious withdrawal," evacuating some 12,000 troops, most of them suffering from dysentery and malnutrition.

The Guadalcanal campaign gave the Americans their first major land victory against the seemingly unbeatable Japanese. For their part, the Japanese were stunned by the defeat. It was as though the myth of their invincibility, to which they themselves had fallen victim, had been shattered at sea in the Battle of Midway and now on land at Guadalcanal.

But Guadalcanal was a costly campaign for both sides. More than 25,000 Japanese died on Guadalcanal, including about 9,000 from disease and starvation. U.S. forces suffered 1,592 killed and 4,800 wounded. There were also many cases of jungle diseases. Hundreds of U.S. Navy men were killed in the 2 aircraft carriers, 7 cruisers, and 14 destroyers sunk in Solomon actions; one Australian cruiser was also sunk. Many Japanese ships were lost, and thousands of Japanese sailors also died in the seas around the Solomons.

The Solomons had not been a target of the Orange war plans, but the capture of Guadalcanal conformed to the overall strategy of the Pacific War, a slow march northward that would continue to the degree that amphibious shipping, troops, and aircraft could be spared from Europe. And although the first steps had been taken on the march, the Japanese home islands were still 3,200 miles away.

Simultaneous with the battle for Guadalcanal, General MacArthur began a limited offensive on New Guinea, some 600 miles to the west of Guadalcanal. Shaped like a prehistoric monster facing westward, its tail, the Papuan Peninsula, pointed toward Guadalcanal and was covered by dense, virtually impassable jungle. In March 1942 the Japanese had moved unopposed across the Solomon Sea from New Britain to occupy the small ports of Lae and Salamaua on the northern side of the New Guinea "tail." On the other side of the mountainous spine of the tail, the Allies held Port Moresby, site of an airfield from which B-17 bombers could fly. The Japanese looked at the naval battle in early May—the Battle of the Coral Sea—as a temporary setback and continued their advance toward Port Moresby, with small naval forces staging down the northern coast of Papua and troops marching overland across the mountains.

General MacArthur's small force of U.S. and Australian soldiers, supported by a few combat aircraft and a group of Australian and American cruisers and destroyers, began a campaign against the Japanese on New Guinea in July 1942. Through the end of the year there were Allied and Japanese landings and counterlandings, the Americans usually making do with coastal cargo ships. Only later would MacArthur have specialized amphibious ships and landing craft. The Navy still was reluctant to allow major fleet units to operate under MacArthur.

When MacArthur's offensive in New Guinea bogged down in December 1942, he appointed the skillful Major General Robert Eichelberger to relieve the commander of the 32nd Infantry Division. Eichelberger had served as secretary to the Army's General Staff when MacArthur was Army Chief of Staff in the 1930s. He told Eichelberger, "If you capture Buna I'll award you the Distinguished Service Cross. I'll recommend you for a high British decoration, and I'll release your name for newspaper publication." After a pause, MacArthur added: "Bob, take Buna or don't come back alive." Buna —halfway up the back of the New Guinea tail—fell to U.S. and Australian troops on January 2, 1943.

Casualties were heavy in MacArthur's six-month Papua campaign. The U.S. Army's 32nd Infantry Division and part of the 41st Division had 13,645 troops in the campaign; they lost 787 killed and 2,172 wounded—a casualty rate of almost 22 percent. The Australians lost another 2,165 killed and 3,533 wounded. In addition, almost 8,000 American troops were "evacuated sick" with a variety of jungle diseases, as were many Australians. The American casualty rate on Guadalcanal was much lower for the same period.

In February 1943, with the capture of Guadalcanal, the South Pacific Force, at the time under the command of Admiral William F. Halsey and subordinate to Admiral Nimitz at Pearl Harbor, was shifted to the operational control of General MacArthur's Southwest Pacific Area. One of the most outspoken and aggressive Navy commanders, Halsey had served in surface warships until 1935, when, at the time a captain at the age of 53, he took flight training, qualified as a pilot—although he often petrified onlookers when he flew— and took command of the aircraft carrier *Saratoga*. When the war began, he was a vice admiral and in command of naval aircraft and carriers in the Pacific, where he won a reputation for being a fast, decisive leader idolized by his men. A war correspondent once called Halsey reckless. When he heard about the accusation, he responded, "Aggressive, yes; audacious, yes; but not reckless."

Halsey had commanded the Doolittle raid, and in October 1942, Nimitz appointed him Commander South Pacific Subarea to complete the Guadalcanal campaign and move northward. Promoted to full admiral in November 1942, he was in the unusual situation of being responsible to Nimitz for his ships, aircraft, and troops and to MacArthur for his strategic direction.

Unlike most senior naval officers, Halsey usually worked well with MacArthur. "Five minutes after I [met him] I felt as if we were lifelong friends," he later wrote. "I have seldom seen a man who makes a quicker, stronger, more favorable impression." During one meeting with Halsey and others, while discussing command of naval forces that would be fully assigned to MacArthur, which came to be designated the Seventh Fleet, MacArthur turned to Halsey and asked, "How about *you*, Bill? If you come with me, I'll make you a greater man than Nelson ever dreamed of being." Halsey replied that he was flattered and would discuss the situation with Nimitz, his boss. Halsey continued to work for Nimitz.

Halsey and MacArthur coordinated operations in the Solomon Islands and New Guinea, beginning in November 1942. And Halsey, like MacArthur, captured the attention of war correspondents. His friends called him "Bill"; the press—impressed with his aggressive attitude—nicknamed him "Bull," but never to his face.

Ashore and at sea, MacArthur and Halsey began to move northward, along the coast of New Guinea and in the Solomons, respectively. The numerous naval battles in these waters were fought by all kinds of warships, but many engagements were at night with only destroyers, light cruisers, and the diminutive motor torpedo boats, called PT boats in the U.S. Navy. In a savage engagement on the night of November 12–13 the American light cruiser *Juneau* was severely damaged by a Japanese ship-launched torpedo and the next day blew up and sank after being hit by another torpedo fired by the submarine *I-26*. Most of the *Juneau*'s crew of 700 were lost, among them the five brothers of the Sullivan family; only ten men survived the attacks and sinking.

On another night in the continuing sea battles in the Solomons, August 1–2, 1943, *PT 109*, moving slowly in the water, looking for Japanese troop barges, was surprised by the Japanese destroyer *Amagiri*, which smashed through its fragile hull. Two American sailors were killed; the *PT 109*'s skipper, Lieutenant John F. Kennedy, and ten others survived after a lengthy swim to an island and rescue a few days later by U.S. forces.

The relentless American drive continued along the northern coast of New Guinea and up the islands of the Solomon chain. Meanwhile, half a world away, the Allies had at last gone on the offensive. On November 8, 1942, U.S. and British troops under the command of Lieutenant General Dwight D. Eisenhower landed at Casablanca, Algiers, and Oran in North Africa. More than 100,000 American and British troops came ashore in the North African landings (code-named Torch), dwarfing the ongoing campaigns against the Japanese in the Solomons and on New Guinea. The Army had a new hero in the making, and MacArthur's island campaigns were all but forgotten.

President Roosevelt and Prime Minister Churchill and their chiefs of staff convened at Casablanca, Morocco, on January 14, 1943, in their first overseas meeting, code-named Symbol. That day, Admiral King expressed his personal view of the future Allied strategy in the Pacific, upon which the American chiefs of staff had not yet come to an agreement. King declared that after the conquest of the Japanese base–fortress complex at Rabaul, the Allies should aim for the Philippines rather than attempting to clear the Japanese from the East Indies. The route to the Philippines, King declared, should be through the Marshall Islands, then to Truk in the Caroline Islands, and on to the Mariana Islands. His proposal closely followed the Orange war plans, developed at the Naval War College that he, like virtually all other American admirals, had attended.

King next raised the issue of resources allocated to the various war theaters. He declared that only 15 percent of the total Allied war effort was being applied to Japan—including the China-Burma-India areas. This was enough only to hold the line, not enough to maintain pressure on the Japanese. King was supported by General Marshall, who reiterated the Navy chief's premise that the only way to defeat the Japanese was to retain the initiative and force them to fight. King and Marshall called for sending 30 percent of the available war matériel to the Pacific, including Burma.

The U.S. Joint Chiefs of Staff did not win British endorsement of their proposal that more effort should go to the war against Japan. The British expressed the fear that "if operations were too extended it would inevitably lead to an all-out war against Japan" for which sufficient resources could not be available at the same time a major effort was being made against Germany.

On January 18 the Combined Chiefs of Staff presented Roosevelt and Churchill with their recommendations for the conduct of the war. It was still a Germany-first strategy, but the capture of Rabaul and operations against the Marshall Islands and Truk, as well as offensive operations in Burma, were approved. With a promised increase in resources for the war in the Pacific, the U.S. Joint Chiefs of Staff developed a five-phase plan for the South Pacific. Under the overall name of Operation Elkton, the plan included capturing New Georgia, Bougainville, Kavieng, and New Ireland and, ultimately, a mass assault on Rabaul at the eastern end of New Britain Island by no less than 23 Allied ground divisions and 45 air groups. The first part of the plan was begun in early 1943 by the forces under General MacArthur and Admiral Halsey moving along the coast of New Guinea and up the Solomon Islands, respectively.

Admiral Halsey's forces, continuing northward from Guadalcanal, seized the smaller islands and, by the end of the year, the large island of Bougainville, just 165 air miles southeast of Rabaul. MacArthur's forces moved up the northern coast of New Guinea through 1943, and on Christmas Day the U.S. 1st Marine Division struck out for the western tip of New Britain across the Vitiaz Strait from New Guinea. Seventy thousand Japanese troops were estimated to be on the island, primarily in the north; 10,000 were in the west. At 7:45 A.M. on December 26, the Marines landed on New Britain, meeting little initial opposition. By the afternoon, however, the Japanese appeared in strength on the ground and in the air, putting up stiff resistance. Their defensive efforts were helped by monsoon rains. But the Marines advanced, taking the airstrip by December 31. Western New Britain was declared secured on April 28, 1944. The Japanese base–fortress complex at Rabaul was surrounded. U.S. aircraft from every available source—bombers and fighters, carrier planes and land-based aircraft—then blasted Rabaul. But the long-planned capture of Rabaul never occurred. Surrounded and reduced to impotency, it was bypassed, its garrison left to subsist on what they could grow and raise on the island.

But MacArthur's New Guinea campaign had moved the Allied front only a short distance in comparison with the Pacific advances under Nimitz. With increased resources allocated to the Pacific and new U.S. ships, aircraft, and troops becoming available, Nimitz had initiated the Central Pacific campaign against the Japanese-held Gilbert and Marshall Islands. The Gilberts, seized by the Japanese from the British on December 10, 1941, were some 2,400 miles west of Pearl Harbor. Under the code-name Operation Galvanic, there would be two landings—one by soldiers from the Army's 27th Infantry Division on Makin Atoll and the main landing by the 2nd Marine Division on Tarawa Atoll. Makin had already been invaded by U.S. Marines. In August 1942 two U.S. submarines had landed men of the 2nd Marine Raider Battalion on a hit-and-run reconnaissance raid. The landing force consisted of 13 officers and 208 enlisted men under Lieutenant Colonel Evans F. Carlson. His executive officer was Major James Roosevelt, a son of the President.

The November 1943 invasions of Makin and nearby Tarawa would be in the conventional amphibious assault mode, the genesis of which were Pete Ellis's research and reports of the 1920s. Based on experience at Guadalcanal, a carefully orchestrated and directed procedure was developed for assault landings in the Pacific. First came detailed reconnaissance of a potential invasion site by long-range American aircraft and by submarines, usually shooting photos through periscopes. Old maps, tourist photos, and traders and sailors who knew the area would be sought out by the intelligence and planning staffs.

Then the cargo ships and transports that were to take part in the assault would be packed with troops, vehicles, guns, equipment, and rations—"combat loaded" for rapid unloading in the order that troops and matériel would be needed ashore. America's best-known war correspondent, Ernie Pyle, was on board an assault transport en route to an island landing in the Pacific when he wrote:

> Our trip had been fairly smooth and not many of the troops were seasick. Down in the holds the marines slept on racks four tiers high. It isn't a nice way to travel, but I never heard anybody complain. They came up on deck on nice days to sun and rest and wash clothes, or lie and read or play cards. We didn't have movies. The ship was darkened at sunset and after that there were only dim lights. The food was good. We got news every morning in a mimeographed paper, and once or twice a day the ship's officers broadcasted the latest news over the loud-speaker.

The assault transports and cargo ships, and later the specialized landing ships—invariably referred to as "amphibs"—bristled with anti-aircraft guns. They sailed in convoys, escorted by destroyers and escorts whose crews kept on the alert for approaching Japanese aircraft and submarines.

As these ships approached their island objective, warships of various sizes —battleships, cruisers, destroyers—closed with the beach and bombarded the objective with intensive gunfire. Their targets were Japanese gun emplacements, bunkers, and other carefully chosen installations. Among the battleships used for shore bombardment in some assaults were several that had been damaged or sunk in the Pearl Harbor attack. Salvaged and rehabilitated, they bombarded the assault beaches with their big guns to destroy enemy bunkers and coastal guns and to strike fear in the hearts of the enemy. It was their principal role in the war.

Later in the war, specialized landing ships and craft armed with rockets and mortars went still closer to the beaches to lend their firepower. Throughout the bombardment period, aircraft from land bases (when they could reach the target) and carrier aircraft fought off any defending fighters and added their salvos of bombs and rockets to the assault on Japanese fortifications. During the bombardment, minesweepers sailed offshore to clear mines from the landing-craft lanes. Small, high-speed boats dropped off highly skilled Navy swimmers of Underwater Demolition Teams (UDTs) —men clad only in swim trunks, webbed flippers, and face masks. They surveyed the near-shore waters and blew up mines and obstacles intended to tear the bottoms out of landing craft.

These preliminaries lasted a few hours or several days, depending on the islands being assaulted. And when the transports and amphibious ships arrived offshore, the troops clambered down their sides into waiting landing craft or tracked vehicles, brought to the assault area on board specialized vehicle-carrying ships. The Higgins-type landing craft, or amphibious tractors (called "amtracs" or LVTs), then circled, awaiting the signal from control craft to form a line, or "wave," for the assault on the beach. The first wave normally consisted of amphibious tanks, the LVT(A)s, followed by waves of LVTs and then small landing craft with ramps (LCVPs) carrying assault troops. Only the LVTs could be used if there was an offshore coral reef, found at many Central Pacific atolls. When there was a coral reef and it was a large assault, there were usually too few amtracs for all of the assault waves. Marines loaded into LCVPs had to transfer at sea into LVTs, a dangerous switch if seas were rough.

Ernie Pyle wrote about the trip to the beachhead in a landing craft:

> The LCVP was so crowded the men just stood against each other. I knew most of them, for they were all from the ship that brought us up. They had been riding for an hour . . . and they were soaked to the skin from the spray. The morning was warm and sunshiny, yet they were all very cold from being wet. Some of them got the cold shakes which wouldn't stop, and they joked with each other about quaking with fear instead of cold. We all smiled in a sickly sort of fashion. We talked most of the way, but I can't remember much of what we said.

After an hour or more in landing craft or amtracs, cold and often seasick as well as scared, the Marines, or soldiers, were disgorged onto the beach, usually under heavy enemy fire. The first men to come ashore were followed by a constant flow of reinforcements. Warships continued to fire at targets identified by the troops ashore. Aircraft were also called in by radio to strike enemy targets if time and circumstances permitted.

Landing craft and LVTs went back to the transports to pick up additional loads of troops and equipment, and on the way out they carried the wounded. Several transports or landing ships waiting offshore served as emergency medical treatment centers. Farther out there might be white-painted hospital ships marked with large red crosses. But most casualties were treated aboard the ships that had brought the assault troops to the area. And there were hundreds and, in many landings, thousands of American casualties.

U.S. soldiers landed on Makin on November 20, 1943. A 6,472-man regimental landing team of the 27th Division took the atoll from the 848 Japanese defenders in four days. U.S. Army casualties were light; the Navy suffered the most casualties at Makin. The light aircraft carrier *Independence* took a hit from a Japanese torpedo bomber on the night of the landing and limped away for repairs. On the morning of November 24 the smaller escort carrier *Liscome Bay* was torpedoed by the Japanese submarine *I-175*. The carrier's bomb magazine blew up, breaking the ship apart. She sank in 23 minutes, taking with her to a watery grave 644 of her crew and pilots.

The relatively easy victory at Makin would not be duplicated on Tarawa, 100 miles to the south. Marines of the 2nd Division landed there on November 20, the same day as the Makin assault, and began a bloody three-day battle. Tarawa, almost midway between Pearl Harbor and the Japanese bastion at Truk, was an obvious target to strategists. The airfield on Tarawa would permit Allied aircraft to control the remainder of the Gilberts. The Japanese saw the value of the Tarawa Atoll and strongly fortified it. The main island of Betio was heavily reinforced, and by the time of the American assault there were 4,836 Japanese Navy troops on the island, including 2,619 men of a Special Naval Landing Force—Japanese marines. They constructed beach defenses of concrete and barbed-wire fences to stop amphibious vehicles and their assault troops. A formidable array of heavy-caliber harbor defense guns also confronted the invaders.

As usual, prior to the landings, Navy ships and aircraft blasted Japanese positions. Planes roared from the decks of three escort carriers to provide close air support for the Makin landings. Five more escort carriers supported the Tarawa assault. The eight small carriers flew 2,278 support sorties during the landings. Marines of the 2nd Division clambered into their amphibious tractors and landing craft in preparation for the assault on Tarawa. It was three and a half miles to the beach, and the sea was choppy. With a covey of minesweepers leading the way, the landing craft headed toward the beach as the enemy shore guns opened fire. Destroyers gave counterfire.

Concussion from the battleship *Maryland*'s 16-inch guns knocked out the ship's makeshift communications center, leaving the Marine assault commander with no direct radio link to the slow-moving landing craft. The LVTs, wallowing in the heavy seas, could not reach the beaches on schedule. Smoke and coral dust, raised by the heavy bombardment, obscured the landing beaches, and the naval commander decided to halt the fire for 30 minutes to allow the smoke to clear. This respite allowed the Japanese to regroup and prepare their defenses. In the extremely low tide even the LVTs had trouble, and the LCVPs had to unload their troops half a mile from the shore. Those Marines waded ashore in a hail of gunfire. It was here that the phrase "Bloody Tarawa" was born.

Marines in the first waves used flamethrowers to clear out the defensive positions. More troops poured onto the beaches; some were trapped in the barbed wire or cut down in the water by the murderous defensive fire. Men left the questionable protection of their standard, unarmored LCVPs to wade ashore through the storm of Japanese fire. Colonel David M. Shoup, who led the assault teams, established a command post near an apparently abandoned Japanese bunker. The original owners were still inside and opened fire, but they were quickly dispatched by Marine grenades. Shoup, wounded, remained there for over two days trying to get the chaos organized. He received one of the four Medals of Honor awarded at Tarawa (and later became Commandant of the Marine Corps).

The night of November 20–21 on Tarawa passed with relative quiet. At 6:15 the next morning more Marines came ashore, wading again into lethal gunfire. As their comrades on the beach watched helplessly, the newcomers floundered in the surf, weighted down with ammunition and equipment. From the hulk of an old, grounded freighter the Japanese poured fire into the men struggling to wade ashore. But enough Marines made it to form up and begin to sweep the atoll, aided by tanks and howitzers. By the end of the second day Shoup declared: "We are winning." By the early afternoon of the fourth day, November 23, Tarawa was fully in American hands.

The cost of taking Tarawa was high; 984 Marines were killed and 2,072 were wounded, plus 29 Navy men killed and another 51 wounded ashore with the Marines. Added to this toll were the sailors lost on the carrier *Liscome Bay* and the soldiers at Makin. Nearly the entire Japanese garrison on Tarawa was wiped out. Only 17 wounded Japanese troops and 129 Korean laborers survived. The other 4,819 Japanese were dead.

U.S. commanders—and Americans back home—were shocked at this heavy toll for a 76-hour battle. War correspondents cabled home a flood of stories describing the horror of Tarawa that prompted a congressional investigation, which was stopped only at the personal request of Lieutenant General Alexander A. Vandegrift, Commandant of the Marine Corps. But suddenly the wisdom of such costly amphibious assaults—the backbone of the strategy to win the Pacific War—came under question. Some U.S. commanders began to think about the use of poison gas as an alternative.

Despite the high cost, Admiral Nimitz and his subordinates began a leapfrog operation in accord with original strategy. The Marshall Islands, the next target, were heavily defended, and Operation Flintlock—the invasion of the islands—would be difficult. Against the advice of his subordinates, who wished to seize outer islands first, Nimitz proposed striking Kwajalein Atoll, the heart of the Marshall group. Majuro Atoll, in the eastern Marshalls, would also be assaulted to provide a logistics base. Through intercepted Japanese radio traffic, Nimitz knew that the enemy had decided to pull back to the Marianas, leaving the 30,000 troops in the Marshalls on their own to repel the invasion or die trying. The two-island Kwajalein Atoll was defended by 5,000 Japanese.

The Army's 7th Infantry Division would land on Kwajalein Island, while the newly established 4th Marine Division would hit Roi-Namur in the northeast corner of the atoll. On February 1, 1944, Marines made the main landings on Roi-Namur, finding little enemy resistance except for a few pockets of Japanese defenders. Roi was quickly taken. However, adjacent Namur was more difficult, with densely wooded areas that hid Japanese bunkers and pillboxes. The Japanese tried to mount a banzai suicide charge but failed. The aim of the wild frontal attack was to kill as many enemy as possible while dying in battle. The charge, usually a desperate final act when facing certain defeat, got its name from the battle cry *Tenno heika banzai!* ("Long live the Emperor!"). On February 2 several Marine tanks came ashore, and behind their armor the troops secured Namur by midafternoon.

To the south, the U.S. Army found Kwajalein Island's defenders more of a problem. The Japanese counterattacked at night in small groups, and it took the Army's 7th Infantry Division four days to secure the island. Defending Kwajalein, the Japanese lost nearly 8,400 men, many of whom committed suicide. Nearly 500 Americans were killed in action. In comparison to the Gilberts, the Marshalls yielded twice as many enemy losses, while exacting only one-half the casualties on the American side. The Americans were learning their trade well, and this kind of "kill ratio" would become a factor in future planning.

The assault of Kwajalein had barely been completed when Operation Catchpole hit Eniwetok Atoll, 325 miles northwest of Roi. According to Admiral Raymond A. Spruance, one of Nimitz's two subordinate fleet commanders, "The Kwajalein operation went so quickly and with such small losses that Admiral Nimitz sent me a radio [message] asking my recommendation on going ahead as soon as possible with the capture of Eniwetok. . . ." Beyond the airfield that could command the area, Eniwetok had a magnificent lagoon that would be invaluable as an advance base for U.S. warships.

Spruance, among America's most capable admirals, had been one of the two U.S. task force commanders in the Navy's victorious carrier battle at Midway in 1942. He now had available to him the reserves not needed for the assault on Kwajalein. The 22nd Marine Regiment and the Army's 106th Infantry Regiment provided the bulk of the assault force for Eniwetok, with support from the 4th Marine Division. The Japanese had reinforced Eniwetok, so that approximately 3,500 Army troops were on the atoll.

First came the usual naval air and gun bombardment. The carrier *Intrepid* —one of five fleet carriers supporting the operation—took a single torpedo launched by a Kate torpedo bomber during a night raid but was able to retire safely. On February 17 the 22nd Marines landed and moved inland behind carefully orchestrated naval gunfire and aircraft strikes. Battleships came to within 1,500 yards of the beach to blast Japanese positions. The defenders fought hard, but by February 23, Eniwetok was in American hands. Almost all of the Japanese garrison were killed. A total of 348 U.S. soldiers and Marines were lost.

With air and naval bases in the Marshalls now available, land-based aircraft, along with occasional carrier strikes, could neutralize most of the Japanese-held Caroline Islands to the west. Accordingly, the island base of Truk, consistently bombed and shelled by U.S. air and naval forces, was not assaulted. Instead, like the Japanese stronghold of Rabaul, it was allowed to "wither on the vine." But there was no evading an assault on the Mariana Islands. They were the gateway to the Philippines and the coast of China.

The Marianas were important for several other reasons. The large islands, especially Saipan and Tinian, would make ideal airfields for Army Air Forces B-29 Superfortress bombers, which could reach the Japanese home islands from the Marianas. And, psychologically, the capture of the Marianas would return Guam, conquered by the Japanese in the dark days after Pearl Harbor, to the American flag and would signify the growing might and momentum of the Allies.

The first moves against the Marianas came from carriers of the U.S. Fifth Fleet under Admiral Spruance. His carrier planes struck the Japanese in February 1944 to destroy enemy installations and take photographs for the subsequent invasion. Set for June 15, the assault was named Operation Forager. The 2nd and 4th Marine Divisions, veterans of earlier Pacific campaigns, and the Army's equally experienced 27th Infantry Division would make the landings. Saipan was the first target, mainly because it offered the closest base to Japan from which to stage B-29 raids. Its capture would also effectively block the Japanese forces on Guam from direct support from Japan.

The U.S. Fifth Fleet, steaming toward the Marianas, consisted of more than 800 ships, including 15 fast carriers and 11 escort carriers as well as a phalanx of 28 submarines driving ahead of the main fleet, seeking out enemy ships. One of the secondary hopes of the huge Forager strikes was that the remaining Japanese fleet would be drawn into one final battle and taken out of the war for good.

In fact, the Japanese *were* coming out for battle. Aware of the importance of the Marianas, they gathered a large fleet, built around their remaining aircraft carriers, for one massive strike at the American fleet in the Philippine Sea. The opposing fleets' aircraft met on June 19 in the last major carrier-versus-carrier battle of the Pacific War. In a running two-day series of strikes and counterstrikes, the Japanese lost nearly all their aircraft and three carriers. The outcome was christened the "Marianas Turkey Shoot" when it was realized that the Japanese had lost 400 aircraft and their pilots. The Americans lost only 100 aircraft, many during the June 20–21 night landing aboard their carriers after a final, long-range strike against the fleeing Japanese ships.

Meanwhile, the amphibious force under Vice Admiral Richmond Kelly Turner approached Saipan carrying 71,000 assault troops. D-Day was June 15. Following the heavy aerial and naval bombardment, within 20 minutes of the first amphibious tractor reaching the beach there were 700 LVTs and 8,000 Marines ashore. The 30,000 Japanese defenders fought ferociously, and the battle was hot and bloody. Before the end of the day, 2,000 Marines were killed or wounded. But 20,000 Marines had landed and were fighting on the island.

The Marines needed reinforcements, and the Army's 27th Infantry Division came ashore. The soldiers took a position on the 4th Marine Division's right flank and helped seize the Aslito airfield. But as Marine and Army troops fought side by side toward a common objective, their respective generals fought their own struggle. The Marine's Lieutenant General Holland M. Smith, whose nickname "Howling Mad" was well earned, was not a tolerant man, especially during interservice conflicts. Dissatisfied with the 27th Infantry's performance and its general's apparent inability to press the attack, Smith relieved his Army subordinate, Major General Ralph Smith, and assumed direct command of the Army operation, much to the disgust and frustration of the Army.

By June 20 the Americans had cleared most of the southern end of Saipan, although the extreme southern tip was a warren of concealed caves and bunkers occupied by Japanese survivors. Three thousand of the remaining Japanese charged the 27th Infantry Division in a vicious attack on July 7. Staggered by the banzai charge, the Americans fell back, but only temporarily. The American assault continued, and two days later, Holland Smith declared Saipan secured.

The loss of Saipan, along with the massive defeat in the carrier battle, brought down the government of the Japanese premier, Hideki Tojo, who resigned on July 18. All but approximately 1,000 of the 30,000 Japanese on Saipan died on the island, some committing suicide at the last moment by jumping from cliffs with civilians who feared the horrible tales of American barbarism told by the Japanese. American casualties numbered 16,525 killed and wounded.

Relations between the Marines and the Army deteriorated on all levels, fanned by the Marines' contempt for what they considered lack of Army aggressiveness in combat. The relieving of Ralph Smith by the Marines' Holland Smith made the matter worse. The conflict eventually reached the Joint Chiefs of Staff in Washington. An Army investigation declared that although Holland Smith could legally relieve Ralph Smith, the action was unjustified. To smooth things over, Holland Smith was given a desk job in Hawaii.

The next target was the smaller island of Tinian, which would offer more airfields for B-29 raids against Japan. The narrow beaches on the northwest edge, flanked by coral cliffs and low bluffs, were selected because landings there would surprise the Japanese, who were expecting landings on favorable beaches. Long-range artillery on Saipan could also provide prelanding bombardment of Tinian. The preinvasion bombardment, intensified on July 23, included the first use of jellied gasoline, or napalm, in combat. Intended to burn away vegetation, the napalm was dropped by the Army P-47 fighters flying from Saipan.

As assault troops of the 2nd and 4th Marine Divisions rode their LVTs onto the beach on July 24, intense Japanese gunfire greeted them. Underwater mines, undiscovered by swimmers from the Underwater Demolition Teams, sank three LVTs loaded with troops, and land mines destroyed many others. Ashore, the Japanese organized fierce banzai charges as the Marines stood fast and dug in. By dawn on July 25, the 4th Division counted 1,241 enemy dead. During the rest of the day more than 40,000 troops came ashore on Tinian. By August 12, the last pockets of Japanese had been eliminated, and Tinian was declared secured.

The assault on Guam—originally planned for June 18, three days after the landings on Saipan—was postponed because of the possible intervention of the Japanese carrier force rushing toward the Marianas and the need to include the Army's 27th Infantry Division in the Saipan assault. Of course, the decisive U.S. victory in the naval battle denied the Japanese fleet any influence on the fighting in the Marianas.

Coral reefs ringed Guam, and steep cliffs rose along the northern coast. Only a 15-mile stretch of beach on the west coast would permit an amphibious landing. The Japanese concentrated their main defense there, moving eight of 11 available infantry battalions and most of their tanks and artillery into that area.

On July 21 the 3rd Marine Division and the 1st Provisional Marine Brigade began the assault, with the Army's 77th Division in reserve. The 3rd Division ran into intense Japanese artillery and mortar fire, as well as machine guns, firing down from the cliffs above the beaches. The Marines struggled up from the beach all day. After midnight, the Japanese charged, shouting, "Banzai!"

The next two days saw the Americans fighting inland against savage opposition. On the night of July 25–26, some 5,000 Japanese, many drunk with sake, stormed across the American lines, engaging the Marines in fierce hand-to-hand combat. The charge was stopped, and the Japanese fell back, leaving half of their force dead and dying. The fierce fighting around Guam's Orote Peninsula and Apra Harbor ran for four days. Eventually, the U.S. flag was raised at the old Marine barracks, and on August 10 the Marines declared Guam secure. But sporadic Japanese resistance would continue as survivors who escaped into the jungles and caves sniped at the Americans. Incredibly, a few Japanese fought their own private war well after the end of the Pacific War, the last old warriors finally surrendering in the early 1970s.

Guam became a major naval base of the Pacific Fleet, and Admiral Nimitz moved his forward headquarters there. Tinian and Saipan were rapidly developed into massive bases for B-29 bombers. Island by island, the interlocking strategies of the plan to defeat Japan were falling into place.

General MacArthur could not forget his promise to return to the Philip- pines. And although the headlines he coveted were telling of events in the European theater of the war and Nimitz's island-hopping campaign in the western Pacific, MacArthur was working to fulfill that promise. By the spring of 1944, as MacArthur's forces were beginning the final drive along the northern coast of New Guinea, his command had nearly 750,000 troops, including Australians, and the U.S. Seventh Fleet, with many of its landing ships and craft manned by the Coast Guard.

MacArthur's New Guinea campaign ended in September 1944. The Japanese had lost some 148,000 troops on New Guinea and adjacent islands and ships en route to the area. During the two-year campaign, MacArthur's intelligence staff under Brigadier General Charles Willoughby (a veteran of his Bataan staff) constantly underestimated Japanese strength on New Guinea despite accurate data often being provided to him by the code breakers. MacArthur himself constantly exaggerated Japanese casualties in his battles. And he always underestimated his own combat casualties, never mentioning the thousands of his troops out of action because of disease and exhaustion from jungle fighting.

In September 1944, MacArthur's forces struck out for Morotai and Peleliu, in the Palau Islands, the westernmost of the Caroline group, halfway between New Guinea and the Philippines. Admiral Halsey, commander of the Third Fleet, had ordered a carrier strike against the southern Philippines. His aircraft sank many Japanese ships, destroyed some 200 aircraft, and discovered, through aerial reconnaissance, that the Philippines were not well defended. Halsey strongly urged cancellation of the Peleliu operation. Although MacArthur agreed to move his Philippine invasion timetable up a month, he wanted to go ahead with the Morotai and Peleliu landings, called Operation Stalemate. Halsey was overruled by Admiral Nimitz because intelligence indicated that Peleliu was lightly defended. There was nearly total ignorance of the Palau Islands, the last detailed information on the islands having come from Pete Ellis, who had died in the area in 1923.

On September 15, Army troops assaulted Morotai, and the 1st Marine Division, supported by the Army's 81st Infantry Division, struck Peleliu. The latter island was heavily fortified, with protective jungle that concealed coral ridges and hundreds of caves—perfect for hiding troops and weapons. The Japanese commanders had told their troops to wait until the invaders were established on the beach and moving inland before opening fire. The Japanese would then establish a defense line in the jungles and run less risk from the massive bombardments that preceded American landings.

Preinvasion bombardment had begun on September 12, but it had done relatively little damage due to inadequate targeting information and the burrowing instincts of Japanese troops. With the help of professional miners, the Japanese had expanded the natural caves into an interlocking defensive system, portions of which could not be reached by naval guns or bombers. The largest cave sheltered 1,000 troops.

The 1st Marine Division troops who came ashore on the morning of September 15 met little initial resistance, which was, of course, part of the

Japanese plan. Then the concealed mortars and machine guns opened fire, initially knocking out 26 LVTs. In the late afternoon the Japanese sent tanks and troops against the 1st and 5th Marine Regiments. The night brought the traditional banzai charges as the Japanese poured from the concealed caves. The Marines were not prepared for the strength of the enemy resistance, especially since intelligence reports had led them to believe that the overall defenses of the island were light. The Marine commander had predicted that Peleliu would be taken in three days. In the first week of fierce combat on Peleliu, the Marines suffered 4,000 dead and wounded. The 1st Marine Regiment was nearly wiped out. Marine survivors joined with the Army's 81st Infantry Division in fighting along the coral ridge, gradually overpowering the weakening Japanese.

"The fighting in the ridges was exhausting and costly," Eugene B. Sledge, a mortarman in the 1st Marine Division, remembered. "Flame throwers were indispensable. Any cave we attacked was covered by heavy Jap fire from other mutually supporting positions and all were interconnected within the ridges. The Japs fought like demons, and shot our stretcher teams—the corpsmen and the wounded. We hated them with a passion known to few antagonists."

Marine-piloted F4U Corsair fighters, newly arrived on the captured airstrip at the southern end of the island, dropped bombs and napalm and strafed the Japanese. The fighting was so close to the airstrip that the Corsair pilots didn't bother to raise their landing gear when they took off for a bombing run. They simply dumped their bombs and rockets on Japanese positions and then banked to come around to land and rearm.

Amid bombs and flamethrowers in the caves and burned-out jungle areas, the carnage—and organized resistance—ended on November 25. The 1st Marine Division suffered 6,786 casualties, including 1,300 men who were killed. Its 1st Marine Regiment suffered casualties amounting to 53.7 percent of its strength; the 5th Marines, 42.7 percent; and the 7th Marines, 46.2 percent. Approximately 12,000 Japanese were dead when Peleliu—six miles long and two miles wide—finally fell to the Americans. And strategists belatedly decided that Peleliu would not be needed for the forthcoming invasion of the Philippines.

The U.S. Army's 81st Division had an easier time taking the smaller, lightly defended island of Angaur, south of Peleliu. The large Ulithi Atoll fell without opposition, concluding the landings in the Caroline group. Ulithi became the principal U.S. fleet base in the western Pacific.

General MacArthur's long-planned grand return to the Philippines was on-again, off-again, as the Navy and Army wrangled with each other about the logistics of the assault. It would basically be an Army operation, although the soldiers would be carried in Navy amphibious ships, brought ashore by

Navy landing craft, escorted by Navy destroyers, with Navy battleships and cruisers for gunfire support and Navy air support from aircraft carriers. Marine participation, important though it was, was to be limited to close air support by planes of the 1st Marine Aircraft Wing.

The Philippines is an archipelago of 7,000 islands, only four of which were of primary importance in the upcoming invasion: Luzon in the north, Mindanao in the south, and Mindoro and Leyte in the central portion. Luzon contained the capital, Manila, as well as important harbors, and it was where most of the Japanese troops were stationed. Besides the 250,000 Japanese troops on Luzon, another 43,000 were on Mindanao, which had an important airfield. Because Leyte offered a geographically strategic link to the other three main islands, it was selected as the first target.

MacArthur used two assault forces containing a total of 500 ships to transport his 202,500 troops to Leyte. H-hour was set for ten o'clock on October 20, and the first waves—troops of the Army's X and XXIV Corps and 1,528 Marines "on loan" from the Fifth Fleet—got ashore with little opposition, although there was some Japanese mortar and machine gunfire. Other waves followed. The tremendous operation successfully brought great numbers of men ashore, and more than 107,000 tons of supplies and equipment were unloaded on the first day. On the following days the unloading pace was even faster, and concern mounted that the Japanese would make after-dark attempts to attack these caches.

Concern was also high over the threat posed by the powerful Japanese fleet entering the area in an effort to oppose the Leyte landings. The fleet was lured to destruction in the decisive Battle of Leyte Gulf on October 24–25, but MacArthur and his staff knew that he still did not have enough aircraft to properly protect further landings against enemy air raids, especially at night. And the captured Japanese airfields were not ready for the massive support operation envisioned for the U.S. squadrons scheduled to come into the Philippines. Mud was everywhere, and it would take the Navy's Seabees many weeks to prepare the strips. An inch of rain fell every day. It took two months to put Leyte's airfields in working condition, and Navy escort carriers remained offshore to provide close air support for the soldiers and Marines. Action on Leyte continued throughout December 1944.

The island of Mindoro to the northwest was the next target. Over 16,000 Army troops landed on December 15, along with another 15,000 construction and Army Air Forces personnel coming ashore to build and operate airfields. Good weather and little opposition from the Japanese allowed the landing to proceed on schedule.

The main landing of the Philippine campaign on the island of Luzon evolved into one of the largest land battles of the Pacific War. With the defeat of the Japanese fleet in the Leyte Gulf battles and the relative ease of the first Philippine landings, the initial JCS plan to bypass Luzon was changed to include a full-scale invasion. The original date of October 1944 for the assault was pushed forward because of the stiffening enemy resistance on Leyte, and the second assault date was set for January 9, 1945. The landing operation was to include the 200,000 troops of the Sixth Army under General Walter Krueger, supported and transported by the 850 ships of Vice Admiral Thomas Kinkaid's Seventh Fleet, with carrier cover by Halsey's Third Fleet. The Japanese had more than 250,000 troops on Luzon, although they were largely disorganized and poorly supplied. And, of course, they could no longer depend on support from the Japanese Fleet.

The Japanese knew that the Americans would land at Lingayen; it was where they themselves had landed in December 1941. The only hope the Japanese had was to fight a costly delaying action that would halt the drive to Japan. For this operation, the Japanese unveiled a new weapon—the suicide plane, which they called kamikaze, a word that had an old, sacred meaning to the Japanese.

In 1274, the great Mongol emperor Kublai Khan, having conquered northern China and Korea, demanded the submission of Japan. Rebuffed, he sent an invasion fleet. Some 40,000 of Khan's troops landed at Hatata Bay on Kyushu, southernmost of the home islands. They fought the Japanese defenders on the beach all day, then withdrew to their ships. A storm drove them out to sea, sinking 200 of the 900 ships.

Seven years later, Khan assembled a greater armada—two fleets totaling 4,400 ships with 142,000 troops—and tried again. This time the Japanese were prepared, with 100,000 men on Kyushu and a 25,000-man reserve on Honshu. And they had built a stone wall eight feet high and 16 miles long. The invaders of the first fleet were repulsed. Weeks later, as the two fleets combined for a massive assault against Kyushu, a typhoon swept across the island, sinking 4,000 ships. Forever afterward, that typhoon would be known as kamikaze, the divine wind. Tradition held that the gods protected Japan from invasion, because never again would an invader succeed. Now, in World War II, as invaders again threatened—and as Kyushu again was a probable invasion site—suicide pilots took the title kamikaze. They would be the divine wind.

The U.S. Navy daily fought off kamikaze air attacks as the huge invasion fleets drew nearer to Luzon. "Jap planes were coming at us from all directions," the young sailor James J. Fahey wrote in his diary soon after his ship, the U.S. cruiser *Montpelier,* reached Leyte Gulf. "Before the attack started we did not know that they were suicide planes, with no intention of returning to their base. They had one thing in mind and that was to crash into our ships, bombs and all. You have to blow them up, to damage them doesn't mean much." From his gun mount, he saw "a tidal wave of suicide planes." His diary continued:

One suicide dive bomber was heading right for us while we were firing at other attacking planes and if the 40 [millimeter gun] mount behind us on the port side did not blow the Jap wing off it would have killed all of us. When the wing was blown off it, the plane turned some and bounced off into the water. . . . Another suicide plane crashed into one of the 5 inch [gun] mounts. . . . A Jap dive bomber crashed into one of the 40 mm. mounts but lucky for them it dropped its bombs on another ship before crashing. Parts of the plane flew everywhere when it crashed into the mount.

Although these suicide raids heavily damaged several U.S. ships, preinvasion bombardment began as scheduled on January 6. The shelling was in concert with attacks by several Marine dive-bomber squadrons now situated in the central Philippines.

At 9:30 A.M. on January 9, assault elements of the Army's XIV Corps landed at Lingayen. The only problems encountered came not from Japanese defenders but from natural obstacles, including fish ponds and flooded rice fields. By nightfall, 68,000 troops had come ashore, and the usual huge supply chain was well into operation. The Japanese had yet to appear in any strength, and American commanders were uneasy. Where was the enemy? The answer lay in the new Japanese tactic of allowing the landings to take place uncontested, thereby avoiding the punishing naval bombardment.

Relief at the lack of enemy opposition on the beaches soon turned to expectant caution as the Army troops moved inland to find an intricate defense system of caves, tunnels, and pillboxes constructed in the now-familiar Japanese manner. Thus began six months of fighting on Luzon, especially around the capital of Manila. Finally, U.S. troops drove into the capital, releasing long-held prisoners of war taken by the Japanese three years before. But heavy fighting continued in what some called the first urban battle of the Pacific War.

When MacArthur began advancing on the city from the north, General Tomoyuki Yamashita, commander of the Japanese forces, ordered a withdrawal from Manila, forbidding unnecessary destruction. While Yamashita got his troops out of the city and into the hills of Luzon, about 15,000 Japanese sailors and Marines and 4,000 soldiers under Vice Admiral Sanji Iwabuchi were encircled in the city by U.S. troops.

Iwabuchi ordered his troops to fight to the last man and to slaughter their enemies, both military and civilian. The Japanese retreated across the Pasig River, which divides the city, and made a stand in the concrete buildings of the business district. They went on a rampage of massacre and torching in the city's residential neighborhoods. U.S. troops and Filipino guerrillas managed to slip behind the Japanese defenses and save thousands of civilians. But to drive the Japanese out of the city meant house-to-house fighting and hand-to-hand combat.

Japanese troops made their last stand in the Intramuros, site of the original Spanish fortified settlement and a place of many churches. It was surrounded by a 25-foot wall about 2½ miles in circumference. When the Japanese refused to surrender, U.S. artillery demolished the place.

On March 3, 1945, after more than a month of fighting that left most of the Japanese, including Iwabuchi, dead, a jubilant MacArthur declared the city secured. But the devastation was so great that his plan for a victory parade was forgotten. About 70 percent of the city had been destroyed, and about 100,000 Filipino civilians had been killed. On June 30, 1945, Mac-Arthur declared most of Luzon secured and the Philippines liberated, although the fighting would continue in the hills of Luzon.

While MacArthur's massive Sixth Army and his Seventh Fleet—supported by Admiral Halsey's Third Fleet—were retaking the Philippines, Admiral Raymond A. Spruance was in Hawaii planning the next assaults of Nimitz's forces: Iwo Jima and Okinawa. (When Spruance went to sea in January 1945, he would sail with the same ships that Halsey had commanded, but they would be redesignated as the Fifth Fleet.)

Iwo Jima's strategic importance made an amphibious assault imperative. The island was 660 miles from Tokyo. Its neutralization would destroy the warning stations that alerted Japan when bomber strikes were coming from Saipan and Tinian, stop Japanese fighters on Iwo from attempting to intercept the bombers, and be useful to the Allies as an emergency base for B-29s as well as a fighter base for operations over Japan.

Iwo is a foul-smelling, pork chop–shaped little island, barely 7½ square miles, its terrain dominated by an active volcano, Mount Suribachi. Planning for the invasion of Iwo Jima began in September 1943, and after the Marianas were taken in 1944, Admiral Nimitz told Lieutenant General Holland M. Smith, no longer exiled to a desk in Hawaii, that his next task would be to land on Iwo. Under Smith were the 3rd, 4th, and 5th Marine Divisions.

Although planning and preliminary aerial reconnaissance of Iwo Jima had already begun, the unexpected heavy Japanese resistance in the Philippines, which tied up the Navy's carrier force, necessitated postponement of Operation Detachment—the name for the Iwo Jima landing—from January 20 until February 19, 1945. Navy ships began shelling Iwo Jima in November 1944, and the U.S. Army Air Forces began a lengthy bombardment on December 8, with B-24s and B-25s bombing the island for an incredible 74 consecutive days. It was the longest preinvasion aerial bombardment of the war. And it was justified. Iwo Jima was the most heavily defended island assaulted in the Pacific War.

U.S. reconnaissance photos revealed a massive Japanese defense network, including more than 600 blockhouses and gun positions and the usual warrens of caves. By February 1, 1945, there were 21,000 Japanese troops waiting on the island, with 120 guns of 75-mm caliber or larger, 20,000 smaller guns, and a vast assortment of mortars, rockets, and anti-aircraft weapons. The Marines who landed on the beaches would immediately come under devastating enemy fire.

Smith later recalled:

> I felt certain we would lose 15,000 men at Iwo Jima. This number was the absolute minimum calculated in our plans made at Pearl Harbor, although some of my officers wistfully predicted a lower figure. So far as the Marines were concerned, we had made every preparation humanly possible to capture the island as expeditiously and as economically as possible. We were to land 60,000 assault troops, and the estimate that one in every four would be dead or wounded never left my mind.
>
> I was not afraid of the outcome of the battle. I knew we would win. But contemplation of the cost in lives caused me many sleepless nights.

On February 19, the morning of the landing brought good weather, a calm sea, and a light breeze from the north. The landings would be made on the southeast shore of Iwo. Secretary of the Navy James V. Forrestal and an entourage of journalists prepared to watch the assault from the amphibious command ship *Eldorado,* and at 9:02 the leading elements of the 4th

Waves of amphibious tractors and landing craft carry Marines to the volcanic beaches of Iwo Jima on February 19, 1945. The island-hopping strategy of the Pacific War was now clear. Would it inevitably culminate in an invasion of Japan?

and 5th Marine Divisions scrambled onto the beaches. Almost mystically, there was only scattered Japanese fire.

The Marine plan was to immediately take Mount Suribachi, the main bastion on the island, at the extreme southern tip, as well as Airfield No. 1, directly inland from the beaches. However, the relatively easy day ended dramatically at 9:45 when tremendous Japanese fire began to rain down on the exposed Marines, now hugging the soft, sootlike beaches. Tanks and wheeled vehicles found it difficult to move in the volcanic ash and were confronted by intense Japanese 47-mm anti-tank gunfire. By nightfall, the Marines had suffered over 2,400 casualties—566 dead, 1,854 wounded—in establishing a beachhead 3,000 yards long and 700 to 1,500 yards deep. Approximately 30,000 troops had come ashore that first day.

On the morning of February 20, the first attempts at taking Suribachi gained only 200 yards. For three days the 28th Marine Regiment battled slowly up the volcano. By 10 A.M. on February 23 they reached the top and raised a small American flag on a piece of Japanese pipe. At the sight of the flag, bells and whistles of the offshore fleet sounded. On board the command ship *Eldorado,* Secretary Forrestal turned to General Smith and said, "Holland, the raising of that flag on Suribachi means a Marine Corps for the next 500 years." Later, a larger flag was sent ashore from an LST, and Associated Press photographer Joe Rosenthal took the famed picture that came to stand for "Marines."

The fierce fighting continued in the days that followed, and the last pockets of Japanese resistance were not overrun until March 16, when Iwo Jima was declared secured. Nearly all of the 21,000 Japanese defenders were killed, but not before inflicting over 23,000 casualties on the invading Marines and 2,800 on the sailors who had brought them there. Among the casualties were 6,821 U.S. dead, nearly all Marines.

Through the reports of war correspondents covering the bloody battles on Iwo, the American public was repulsed by what appeared to be the senseless loss of huge numbers of American lives. Criticism ran high against the men who had planned and led the assault and the monthlong battle. The Hearst newspaper chain especially questioned the tactics, and an outraged group of Marines invaded the editorial offices of the *San Francisco Examiner* to demand an apology. In praise of the men who fought on Iwo Jima, Admiral Nimitz said, "Uncommon valor was a common virtue." It was true. Twenty-seven Medals of Honor were won by Navy and Marine personnel at Iwo Jima, the most for any single operation of the war.

On March 4, even before the island was secured by the Marines, the first B-29 made an emergency landing on Iwo Jima. Within three months of Iwo Jima's capture, more than 850 B-29s had also made emergency landings on the island. By early April, P-51 Mustang fighters were flying from Iwo Jima to escort B-29s on their raids to Japan. In all, the number of emergency B-29 landings on Iwo Jima would total 2,400, some being multiple landings by the same plane. One B-29 crew landed on the island five times during its 11 combat missions. Certainly not all of those B-29 crews would have gone into the sea if Iwo Jima had not been captured, and of those who came down, many would have been rescued by U.S. submarines and seaplanes. But hundreds of the "Superforts" and thousands of their crews were saved because Iwo Jima was in American hands.

Those "Superforts" and an aerial armada of thousands of other warplanes were providing a new dimension to the Pacific War. The route to Japan would be aloft. The B-29s would reach Tokyo far ahead of the slogging soldiers and Marines. Aerial bombardment had always been a key ingredient in the plans to defeat Japan. And now that it could, in fact, take place—and on an increasingly massive scale—advocates of air power would claim that these planes and their intrepid crews could themselves win the war.

CHAPTER 3

WINNING WITH AIR POWER

Incendiary bombs stream from B-29 Superfortress bombers onto a Japanese city. Air-power advocates believed that sustained aerial bombardment, along with a naval blockade, would lead to the defeat of Japan without an invasion of the home islands.

The belief, prevalent in 1945 among the leaders of the U.S. Army Air Forces, that air power alone could end the war against Japan was based on three convictions: that an independent air force was the best way to achieve victory in any wartime situation, that long-range bombers were unstoppable, and that daylight precision bombing was possible.

The champions of air power had long asserted that they were the warriors of the future—a future that had been forecast many years before. The concept that "National defense can be assured only by an Independent Air Force of adequate power" originated with the Italian general Giulio Douhet, whose 1921 book *Command of the Air* became the touchstone of American (and British) air-power advocates. On page after page of his original work and subsequent revisions and articles, Douhet insisted time and time again that "an Independent Air Force functioning completely independent of the army and navy is of paramount importance." This air force would use long-range bombers that could attack an enemy's cities, cowering the populations and destroying his war-making apparatus. Such attacks would be "the best way to assure victory, regardless of any other circumstances whatever...."

The second conviction, that the bomber would always get through, was believed (in the West) as early as 1932, when British Prime Minister Stanley Baldwin told the House of Commons, "I think it well also for the man in the street to realize there is no power on earth that can protect him from bombing, whatever people may tell him. The bomber will always get through...."

In the United States, Brigadier General William Mitchell, an air-service leader in World War I, became Douhet's most vocal disciple. Younger airmen read Douhet at the Army's Air Corps Tactical School and watched with vain hopes as Billy Mitchell fought for an air arm independent of the Army in the 1920s. But while they lost that battle, air-power advocates of the 1920s and 1930s continued to embrace the long-range-bomber concept, even to the exclusion of fighters and their advocates.

But could long-range bombing really destroy an enemy's means and will to fight? The failure of Hitler's Luftwaffe to force the surrender of Britain in the Blitz of 1940–1941 or failure of the combined British-American bomber offensive of 1942–1945 to bring about the fall of Germany did not dissuade air-power advocates from believing that, given the proper weapons and bases, they could indeed destroy Japan through aerial assault.

76

And contrary to their conviction that the bomber would always get through, in the aerial campaign against Germany, which the British began in 1940, the bomber often had a hard time doing so. The British were soon forced to shift from daylight to night bombing to survive over the German-dominated skies of Europe. Night attacks meant a considerable loss in accuracy, and that loss meant that "area" targets, including civilian areas, had to be attacked.

American airmen persisted in daylight bombing attacks. The cost was heavy. During 1943, when American commanders sent B-17 Flying Fortress bombers to strike targets in Germany in daylight attacks in mass formations, they lost 60 bombers on a single mission over the industrial city of Schweinfurt in August and 60 more over Schweinfurt on a raid in October. Each bomber that went down in flames took with it ten trained airmen, condemned to death or captivity. Hundreds more ten-man bombers were lost over other targets between the two Schweinfurt strikes.

Daylight raids over Germany were halted. And not until December 1943, when sufficient P-51 Mustang fighters were available to escort the B-17s from Britain all the way to targets in Germany, were the long-range strikes resumed. The toll of strategic bombers during the European War was enormous. Some 9,950 American bombers were lost during the aerial campaign over German-controlled Europe; 49,000 U.S. bomber crewmen were killed, and more than 30,000 others were captured by the Germans. One out of every five American soldiers killed in combat during the war—in all theaters—was a bomber crewman in the European theater. The bomber did get through, but only with fighter escorts and after tremendous losses.

Advocates of American air power had come to believe in the effectiveness of daylight precision bombing during the 1930s, and the tool that would make it possible was the Norden bombsight, developed for the Navy by C.L. Norden, a civilian consultant. The bombsight was adopted by the Army Air Forces, and spokesmen soon boasted that it could "drop a bomb into a pickle barrel from 25,000 feet." When visibility was good and the aircraft could fly a straight and level course on the bomb run, the bombsight did give a bomber a high degree of accuracy. But in cloudy weather or when the target was otherwise obscured—as most of the time over Europe—and when the plane was being shaken by anti-aircraft bursts, the bombsight was not effective. In reality, only one in five aimed bombs dropped by American bombers during the war fell within 1,000 feet (about three city blocks) of the target.

Usually a bomber group's "lead bombardier" would sight the target, and the release of his bombs would be the visual signal for the rest of the planes in the formation to drop their bombs—in effect, area bombing. The frequency and volume of aerial bombardment, not its accuracy, wrought devastation on Germany. The destruction of workers' housing, utility services, and transportation facilities was more effective in stopping industrial production than attempts to precision-bomb the factories.

Still, air-power advocates in the Pacific theater in 1945 continued to insist that Japan could be bombed into submission, and if experience in the European theater contradicted that point of view, one very powerful presumption supported it. If the enemy's war-making capacity could be destroyed by precision bombing and air power could force Japan's surrender, not a single American or Allied soldier would have to assault the heavily fortified home islands and fight his way to the capital.

Army Air Forces planners in 1943 had considered a number of potential bases for the strategic bombing of Japan. The bomber that would be used against the Japanese Empire—including the home islands—would not be the B-17 Flying Fortress and B-24 Liberator that were being battle-tested in Europe as well as in the Pacific. The bomber of Japan would be a new aircraft, the B-29 Superfortress.

The Boeing-designed B-29 was a huge, streamlined four-engine bomber. Its maximum takeoff weight of 135,000 pounds, including up to ten tons of bombs, compared to a maximum of three tons carried by the B-17G. The new bomber could fly 1,500 miles on a bombing mission—more than twice the range of the B-17. And the plane was virtually invulnerable to attacking Japanese fighters because of its greater speed, higher operating altitude, and defensive armament of eight or ten .50-caliber machine guns in four remote-control turrets, plus a tail turret mounting two machine guns and one 20-mm cannon.

The bases considered by American planners for the B-29, which would become available for use in mid-1944, included the Mariana Islands, Soviet Siberia, Manchuria, Korea, Japan itself (the northern island of Hokkaido), Formosa, and the Philippines. The plan, adopted in mid-1943 for attacks on Japan, called for also basing the B-29s in China and, after its capture, on Formosa. As for fighter and tactical bomber bases, the plan said the Allies would "have to rely almost entirely on carrier-borne air support for the invasion of Japan." In fact, the planners emphasized the importance of carrier aviation, stating that the "increased use of this type of support offer[s] the most helpful prospect of accelerating the date by which we [could] undertake the invasion."

Thus, not all air-power advocates presumed that an invasion would be unnecessary, but the August 1943 plan provided for an aerial offensive against Japan that would so destroy her ability to resist that the home islands could be occupied by the fall of 1945, a year after the assumed defeat of Germany. By an ingenious method of calculation, it was estimated that approximately 130,000 tons of bombs would reduce Japan to virtual helplessness. It was further postulated that one 45-plane group of B-29 bombers flying from China could average 700 tons of bombs per month. It would therefore require 186 "group months" to deliver the total amount of destruction. There would be four groups of B-29s based in China in June 1944, increasing to 20 groups by May 1945—some *nine hundred* B-29s. In addition, it was envisioned that two B-29 groups would be based in the Aleutians to bomb the northern Japanese islands.

A key player in the plan to build bomber bases in China was Major General Claire L. Chennault. An airman who had specialized in fighter tactics in the 1930s and ran afoul of the bomber advocates who led the Army Air Corps, Chennault had retired from the Army in 1937 because of deafness caused by flying in open-cockpit planes. Before the American entry into the war he had accepted an offer from Chiang Kai-shek to train fighter pilots for China. Chennault returned to the United States in early 1941 and with the full, albeit somewhat secretive, approval of the U.S. government, including President Roosevelt, recruited American pilots for the American Volunteer Group. Highly publicized as the "Flying Tigers" after the toothy snouts of tiger sharks painted on the noses of their P-40 fighters, the volunteers began flying against the Japanese on December 20, 1941.

In April 1942, Chennault was recalled to active U.S. service, promoted to brigadier general, and given command of the U.S. Fourteenth Air Force in China. There he frequently clashed with Lieutenant General Joseph W. (Vinegar Joe) Stilwell, the senior U.S. officer in China, military chief of staff to Chiang Kai-shek, and a man highly regarded by General Marshall. In simplest terms, the feuding between Chennault and Stilwell was a feud between air power and land power.

Chennault, a ruggedly handsome airman with the cold eyes of a zealot, quickly won the admiration of Chiang Kai-shek, for whom air power had a magic quality. He would not need to raise and finance large land armies led by potentially treacherous warlords. He could beat his enemies—the Chinese communists came first, Japanese conquerors second—by bombing them. Chiang and Chennault, in their persistent demands for victory through air power, ignored the fact that U.S. air bases were extremely vulnerable. As General Marshall tried to explain to President Roosevelt, "As soon as our effort hurts the Japs, they will move in on us, not only in the air but also on the ground." And the Chinese Army was too feeble to protect U.S. bases.

Chennault and Stilwell were temperamentally similar. Both had a stubborn faith in themselves and in their views of Chiang. Chennault, flattered by the Chinese leader and his American-educated wife, saw Chiang as the champion of Western values and a foe of communism. Stilwell saw Chiang as just another warlord exploiting his people. Although Roosevelt did not like Stilwell's acerbic style, he did admire Chennault, who had a genius for getting himself and his Flying Tigers into the newspapers and the newsreels.

Chennault in China, like General Hap Arnold in Washington, made extravagant claims for the war-winning ability of air power. Chennault believed in the gospel of Douhet and Mitchell, that air power was the decisive, if not the sole winning, factor. The emphasis in China, he believed, should therefore be on air power, not ground forces, and he, not Stilwell, should be the senior American commander in China. Chennault's advocacy of air power gained the support of Chiang and his influential wife, and he eventually won out over Stilwell, his nominal superior.

Chennault got a chance to push his theories to the highest levels of American command in October 1942, when Wendell L. Willkie, the Republican presidential candidate Roosevelt had defeated in 1940, arrived in Chungking on a fact-finding tour for Roosevelt. Chennault gave Willkie a letter for the President in which he said that if he were made "American military commander in China," he could "cause the collapse of Japan" with an air force of only 105 modern fighters, 12 heavy bombers, and 30 medium bombers. The "downfall of Japan," he wrote in his letter of October 8, would occur "probably within six months, within one year at the outside." General Marshall later dismissed Chennault's claims as "just nonsense; not bad strategy, just nonsense." After hearing Chennault's plans, even Arnold had to remark, ". . . to my astonishment, in spite of [Chennault's] Air Corps and Tactical Training School training, he was not realistic about the logistics of his operations."

But the letter intrigued Roosevelt. The President was also being lobbied by his key adviser, Harry Hopkins, who supported the idea of using bases in China to fight Japan. And, in April 1943, Chiang asked Roosevelt to bring Chennault to Washington to present a new plan for an air offensive from China. Other senior U.S. and British commanders were summoned to Washington and met with the President, Prime Minister Churchill, and their chiefs of staff at the Trident Conference in Washington in May. Two strategies were presented. Stilwell wished to use all available Allied resources toward regaining Burma, opening a truck road to China, and using much of its tonnage to equip a large Chinese ground army to drive the Japanese out of China. Chennault's plan called for a greatly increased airlift from India into Kunming, with most of the additional tonnage going to an augmented air force flying from Chinese bases.

Chennault's viewpoint won the Washington strategy debate. Thus was born Operation Matterhorn, officially the Joint Planning Staff's plan for "Early Sustained Bombing of Japan." The plan, completed in early November 1943, advocated bringing the four-engine "Superforts" into the war against Japan as soon as possible. There were immediate objections to Matterhorn, from the Army's leadership, the Navy, and the British. Still, the attractiveness of using air power rather than ground troops to win the war was too appealing, and on November 11, President Roosevelt approved the plan in principle and advised Churchill and Chiang of its general features.

Matterhorn would be carried out from forward bases in China, with the main B-29 bases and their massive logistic support structure established in India. By May 1944, after vast expenditures of U.S. funds and the labors of some 400,000 Chinese, four bases for B-29s had been built in the Chengtu area, along with several bases for fighter aircraft to protect the bomber fields. Thousands of support personnel—mechanics, armorers, cooks and bakers, warehousemen—had to be brought to the bases, along with spare parts (including replacement engines), bombs, provisions, and even fuel. To launch an attack with 100 B-29s from the Chinese bases required some 2,300 tons of flown-in supplies, besides what the bombers themselves had to carry when they flew into China from the rear bases in India.

China-based XX Bomber Command B-29s flew raids against Japanese targets in Southeast Asia and, on June 15, 1944, made their first strike against the Japanese home islands. The target was the Yawata steelworks on Kyushu, the southernmost island. The plant produced an estimated 24 percent of Japan's rolled steel.

Seventy-five planes were to make the raid. The round-trip flight of 3,200 miles restricted the planes to only two tons of bombs each; and the long distance required the planes to fly individually, in a stream rather than in a formation. Also, the strike would be flown at night to reduce the threat from Japanese fighters and anti-aircraft guns. Only 47 B-29s reached the target. There was some fighter interference and anti-aircraft fire, but despite damage, none of the planes was downed by enemy fire, although three more were lost on the return flight. Robert Schenkel, a *Newsweek* correspondent, died in one of the crashes.

A photo-reconnaissance B-29, sent over Yawata a few days later, found the damage was "unimportant," according to the official Army Air Forces history. Three hundred and seventy-six 500-pound bombs were dropped on the target that night. Only one hit in the main plant area.

The XX Bomber Command planes continued to strike Japanese targets in the Southeast Asia area and periodically returned to bomb targets in Japan. But given the logistics required to support the B-29s and their ineffective high-altitude daylight bombing tactics, raids from Chinese bases were hardly worth the effort, and air strategists finally realized that only the Marianas could provide effective bases for B-29s. The American conquest of Guam, Tinian, and Saipan in mid-1944 provided airfields only 1,200 miles from Tokyo. There was no threat from Japanese air or ground attack, and cargo ships and tankers could bring in the bombs, supplies, parts, and fuel without the cost and time of air transport to the B-29 bases in China.

Even as General MacArthur's troops were recapturing the Philippines, the XXI Bomber Command with B-29s was established on bases in the Marianas in the fall of 1944. On October 28 the command sent out its first strike—18 aircraft against the submarine base at Truk, the Japanese air- and naval-base complex in the Caroline Islands. Other small-scale B-29 strikes were flown from Saipan against Japanese-held islands during October and November. Also taking off from Saipan, a single F-13 aircraft, the photo-reconnaissance version of the B-29, piloted by Captain Ralph D. Steakley, flew over Japan on October 13, 1944. It was the first American plane to fly over Tokyo since the Doolittle raid. Named *Tokyo Rose,* the photo plane overflew several urban areas, spending 35 minutes over Tokyo. The plane's cameras took thousands of photographs. "We got the best pictures we could have hoped for. There wasn't really another chance like that for the rest of the war. Those photographs were a godsend," Major General Curtis LeMay later wrote.

The second B-29 raid on Japan occurred on November 24 when 88 B-29s flying from Saipan attacked Tokyo. Their primary target was the Nakajima aircraft engine works in the densely populated northwest Tokyo suburb of Musashino, some ten miles from the Imperial Palace. The plant manufactured over 30 percent of Japan's aircraft engines. The bomber crews were sternly briefed not to bomb the Imperial Palace.

In a classic daylight precision-bombing attack, the planes flew over the target at 30,000 feet, each B-29 dropping some 2½ tons of bombs, about one-third incendiary and two-thirds high explosive. Only 24 of the B-29s actually bombed the Nakajima plant, and few bombs found their target because of mechanical problems, cloud cover, and high winds. Aerial photos indicated that just 16 of the 500-pound bombs had hit the target (although postwar investigations showed that 48 bombs—three of them duds—had landed within the factory area). The incendiaries started secondary fires that burned out about one-tenth of a square mile of suburban Tokyo. It was another poor showing for the world's most capable bomber. Indeed, during the next 3½ months the bombers would return again and again to strike the Nakajima engine complex without being able to halt the production of aircraft engines.

Poor high-altitude bombing performance was repeated time and time again over Japan. There were also maintenance problems with the B-29, which forced many planes taking off from the Mariana bases to turn back before reaching their targets. The attacks were also hampered by poor intelligence about Japanese industry and a lack of maps. Attempts at "precision bombing" raids against Japan by B-29s continued with little success until Curtis LeMay arrived in the Marianas on January 7, 1945.

In 1942, as a colonel, LeMay had trained the 305th Bomb Group to fly the B-17 Flying Fortress and then led the group against German targets from bases in England. Promoted to brigadier general, in July 1943 he moved up to command the 3rd Air Division of the Eighth Air Force in England. He pioneered the development of advanced bomber tactics—high-level, precision daylight strikes against German industrial targets.

LeMay took charge of the XX Bomber Command in the China-Burma-

When high-altitude precision bombing proved ineffective, General Curtis LeMay sent his B-29s in low, at night, to firebomb and devastate Japanese cities.

India theater in September 1944, but his China-based B-29s flew strikes against targets in Formosa, Manchuria, and Japan with little effect. The B-29s in the Marianas were not hampered by the incredible logistic problems that plagued B-29s flying from China, but the Mariana-based bombers had other problems and were not producing results. Brigadier General Haywood S. Hansell, commander of the XXI Bomber Command in the Marianas, was fired, and LeMay was given the command of the most powerful bomber force ever assembled. Hansell was 41, LeMay just 39, reflecting the extremely young age of the American bomber commanders who bore such tremendous responsibilities in the war.

LeMay, rarely seen without a cigar clenched in his mouth or carrying a pipe, had grown up tough in a drifting life that gave him little childhood. He worked his way through college, joined the Army's reserve officers' training program, and got his pilot's wings in 1929. "I'll tell you what war is about," he once said, "—you've got to kill people, and when you've killed enough they stop fighting."

He ordered more high-level daylight raids flown against targets in Japan so that he could determine the reason for the failures. The results continued to be marginal. The B-29 was the most advanced bomber in the world; it had the famed—and overly lauded—Norden bombsight as well as a radar bombsight. With the Norden device the bombardier had to sight the target visually, and the aircraft had to fly straight and level. The heavy cloud cover and strong winds over Japan severely reduced the effectiveness of the Norden sight. And the B-29's original radar bombsight, which showed the ground terrain, was useful for navigation but not good enough for precision bombing because strong ground contrasts, such as shorelines, were needed for it to provide precise positions.

By the first week of March 1945, the B-29s, which had already lost 102 of their number to enemy fighters since the previous November, had accomplished relatively little in return for tremendous logistic and operational efforts. LeMay sought another method of employing his B-29s. He realized that the Japanese did not have large numbers of 20-mm and 40-mm antiaircraft guns that threatened low-flying bombers. Without this "light flak" he could send his bombers in low over Japanese targets, where they could bomb with more accuracy. At the same time he was under pressure to improve the performance of the XXI Bomber Command. General Arnold sent Brigadier General Lauris Norstad to talk to LeMay, who later recalled:

> General Arnold needed results. Larry Norstad had made that very plain. In effect he said: "You go ahead and get results with the B-29. If you don't get results, you'll be fired. If you don't get results, also, there'll never be any Strategic Air Forces of the Pacific. . . . If you don't get results, it will mean eventually a mass amphibious invasion of Japan, to cost probably half a million more American lives."

LeMay went to work to exploit the potential of low-level bombing. His intelligence staff and, he noted, the *National Geographic* described a unique characteristic of Japanese cities: ". . . ninety percent of the structures in

Tokyo are built of wood. . . . Very flimsy construction." LeMay decided to do the unorthodox, to bring the B-29s down to a few thousand feet and attack Tokyo with incendiary bombs.

The Army Air Forces had some interest in incendiary weapons, although high-explosive bombs were the preferred weapon for precision bombing. Earlier in the war, in the desert wasteland of Utah, including part of the Dugway Valley, the Army began testing various types of improved incendiary bombs, including jellied gasoline—generally called napalm (for *na*phthene and *palm*itate), consisting of gasoline and a thickening material. Facsimiles of German and Japanese buildings were erected at Dugway to test such bombs. These mock-ups of enemy structures—including residential buildings built at the specific direction of President Roosevelt—were intended to test the new incendiary bombs, especially the M69, a six-pound napalm-filled projectile.

The Dugway mock-ups were referred to as the "Nazi and Jap Villages," the latter consisting of "Japanese pagoda-type homes . . . [of] much flimsier make [than the German]. There are 12 individual houses, all about 20 feet high and 24 feet long; ranging from 14 to 30 feet wide. Outside walls are of plaster or adobe, but partitions are paper or very light wood." Inside, the buildings in "Jap Village" were furnished with tatami mats, low tables, and pillows for chairs.

The small M69 napalm bombs, particularly effective in tests against the lightly constructed Japanese structures, were assembled in 500-pound clusters. A B-29 was able to carry 24 such bundles, a six-ton bombload that the four-engine Superfortress could carry from the U.S. airfields in the Marianas to Tokyo.

General LeMay ordered most of the guns and ammunition removed from his B-29s and sent them against Japanese cities at low level, at night, to spread incendiary bombs. On the night of March 9–10, 1945, he struck Tokyo with 279 B-29s, which flew at altitudes of 5,000 to 8,000 feet instead of at their normal bombing altitude of some 30,000 feet. As the planes reached their target—marked by fires started by pathfinder bombers using large incendiary bombs—they released 1,665 tons of the napalm incendiaries on Tokyo, mostly the diminutive M69 bombs. Fierce fires took hold and, fanned by 20 mph winds, precipitated a firestorm. The later waves of bombers heading for Tokyo that night suffered from poor visibility due to the mass of smoke, and their bomb runs were made difficult by turbulence created by the intense heat waves. As the planes flew away from Japan, their tail gunners could see the glow of Tokyo fires for 150 miles.

B-29s flew over Tokyo for three hours that night. There was considerable anti-aircraft fire, but the fire from the smaller, automatic weapons was too low, and the heavy flak guns fired too high. Few Japanese fighters were sighted. Fourteen B-29s were lost to anti-aircraft fire, none to enemy fighters. Five of their crews were rescued at sea.

"The Great Tokyo Air Raid," as the Japanese called it, completely burned out almost 16 square miles of the capital. More than a million people—one-seventh of the capital's population—lost their homes. Japanese records show that 83,793 people were killed and almost 41,000 injured in that raid. Some Japanese reports put the toll of dead and missing as high as 197,000. The raid inflicted not only great loss of life and physical damage on the Japanese; it was also a devastating blow to public morale.

Twenty-nine hours after the last B-29 returned from the incendiary attack on Tokyo, LeMay launched his second firebomb raid. This time 285 bombers struck Nagoya, the principal aircraft production center of Japan. The March 11–12 nighttime strike released 1,790 tons of incendiaries over the city, 125 tons more than on Tokyo, but the damage was far less than in Tokyo because many aircraft dropped their bombs short of the target and there were no winds to fan a firestorm. Still, the implications of what was to come were clear to the Japanese. Only one B-29 was lost; it came down at sea soon after takeoff; about 20 other bombers were damaged by anti-aircraft fire.

On the night of March 13–14, Osaka, Japan's second-largest city and a major industrial center, was bombed by 274 B-29s dropping incendiaries. The targets included the massive Osaka arsenal, and secondary explosions of munitions at the arsenal tossed the B-29s around in the night sky. A B-29, appropriately named *Topsy Turvey,* was blown 5,000 feet straight up by a shock wave, turned upside down, and fell 10,000 feet before the pilot regained control of the aircraft! The 1,732½ tons of bombs dropped on Osaka devastated eight square miles in the heart of the city. Factories and whole residential districts were burned out, killing more than 4,600 Japanese. Osaka was crippled. Three nights later, on March 16–17, a raid by 331 of LeMay's B-29s dropped 2,350 tons of incendiaries on the port city of Kobe —the largest bombload yet carried to Japan. Two nights later, 290 planes returned to firebomb Nagoya a second time.

Not only were the firebomb raids devastating military and industrial installations that daylight precision bombing had failed to destroy; they were also obliterating the small home workshops that were producing parts for Japan's precarious war machine. "We were going after military targets," LeMay wrote in his memoirs.

> No point in slaughtering civilians for the mere sake of slaughter. Of course there is a pretty thin veneer in Japan, but the veneer was there. It was their system of dispersal of industry. All you had to do was visit one of those targets after we'd roasted it, and see the ruins of a multitude of tiny houses, with a drill press sticking up through the wreckage of every home. The entire population got into the act and worked to make those airplanes or munitions of war . . . men, women, children. We knew we were going to kill a lot of women and kids. . . . Had to be done.

Survivors could not work. They had to locate family members who might still be alive and find food and a place to sleep. Throughout Japan the government ordered officials of major cities to tear down thousands of houses to make firebreaks to stop future conflagrations from engulfing whole, flimsily built areas of the cities.

Thus, between March 9 and 19 young LeMay had directed five great incendiary raids against four major Japanese cities. These raids stopped only because the XXI Bomber Command ran out of incendiary bombs. LeMay then sent his B-29s on visual precision-bombing strikes at night with high-explosive bombs, striking targets illuminated by flares and fires ignited by pathfinder aircraft. Again the results of these precision-bombing efforts were not particularly effective, and LeMay soon discontinued them. Instead, the B-29s flew combinations of medium-altitude bombing attacks (12,000 to 18,000 feet) in daylight and, as more incendiaries arrived in the Marianas, low-level incendiary attacks at night.

The B-29s returned to Tokyo four times during early April in relatively small raids (68 to 105 planes), dropping high explosives on aircraft factories. Then, on Friday, April 13, shortly before midnight 327 of the giant bombers dropped 2,139 tons of high-explosive and incendiary bombs on Tokyo's arsenal district, northwest of the Imperial Palace. The bombs and ensuing fires burned out another 11 square miles of the city, killing almost 2,500 people, injuring twice that many, and leaving another half million persons homeless.

Among the hundreds of buildings razed in the April 13 raid were portions of the Riken laboratory in Tokyo, a key site of Japanese atomic bomb research. Since 1940 both the Japanese Army Air Force and Imperial Navy had seen the possibilities of an atomic bomb and sponsored some atomic research. Only the Navy's program endured, and even that was a pathetically small effort by what was known as the N-group, working under Navy sponsorship at the University of Kyoto as well as the Riken laboratory in Tokyo. Plagued by severe shortages of scientists, engineers, and equipment, the effort came to an end on the night of April 13–14 as B-29 bombs ignited fires that devoured much of the Riken laboratory complex. Building No. 49, which housed Japan's single uranium separator, appeared to have survived the bombings and fires. But after the fires were extinguished and the firefighters and laboratory staff were resting, the wooden building suddenly broke into flames and was totally destroyed. Either a smoldering fire had flamed up or a bomb had belatedly detonated. Regardless, the B-29s had destroyed Japan's atomic bomb effort.

The B-29s again struck Tokyo on the night of April 15–16, when 109 bombers delivered more incendiaries. Another six square miles of the city were burned out, as well as adjacent areas of the cities of Kawasaki and Yokohama. More bombs would fall on the nights of May 23–24 and again on May 25–26 as LeMay sent the B-29s back for a "final one-two knockout blow" against the capital. Four previous area raids had struck Tokyo with more than 5,000 tons of incendiaries and destroyed 34 square miles of the city; the last two firebomb raids dropped another 6,900 tons, burning out another 22 square miles. In total, just over 56 square miles had been destroyed—half of the city.

The firestorm of May 25–26 burned out Tokyo's financial, commercial, and government districts. The Foreign Ministry, the premier's official residence, and Navy Ministry buildings were destroyed. Tokyo's army prison was also devastated, killing numerous Japanese prisoners and 62 captured American fliers. Flaming debris from the fires hurdled across the moat of the Imperial Palace. Surrounded by moats and wooded areas, the palace was initially constructed in 1888 when the Meiji Emperor moved from Kyoto to Tokyo. Despite the best efforts of some 10,000 firefighters, troops, and government workers to extinguish the flames, 27 palace buildings were destroyed in less than four hours. Twenty-eight members of the Imperial staff were killed in the flames, while the Emperor, Empress, and their senior attendants cowered in a newly built shelter 60 feet beneath the palace library.

There were no more raids on Tokyo until a small one on August 8 because no significant targets were left. Not knowing that the XXI Bomber Command planners had shifted their efforts to other targets and with few industrial activities remaining in the city, on July 2 the Japanese government ordered a mass evacuation of what was left of the Tokyo metropolis. All but some 200,000 men and women were forced to leave. Before the war the city's population had been about eight million.

There was one deliberate, although unauthorized, American effort to bomb the Imperial Palace: on July 20 by a B-29 named *Straight Flush* from the 509th Composite Group, the unit preparing for atomic bomb strikes. Unaware of the true purpose of their mission, the *Straight Flush* crewmen were practicing atomic bomb delivery techniques. They thought that they and other 509th crews were bombing targets with a new weapon, which they nicknamed the pumpkin bomb for its orange color and odd shape. But the single 5,500-pound, high-explosive bomb they dropped was a stand-in for the "Fat Man" nuclear weapon. The plane's assigned target was obscured by clouds, and Sergeant Jack Bivans, the assistant flight engineer, suggested that they bomb the palace. The B-29's pilot, Major Claude Eatherly, took a vote of his crew over the plane's intercom, and the B-29 turned toward the palace. Tokyo, too, was clouded over. The plane dropped its single high-explosive bomb by radar.

The bomb missed the palace, and upon returning to Tinian, the crew was severely rebuked. The news of the attack reached the Tinian headquarters via a Tokyo radio newscast.

. . .

The XXI Bomber Command's B-29s were also attacking Kyushu. Because it was an almost inevitable choice for an American invasion, the Japanese had been building up defenses there, and ground, air, and naval bases dotted the island. Kamikaze pilots trained at Kyushu bases and flew off from there on suicide attacks against U.S. ships of the Okinawa invasion fleet. Between April 17 and May 11, B-29s attacked Kyushu airfields every day, with strikes averaging from 75 to 100 bombers. Air opposition was more determined than ever as Japanese fighters rose to defend their bases, and 22 B-29s fell to Japanese fighters in this period—still a loss rate of only about one percent, compared to mission loss rates as high as ten percent and more for U.S. daylight bombing in Europe. The B-29s reduced many of Kyushu's airfields to rubble, and the kamikaze attacks against the U.S. fleet off Okinawa fell off considerably.

The B-29s then returned to industrial targets, using mostly incendiaries to destroy factories, electric generating plants, railroad yards, and oil refineries. Damage was heavy, and many hundreds of civilians were killed every day and night. By early August, more than 105 square miles had been destroyed in the six major Japanese urban areas, which overall encompassed 257 square miles. By that time American bombs and the fires that they ignited had killed more than 240,000 Japanese—men, women, and children—and injured more than 300,000.

Starting on February 16, 1945, U.S. Navy carrier-based aircraft periodically attacked targets in the Tokyo area. Up to 16 aircraft carriers, operating as close as 60 miles to the Japanese coast, launched several hundred fighters and bombers in the first series of strikes. The planes ranged freely over Honshu and inflicted major damage on the Nakajima engine factory complex at Musashino, which at that time had suffered little damage from the B-29 high-altitude strikes. There were no Japanese counterattacks against the U.S. carriers.

Beginning on April 7, P-51 Mustang fighters flew from Iwo Jima to escort B-29s on their raids to Japan, brushing away the few Japanese fighters that rose to attack the bombers. Periodically, fighter pilots tried to crash into the B-29s over Japan. Two suicide pilots who crashed into B-29s, bringing them down, survived by landing their crippled planes at sea, where they were rescued. They were hailed as heroes.

These tactical aircraft from carriers and Iwo Jima, soon joined by other Army as well as Marine bombers flying from Okinawa, covered the landscape of southern Japan during daylight hours, bombing and strafing military facilities, airfields, and even military vehicles.

. . .

With General LeMay's firebomb raids, American strategic bombing was at last having an effect: not high-altitude, daylight precision bombing, but low-level, night area destruction that was burning out the core of Japanese cities. "I was not happy, but neither was I particularly concerned, about civilian casualties on incendiary raids," LeMay later wrote. "I didn't let it influence any of my decisions because we knew how the Japanese had treated the Americans—both civilian and military—that they'd captured in places like the Philippines."

The largest B-29 raid of the war came on August 1, 1945, when 836 aircraft were launched from bases in the Marianas; 784 reached targets in Japan, most striking urban areas with incendiaries. In addition to dropping almost 170,000 tons of bombs during 14 months of war, B-29s laid more than 12,000 aerial mines in Japanese and Korean waters to hamper the movement of troops, military equipment, and foodstuffs between the Asian mainland and the home islands. The five-month mining effort—dubbed Operation Starvation—halted most seaborne traffic. Some reports contend that 670 Japanese ships, mostly coastal vessels, were sunk in that operation; 16 B-29s were lost in the effort's 1,528 sorties (nine to enemy action, the rest operational).

By August 1945, LeMay had 1,000 B-29s on the airfields in the Marianas. Meanwhile, Lieutenant General Jimmy Doolittle had arrived on Okinawa in July 1945. After his Tokyo raid, Doolittle had been assigned to General Arnold's staff. In September 1942 he took command of the Twelfth Air Force in England, which went to North Africa later that year. After commanding strategic air forces there, in January 1944 he took command of the Eighth Air Force in England, flying heavy bombers against European targets. Now his target would be Japan. By August 1, 1945, Doolittle had 42 B-29s on Okinawa, and plans called for him to have 600 of the large bombers by November for attacking Japan.

More B-29s were coming off American production lines, and hundreds of crews, many of them B-17 and B-24 veterans from the European War, were being trained to fly B-29s in the Pacific. This massive buildup of long-range bombers in the Pacific had led to a major reorganization of the air forces. In April, General MacArthur had been named head of all Army forces in the Pacific; Nimitz, the commander of all naval forces. Except for the B-29s, Army land-based aviation came under MacArthur's purview. General Arnold had always fought to keep an independent strategic bomber force in the Pacific. After considerable discussion the Joint Chiefs of Staff agreed to create the Twentieth Air Force to operate the B-29s (through the XX and XXI Bomber Commands). But there was a catch: The Twentieth Air Force would report directly to the Joint Chiefs of Staff, with General Arnold as the nominal commander and the JCS executive agent for B-29 operations. With Arnold in Washington, suffering from a heart ailment, it was an awkward arrangement.

Even before the MacArthur-Nimitz division of American forces in the Pacific, Arnold had been arguing for a single air commander in the Pacific for all land-based aircraft, long-range and tactical, possibly including Navy and Marine Corps planes flying from land bases. It sounded like a logical proposal, but it was obviously unworkable because ground and naval commanders had to have control of the planes that worked directly with their respective forces.

While Arnold sought a supreme air commander with coequal status with MacArthur and Nimitz—a proposal unacceptable to either the Army or Navy theater commander—some reorganization was needed because of the imminent movement to the Pacific of many of the Army Air Forces units that had fought in Europe. The JCS decided that the strategic bombers would be combined under a new command, the U.S. Army Strategic Air Forces in the Pacific—USASTAF in military jargon. There had been a similar setup in Europe, where it was necessary to coordinate U.S. and British long-range bombers flying from Britain and North Africa.

USASTAF was established on July 16, 1945, with General Carl A. (Tooey) Spaatz as Commander in Chief, with headquarters on Guam, where Nimitz now had his advance headquarters. A World War I fighter pilot, Spaatz was a brilliant aviation strategist who had commanded the U.S. Strategic Air Forces in Europe from January 1944 to March 1945. He was 54 years old when he assumed the Pacific post.

As an official U.S. observer in London in 1940, Spaatz had lived through the Battle of Britain and knew, from the ground, what city bombing meant. He was a committed believer in bombing as a strategic, rather than tactical, weapon. In D-Day planning he had opposed General Eisenhower, who wanted Spaatz's bombers to hit the French railway system to thwart the movement of German reinforcements to Normandy. Spaatz, who won the support of Arnold, argued against the move, which essentially gave Eisenhower direct control of the bombers. So strong were Spaatz and his British air-power colleagues that Churchill and Roosevelt had to intervene, ordering that the bombers be put under Eisenhower's "direction."

As head of strategic bombers in the Pacific, Spaatz reported directly to General Arnold, who was the JCS executive agent for strategic bombers. But direct command of the B-29s was now moved from Arnold's office in the Pentagon to Guam. LeMay, who had led the B-29s to their greatest success, was not told of the changes by Arnold. He found out when Lieutenant General Nathan Twining arrived in July to take command of the Twentieth Air Force under Spaatz. LeMay asked Twining, "What are you doing out here?"

Twining later said, "Taking over the outfit from Curt LeMay is about like taking over the Notre Dame football team from Knute Rockne." LeMay became Spaatz's chief of staff, a role that would keep his active mind involved in strategic bombing operations against Japan. The Spaatz-LeMay team would direct Twentieth Air Force B-29s in the Marianas and Doolittle the Eighth Air Force B-29s on Okinawa in the intensified bombing of Japan. In addition, under Army (MacArthur) control was the Far East Air Forces, commanded by Lieutenant General George C. Kenney, directing the Fifth, Seventh, and Thirteenth Air Forces with several thousand fighters, medium bombers, and the "heavy" four-engine B-24 Liberators and B-32 Dominators, most of which could reach targets in Japan. The B-24s, flying from airfields on Okinawa, began bombing Japan on July 10. The B-32, developed as a backup in case the B-29 encountered development problems, only flew photo-reconnaissance missions.

Similarly, Nimitz's carrier-based aircraft as well as the guns of his battleships and cruisers were adding to the bombardment of the home islands. With some 20 U.S. and four British fleet carriers available in mid-1945 (and more coming out), there were some 1,200 fighters and attack planes at sea.

And the British were coming. The Royal Air Force (RAF) planned to shift heavy bombers to the Pacific, and a mostly Australian tactical air force was getting ready to support the Commonwealth Corps for the planned invasion of Honshu in 1946. The RAF's most capable strategic bomber, the four-engine Lancaster, had the largest bomb capacity of any aircraft flying except the B-29, able to carry up to seven tons in its normal configuration. Some Lancasters were modified for "big" bombs, including the 22,000-pound "Grand Slam," the biggest conventional bomb ever made. Ten tons was the maximum bombload for a B-29 with a reduced range.

The RAF was assembling the so-called Tiger Force of Lancaster Mark VII bombers, which would be based on Okinawa with Doolittle's Eighth Air Force. The modified RAF bombers were to begin arriving on Okinawa's crowded airfields on about September 1945. Between 30 and 36 squadrons, each with 16 aircraft, were to comprise the Tiger Force, adding a few hundred more bombers to the assault on Japan.

Thus, the strategic bombers attacking Japan in the latter half of 1945 and into 1946 would number perhaps 2,000 B-29s and Lancasters plus the several hundred B-24s and B-32s of Kenney's commands. At the Yalta Conference in February 1945, Stalin had acceded to President Roosevelt's request for two bases in the Far East for B-29 operations. Although logistic support of B-29s in eastern Siberia would have been very difficult, if not impossible, those airfields could have served as emergency or "shuttle-bombing" bases for the U.S. planes.

By mid-1945 the U.S. military services were developing a plan to bombard Japan with guided missiles—U.S. versions of the V-1 "buzz bombs" that the Germans had begun launching against London in June 1944. These missiles, called "doodlebugs" by the British, had a 1,870-pound high-explosive warhead. During an 80-day period, when 2,149 V-1s fell on England, the missiles killed 6,184 persons, seriously injured another 17,981, and wrecked or damaged more than one million buildings.

In July 1944 salvaged German V-1 parts were flown from England to the United States and were quickly copied by the Army. The first American versions were delivered within three weeks of the order to produce the missile, which was given the American designation JB-2 for Jet Bomb. It was a relatively slow (subsonic), low-altitude "cruise," or guided, missile with an air-breathing combustion engine. These missiles followed a preset flight path to a fixed target, and the lack of terminal or homing guidance made it a "terror weapon" rather than an effective precision weapon.

By the end of July 1945 the Army had ordered 1,000 JB-2s, with plans being made for the monthly production of that number, to increase to 5,000 per month by the fall of 1945. General Arnold envisioned eventually bombarding Japan with *500 missiles per day* by 1946, the missiles being launched from captured bases in South Korea and from tank landing ships (LSTs). In the competition to adopt new weapons, the U.S. Navy looked at bombarding Japan with JB-2s—which it called the Loon—from small aircraft carriers and LSTs. Thus, by the spring of 1946 hundreds of V-1 missiles could be pounding Japan every day and every night in addition to the waves of bombers and tactical aircraft.

Some even more unconventional air attacks against Japan were contemplated. Dr. Lytle S. Adams, a Pennsylvania dental surgeon who was inspired by a visit to Carlsbad Caverns, New Mexico, the home of millions of bats, proposed using "bat bombs" against the wood-and-paper homes of the Japanese. Adams wrote to the White House, which passed the idea to the Army's Chemical Warfare Service. According to the official history, "President Roosevelt OK'd it and the project was on."

After experimenting with several bat species, Adams and a team of naturalists selected the Mexican free-tailed bat *(Tadarida brasiliensis),* which was found at Carlsbad. The freetails, which weigh up to half an ounce, could fly with a one- or two-ounce bomb. The task of making weapons out of the bats fell to the Army Air Forces, which turned to Dr. L.F. Fisser of the National Defense Research Committee.

Fisser designed two incendiary bombs for the bats. One, weighing just over half an ounce, would burn for four minutes; the other, a two-ouncer, burned for six minutes. The bombs were filled with jellylike kerosene and were set off when a chemical corroded a spring-held wire that propelled a firing pin to the bomb's igniter head. The bomb was attached by string and a surgical clip to loose skin on the bat's chest.

The armed bats were to be frozen or hibernated in ice-cube trays and loaded, about 180 at a time, in cardboard containers that would be dropped from bombers and set to open at an altitude of about 1,000 feet. Because bats eat several times their own weight in insects each day, they had to be frozen so they would not have to be fed. The bats, according to the Army history, were to "fly into hiding in dwellings or other structures, gnaw through the string, and leave the bombs behind."

The bats' first test missions, carrying dummy bombs, were flown in May 1943 from a B-25 Mitchell bomber. In the bat-drop tests, many bats disappeared, and others fell directly to earth. An aircraft hangar and general's car were set afire by real bat bombs before the Army Air Forces decided in August 1943 to give the project to the Navy, which called it Project X-Ray and soon passed it to the Marines. Full-scale tests of the bat bombs were planned for August 1944, but the project was finally canceled in March 1944 by Admiral King when he learned that it would be 15 months more before the bats could be used in combat. About $2 million and an unknown number of bats were lost on the project.

Still another proposal was to bomb Japanese volcanoes to cause eruptions that would destroy nearby military and industrial facilities. An Army study looked at the effects of exploding bombs in the 50 active volcanoes in Japan. The structure of volcanoes, the study concluded, was not vulnerable to bombing, although "If the *time* when an eruption of a given volcano is almost due could be predicted, a bomb explosion *might* theoretically act to hasten the eruption. There is but one chance out of a million that such a coincidence could be brought about since volcanologists *cannot* predict the next volcano to erupt nor when it will erupt." This scheme was also dropped. The bombing effort against Japan would be continued with conventional high-explosive and incendiary weapons.

In the early summer of 1945, it seemed that the visions of the advocates of air power were being realized. Although it was not under independent command and daylight precision bombing had proved ineffective, an air force of overwhelming strength was getting through to its targets, destroying the enemy's cities, and crippling its war-making ability. Victory through air power, the dream of Giulio Douhet and his followers, appeared to be at hand. The U.S. Army Air Forces—from General Arnold to the pilots of the B-29s and their air crewmen and ground mechanics—had little doubt that sustained aerial bombardment would bring the Japanese to full surrender without any need for an invasion of the home islands.

CHAPTER 4

350 MILES TO DOWNFALL

Waves of amphibious tanks pass a
battleship as American troops assault
Okinawa on April 1, 1945. The attack
was a shocking preview of an invasion of
Japan—in both the great number of
American casualties and the ferocity of
Japanese resistance.

The American assault on Okinawa was to be the penultimate campaign of World War II, the prelude to the final battle—the subjugation of Japan by whatever means necessary. Despite the optimism of the air-power advocates, an invasion of the Japanese home islands still was a possibility, and Okinawa became an obvious final steppingstone. The island offered several fleet anchorages and airfields that would make Okinawa an advanced staging base for an invasion of Japan. And the island's five airfields could be expanded to accommodate several hundred American planes, including the giant B-29 Superfortresses.

Many American commanders believed that the Okinawa assault would be a model for the invasion of Japan. Okinawa, the main island of the Ryukyu chain, was only 350 miles southwest of Kyushu, the southernmost of the Japanese home islands, which put Okinawa within range of fighter aircraft based there. Okinawa was Japanese territory, and the Okinawans were Japanese citizens, unlike the conquered peoples encountered in most previous Pacific assaults. Okinawa had been annexed in 1879, and its people were integrated completely into the Japanese political and economic structure. Its population was 435,000 when the war began.

But if the invasion of Okinawa could be likened to an invasion of Japan, its conquest would be quite different from previous landings in the Pacific. Okinawa was a large island compared to many other Pacific island targets— 60 miles long and from 2 to 18 miles in width, with an area of 485 square miles. And because of its strategic importance and proximity to Japan, it was heavily fortified. The assault planners anticipated that the Japanese troops and paramilitary civilians on Okinawa would fight fiercely in a series of costly delaying actions and suicidal attacks, supported by the last remaining major warships of the Imperial fleet and massive aerial kamikaze raids. The battle slogan of the 32nd Army, charged with defending Okinawa, was:

> One Plane for One Warship
> One Boat for One Ship
> One Man for Ten of the Enemy or One Tank

The man commanding the defenses of Okinawa, Lieutenant General Mitsuru Ushijima, had taken over the Okinawa-Ryukyu Islands command in August 1944. His chief of staff was Isamu Cho, recently promoted to lieutenant general and reputed to be one of the most competent officers of the Japanese Army. Ushijima, slated for promotion to full general in August 1945, was a man of great integrity and character. He demonstrated a quiet competence, inspiring confidence, loyalty, and respect from his subordinates. Cho, known for heavy drinking and chain-smoking, was a fiery, ebullient, and hard-driving officer who spared neither himself nor his staff. He was already infamous for having issued the orders for the execution of all Chinese prisoners at Nanking in December 1937 (apparently on instructions from Prince Yasuhiko Asaka, uncle of Emperor Hirohito). Together Ushijima and Cho were considered an effective and formidable command team.

Although Ushijima worked on the defenses of Okinawa with fervor, he was badly handicapped. He had been forced to transfer his veteran 9th Infantry Division to Formosa in December 1944 when it appeared that the Americans might land there after the conquest of the Philippines, and it had been only partially replaced. That same month, an accidental explosion destroyed half of the 32nd Army's ammunition, and that was not replaced. Indeed, fearing that the home islands would be the next target of American assaults, the Japanese high command sent few replacements to Okinawa.

Nevertheless, when American soldiers and Marines came ashore on Okinawa and adjacent islands, they would find the 32nd Army well entrenched, but not on the beaches. Short of troops after the 9th Division was taken from him, Ushijima deployed his forces inland. His regular Army troops numbered 66,600 men, and the naval-base force contributed another 8,800 men to the defenses of the island, although they had little training, lacked weapons, and were used mainly to man anti-aircraft and coastal-defense guns. But these troops, as well as Okinawan conscripts, were desperately needed because of Ushijima's shortage of troops after the departure of the 9th Division.

In another harbinger of what planners anticipated would happen in the assault on the home islands, Okinawa civilians—including some women—were mobilized into the home guard, or *Boeitai,* which numbered 17,700. About 750 male students, 14 years of age and older, were organized into volunteer youth groups called *Tekketsu* (Blood and Iron for the Emperor Duty Groups) and assigned to front-line or communication units or prepared for guerrilla warfare behind American lines. Female students were given rudimentary training to care for the wounded. Many Okinawans cooperated in the defense of the islands because after years of being looked upon as inferior by Japanese, they saw the battle as an opportunity to prove with their lives that they were loyal Japanese subjects. Including all of these quasi-military groups and some 2,300 Okinawan engineer units, more than 23,000 Okinawan men, women, and children were formally mobilized for the defense of the island. Thus, some 100,000 American troops were to assault an island held by 100,000 defenders.

. . .

The Allied lineup for the Okinawa assault—Operation Iceberg—consisted of a huge fleet of warships and amphibious ships, the latter carrying Admiral Nimitz's Tenth Army, which was commanded by Lieutenant General Simon B. Buckner, a veteran of the recent campaign to clear the Japanese from the Aleutian islands they had seized in June 1942. Created in June 1944, the U.S. Tenth Army was half Army and half Marine, consisting of the Army's XXIV Corps (with three divisions) and the III Marine Amphibious Corps (with two divisions). A third Marine division would fake a diversionary landing on the southern coast and with another Army division, also embarked in ships, form an afloat reserve to come ashore if needed. With troops assigned to the Tenth Army and the two corps, the assault force totaled more than 100,000 men, embarked in 434 assault transports, cargo ships, and landing ships. Close air support would be provided by a combined Army-Marine tactical air force as well as carrier-based aircraft.

The Okinawa invasion fleet consisted of the largest number of ships involved in a single amphibious operation of the Pacific War—nearly 1,500 U.S. combatant and auxiliary ships. In addition, the British sent a fast carrier task force of 22 ships with 244 aircraft on four fleet carriers to supplement the American total of almost 1,000 carrier aircraft. All told, a half million men—Army, Navy, Marines, and Royal Navy—would participate in Operation Iceberg. The size of the amphibious landing on Okinawa was exceeded only by the Philippine and Normandy landings the year before. But the Normandy invasion could not compare to the distances and logistic problems involved in Operation Iceberg.

The Okinawa invasion was originally scheduled for March 1, 1945, but delays in the Philippine and Iwo Jima campaigns set Operation Iceberg back to April 1, Easter Sunday. In an effort to destroy Japanese aircraft assigned to attack the landing, two weeks prior to the invasion, the fast carriers of Admiral Raymond Spruance's Fifth Fleet bombed and strafed the Japanese home island of Kyushu. Beginning on the morning of March 18, fighters from the carriers struck the Kyushu airfields, while scouting planes fanned out to find Japanese warships that were hiding.

The principal U.S. targets were the 45 airfields in the area. Few Japanese planes were found, most having fled to northern bases to escape attack. Still, that day, 50 Japanese planes carried out sporadic bombing and suicide missions against the U.S. ships that lasted almost six hours. But the defensive fighters and intense anti-aircraft fire from the ships let few suiciders get through to their targets. Seven sailors were killed and some were wounded on ships, but the damage was minor.

The next day, the carrier planes struck at the anchored Japanese ships sighted the previous day; 16 were hit, among them the super battleship *Yamato,* although damage to the survivors of the Japanese Fleet was light.

Admiral Nimitz would command Allied naval forces for the invasion, the final and most brutal test of Allied military might.

Flying strikes against these anchored ships reduced the air attacks on Japanese airfields, and the carriers paid for this oversight. Shortly after sunrise on March 19, Japanese planes began to appear over the carrier force. A single bomb from a Japanese plane struck the new carrier *Wasp,* penetrating to the hangar deck and a berthing area before exploding in a galley. Fires flared on five decks. Although her insides were torn up and 102 men were dead or dying and another 269 were injured, the fires were extinguished in 15 minutes, and the *Wasp* continued flight operations.

Not so with the carrier *Franklin.* At almost the exact moment the *Wasp* was hit, another Japanese plane made a low-level run on the "Big Ben" and hit the ship with two small bombs. The first one exploded on the hangar deck forward, wrecking the elevator, killing everyone in the area, and igniting fires that quickly enveloped armed and fueled aircraft. The second bomb exploded in the hangar, starting more fires among aircraft readying for launch on the flight deck and spreading flames and destruction through the rest of the hangar. At 7:09 A.M.—one minute after the bombs hit—the *Franklin* was rocked by the first of a five-hour-long series of explosions by bombs and rockets on aircraft being readied for launch. The flames exploded ammunition in gun mounts and lockers. These explosions and streaking bullets prevented firefighters from reaching the flames.

The ship's forward magazine was flooded; the after magazine was not because, unknown at the time, the sprinkler system had failed. The *Franklin* writhed in agony, bellows of black smoke pouring skyward. But she survived. Superhuman effort by her crew brought the fires under control as the ship drifted only 55 miles from Kyushu. Other ships came alongside to help fight the fires and take off unneeded crewmen.

Again able to get up steam, the battered *Franklin* headed away from Japan. She had suffered more damage than any other carrier that survived the war—and many that did not. Her dead numbered 832; her wounded, 270. Among the living was the ship's chaplain, Lieutenant Commander Joseph O'Callahan, who not only administered last rites to the dead and dying but also helped direct fire-fighting parties. For his valor he became the only chaplain in the war to be awarded the Medal of Honor.

The Okinawa campaign had claimed its first casualties. But U.S. pilots reported destroying 482 Japanese aircraft in the two-day raid (a slightly inflated score). After three damaged carriers and their escorts withdrew, the 13 remaining U.S. carriers and their array of escorting ships refueled at sea and headed toward Okinawa to provide air support for the invasion.

Ten outdated U.S. battleships—many veterans of the Pearl Harbor attack —9 cruisers, 23 destroyers, and 177 gunboats and rocket craft began a preinvasion bombardment of Okinawa a week before the landings. The Japanese returned only light artillery and mortar fire, without effect. On March 26–27 five small islands of the Kerama Retto group to the west of Okinawa were seized by troops of the Army's 77th Infantry Division so as to cut off a force of enemy suicide boats and to establish a preliminary anchorage for U.S. ships. Japanese opposition was determined but light. On one of those islands, Tokashiki Jima, the garrison commander, Yoshitsugu Akamatsu,

> . . . ordered local inhabitants to turn over all food supplies to the army and commit suicide before U.S. troops landed. The obedient islanders, 329 all together, killed each other at the Onna River with razors, hatchets, and sickles. U.S. forces occupied nearby Iejima [Ie Shima] and used some of the local people to take surrender appeals to Akamatsu's unit on Tokashiki-jima. Akamatsu's men killed the emissaries and many members of the island's self-defense unit for allegedly violating orders.

On the adjacent island of Zamami Jima, a commander named Umezawa ordered the island's elderly and children to commit suicide in front of the memorial to local men killed in Japan's wars with China and Russia.

The main U.S. landings on Okinawa began at 4:06 on Easter Sunday morning, starting with a feint toward the southeastern shore by the 2nd Marine Division. The real landing came on a five-mile stretch of beach on the southwestern coast, near the village of Hagushi, a site chosen because of the proximity of two airfields. Capturing those airfields as quickly as possible would help relieve the pressure on the covering carrier task forces providing close air support.

The battleship *Tennessee* steamed in to within 1,900 yards of the beach so that her 14-inch guns could provide covering fire for the landing force. Several other battleships farther offshore fired salvo after salvo of 14-inch and 16-inch rounds at the Japanese defenses. Only an occasional Japanese mortar or machine gun fired in response. Indeed, the Marines and Army troops came ashore with virtually no opposition. Ernie Pyle, who went ashore with the seventh assault wave, wrote: "We landed absolutely unopposed, which is indeed an odd experience for a marine. It was incredible; nobody among us had dreamed of such a thing. We all thought there would be slaughter on the beaches. There was some opposition to the right and left of us, but on our beach, nothing, absolutely nothing."

Within four days the American troops—with little enemy opposition— had gained most of their objectives along the west-central coast of the island. The lack of opposition to the landing was unexpected, but it had happened before, at Guadalcanal, at times in New Guinea, and in the Philippines. The two airfields were taken without much effort. Navy Seabees and Army engineers were soon reconditioning the airfields at Yontan and Kadena for American use, and early on April 2, Marine-piloted Piper Cub–type "grasshopper" artillery-spotting planes began using the airfields. They were joined ashore on the afternoon of April 7 by gull-wing F4U Corsair fighter-bombers.

The initial Japanese response to the landings came in the form of intense kamikaze air attacks on the naval forces standing offshore. More than 1,900 kamikaze sorties would be flown against the Allied ships off Okinawa in the three months of Operation Iceberg. While kamikaze pilots were volunteers, Rear Admiral Toshiyuki Yokoi, chief of staff for the Kyushu-based Fifth Air Fleet, would later write:

> . . . when it came time for their take off, the pilots' attitudes ranged from the despair of sheep headed for slaughter to open expressions of contempt for their superior officers. There were frequent and obvious cases of pilots returning from sorties claiming that they could not locate any enemy ships, and one pilot even strafed his commanding officer's quarters as he took off.

Most kamikaze pilots, however, went on their last missions with courage and determination. Special ceremonies were held before takeoff, with cheers for the Emperor. Kamikaze pilots would wear a *hachimaki,* a cloth wrapped around their heads, as a mark of courage and composure, as ancient samurai warriors had wrapped a folded white cloth around their heads before battle to hold back their long hair and keep perspiration from their eyes. Pilots' hair and fingernail cuttings were left with their carefully packed belongings, to be sent to their families. The pilots would then man their planes and take off to the salutes of those left behind. On occasion, when his plane had engine trouble, a kamikaze pilot would come running to his commanding officer screaming, "Commander, engine trouble! Give me another plane!"

Kamikaze pilots were usually teenagers or barely in their twenties. An older pilot, who had children five and three years old, left a letter that told them not to envy boys who had fathers. "Always be a good brother and sister. . . . Your father has become a god and will be watching over you."

The Japanese aerial assault—called Operation *Ten-Go*—was delayed because of the carrier and B-29 strikes against Kyushu airfields. Still, some kamikazes began attacking as soon as the fleet appeared off Okinawa. On March 31 a suicider hit Admiral Spruance's flagship, the cruiser *Indianapolis*. The admiral shifted his staff to an old battleship, and the cruiser steamed off for temporary repairs, after which she headed to the West Coast of the United States and more extensive work. (When she returned to the war zone in July 1945, she would be carrying components for the atomic bomb.)

Operation *Ten-Go* called for 4,500 aircraft to fly both conventional and suicide attacks against the U.S. ships off Okinawa. The primary targets for the suiciders were the U.S. destroyers on radar picket stations around the island and then the aircraft carriers, transports, and landing ships that the destroyers guarded. Although suiciders began to appear as soon as American warships arrived off Okinawa, the first of ten massed air attacks began on the afternoon of April 6. When the suiciders singled out the radar picket destroyers for attacks, additional landing craft were sent out to work with them. The smaller craft were soon called "pallbearers"; they clustered around the destroyers to help the larger ships fight fires and, if sinking, take off survivors.

One after another the picket destroyers were smashed. On April 6—the day of the first massed air attack—the destroyer *Mullany* was hit. Then *Newcomb, Leutze, Howorth, Hyman, Morris,* and *Haynsworth.* The destroyer *Harrison* was scorched by a near miss. Two destroyers, *Bush* and *Calhoun,* both struck by two or more kamikazes, sank. The *Bush* lost 94 officers and enlisted men killed and many wounded; the *Calhoun* lost 35 killed. The destroyer-minesweeper *Emmons,* steaming at 25 knots to assist her sister ship *Rodman,* which had just been hit by a suicider, was struck by no less than *five* Japanese aircraft. She went down with 64 of her crew. Two destroyer escorts, *Fieberling* and *Witter,* were also hit by kamikazes that day.

The heavily damaged destroyer *Leutze,* in danger of sinking, was taken in tow by the large minesweeper *Defense,* which had just been hit by two kamikazes and had shot down a third. Upon reaching a repair ship anchored near an offshore island, her skipper, Lieutenant Commander Gordon Abbott, signaled: "Sorry to be late, have scratched a kamikaze and taken two on board. Now have a destroyer in tow."

During the late afternoon and night of April 6, suiciders crashed into a total of 19 ships. Two destroyers, a destroyer-minesweeper, an LST, and two ammunition-laden merchant ships were sunk. Beyond the men killed, there were large numbers of wounded on the ships, many badly burned, often the result of flaming aviation gas from the crashed aircraft. While no accurate count of the number or means of destruction of the attacking Japanese aircraft was possible, it was estimated that more than half of the almost 700 planes in that first mass attack were destroyed.

Day after day the kamikazes and conventional attackers returned. Although hundreds were shot down, ship after ship was struck by suiciders and bombs. On April 12 a new aerial kamikaze appeared off Okinawa. The clear day brought out an estimated 185 suiciders plus almost 200 conventional attackers. A Zero fighter smashed into the destroyer *Mannert L. Abele,* breaking the ship's keel and leaving her dead in the water. One minute later she was hit by a Baka—a manned flying bomb.

The new weapon was called *Ohka,* or Cherry Blossom, by the Japanese and given the Allied code-name Baka—the Japanese word for "fool." The flying bomb was the idea of Ensign Mitsuo Ohta, a Navy transport pilot, who, during the summer of 1944, saw the superiority of U.S. forces and conceived a manned flying bomb that could be used to attack American ships. The small aircraft was carried into the battle area under the belly of a twin-engine bomber ("mother" plane). After release from the mother plane, the rocket-powered Baka would accelerate to a speed of 400 mph and streak toward its target ship, often reaching a much higher terminal speed as it dived to destruction.

The *Mannert L. Abele* sank five minutes after being hit by the Baka. Seventy-nine of her crew were dead or missing. The same day, another Baka hit the destroyer *Stanly,* smashing through her bow before exploding on the other side of the ship. The destroyer was hurt but kept moving and shooting. Within ten minutes a second Baka zoomed toward her, ripped the national ensign off the gaff, and hit the water 2,000 yards away. A Zero then dived on the *Stanly,* was hit by 40-mm gunfire, and broke apart over the ship, the fuselage and bomb falling 15 yards from the ship.

The Bakas returned periodically to plague the U.S. ships off Okinawa. But their effectiveness was limited, in large part because of the vulnerability of the mother planes while en route to the attack area. Often the Bakas were jettisoned, or the carrying bombers were shot down far short of their targets. More dangerous were the Navy single-engine fighters and dive bombers pressed into the kamikaze role and the Army Air Force *taiatari* (suicide) role. Between mid-March and the end of June, some 1,900 Army and Navy planes made suicide sorties against the fleet off Okinawa.

The intensive aerial attacks continued day after day. Soon radar operators aboard ships off Okinawa were bleary-eyed, and all crewmen of the warships were exhausted as they stood at battle stations around the clock. Ship after ship was hit. While aircraft carriers, battleships, and cruisers were damaged in *Ten-Go,* destroyers—13 of them—were the largest U.S. warships to be sunk. Another 37 destroyers were heavily damaged, nine of them too seriously to be repaired. The Japanese claimed that *Ten-Go* had sunk five large carriers, three smaller ones, and 12 battleships in addition to lesser ships.

The destroyer *Laffey* had the dubious distinction of surviving the most intensive air attack on a single warship off Okinawa. On April 16 the third mass attack began with 165 kamikazes falling on the American ships. The 2,200-ton *Laffey,* already a veteran of the Normandy invasion as well as Pacific action, was steaming on radar picket station No. 1, northwest of Okinawa. The destroyers *Bush* and *Morrison* had already been sunk while on that station.

The *Laffey*'s skipper, Commander Frederick J. Becton, recorded the action beginning at 8:27 A.M. From first light there were enemy planes on her radar screen, and at one point her radar operators counted 50 planes closing from the northern quadrant. The kamikazes came in from every quarter of the compass. Defensive fighter aircraft shot down several attacking planes outside the range of the ship's guns and boldly flew into the gunfire area to make intercepts. But during a period of 80 minutes, in 22 separate attacks plotted by the *Laffey*'s crew, the ship was hit by six kamikazes, by four bombs, and by strafing. Another bomb was a near miss and a seventh kamikaze splashed close aboard.

The *Laffey*'s tireless gunners shot down nine aircraft and undoubtedly damaged others. When the last attack ended at 9:47 A.M., the ship had only four 20-mm guns still in action. The attack had knocked out her three 5-inch twin gun mounts, all of her 40-mm anti-aircraft guns, and most of the 20-mm guns. She was on fire down by the stern, and her rudder was jammed. Thirty-one of her crew were dead, and another 72 were wounded. Still, the *Laffey* remained afloat and was towed out of the battle zone for temporary repairs that enabled her to steam under her own power back to the United States, where she was rebuilt.

Beyond actual ship losses, the kamikazes had a devastating psychological effect on the sailors of the invasion fleet. "The strain of waiting, the anticipated terror, made vivid from past experience, sent some men into hysteria, insanity, breakdown," a correspondent later wrote. Could the kamikazes have won the battle of Okinawa? Captain Rikihei Inoguchi, in charge of training kamikaze pilots for the Tenth Air Fleet based in Kyushu, later said, "At the time of these operations, in the Tenth Air Fleet it was not believed that the American forces could be decisively defeated by suicide actions alone. However, it was thought that if enough damage could be done to American ships and enough American casualties resulted perhaps there

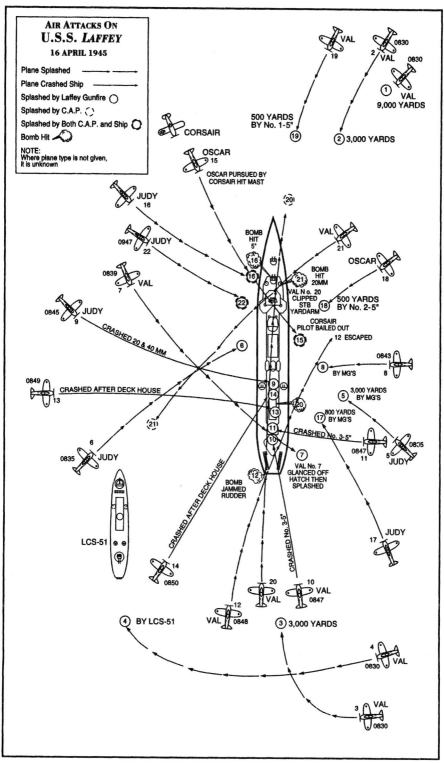

would be a 'new deal' later in which some form of victory might be salvaged from the war."

Perhaps the most dramatic—and futile—kamikaze effort was the vainglori-ous attempt to use the super battleship *Yamato* to attack the American invasion fleet off Okinawa. One of the two biggest battleships ever built, the *Yamato* was armed with nine 18.1-inch guns, the largest ever mounted on a warship. The *Yamato* was completed in December 1941 and participated in several battles, although she never fired her 18.1-inch guns against a major enemy warship.

The suicide plan was for the *Yamato* to fight her way through the Allied ships around Okinawa, bombard the amphibious ships with 3,200-pound projectiles from her 18.1-inch guns, and then run aground on the island; she had only enough fuel for a one-way trip. Her guns—if ammunition remained—could support the troops ashore, and unneeded sailors would be sent to reinforce the ground forces. When Lieutenant General Ushijima on Okinawa was advised of the operation, he is said to have dictated a message demanding cancellation of the battleship's kamikaze mission. It was, he felt, ridiculous and a waste of ships and men. It is not clear if the message was ever dispatched or, if so, was received at naval headquarters.

On the eve of her sailing, the officers and enlisted men of the *Yamato* were exuberant about their mission. The commanding officer, Rear Admiral Kosaku Ariga, who usually dined alone in his cabin, invited himself to the main wardroom. He feasted with 200 officers and joined in drink after drink of warm rice wine. There was plenty to drink aboard the *Yamato*. Some supply officers quipped that *if* the *Yamato* should ever sink, the fish for miles around would be drunk.

The *Yamato* departed Tokuyama on the Inland Sea on the afternoon of April 6, carrying in addition to her crew of 2,718 officers and enlisted men 49 newly graduated cadets from the Etajima Naval Academy. Accompanied by a light cruiser and eight destroyers, the *Yamato* steamed at high speed toward Okinawa, reaching the halfway mark at noon on April 7. Twenty minutes later, the battleship's radar detected a mass of approaching aircraft. In moments, hundreds of American carrier planes fell on the hapless Japanese ships.

The *Yamato* was quickly hit by at least five bombs and ten torpedoes. Efforts were made in vain to control the damage. A junior officer who survived the *Yamato* wrote of the efforts to keep the ship afloat:

> The order was given to pump sea water into the starboard engine and boiler rooms. These were the largest and lowest ones in the ship and their flooding should produce optimum results toward correcting the list. I hastily phoned these rooms to warn the occupants of the flooding order, but it was too

late. Water, both from the torpedo hits and flood valves, rushed into these compartments and snuffed out the lives of the men at their posts, several hundred in all. Caught between cold sea water and steam and boiling water from the damaged boilers they simply melted away—a thankless end to all their days of toil in the scorching heat and deafening noise of their laborious duty.

The sacrifice of the engine room personnel scarcely affected the ship's list.

Admiral Ariga and several other officers had themselves tied to the bridge to be assured of going down with the ship. The fleet commander on board the *Yamato*, Vice Admiral Seiichi Ito, shook hands with his staff officers and then went into his cabin. He was never seen again.

As she sank, the *Yamato*'s after magazine exploded, tearing the ship apart and creating a mushroom-shaped cloud that rose to 20,000 feet—visible from southern Kyushu, 320 miles away. The giant *Yamato* went down with all but 269 of the 2,767 officers, enlisted men, and cadets on board. The Japanese light cruiser and four of the destroyers were also sunk.

This suicide of the *Yamato* force killed almost 4,000 Japanese and accomplished absolutely nothing. U.S. carriers lost only ten aircraft and a dozen fliers in sinking the behemoth. It was the last surface operation by the vaunted Imperial Japanese Navy, which had ruled the Pacific and Indian Oceans three years earlier. Purportedly, the rationale for this useless mission was to help the gallant defenders of Okinawa. But one of the senior officers who survived wrote that the Chief of Staff of the Combined Fleet had told Rear Admiral Ariga that "the whole nation would hate the Navy if the war should end with *Yamato* still intact." Through no fault of Ariga's, the *Yamato* had been out of action for three years prior to the Leyte Gulf battles in October of 1944 and was being spoken of as "a floating hotel for idle, inept admirals."

Ashore on Okinawa the Japanese had foregone the heretofore meaningless suicide charges, allowing the Americans to establish their beachhead unmolested. Under Lieutenant General Ushijima's direction, the main Japanese forces had withdrawn to the southern half of the island, building concentric defense lines radiating out from the town of Shuri in the center of the island, a barrier to the American conquest of the southern half of Okinawa.

With the sinking of the *Yamato* and the relatively light resistance ashore, on April 8, Vice Admiral Richmond Kelly Turner, commander of U.S. amphibious forces in the Pacific, sent a message to Admiral Nimitz: "I may be crazy but it looks like the Japanese have quit the war, at least in this section." Nimitz curtly replied: "Delete all after 'crazy.' " Nimitz was right.

The Japanese defenders were dug into caves and tunnels in the mountains around Shuri. In one typical defense sector, an area 2,500 by 4,500 yards, a network of caves and bunkers bristled with 16 grenade launchers, 124 machine guns, 7 anti-tank guns, and 8 artillery pieces. Three U.S. Army divisions and two Marine divisions fought for two weeks to penetrate the outermost defense ring atop a mountain ridge. U.S. warships offshore and artillery on Okinawa opened the assault on the five-mile defensive line on April 19 with a barrage of 19,000 shells, the greatest single concentration of artillery in the Pacific War. The Japanese defenses withstood the bombardment as well as continuous attacks by American fighter and attack aircraft.

American troops struggled up the ridge while under fire from hidden machine guns and cannons that were lobbing shells from the reverse slope of the mountain. Of one company of 89 men attempting to scale the ridge, only three made it back unwounded. Marines used flamethrowers and satchel charges to advance to the crest of a hill. Then Japanese surged upward from the reverse slope, driving the Marines downhill with mortar fire, grenades, and bayonets.

In the midst of the killing and hand-to-hand combat, a few of the Japanese commanders still enjoyed what few comforts were available. Colonel Take-hiko Udo "continued his plush lifestyle in the trenches, with three women serving him hand and foot." The chief of staff of the 32nd Army, Lieutenant General Cho, "drank even in the trenches and had girls from the brothel area in Naha."

But few of the Japanese fighting on Okinawa had such opportunities. Finally overwhelmed by the American assaults, the defenders pulled back, shedding American blood for every yard of their advance. In wild, suicidal banzai charges, Japanese troops fought to kill as many Americans as possible while dying in battle. Superior U.S. firepower could not stop them. "We poured a tremendous amount of metal in on those positions," a Marine officer remembered. "Not only from artillery but from ships at sea. It seemed nothing could possibly be living in that churning mass where the shells were falling and roaring but when we next advanced, Japs would still be there, even madder than they had been before."

The Japanese had established a defense line which became known as the Shuri Line, from the ancient nearby castle. Running east-west, north of Naha on the southern tip of Okinawa, the Shuri Line had its first test on April 4, when Army troops ran up against massive defenses on Kakaza ridge. Eight days of heavy fighting were needed to take the ridge. Americans cleared Japanese from these positions cave by cave. The fighting continued with only a brief pause as, on April 12, word was passed from American position to American position that President Roosevelt was dead. The battle-hardened soldiers and Marines at first refused to believe the news. Slowly, they accepted it, most often with tears coming to their eyes before they rubbed them dry and went back to their deadly work. A few, upon hearing that Harry Truman was now President, asked simply, "Who the hell is he?"

At one point the American commanders considered a second amphibious landing to bypass the Shuri Line. General Buckner, however, decided against it because of the supply and logistic problems. Buckner, of course, was under the command of Admiral Nimitz, and the Navy supported him, infuriating the Marines, who from the outset had questioned the wisdom of putting an Army officer in command of an amphibious operation of this magnitude. Internal disagreements again emphasized the rift between the Army and Marines and the Marines and the Navy.

Buckner ordered a major offensive against the Shuri Line on May 11, but again his men failed to break the Japanese defenses. Finally, the 1st Marine Division took Shuri Castle on May 29. By that time Japanese strength was failing. More than 62,500 Japanese and Okinawans had been killed around Shuri.

The enemy evacuated Shuri, moving farther south to establish still another defensive line at Yaeju Dake and Yazu Dake. The battle for Okinawa continued as the Japanese, with no hope of relief or victory, fought on. Even the deaths of both the U.S. and Japanese force commanders within five days of each other had no effect on the final outcome. General Buckner died from shrapnel wounds suffered on June 18 when he visited an observation post that came under Japanese shelling. He was the highest-ranking American officer killed by the enemy in World War II.

On June 22, Lieutenant General Ushijima and Lieutenant General Cho, his chief of staff, followed an ancient code. Cho stepped from the cave that was the last Japanese command post and said, "Well, Commanding General Ushijima, as the way may be dark, I, Cho, will lead the way." Ushijima had donned his full field uniform, with decorations; Cho wore a white kimono on which he had written: "The offering of one's life is to fulfill the duties towards the Emperor and the country." Cho spread a white cloth at the mouth of the cave, and there the two generals drew their daggers and performed the rite of *seppuku,* cutting open their bellies. An adjutant then decapitated the generals. Their bodies were secretly buried in previously dug graves.

The fighting on Okinawa continued until June 21, when Marine Lieutenant General Roy Geiger, who had succeeded General Buckner as commander of the Tenth Army—the only instance of a U.S. Marine leading a field army —finally declared Okinawa "secure." The campaign was officially completed on July 2.

Both sides suffered horrendous casualties on Okinawa, as did the U.S. fleet offshore. An estimated 107,539 Japanese troops, Okinawan military personnel, and civilians died; thousands more civilians were injured. As the battle ended, many Japanese troops, including the wounded, took their own lives with hand grenades or by using a toe to shoot themselves with their rifles.

Almost 4,000 Japanese troops were taken prisoner, most captured because they were wounded. Another surviving 4,000 troops hid in the hills to conduct guerrilla attacks; they later surrendered.

U.S. Tenth Army losses were put at 7,613 soldiers and Marines killed or missing in action and another 31,807 wounded, plus 4,907 dead and 4,824 injured on board U.S. ships. The Marine numbers include 118 Navy medical personnel—"medics"—killed while serving with Marine units. There were also more than 26,000 "nonbattle" American casualties, mostly combat fatigue, attributed to the intensity of the fighting and the persistent Japanese artillery and mortar fire.

The Okinawa campaign brought the Allies to Japan's doorstep. But the equivalent of less than three Japanese divisions, with no possibility of relief or victory, heavily pounded by American aircraft and naval bombardment, had held out for more than 100 days against a larger U.S. ground force with massive air support. The toll that Lieutenant General Ushijima took of American lives—12,520 dead and 36,631 wounded—was greater than in any other Pacific assault or battle. And one war correspondent was killed. After watching the main Okinawa campaign, Ernie Pyle traveled to the island of Ie Shima off the west coast of Okinawa. He was with U.S. Army infantrymen on the tiny island when Japanese snipers fired on a jeep in which he was riding. Pyle dived into a ditch. When he raised his head, a machine gun erupted, and he was shot in the left temple. He was buried on the island.

The heavy U.S. losses on Okinawa and aboard U.S. ships offshore would become a major factor in American decisions about how the war against Japan should be continued. If the casualty lists from Okinawa were indicative of the ferocity of Japanese resistance, what would be the cost of an assault against Japan itself?

CHAPTER 5

TRUMAN'S WAR

President Franklin D. Roosevelt and his chief of staff, Admiral William Leahy (second from right), met in Pearl Harbor in July 1944 with General Douglas MacArthur (left) and Admiral Chester Nimitz to discuss the final stages of the Pacific War—which Roosevelt would not live to see.

As Vice President Harry S. Truman was presiding over the Senate on February 20, 1945, he heard a rumor that President Roosevelt had died. The rumor, Truman later wrote, "swept through the corridors and across the floor." Stunned but trying to look calm, Truman left his place on the Senate dais and hurried to the office of Les Biffle, secretary of the Senate.

"I hear the President is dead," Truman said to Biffle. "What will we do? Let's find out what happened." Years later, writing about these moments, Truman did not reveal his own emotions, but he did say that it was Biffle, not he, who called the White House. Biffle turned to Truman and told him that Major General Edwin M. (Pa) Watson, Roosevelt's appointments secretary, was the man who was dead. He had died on board the heavy cruiser *Quincy*, which was bringing Roosevelt and his aides back from the Big Three conference at Yalta in the Soviet Crimea. The Big Three, as the press had dubbed them, were Roosevelt, British Prime Minister Winston Churchill, and Marshal Joseph Stalin, dictator of the Soviet Union.

Truman had never met Churchill or Stalin. Indeed, since becoming Vice President on January 20 he had not met with Roosevelt. They saw each other briefly, hardly doing more than exchanging greetings, when Roosevelt returned from Yalta. Roosevelt's appearance shocked Truman. "His eyes were sunken. His magnificent smile was missing from his careworn face," Truman wrote. "He seemed a spent man. I had a hollow feeling within me. . . ." Deep in his soul, Truman sensed that he would soon become President. But Roosevelt, entering his unprecedented fourth term in perilous health, had not made any effort to educate Truman to succeed him in the role of Commander in Chief.

Roosevelt had had that role since the European War began in September 1939, and in the years that followed, in agreement with Churchill, he had pursued a "Germany-first" strategy. The defeat of Germany was also Stalin's top priority. And at the Tehran Conference in November 1943, he sought to pressure the Allies into launching an early invasion of Western Europe, a move that Churchill opposed. Roosevelt, in turn, was urged by his advisers to get a commitment from Stalin to enter the Pacific War. And in the end a compromise was effected. Stalin won Roosevelt's support for the long-awaited "second front" in Europe, and Roosevelt won from Stalin this promise, which was not made public at the time: "Once Germany was finally defeated, it would be possible to send the necessary reinforcements to Siberia and then we shall be able by our common front to beat Japan." Roosevelt, eager to get a down payment on the promise, handed Stalin two planning papers on future Allied air and naval operations against Japan in the northwestern Pacific, which presumably would lead the Soviets into joint planning for later operations against Japan.

Roosevelt envisioned the United States and the Soviet Union fighting side by side in the Pacific, and to realize that vision, he told Stalin that he hoped to launch U.S. bombing raids on Japan from the Soviet Pacific coast and allow Soviet Navy ships to use the same Pacific bases used by the U.S. Navy. The President also sought intelligence reports and information about weather, housing, and communications in the Soviet maritime provinces. Roosevelt hoped for Soviet cooperation in a U.S. bombing campaign against the Japanese-held Kuril Islands and said that the U.S. military mission in Moscow could take up these matters with the Soviet General Staff. No such staff talks ever materialized, and the Soviets never gave Roosevelt what he had asked for. Nevertheless, the United States continued to consider Soviet participation in the Pacific War as a strategic necessity.

Roosevelt also saw China, under Chiang Kai-shek, as a major ally in the Pacific War. In reality, Chiang's Nationalist Army was incompetent and unreliable. Warlords allowed Chiang to use their armies at their discretion, not on his orders. Typically, nearly half of the young men conscripted into Chiang's army died or deserted without reaching their units. Officers stole and sold off their troops' rations. And Chiang himself was more interested in fighting the Chinese communists than the Japanese invaders, who had brutally seized vast territories in China, including all major ports and cities. But popular—and congressional—faith in China persisted. China's struggle against the Japanese had long been a staple of American newspapers, magazines, movies, and newsreels, whose images of the Chinese women and children killed by Japanese bombs had shocked Americans long before Pearl Harbor.

After the Pearl Harbor attack, the United States put pressure on Chiang to fight the Japanese, on the simple theory that every Japanese soldier on mainland China was a soldier not fighting American forces elsewhere. And both Roosevelt and General Marshall believed that China would be a vital player in an Allied invasion of Japan. Attempts were made to aid China's war effort, but American arms, money, and advisers accomplished little. Chiang squandered the money, did little with the arms, and antagonized his principal American adviser, General Stilwell, who admired the Chinese peasant but distrusted Chinese leadership. He quickly got on bad terms with Chiang, whom he referred to as "the Peanut." As for Chiang, he believed that China was being shortchanged by the United States. In 1942, when he was told that an air raid on Tokyo was being planned, he tried to have it canceled, expecting Japanese retribution in China. He was right. The Japanese were outraged, killing hundreds of thousands of Chinese suspected of aiding the American fliers who had crash-landed in China.

In the aftermath of the Doolittle raid, Chiang became distrustful of Americans. Infuriated by perceived slights, he made what became known as the Three Demands: three U.S. Army divisions to fight in China; 500 U.S. combat aircraft to operate from China; and the monthly air delivery of 5,000 tons of supplies across the Hump, the airlift route over the Himalayas from Assam, India, to Kunming, China. (The airlift, begun on April 8, 1942, was then carrying about 700 tons a month.) If the United States failed to meet these "minimum requirements," Chiang warned, China would have to make "other arrangements." To back up the implied threat of a separate peace, Chiang's agents spread rumors that Chinese and Japanese negotiators were already discussing China's withdrawal from the war.

U.S. officials saw the demand as a bluff but did step up the delivery of supplies and increase the size of the U.S. air forces in China. Still, Chiang remained preoccupied with maintaining his own position of power. During the summer of 1943, Soviet diplomats told U.S. and British officials of reports of firefights between Chiang's troops and forces led by his communist rivals. In September the U.S. Embassy in Chungking predicted "civil war at some undetermined future date." But Chiang was invited to the next Roosevelt-Churchill meeting, at Cairo, in November 1943, as a morale-building concession. In what was called the Cairo Declaration, China was promised the return of all Chinese territory that had been occupied by Japan. Chiang went home, and Roosevelt and Churchill went on to Tehran to meet with Stalin (who did not want to meet with Chiang).

There Stalin made his promise that he would enter the war against Japan as soon as Germany was defeated. And that promise, which was not passed on to Chiang, considerably diminished the importance of China in future U.S. war plans in the Pacific. At Tehran the Big Three also agreed that U.S. and British forces would invade Europe the following spring. Thus, the Pacific War was still being relegated to second place, and if Allied planners were envisioning a similar invasion of Japan, they would have been wise to discount any assistance from an ineffectual Chiang or rely on the promises of a duplicitous Stalin.

The year 1944 would see not only the dramatic invasion of Normandy on D-Day, June 6, but also a presidential election. Roosevelt, who had broken precedent by running for a third term in 1940, was expected to run again in 1944. Ailing but determined to live to see the end of the war, he was not taking any chances as he set the stage for the 1944 November election.

When the presidential election year began, Senator Harry S. Truman of Missouri got a small political favor. Secretary of the Navy Frank Knox selected the senator's daughter, Margaret, to christen the battleship *Missouri* on January 29, 1944. There were also major political moves, most of them revolving around the fate of Roosevelt's Vice President, Henry A. Wallace. Many Democratic leaders had grown disillusioned with Wallace, viewing him as overly liberal and somewhat of a mystic. In March, while anti-Wallace Democrats quietly looked for a replacement Vice President, Roosevelt sent Wallace to China to talk to Chiang Kai-shek, whose control over China had become so shaky that Roosevelt feared he might really negotiate a separate peace with Japan.

Roosevelt knew that Chiang's important friends in Washington would create a political uproar if it appeared that the United States was losing faith in China. Wallace's trip did little more than provide public proof of Roosevelt's sympathy toward China. The trip would have no influence on U.S. policy, but it would mute some of the Republican criticism of Roosevelt's conduct of the Pacific War.

Conservative Republicans had long focused on the Pacific War as a "forgotten front," neglected by Roosevelt. Fanning the criticism, General MacArthur allowed himself to be pictured as the victim of the Germany-first strategy. Fighting to retake the northern coast of New Guinea from Japanese garrisons —even in the Pacific, a secondary theater—he slogged through muddy, dank jungle warfare.

Still, he was a hero. He was remembered as MacArthur of the Philippines, the man who defended the island fortress of Corregidor under Japanese bombardment. Ordered out by President Roosevelt, he made a harrowing escape by PT boat and then B-17 bomber. He had arrived in Australia to be hailed as that country's savior. Ramrod-straight, invariably pictured with a corncob pipe jutting from his mouth above a firm chin, he was the epitome of an American hero. And, to some Republicans, he was more than a hero; he was presidential timber, a general whose rightful rank was Commander in Chief.

Colonel Robert R. McCormick's *Chicago Tribune,* Joseph M. Patterson's *New York Daily News,* and Cissy Patterson's *Washington Times-Herald,* along with the Hearst newspaper chain, pounded the publicity drums for MacArthur. Many newspapers published excerpts from the laudatory books that were being published about the general. (One was titled *MacArthur the Magnificent.*) He also received the endorsement of such virulent Roosevelt enemies and hate mongers as Gerald L.K. Smith and Father Charles E. Coughlin.

MacArthur refused to comment publicly about the presidential boom. Off the record, aides said the general had no interest in politics. But when a journalist interviewed him and reported that MacArthur would accept the Republican nomination, he did not call in those aides and order a statement released denying his interest. And when he was entered in the Illinois presidential preference primary, he did not ask that his name be removed. He received 76 percent of the Illinois vote. The primary did not prove he

General MacArthur wading ashore at Leyte, in the Philippines, on October 20, 1944, fulfilling his vow: "I shall return." His next assignment: command of Operation Downfall, the planned assault of the Japanese home islands.

was a winning candidate—neither Wendell L. Willkie, the 1940 Republican candidate, nor Thomas E. Dewey, the governor of New York, had bothered to enter—but it did show that he was in the race.

An enthusiastic Republican congressman, Albert L. Miller of Nebraska, wrote MacArthur, "You owe it to civilization and to the children yet unborn" to defeat Roosevelt. Otherwise, "our American way of life is forever doomed." MacArthur replied, "I do unreservedly agree with the complete wisdom and statesmanship of your comments." And he, too, was concerned about "the sinister drama of our present chaos and confusion."

In another letter, Miller said he wanted MacArthur to "destroy this monstrosity . . . which is engulfing the nation and destroying free enterprise and every right of the individual." MacArthur replied: "Your description of conditions in the United States is a sobering one indeed and is calculated to arouse the thoughtful consideration of every true patriot."

On April 14, just as MacArthur was about to lead the invasion of Hollandia in New Guinea, Miller made the correspondence public, and newspaper accounts of the general's intemperate and insubordinate words abruptly ended the MacArthur-for-President campaign. On April 30, he asked that "no action be taken that would link my name in any way with the nomination." In June, at the Republican National Convention that nominated Dewey, MacArthur got one vote.

The following month, Roosevelt announced that he was running for a fourth term, and while privately assuring Wallace of support, he did not stop Democrats from seeking another vice presidential candidate. James F. Byrnes, director of the Office of War Mobilization, whom Roosevelt referred to as his "assistant president," thought he had the President's backing. Roosevelt, however, did not make any public commitments, saying he preferred an open convention.

Harry Truman had repeatedly said that he did not want to run for Vice President. But when the Democratic National Convention opened on July 19, he was a favorite. Roosevelt, hearing that Truman was balky, called the party's national chairman, Robert Hannegan, who held the telephone receiver so that others in the hotel room, including Truman, could hear the President's voice. "Bob," Roosevelt asked, "have you got that fellow lined up yet?" Hannegan said he hadn't. "Well," Roosevelt replied, "tell him that if he wants to break up the Democratic Party in the middle of the war, that's his responsibility."

Truman accepted, but he did not think it much of an honor. It was, he said, a job for a man who "simply presides over the Senate and sits around hoping for a funeral." As for Roosevelt, he showed remarkably little enthusiasm for Truman. Roosevelt's son James, a Marine officer, said his father professed not "to give a damn" whether the delegates nominated Supreme Court Justice William O. Douglas, Byrnes, or Truman.

By the time the convention ended, Roosevelt was on board the heavy cruiser *Baltimore,* heading for Pearl Harbor and a meeting with MacArthur. Ostensibly, Roosevelt went to Pearl Harbor to have a council of war with Nimitz and MacArthur, his Pacific commanders. But he had started his campaign for a fourth term, and photographs of the Commander in Chief with Admiral Nimitz and General MacArthur made for good political publicity.

The meeting would greatly influence the waging of the Pacific War, which was at a strategic crossroads in the summer of 1944. Roosevelt's top military advisers, General Marshall and Admiral King, still believed that China, given munitions and other aid for its massive army, could go on the offensive against the Japanese, tying down troops that otherwise would be hurled against U.S. forces if an invasion of Japan was ultimately necessary. King also argued for an assault against Formosa, which, he believed, would guarantee

U.S. domination of "the sea lanes by which Japan received essential supplies of oil, rice and other commodities from her recently conquered southern empire." The Navy, King added, "had no interest in fighting the Japanese on land in the home islands. . . ."

Roosevelt arrived at Pearl Harbor without King or Marshall, bringing along only Admiral Leahy, interlocutor between the President and the Joint Chiefs. He found his two top Pacific commanders at odds. When Nimitz and Mac-Arthur presented their cases to the President, Nimitz concentrated on the military aspects of Pacific strategy, while MacArthur focused on what he saw as America's moral commitment to the Philippines. He had said, "I shall return," and that was what he intended to do.

Nimitz and MacArthur had once been in agreement on a Pacific strategy. But Nimitz now had no choice but to support the thinking of King, who urged the "use of China as a base—and of Chinese manpower to secure and maintain the base." King also gave priority to clearing the Mariana Islands, an arc of Japan's inner ring of defense. Then, on King's timetable, would come the liberation of the Philippines. In his emphasis on the Marianas, King was supported by General Arnold, who wanted the islands for his new B-29 Superfortress bombers to strike the Japanese home islands.

The conquest of the Marianas had already begun when Roosevelt arrived for his meeting with Nimitz and MacArthur. Now the strategic issues they had to settle involved the pathways and sequence of military operations that would lead up to the doorstep of Japan. But because of MacArthur's obsession with the Philippines, that was the subject that dominated the talks.

Roosevelt, MacArthur, Nimitz, and Leahy gathered before a large wall map of the Pacific in a room of a private mansion. Nimitz and MacArthur spent the night presenting their cases—military for the admiral, morality for the general. To bypass the Philippines, MacArthur argued, meant leaving its people to Japanese troops who would continue to "steal the food and subject the population to misery and starvation."

At some time during the conference—accounts differ as to when—Mac-Arthur managed to get Roosevelt alone. He asked the President whether he was willing "to accept the responsibility for breaking a solemn promise to 18 million Christian Filipinos that the Americans would return." By one of MacArthur's two accounts, Roosevelt's last words to him were: "Well, Douglas, you win! But I'm going to have a hell of a time over this with that old bear, Ernie King."

Whether or not it was sound military strategy, Roosevelt thus deprived conservative Republicans of the "MacArthur martyrdom" issue. MacArthur, in a highly publicized display of bravado, would wade ashore from a landing craft at Leyte on October 20, making good his "I shall return" vow on the eve of the presidential election. And although fighting on Leyte would continue until early in 1945, MacArthur, nine days before Election Day, told war correspondents that the fighting there was nearly over.

Roosevelt's Pearl Harbor meeting with MacArthur undoubtedly helped to reinforce his image as the Commander in Chief, and back in the United States he continued to campaign as a leader of a war nearing a victorious climax. General Dwight D. Eisenhower's sweep into Germany and MacArthur's success in the Philippines inspired Roosevelt's political aides to say, "Ike and Doug are our two ablest campaigners." Not so Chiang.

By the end of 1944, Chiang had been discounted as an effective ally. A Japanese offensive in eastern China had taken eight more provinces, placed 100 million more Chinese under enemy control, forced the abandonment of U.S. air bases, and sealed off China's eastern coast. General Stilwell, soon to be ordered out of China, wrote in his diary on October 4: "War Department is with me apparently, but this theater is written off and nothing expected from us."

Stilwell, recalled from China at Chiang's insistence, was a potential embarrassment in Roosevelt's reelection campaign. Although not as lionized as MacArthur, Stilwell was a popular figure, and his "firing"—for that was what the press would call it—became an eleventh-hour campaign issue. Purportedly for security reasons, he was kept out of sight—and hearing—until Election Day.

The campaign also saw the unprecedented involvement of the Army Chief of Staff in politics, albeit in total secrecy. Army intelligence officers heard rumors that Dewey, who was making Roosevelt's conduct of the war an issue, planned to say that the United States had deciphered Japanese codes before Pearl Harbor and that, by inference, Roosevelt knew of the attack in advance. On General Marshall's orders, Colonel Carter W. Clarke, an intelligence officer, was to meet with Dewey and hand him a personal letter. Clarke, wearing civilian clothes, found him in Tulsa, Oklahoma. In the letter Marshall said that he was acting "without the knowledge of the President" and told Dewey of the value of code breaking in Pacific battles and in Europe. He asked Dewey to not mention the code breaking because of the "tragic results" of such a disclosure. Dewey agreed. Clarke later delivered a second letter to Dewey in Albany. Dewey did not bring up the issue in the campaign.

Another secret was preserved during that presidential election year. In February 1944, Stimson, Marshall, and Vannevar Bush, director of the Office of Scientific Research and Development, met in the office of Sam Rayburn, Speaker of the House and the most powerful Democrat in Congress. With Rayburn were the Democratic majority leader, John McCormack, and the Republican minority leader, Joe Martin.

Stimson told the triumvirate of House leaders that the United States was engaged in a crash program to build an incredibly potent weapon before Germany did. Stimson then decided to have Marshall, not Bush, describe the atomic bomb. Bush, a distinguished scientist and engineer, probably would have given too technical a discourse. After telling about the bomb and the race against the Germans, the delegation got to the point. The bomb program needed $1.6 billion more from Congress. The legislators agreed, in Martin's words, that the funds would "be provided without a trace of evidence to show how it was spent." Senator Truman had not been invited to the meeting.

Roosevelt did not tell his running mate about the bomb. In fact, Roosevelt and Truman saw little of each other during the campaign, which ended with Roosevelt beating Dewey by more than 3.5 million votes and carrying 36 of the 48 states.

Between Election Day and Inauguration Day, Roosevelt focused on his long-planned meeting with Churchill and Stalin at Yalta, and again there was not much time for Truman. Then, two days after the January 20 inauguration, Roosevelt secretly left Washington aboard a train that took him to Norfolk, Virginia, where he boarded the *Quincy,* sailed to Malta, and from there flew to Yalta. Truman was not told about the Big Three conference and had been barely informed about Roosevelt's itinerary. The Vice President had not even yet met Secretary of State Edward Stettinius. He knew nothing about the complex commitments Roosevelt had made with Churchill and Stalin at any of their meetings.

If the President gave no thought to his mortality, others were deeply concerned about his health. Stettinius had noted that Roosevelt had been trembling during his inauguration address. "It was not just his hands that shook," he observed, "but his whole body as well." The frailty of Roosevelt, who had suffered a seizure the previous July, was another well-kept secret of the presidential campaign. Before the Democratic National Convention, one Democratic leader said he feared that "the man nominated to run with Roosevelt would in all probability be the next President."

The man who was nominated, Senator Truman of Missouri, had been a field artillery captain in France in World War I. He retained his reserve commission, and soon after the Japanese attacked Pearl Harbor, he had asked Army Chief of Staff Marshall to order him to active duty. As Truman recalled the conversation, Marshall told him he was "too damned old." Truman pointed out that Marshall, then 61, was older than he was by four years. The general ended the conversation by diplomatically suggesting that Truman was of greater value to the nation in the war job he already had. He was chairman of the Special Committee to Investigate the National Defense Program.

The Senate committee, created in February 1941, was better known as the Truman Committee, the scourge of waste and corruption by war contractors. By some estimates, the committee saved taxpayers more than $15 billion, and Truman became so well known that in 1944 a poll of newspaper reporters rated him second only to the President in contributions to the war effort. His popularity had helped win him his nomination for Vice President.

One of the Truman Committee's investigations had led to a mysterious, extremely costly enterprise known as the Manhattan Project. And, on June 17, 1943, Truman himself telephoned Secretary of War Stimson and asked him about the project. "Now that's a matter which I know all about personally," Stimson said, "and I am the only one of the group of two or three men in the whole world who know about it."

"I see," Truman replied.

"It's part of a very important secret development."

"Well, all right, then—"

"And I—" Stimson began.

Truman interrupted: "I herewith see the situation, Mr. Secretary, and you won't have to say another word to me. Whenever you say that to me, that's all I want to hear." Rumors about the project continued to reach Truman through his staff, but, true to his word, he did not pursue them. Stimson, however, still worried. "Truman is a nuisance and a pretty untrustworthy man," he confided to his diary. "He talks smoothly but he acts meanly."

Few in government would assess Truman as harshly as Stimson. In the Senate and in his home state he had a reputation for unflinching honesty as well as blunt talk. His reputation as an effective legislator had helped to get him the vice presidential nomination, and Roosevelt knew that Truman would be of inestimable value as the administration's man in Congress. Still, even after his return from Yalta, he did not take Truman into his confidence about the progress of the war.

In his report to Congress on March 1 about the Yalta Conference, Roosevelt spoke from a seat in the well of the House because, as he wearily explained, "it makes it a lot easier for me in not having to carry about ten pounds of steel around on the bottom of my legs, and also because of the fact that I have just completed a 14,000-mile trip." It was a rare reference to the paralyzing polio that had struck him in 1921. After a faltering performance, Roosevelt briefly spoke with Truman. "As soon as I can," Roosevelt said, "I will go to Warm Springs [Georgia] for a rest. I can be in trim again if I can stay there for two or three weeks."

Roosevelt's report to Congress drew applause when he reiterated the Allied demand for unconditional surrender. He mentioned a compromise over Poland, but he gave little time to political decisions that the Big Three had made at Yalta. In a top-secret compact with Roosevelt and Churchill, Stalin had reaffirmed his promise to enter the war against Japan "two or three months" after the defeat of Germany. But for this promise he extracted concessions: return of the southern part of Sakhalin Island and the Kuril Islands, given to Japan in 1875 by Russia in exchange for northern Sakhalin Island; restoration of the lease of Port Arthur (now Lüshun), at the end of the Liaodong Peninsula in Manchuria as a Soviet naval base; internationalizing of the adjacent port of Dairen (now Dalian); and joint Soviet-Chinese administration of the Manchurian railroads.

On March 8 and March 19, Truman had two short, inconsequential private sessions with Roosevelt in Washington. He still knew nothing that had not been made public about the Yalta Conference, and he was not told about the secret agreement promising Soviet entry into the Pacific War. Then, on March 30, Roosevelt left by train for a place that always had restored him, the "Little White House" in Warm Springs. For two weeks he rested, signing papers brought from Washington by courier, keeping in touch with the war situation but never communicating with his Vice President. His personal physician said that Roosevelt was well rested and had begun "to eat with appetite, rested beautifully, and was in excellent spirits." But around 1 P.M., Eastern War Time, on April 12, Roosevelt put his left hand to his head and in a low voice said, "I have a terrific pain in the back of my head." Shortly before 3:30 he died. He had suffered a cerebral hemorrhage.

Shortly after five o'clock on April 12, while mixing a drink in Sam Rayburn's Capitol hideaway, Truman received a telephone call telling him to report at once to the White House. There Eleanor Roosevelt informed him of the President's death. He was taken to the Cabinet Room and immediately sworn in as President. The only senior military officer present was Admiral Leahy.

Moments later, the new Commander in Chief called his first Cabinet meeting, at which he said he intended to carry on the policies of President Roosevelt. As the somber members of the Cabinet silently left the room, Stimson lingered behind. "He asked to speak to me about a most urgent matter," Truman recalled. "Stimson told me that he wanted me to know about an immense project that was under way—a project looking to the development of a new explosive of almost unbelievable destructive power. . . . his statement left me puzzled." Truman apparently did not connect Stimson's remark with the cryptic conversation they had had back in 1943 about something called the Manhattan Project.

On the evening of April 13, Truman ended his first full day as President by reading a State Department briefing on U.S. relations with friends and foes. With victory in sight in Europe, the report, written to educate the new President, discussed America's postwar plans for Germany, Austria, Italy, Poland, and the Balkans. Amazingly, however, there was no discussion of the Pacific War. Nor was there mention of Stalin's promises to enter the Pacific War or of the massive military venture tied to that promise—the possible invasion of Japan.

The events and personalities of Roosevelt's war—and the military strategies that had been devised to win it—were largely unknown to Truman on April 12, 1945, when the war became Truman's war. The new President began educating himself in the Map Room, the secret White House office where Roosevelt had centered his conduct of the war. Until April 17, Truman had never entered the Map Room. "Detailed maps showed the battle lines everywhere," a fascinated Truman noted, "and from the center of the room it was possible to see at a glance the whole military situation. . . . And certainly it helped me quickly to visualize the world situation and to grasp the basic military strategy."

Roosevelt habitually had begun his day by coming down from his living quarters in his wheelchair and then rolling across the hallway to the Map Room on the ground floor of the White House. There he followed the progress of the war. Maps lined the walls. Blackout curtains covered the windows. The National Geographic Society had provided a set of roll-up maps in a wooden case, arranged so that Roosevelt in his wheelchair could pull them down and study them.

The room was manned twenty-four hours a day by military personnel cleared for handling the nation's most vital secrets. Access was limited, and much of the information in the room could be shown only to the President, his military aides, and his chief adviser and confidant, Harry Hopkins. Privileged White House visitors like Rear Admiral Samuel Eliot Morison, the distinguished naval historian and a friend of Roosevelt's, were denied entry. Winston Churchill was the only foreigner known to have had access. The maps, updated constantly by the Map Room staff, showed the ebb and flow of Allied and German armies in Europe, the routes of convoys across the Atlantic, and the islands being fought for in the Pacific.

Most of these maps were in millions of American homes; they came with issues of the *National Geographic* magazine. One such map, distributed with the April 1944 issue, was labeled "Japan and Adjacent Regions of Asia and the Pacific Ocean." In the Map Room, it was marked "Top Secret" because it bore handwritten information about plans for the possible invasion of Japan.

In Truman's recollections of the Map Room, he did not specifically mention this map, although it was in the room when he became President. Whether or not he saw the map, it reflected the Pacific strategy that Truman had inherited from Roosevelt. Whatever the problems with Chiang Kai-shek and Stalin, both China and the Soviet Union were expected to be vital players in an invasion of Japan.

Written on the map in a precise military hand were three boxes placed adjacent to the geography they referred to:

1. Seize Philippines, occupying Luzon, late this year [1944].
2. Seize Objectives between Philippines and Japan, including those on China coast without committing major forces.
3. Invade Jap Homeland Fall of 1945.

Scattered about the empty expanse of the Pacific Ocean were other notes, including details of logistics for the invasion, estimates of the strengths of Japanese and Soviet ground forces, and indications of expected Soviet cooperation. One note, for example, listed how many tons of supplies could be transported on the Soviet Union's Trans-Siberian Railroad for the forces assaulting Japan.

Truman, usually accompanied by Admiral Leahy, frequently went to the Map Room to study the world situation and read messages, including communications between Roosevelt and Churchill and Stalin. W. Averell Harriman, U.S. ambassador in Moscow, had rushed to Washington after Roosevelt's death to brief the new President on deteriorating U.S.-Soviet relations. Harriman, meeting with Truman for the first time, was concerned that Truman would be ignorant about recent, fast-moving events. "My fear was inspired by the fact that you could not have had time to catch up with all the recent cables," Harriman told Truman. "But I must say that I am greatly relieved to discover that you have read them all. . . ."

What Truman could not learn from any map was the status of the atomic bomb. His mentor would be Stimson, the man who nearly two years before had dismissed Truman as an untrustworthy nuisance. Stimson, in his seventy-seventh year, was the elder statesman of Washington officialdom. President Taft had appointed him Secretary of War in 1911, and he became President Hoover's Secretary of State in 1929. In 1940, Stimson had been named Secretary of War by Roosevelt, who had also appointed Frank Knox Secretary of the Navy to get two prominent Republicans in the Cabinet as America geared up for war.

Stimson, entrusted by Roosevelt with the overall supervision of the Manhattan Project, had kept the secret well, as had Stimson's atomic bomb manager, Major General Leslie R. Groves, the head of the Manhattan Project. In October 1941, Roosevelt had created a secret committee, the "Top Policy Group," to advise him on the development of the atomic bomb. The members were Stimson, General Marshall, Vice President Wallace, Vannevar Bush, and James B. Conant, chairman of the National Defense Research Committee. (Wallace had first learned about the project in July 1941 when Bush decided to consult the only scientist in the Cabinet; Wallace, formerly Secretary of Agriculture, had been a plant geneticist.) The Top Policy Group decided that the U.S. Army's Corps of Engineers should direct the A-bomb effort. Groves, who had just been in charge of constructing the Pentagon, was named to head the project, running what would become a gigantic enterprise involving about 120,000 people at 37 facilities.

Despite its size, the Manhattan Project remained unknown not only to Senator Truman but also to most members of Roosevelt's Cabinet and nearly all senior military commanders. Although Vice President Wallace was in the small circle that knew about the bomb, Roosevelt did not feel that Truman, as Wallace's successor, warranted that knowledge. Byrnes, as a key Roosevelt aide and director of the Office of War Mobilization, had learned some details about the Manhattan Project and, the day after Truman's first Cabinet meeting, passed them on to the new President, telling him that the United States was "perfecting an explosive great enough to destroy the whole world."

So Truman knew a little about the bomb when he received a note on April 24 from Stimson asking for a meeting "as soon as possible on a highly secret matter." The note went on to say that Stimson had mentioned the matter shortly after Truman took office but had not brought it up because of the pressure he had been under. "It, however, has such a bearing on our present foreign relations and has such an important effect upon all my thinking in this field that I think you ought to know about it without much further delay."

Stimson and Truman met at noon the next day, April 25. General Marshall declined to join in the briefing, believing that if he arrived with Stimson the press would speculate about some major development in the war. For similar security reasons, Groves did not arrive with Stimson, but entered the White House through another entrance.

While Groves waited in an outer office, Stimson told Truman, "Within four months we shall in all probability have completed the most terrible weapon ever known in human history, one bomb of which could destroy a whole city." Stimson then discussed eight other points about the bomb; all had to do with problems of diplomacy that the United States needed to solve "to bring the world into a pattern in which the peace of the world and our civilization can be saved." Stimson, Truman noted, "seemed at least as much concerned with the role of the atomic bomb in the shaping of history as in its capacity to shorten this war." Truman, the old artillery officer, saw the bomb as a weapon and was impatient about hearing talk of the bomb's role in the postwar world.

Stimson asked that Groves be called in. The general handed Truman a 24-page report and asked the President to read it. When Truman said he did not like to read long reports, Groves, by his account, insisted, saying, "Well, we can't tell you this in any more concise language. This is a big project." Truman read the report, frequently asking Groves questions. In his memo on the meeting, Groves did not say what the questions were, nor did he mention the use of the bomb as a weapon.

Shortly after the meeting with Stimson and Groves, Truman turned to Byrnes, a shrewd politician who would soon become Secretary of State. Byrnes had been a member of both the House and Senate and had later resigned from the Supreme Court to work for Roosevelt. Truman asked him to look into the $2 billion project and decide whether or not the atomic bomb would be an effective weapon.

Among the people Byrnes talked to was Admiral Leahy, who remained presidential chief of staff under Truman. Leahy had known about the bomb since at least September 1944 and was not convinced that it was worth all the effort or even if it would ever work. "The damn thing will never go off, and I say that as an expert on explosives," Leahy reportedly said before the testing of the bomb. During his Navy career Leahy had headed the Navy's Bureau of Ordnance. To him, "bomb" was not the right word for the weapon that Byrnes described. "It is not a bomb. It is not an explosive," Leahy believed. "It is a poisonous thing that kills people by its deadly radioactive reaction, more than by the explosive force it develops." Leahy's faith was in the Navy's sea blockade, which he believed could bring Japan at least to the verge of defeat.

Truman accepted Stimson's suggestion that he form a secret group—Stimson called it the Interim Committee—to give advice on atomic matters, including possible uses of the bomb. But the new President was so weighed down with other problems—the Soviets' unyielding stand on Poland, the upcoming United Nations Conference in San Francisco, the political and military aspects of a German surrender—that he seemed to have given little immediate thought to the atomic bomb. Like the military advisers he was getting to know, he focused on Europe and put the Pacific in its usual second place.

In their initial briefing of the new President, the Joint Chiefs had told him that the war in Europe might last six months; the Pacific War, a year and a half. Marshall and King both feared that the end of the European War would, in Marshall's words, produce "great impatience." He wondered if the American people were ready to face the "stern necessity of maintaining the momentum of the war in the Pacific in order to shorten it by every possible day." King had said privately that he feared that the American people would weary of the war: "Pressure at home will force a negotiated peace, before the Japs are really licked."

The possibility of a negotiated peace with Japan, however, had been politically unlikely since April 16, when Truman addressed Congress for the first time as President. "The armies of liberation are bringing to an end Hitler's ghastly threat to dominate the world," he had said. "Tokyo rocks under the weight of our bombs. . . . I want the entire world to know that this direction must and will remain—unchanged and unhampered. Our demand has been, and it remains—unconditional surrender."

Members of Congress responded with thunderous applause. *Unconditional surrender.* That was the policy of Roosevelt, and now it would be the policy of Truman. There would be no retreat, no compromise. And, translated into military terms, unconditional surrender also meant that an invasion of Japan was almost inevitable. That assessment was spelled out in an intelligence report submitted to the Joint Chiefs a week after Truman's address. The report warned that if Japan were not invaded, it was "probable that unconditional surrender could not be forced upon the Japanese before the middle or latter part of 1946."

Truman, simultaneously learning about the war and trying to run it, had to keep a tight focus on Europe, where, in a sequence of swiftly moving events, German forces surrendered in Italy, Russian troops encircled Berlin,

Hitler killed himself in his Berlin bunker, Italian dictator Benito Mussolini was killed by Italian partisans, and German forces in Holland, Denmark, and northwest Germany surrendered. Finally, on May 7, German officers signed a military surrender of all remaining forces. But Stalin, in a petulant show of power, insisted that the Big Three delay the announcement until May 8. Churchill wanted to defy Stalin, but Truman insisted on humoring him. The decision made Churchill "as mad as a wet hen," Truman said in a letter to his mother.

On May 8, after announcing that one war had ended—"The flags of freedom fly all over Europe"—President Truman reminded Americans that "our victory is only half over." Some of his advisers believed that the reminder was necessary, for they foresaw what Marshall called "the possibility of a general letdown in this country" after Americans finished celebrating VE-Day.

During the battle for Iwo Jima in February 1945, Japanese defenders had killed 6,821 Americans, most of them Marines, in the bloodiest fighting of the war. The three-month assault on Okinawa, under way when Truman succeeded Roosevelt, was even more costly. On April 5, in the wake of the initial landings, the Japanese Cabinet fell, and the new premier, Baron Kantaro Suzuki, a 78-year-old retired admiral, had called upon the Japanese people to fight to the death.

How many Americans would die in an invasion of Japan? That was the single question that dominated Truman's thoughts as he turned from Europe to the Pacific War.

CHAPTER 6

CLIMBING OLYMPUS

Hundreds of ships and countless landing craft were assembling for the Downfall assaults, which in size and complexity would far surpass the Normandy landings of June 1944.

For more than three decades U.S. Army and Navy officers had planned to defeat Japan without an assault on the island nation, which had never before been successfully invaded. The various Orange war plans had called for a blockade of the Japanese home islands after the decisive fleet encounter, forcing Japan into negotiations that would favor the United States. When aerial bombardment was added to the strategic equation, many planners thought that alone would force Japan to negotiate a peace settlement. There was, however, a problem that was political, not military: the doctrine of unconditional surrender. The American government and public would not accept a negotiated peace with Japan.

Preliminary American planning for the defeat of Japan had been started during August 1942 by a team within the U.S. Joint Chiefs of Staff. This effort led to a working paper, produced in April 1943, which declared that "achieving the unconditional surrender of Japan might require actual invasion of the Japanese homeland." The following month the U.S. Joint War Plans Committee (JWPC), representing the Army, Navy, and Army Air Forces, formally outlined a strategy for the defeat of Japan. In a draft of the plan the JWPC reiterated that "the unconditional surrender of JAPAN may require the invasion of the Japanese homeland."

The planners refrained from saying that an invasion would be unavoidable, stating that if the Allies gained undisputed control of the seas or carried out a sustained bombing effort against the home islands, the Japanese might surrender without the need for an invasion. The planning document, known as JWPC 15, held that the end of the war could come only after the Allies had the sea power to blockade Japan and the air bases to bomb the home islands at will. The plan said that the war could be won in six momentous phases:

Phase One: Increase U.S. aid to China to pin down and ultimately defeat the massive Japanese Army in China. Meanwhile, British forces, aided by China and the United States, would liberate Burma, and U.S. forces would sweep across the Central Pacific to gain control of the Celebes Sea, a pocket of the Pacific enclosed on the north by the Philippines' Sulu Archipelago and the island of Mindanao.

Phase Two: The British would gain control of the Strait of Malacca, between the southern Malay Peninsula and the island of Sumatra, dividing

Japanese forces in the region. At the same time, the United States would liberate the Philippines.

Phase Three: The British would advance from Burma to gain control of key positions in Southeast Asia; the United States would help China take Hong Kong while simultaneously driving the Japanese Fleet from the South China Sea.

Phase Four: China, aided by the United States and Great Britain, would liberate eastern China from the Japanese and set up air bases there for a bombing campaign against Japanese cities. The bombing campaign constituted *Phase Five,* which might in itself be enough to end the war, and if that happened, *Phase Six*—the invasion of Japan—might not be necessary.

The U.S. Joint Chiefs of Staff unveiled JWPC 15 at the Roosevelt-Churchill strategy conference—code-named Trident—held in Washington, at the White House, beginning on the afternoon of May 12, 1943. On May 20, when the discussions at Trident began to address the war in the Pacific, the British Chiefs of Staff politely questioned details of JWPC 15 and began to dissect it, hoping that the process would kill it. Unable to agree on a Pacific strategy, the Allies shelved JWPC 15 and decided to try again in June 1943 at a strategy conference of the Combined Chiefs of Staff in London and at another session in Washington in July. Meanwhile, the U.S. Joint War Plans Committee unilaterally continued its "own studies on the defeat of JAPAN, with a view to *retaining* the *initiative* and *leadership* now established in relation to the British." As the official JCS history observed, the U.S. planners "did not want British interference in Pacific strategy."

When Churchill and Roosevelt met again in Quebec in August 1943—a meeting code-named Quadrant—the leaders stated, "From every point of view operations should be framed to force the defeat of Japan as soon as possible after the defeat of Germany. Planning should be on the basis of accomplishing this within twelve months of that event." Here, then, was the schedule for the defeat of Japan, which might be further accelerated, based on a Soviet commitment to join in the war against Japan after the defeat of Germany. At Quadrant the U.S. planners were directed to prepare by October 15 a plan for the defeat of Japan.

Meanwhile, the Allied offensive against Japan continued in the Pacific. By mid-1943 the United States was able to muster in the Pacific a huge armada led by aircraft carriers. Although the European theater had priority for Army troops and aircraft, geography made it possible for a few Marine and Army divisions—ably assisted by Allied code-breaking efforts—to advance against the Japanese holdings on several fronts. Furthermore, by the end of 1943 the demonstrated impotence of Chiang Kai-shek's troops and the difficulties of supplying forces in China made it clear to most Allied planners that the main approach to Japan would be across the Pacific Ocean rather than from the Asiatic mainland.

On October 25, 1943, a team of Anglo-American planners completed a

General of the Army George C. Marshall, Army Chief of Staff and President Truman's most trusted military adviser. Despite the enormous cost, Marshall saw no alternative to a direct assault against Japan.

revised strategy for the defeat of Japan, calling for the invasion of the Japanese northern island of Hokkaido in the summer of 1946, to be followed by an assault against Tokyo on the island of Honshu in the fall of 1946. This plan was promptly assailed by a variety of Allied staff officers. Representatives of the Army Air Forces still continued to believe that intensive B-29 bombing of Japan would make an invasion unnecessary, while Navy staffers still considered a combination of carrier strikes and blockade as the most efficient way to force a Japanese surrender.

However, the concept of an invasion survived, and in early November 1943 the planners recommended to the Joint Chiefs of Staff that Hokkaido be invaded before the end of 1945 and the main island of Honshu the following spring. Priority would be given to forces under Admiral Nimitz undertaking the capture of the Mariana Islands—Guam, Saipan, and Tinian —for use as strategic bomber bases to pound Japan. General MacArthur would be directed to continue his advance toward the Philippines. And preparations would be made to occupy the Kuril Islands in the event that the Soviet Union entered the war and a shipping route to Siberia was needed.

A 47-island archipelago, the Kurils stretch from Siberia southward to the northernmost Japanese island of Hokkaido. The Kurils, which lie 640 miles west of Attu in the Aleutian Islands, would be attacked by American aircraft based in the Aleutians, along with the Navy's North Pacific Force. The neutralization of the Kurils would permit the shipping of war matériel to the Soviet Far East and support the U.S. invasion of Hokkaido.

When this plan reached the Joint Chiefs of Staff, en route to the Churchill-Roosevelt Cairo conference (Sextant) in November 1943, none of the senior U.S. military officers was pleased with it. Admiral King was "astounded" at the proposal to invade Hokkaido rather than Formosa in 1945. He favored an accelerated move to assault Formosa (rather than Luzon, the northernmost of the Philippines) or use Allied forces directly in an assault on Kyushu, both of which would be more logical steps toward the invasion of the principal Japanese island of Honshu.

Admiral Leahy questioned whether Japan could even be invaded and defeated within a single year. Generals Marshall and Arnold said little except that Marshall raised the issue of the possible effects of depriving Japan of oil in an intensified blockade. All of the military chiefs agreed that the proposed plan to defeat Japan had to be reconsidered. Even at the strategic level, planning was difficult for an assault some two years in the future.

President Roosevelt had favored an invasion of Japan that would team up U.S. forces with those of China and the Soviet Union. But such an invasion, while politically attractive to Roosevelt, would be a logistic nightmare. Even with a Soviet conquest of Manchuria and with Formosa and the Korean coast cleared of Japanese troops—a massive combat endeavor—an invasion force would still need a staging area that could accommodate the men and matériel flowing from the United States and U.S. Pacific bases. Troops and supplies being shipped eastward from Europe would overtax the already stressed Trans-Siberian Railroad. But assuming heroic U.S.-Soviet efforts to upgrade the railroad, considerably more work would be needed to make railway passage practical in Manchuria and southward through Korea. If Pusan, on the southern tip of Korea, were chosen as the invasion jump-off, it would have to be enlarged and modernized into a port comparable to Amsterdam, the Dutch port the Allies fought to take as a logistics megalopolis for supplying the invasion forces sweeping across Western Europe. Such an invasion route to Japan could have taken the Allies on the order of two years to prepare and win.

By March 1944 the Joint Chiefs of Staff had issued final instructions to the Pacific commanders for a continued dual advance. General MacArthur's forces attacking the southern Philippines and Admiral Nimitz's forces moving on the Marianas and Palaus were to meet somewhere in the Formosa-Luzon area by February 1945.

The multiple Allied offensives in the European and Pacific theaters moved rapidly in the first half of 1944, reaching a peak in mid-1944. On June 6 the Allies hurled six divisions against the beaches of Normandy; another three airborne divisions were parachuted behind German lines. Halfway around the world, on June 15, two Marine divisions and an Army division assaulted the island of Saipan in the Marianas. The success of the Allied landings at Normandy, the Soviet advances on Germany's eastern front, and the massive Anglo-American bomber offensive against the Third Reich led some Allied commanders and planners to estimate that the war in Europe could be over by the end of 1944. Soldiers in training in the United States were caught up in the optimism. Many believed that if they were sent off to Europe they would be just in time for victory celebrations, while shipment to the Pacific meant participation in amphibious assaults and, ultimately, landing on the beaches of Japan. Unaware of the big strategic picture, they did not know which divisions were to go where.

The 75th Infantry Division, nicknamed the "Diaper Division" because so many of its men were 18-year-old boys, was finishing its combat training at Camp Breckenridge, Kentucky, in the fall of 1944. "We got on a train one day," former private Harvey Katz remembered, "and we all sat there wondering if the train was going to go east or west. When it became apparent that we were going east, everybody cheered. Europe then was the war of choice."

At the same time as the Normandy and Saipan landings, in Washington the JCS planners completed an extensive inquiry into Pacific strategy and issued JPS 476, a comprehensive study that incorporated the Army's view about the necessity for an invasion of Japan. In fact, it went well beyond the Army planners' original position and came out with a detailed strategic study leading to an assault on Honshu's Tokyo (Kanto) Plain *by the end of 1945*.

Germany, however, was far from finished. The first major indication that the war in Europe would not be over by year's end came on September 17, 1944. In an effort to rapidly cut through northern Holland, the British 21st Army Group under Field Marshal Bernard Montgomery undertook a thrust 60 miles into German-held territory. British, American, and Free Polish paratroopers were dropped behind German lines in an attempt to capture five sets of bridges over rivers and canals (Operation Market-Garden). The third (and last) parachute and glider assault—to seize bridges at Arnhem in Holland—failed. Described as "a bridge too far," the failure brought Montgomery's advance to a complete halt.

Then, on December 16, the surprise German offensive in the Ardennes—the Battle of the Bulge—caused massive American battle and noncombat casualties, creating a U.S. Army manpower crisis in Europe. The 75th Infantry Division, whose men had cheered their orders to Europe, went into the Battle of the Bulge on Christmas Eve, fighting in deep snow and bitter cold. The 75th was blooded in fierce fighting in the Amonines area, where the Germans came so close to breaking through American lines that, according to one U.S. commander, they could have done it with only three more riflemen.

Of the 600,000 U.S. soldiers involved in the Battle of the Bulge, almost 19,000 were killed, another 15,000 were captured, and some 40,000 were wounded. Two U.S. infantry divisions were annihilated. In one of them, the 106th, 7,500 men surrendered in the largest mass of American troops in the war other than the capitulation on Bataan, when 12,000 American and 64,000 Filipino troops surrendered.

In January 1945, General Marshall offered to speed up the transfer to Europe of four divisions in the United States intended for that theater. General Eisenhower was desperate for troops, and he immediately said yes. Eisenhower also got the 86th and 97th Infantry Divisions, which had been scheduled to go to the Pacific. When those two divisions arrived in Europe in March 1945, there were no Army divisions left in the United States. Of 89 Army combat-ready divisions, 68 were now in the European-Mediterranean area and 21 were in the Pacific; all six Marine divisions were in the Pacific.

By the beginning of 1945 ground personnel from the Army Air Forces were being retrained as infantry, and black troops began training as riflemen, a role previously denied to most black troops in the largely segregated U.S. Army. And there was a severe shortage of ammunition. The Allied setbacks and shortages in northwestern Europe delayed the shifting of men, guns, tanks, and aircraft to the Pacific. This, in turn, meant that the assault against the Japanese home islands would be delayed.

Meanwhile, in Washington the U.S. senior military commanders were continuing to disagree over strategies for winning the Pacific War. But General Marshall still held to the view that Japan had to be invaded, and his advocacy prevailed. Earlier, the War Department's operations division had developed the basic Army position on this issue: "a. The collapse of Japan as a result of blockade and air bombardment alone is very doubtful. b. The collapse of Japan can be assured only by invasion of Japan proper."

If the fighting in Western Europe at the start of 1945 was bloodier than Allied leaders had envisioned, operations in the Pacific were going better than expected. When Churchill and Roosevelt met on Malta and then with Stalin in Yalta in January-February 1945 (code-named Argonaut), General Marshall and Admiral King reported that plans were being readied for an attack on the islands of Kyushu and Honshu before the end of 1945. The Kyushu invasion was code-named Olympic; the massive assault to be launched against Honshu and Tokyo itself was code-named Coronet. Marshall and King stressed that both operations depended on the redeployment of troops, planes, and matériel from Europe, which they estimated would take four to six months after Germany's defeat.

The British needed specific dates to help their industry, employment, and logistic planners. Accordingly, at Argonaut the combined Anglo-American chiefs of staff recommended that—for planning purposes—the end of the war against Japan would come 18 months after the defeat of Germany, which was expected sometime after July 1, 1945. It was a conservative formula; the senior Allied military leaders envisioned that the invasion of Japan would begin about the end of 1945 and that victory in the Pacific would finally come at the end of 1946.

Early in 1945 both the Soviet and Anglo-American armies were advancing against a Germany that had spent its last effective combat forces in the Battle of the Bulge. Brigadier General George A. Lincoln, one of the Army's leading planners, in February 1945 advised his subordinates that they must adhere to the "view to maintaining our stand that we must be prepared to switch at once to the Pacific any day from today forward since there is a possibility, increasing with every week, that this war in Europe may fold up ahead of 1 July." In March, Marshall told MacArthur: "CORONET [the invasion of Honshu] will be the decisive operation against Japan and will be concurrently supported and assisted by continuation of OLYMPIC [the invasion of Kyushu]. . . . Based on assumption the European war ends by 1 July 1945, planning is aimed at making possible target dates for OLYMPIC and CORONET of 1 December 1945 and 1 March 1946, respectively."

While approving the planning for the assault against Japan, the Joint Chiefs also took up the politically difficult decision of establishing the command structure for the invasion. There was some discussion in Washington about giving command of the overall operation—viewed by some as a series of amphibious landings—to Admiral Nimitz, who had directed the assaults against the Solomons, Marshalls, Gilberts, Marianas, Iwo Jima, and Okinawa. Army as well as Marine assault troops and Army aircraft had been involved in most of those operations.

General MacArthur protested vigorously. He believed that the invasion of Japan would be primarily a land campaign. He had directed scores of amphibious landings during his campaigns in New Guinea—mostly small amphibious operations against limited opposition—and the Philippines. Since December 1944, however, MacArthur had been advocating that all Army troops in the Pacific be placed under one command—his—and all naval forces under Nimitz. MacArthur concluded:

> Only in this way will there be attained that complete flexibility and efficient employment of forces that is essential to victory. . . . I recommend most earnestly that immediate consideration be given to this recommendation and earliest action taken. It is based upon three years of hard experience which has led me to the considered professional opinion that failure to simplify the command structure . . . will jeopardize our ultimate victory.

In Washington the Joint Chiefs debated the issue. MacArthur had few real friends in Washington, although Marshall was an unfailing supporter. As they did during his ill-fated flirtation with the Republican presidential nomination in 1944, MacArthur's civilian friends carried his banner. John Callan O'Laughlin, publisher of the highly accredited *Army & Navy Journal,* reportedly called on General Marshall in February 1945 and subsequently wrote to former President Herbert Hoover. According to O'Laughlin, Marshall called MacArthur "obstinate and ambitious . . ." and

> he said that there must be organized for that region another Supreme Headquarters Allied Expeditionary Force, with British representation as in Europe. . . . One rumor is that Marshall or King, neither of whom have [*sic*] led troops nor fleets in battle, may be sent in Supreme Command. Marshall, a 5-star General, is senior to MacArthur of the same rank.

It was preposterous to believe, however, that Marshall—who had not taken command of the Normandy invasion when President Roosevelt offered it to him—would take command of the invasion of Japan. As for King, he was promoting not himself but Nimitz for the supreme Pacific command. Nimitz, of course, had directed major amphibious operations far larger and more complex than those carried out by MacArthur's forces.

The debate over command of the invasion of Japan continued into the spring of 1945, with MacArthur and Nimitz as the leading contenders. There was never an effort by Marshall or any of the Joint Chiefs to establish an Anglo-American command in the Pacific as there was in Europe, since the British contribution in the Pacific theater was minuscule.

MacArthur's air commander, Lieutenant General George C. Kenney, visited the United States in March 1945 to discuss aircraft deliveries and other issues affecting his command. On March 20 he made a call on President Roosevelt to brief him on events in the Pacific and to express his appreciation for having been nominated for four-star rank. Kenney recalled:

> As I shook hands with him to leave, he thanked me for coming in, congratulated me on my job in the Pacific, and then said, "I suppose you would like to know whether MacArthur or Nimitz is going to run the campaign when the landing is made in Japan." I admitted that I was a bit curious. He laughed and said, "You might tell Douglas that I expect he will have a lot of work to do well to the north of the Philippines before very long."

When Kenney arrived in Manila a week later, he told MacArthur he had "heard a rumor" that MacArthur would command the assault on Japan. MacArthur snapped back, "I don't believe it. My information is that Nimitz will be in charge and that I am to clean up the Philippines and then move south into the Dutch East Indies." Kenney then revealed the source of his "rumor." MacArthur, wrote Kenney, "tried to keep the same expression but it was no use. He was as pleased as I was." Asked if he knew when the decision would be announced, Kenney replied that the "rumor" monger had said "soon."

The solution to unified command in the Pacific theater was "reached after prolonged and exceedingly difficult discussion," Marshall wrote to MacArthur in a "for his eyes only" message. "The final document has, however, been amicably agreed upon. It constitutes a major retreat by the Navy from their original stand," continued Marshall in his inimitable manner of handling the highly sensitive and vain MacArthur. But Marshall did note, "It has been necessary for us to make minor concessions in order to secure agreement on the major matters."

MacArthur's view that there should be a single commander for ground forces and one for naval forces throughout the Pacific was basically accepted. On April 6, 1945, the Joint Chiefs of Staff named him Commander in Chief U.S. Army Forces Pacific (in addition to his role as Commander in Chief Southwest Pacific Area), with Nimitz remaining as Commander in Chief U.S. Pacific Fleet as well as Pacific Ocean Areas. In essence, all ground forces (Army and Marine) and their tactical air commands would be placed under MacArthur, while Nimitz would command all naval forces in the Pacific. MacArthur immediately had his staff begin planning for assaults on the Japanese home islands, which was then given the overall code-name Downfall.

Nimitz gained little new authority. MacArthur would get Nimitz's Tenth Army, a joint Army-Marine command that was locked in bloody combat on Okinawa and would not be formally transferred to MacArthur until early August. He also got Nimitz's land-based Seventh (Army) Air Force and the

Army troops in rear areas. Nimitz would eventually get the Seventh Fleet, which was supporting MacArthur's amphibious landings, in time for the invasion of Japan. While Nimitz retained control of the Navy's large land-based air arm, General Kenney, MacArthur's air commander, would direct all land-based Marine and Army aircraft in the Pacific theater, except for the giant B-29s flying from the Marianas and soon to fly from bases on Okinawa. Continued was the awkward command structure under which the Twentieth Air Force's B-29s were directly controlled by the Joint Chiefs of Staff, with General Arnold in Washington as the JCS agent for their deployment.

The formal MacArthur-Nimitz division of commands did not end Mac-Arthur's long-standing feuds with the Navy and, indeed, with the Joint Chiefs of Staff, whom he had continuously criticized for favoring other commands, especially those in the European theater, over his own. MacArthur sent his chief of staff, Lieutenant General Richard Sutherland, to Nimitz's headquarters on Guam to set forth MacArthur's ideas on the reorganization. After three days Sutherland left empty-handed. Nimitz refused to simply concede all points to MacArthur's representative, as he had been expected to do. The turnover of Army units serving under Nimitz would be complex because the troops were spread throughout his vast Pacific command. There was also a shortage of bases in MacArthur's forward areas and a need for better scheduling of transport ships to move the troops and their equipment.

The continued haggling led Marshall to send another "For General Mac-Arthur's Eyes Only" message a month after the JCS had directed the restructuring of command. Marshall wrote:

After considering the messages concerning the progress being made in the reorganization in the Pacific, I believe that you personally should meet with Admiral Nimitz in the near future in a personal effort to resolve between yourselves the problems which have arisen rather than depending upon your respective staff officers. This seems particularly important since the JCS are considering the immediate issuance of a directive to execute Olympic not later than 1 November.

Informal reports that come to me from various sources indicate so much opposition and expression of strong feelings in staff meetings[;] that situation should be gotten under firm control before great harm is done. I feel certain that you personally can handle the situation and avoid a breach that might well have tragic consequences.

MacArthur would not go to Guam. Nimitz flew to MacArthur's headquarters on Luzon, where fighting was still raging. Professor E.B. Potter, Nimitz's friend and biographer, would later write that at earlier meetings "Admiral Nimitz found MacArthur highly intelligent, with a magnetic personality, but also with an unfortunate tendency to strike poses and to pontificate. The general's sometimes pompous manner impressed some people and irritated others. Nimitz seems to have been amused." One particularly annoying incident between MacArthur and Nimitz had arisen in December 1944, on an earlier Nimitz visit to MacArthur's Leyte headquarters. The admiral wore the five-star insignia that he, MacArthur, and five other officers had been awarded the previous month. "The general was in a jovial mood, having just announced the end of organized Japanese resistance on Leyte," Potter related. "MacArthur was instantly irked, however, when he perceived that Nimitz was wearing his five-star insignia, while he did not have any. That evening, he ordered his aides to see to it that he had his own five-star insignia by early the next morning."

Nimitz owed his allegiance to Admiral King, his naval superior, and to the Joint Chiefs of Staff. Although deceptively soft-spoken, he held strong views of his own, which he would subordinate only to those of King and the JCS. MacArthur, however, believed that his dual charter as Commander in Chief of both the Southwest Pacific Area and U.S. Army Forces Pacific made him independent of all superiors save Roosevelt, *the* Commander in Chief.

MacArthur and Nimitz met again in Manila on May 15 to discuss the invasion of Japan. The two men got on well; they were both strong-willed but professional. In two days of face-to-face talks it appeared that most of the problems were settled, and the issue of command was agreed upon. Admirals would command the separate invasion forces until the ground commanders were ashore and had established their headquarters. Then the generals would assume command of operations.

But it was soon apparent that controversy was not over. On May 21, MacArthur told Marshall that "it became evident [at the meetings] that the matter of command is not RPT [repeat] not adequately covered by the directives already issued." He pointed out the success of his amphibious operations—as he often did. Then he cited Nimitz's "inflexible attitude" and called for clarification of the Army position that he would have "the primary responsibility for the entire operation" and that there would not be two parts to the operations, as dictated by the JCS—the naval-amphibious phase. After discussing other points of difference, MacArthur reiterated: "This campaign is essentially an Army campaign with important naval phases and the command responsibility should be definitely fixed and assigned to that service." MacArthur had returned to his call for total command to be placed in his hands.

Clarification came from the JCS on May 26. They favored MacArthur's position, and he was "charged with the primary responsibility for the conduct of the operation Olympic including control, in the case of exigencies, of the actual amphibious assault through the appropriate naval commander." Nimitz was again given "the responsibility for the conduct of the naval and amphibious phases of the Olympic operations...."

Thus, MacArthur was chosen to lead the invasion of Japan. His only competitor had been Nimitz. But the flamboyant MacArthur was much better known to the American public than the soft-spoken Nimitz. MacArthur had outperformed Nimitz during their Pearl Harbor meeting with the President in July 1944, and Marshall, MacArthur's only high-ranking supporter, had been more clever than Nimitz's advocate, Admiral King, at Washington infighting.

During the debate over the Pacific command structure, on April 6, Marshall advised MacArthur that he was considering sending General Omar N. Bradley, commander of the 12th U.S. Army Group in Europe, to the Pacific. "On the Normandy Beach the fourth day after the landing, General Bradley asked me to have him in mind for service in the Pacific, incidently [sic], the only personal request of any kind he has ever made," wrote Marshall. Bradley, like Eisenhower, had risen in his career primarily because he had earned a place in Marshall's little black book. Marshall also mentioned that other senior officers were asking for duty in the Pacific, among them the irascible George Patton, a friend of Marshall's since World War I. Marshall added that Patton, who commanded the Third Army in Europe, was willing to step down to command of a division to go to the Pacific War.

MacArthur's rapid response was cordial, saying that "the integration of proven personnel from the European to the Pacific theater should not RPT [repeat] not prove too difficult." But then he immediately qualified that statement by pointing out that there would be some difficulty in absorbing the more senior European officers because of their rank and the smaller size of the U.S. ground forces in the Pacific.

Marshall persisted, and on April 24 he advised MacArthur that he was dispatching from Europe an army-level headquarters unit and special troops (such as artillery, engineer, and signal units) to help command the divisions being shifted to the Pacific. And, added Marshall, "I have tentatively in mind allocating Bradley with his group headquarters . . . for the Pacific."

Within hours MacArthur also shot down that idea. The "fronts" in the Coronet landings would be too small to warrant army group commands; Bradley "should come as an army and not repeat not as an army group commander." He further noted that Bradley was junior to General Walter Krueger, who commanded the Sixth Army in MacArthur's theater. And, wrote MacArthur, Krueger "in my opinion is not repeat not only the more competent officer of the two but is entirely familiar with this theater and its personnel . . . and with the intricate procedures of amphibious warfare peculiar to the Pacific." He concluded that he would be "delighted" to welcome Bradley as well as General Courtney H. Hodges from Europe, *both* as army commanders.

Marshall told Bradley that MacArthur would take him as an army rather than army group commander. Reportedly, General Eisenhower, Bradley's boss, "was completely infuriated by the suggestion. He began writing Marshall a steamy letter that said that to relegate [Bradley] to army commander 'would make it appear to all soldiers in this theater and to the public that this was rather a minor league affair and would have the further effect of diminishing Bradley's stature in the postwar Army and public opinion.'"

Bradley, Eisenhower's senior American field commander, did not go to the Pacific. Marshall replied to Eisenhower: "My intention was not to move Bradley to the Pacific unless he desired to go. In view of your message he will no longer be considered for such an assignment." If Marshall backed down on Bradley, he did not on General Joseph W. Stilwell, who had just spent almost three years in China as commander of U.S. forces in the area and deputy to Generalissimo Chiang Kai-shek. Marshall had many years before pronounced Stilwell "farsighted. Highly intelligent . . . a leader . . ." and "one of the exceptionally brilliant and cultured men of the army" who was "qualified for any command in peace or war." Stilwell's intolerance for failure and duplicity had earlier earned him his nickname, "Vinegar Joe." After his difficult tenure in China and Burma, Marshall proposed Stilwell to MacArthur to command the Tenth Army, which was completing the campaign on Okinawa under Nimitz and was then to shift to MacArthur's command.

Stilwell had returned from China to Washington in November 1944 under a cloud. He had alienated Roosevelt because of his candid and pessimistic reports on China, and the President refused to see him, although he normally met with all three- and four-star generals returning from the battlefronts. Marshall gave Stilwell command of the Army Ground Forces, responsible for training and organizing troops to fight in Europe and the Pacific. But Stilwell did not want a desk job; he wanted to go back to the war. He wrote a two-page memo to Marshall in May 1945 about the pending assault on Japan that succinctly suggested factors to be considered in the forthcoming invasion, demonstrating that his keen mind was already at work on invasion issues. Stilwell then undertook a survey of U.S. Army forces in the Pacific.

At about the same time that Marshall's recommendations reached Mac-Arthur, Stilwell was at his headquarters in Manila. MacArthur asked him if he would become his chief of staff, a position held since the start of the war by Sutherland, who was now becoming estranged from MacArthur, although he would serve him through late 1945. Stilwell told him no, because, as he put it in his diary, "I fancied myself as a field commander." MacArthur asked if he would take a field army, to which Stilwell replied that he would take a division (a two-star assignment) to be with troops. "Pooh pooh," replied MacArthur, "if you would take an Army I would rather have you than anyone else I know."

But in his response to Marshall's suggestions for commanding general of the Tenth Army, MacArthur said his *first* choice was Lieutenant General Oscar Griswold, who was "eminently qualified in every respect . . . completely familiar with the problems involved in amphibious warfare . . . intimately acquainted with the personnel in the theater. . . ." He added that his preference for officers from outside the theater was Stilwell, first, and then the others (except that Patton was not mentioned in MacArthur's message).

Marshall's response was to assign Stilwell to command the Tenth Army after Marine Lieutenant General Roy Geiger completed operations on Okinawa. But MacArthur would have the last word. Stilwell took command of the Tenth Army on June 23, 1945—the day after the completion of the conquest of Okinawa. It was formally transferred from Nimitz's command to MacArthur on August 4, 1945. Stilwell expected to lead that force in the 1946 invasion of the main Japanese island of Honshu. In planning the invasion, however, MacArthur would strip the Tenth Army of its combat units and assign them to the other commands that were to assault Honshu. Thus, Stilwell, with three years of hard experience fighting the Japanese, was to have been left on Okinawa in an occupation-support role. Neither Bradley nor Patton went to the Pacific.

Meanwhile, other Army ground and air commanders and units were going to the Pacific. One of the first senior officers to arrive was Lieutenant General Jimmy Doolittle, leader of the historic Tokyo raid and commander of the Eighth Air Force in Europe since January 1945. He was transferred to Okinawa in July to prepare for the arrival of his B-29s, which would join in the Twentieth Air Force's strategic bombardment of Japan. While Doolittle's B-29s and other commanders, airmen, and planes from Europe would smash the Japanese home islands from the air, most of the troops that were to invade Kyushu beginning on November 1 were already in the Pacific, as were the ships that would carry and support them.

As plans progressed for Operation Coronet, the issue of British and other Allied participation in the final assault on Japan was again raised. At Casablanca in January 1943, Prime Minister Churchill had pledged full British participation in the war against Japan as soon as the German legions were vanquished. Then, in mid-1944, believing that Germany could be defeated before the end of the year, the British government proposed for planning purposes a force of six British and two Dutch divisions—plus British dominion troops—for the final campaigns against Japan. This was in addition to British troops fighting in Burma under Lord Admiral Louis Mountbatten, the Supreme Allied Commander in Southeast Asia. However, the British requirements for support of the divisions that would participate in Downfall were considerable, including establishing bases for almost a half million troops. Moreover, the British could provide shipping for only three divisions (about 50,000 troops), meaning that U.S. amphibious ships would be needed to carry the additional units from Europe to the Pacific and then land them on enemy beaches. And the British sent the U.S. Joint Chiefs lengthy lists of equipment that would be needed from America in 1945 for the divisions that would go to the Pacific theater. These lists, above the requirements already submitted for the war in Europe, included everything from thousands of tanks, trucks, and railroad cars to 1,708,000 cotton drawers, 16 million razor blades, and 1.5 million toothbrushes.

This ambitious shopping list was duly noted by the American military planners, but as the war in Europe continued into 1945, the size of the proposed British contribution to the invasion of Japan was scaled back considerably. By the time planning began in earnest in the summer of 1945, Churchill had been voted out of office. And with victory in Europe after a struggle of almost six years, Britain was worn, tired, financially bankrupt, and looking inward. The British people—their soldiers still fighting in Burma—had very little interest in fighting another war in the Pacific.

Although the movement of their heavy bombers to Okinawa for the intensified bombing of the Japanese home islands began almost as soon as the war in Europe was over, the British would be unable to mount a ground force in time for Olympic, the invasion of Kyushu in November 1945. But the British fully intended to participate in Coronet, the landing on Honshu in March 1946 and the subsequent ground-air battle for Tokyo.

By mid-1945 British planning called for three Commonwealth divisions to land in the Honshu assault, with another two or possibly three divisions available for the subsequent land battles. To avoid the cost and time of building advance bases in the Philippines or on Okinawa to support their contribution, the British high command envisioned a floating reserve of about 15 merchant and store ships carrying additional guns, vehicles, ammunition, packaged fuel, and other supplies to sustain the troops once ashore. Still, the minimum British support base and hospitals in the Philippines would require some 7,000 engineers to build the facilities and 4,000 troops to man them. Even that effort would require American construction material and some U.S. construction troops.

The British initially proposed that British, Australian, Canadian, New Zealand, and Indian divisions participate in Coronet, but General MacArthur objected to the Indian troops: "I doubt the advisability of employing troops of native origin in this complex operation where homogeneity of language within the corps in required. . . . Likewise, there is a question of the advisability of utilizing troops of tropical origin in a temperate zone without an extended period of acclimatization, hence the acceptance of Indian troops is not concurred in. The British division [sic] should be Anglo-Saxon."

Thus, the Commonwealth Corps that would participate in the Honshu operation would consist of British, Australian, and Canadian divisions—some 75,000 men, supported by an air group of some 7,500 men with 250 aircraft under Australian command. But it was questionable if even a single British division could be ready in time for Coronet. The British Army then numbered 2,920,000 men and women, but because of the British scheme for releasing service personnel, the War Office was having "considerable difficulty in providing a division with the necessary nucleus of battle experienced personnel who are at the same time eligible for service in the Far East."

Nevertheless, British staffs worked fervently to find a single infantry division—some 20,000 men—that could be sent to the United States, re-equipped, trained in amphibious warfare, moved to a staging area in the western Pacific, briefed, and embarked in amphibious assault ships by early March 1946. The 3rd Infantry Division was tagged as the unit that could come closest to meeting the Coronet schedule. The X Corps headquarters and support troops—about 15,000 men—would also have to be moved from Britain and Western Europe to the Pacific.

The issue of including an Australian division was a particularly sensitive and controversial one. From the moment that MacArthur arrived in Australia after fleeing from Corregidor in March 1942, Australian troops had been a major component of his forces. They had fought bravely under his direction in the lengthy New Guinea campaign and in other operations of his Southwest Pacific Area command. Indeed, General Sir Thomas Blamey, the head of the Australian Army, was appointed MacArthur's Allied Land Forces Commander in 1942. With extensive Middle East combat experience, Blamey was responsible for the administration and training of all U.S. and Australian troops, although command in combat of MacArthur's forces always went to U.S. generals, unless it was a small Australian-only operation.

Despite this close association, by 1944 MacArthur was declining the use of the Australian troops offered to him except for "mopping up" operations in the Southwest Pacific. This refusal—sometimes by MacArthur and sometimes by his chief of staff, Sutherland—left the Australian political and military leadership perplexed. By the fall of 1944 the 1st Australian Corps was available for combat in the Philippines; the corps consisted of two infantry divisions, an armored brigade, and various support troops, some 90,000 men in all. The Australian government wanted the two divisions, the 7th and 9th, to be used by MacArthur in the Philippines "as an acknowledgement of American assistance to Australia." But despite several statements by MacArthur of the importance of Australian troops to future Pacific operations, including Olympic and Coronet, he apparently did not plan to include them until forced to do so by the Joint Chiefs of Staff, and then as part of the British Commonwealth Corps. (MacArthur did have some Australian naval ships in his Seventh Fleet and said that if Australian naval forces were still under his command, he would be in an Australian warship for either the Olympic or Coronet landings.)

The British and Australian governments chose the 10th Australian Division, in Borneo at the time and already trained in amphibious operations, for the Commonwealth Corps for the Honshu campaign. The division's officers and enlisted men had already fought beside Americans in the Southwest Pacific.

. . .

The 35,000 British soldiers who would participate in the Commonwealth Corps were but a small part of the men and matériel that had to be moved across the Atlantic and Pacific Oceans. Movement was already under way for the approximately 90,000 men—air crews, maintenance men, construction troops, and others—who would support the British bomber force moving to Okinawa. The construction troops who would build the forward facilities for the ground troops and the rear-echelon administrative, supply, communications, and medical troops increased to perhaps 200,000 the British personnel that would have to be moved to the Pacific.

Planned American troop movements from Europe directly to the Pacific through the spring of 1946 would total almost 400,000 men, plus another 408,000 who would be shipped from Europe to the United States and then on to the Pacific. In addition, almost 100,000 troops would be sent from the United States to the war zone every month as attrition and rotation replacements. Counting their equipment, weapons, vehicles, provisions, and fuel, the shipping requirements were staggering. Further complications were the need to bring home more than two million American troops from Europe who were not going to the Pacific, the return of Commonwealth troops from Europe to their scattered homes, and repatriation of German and Italian prisoners of war from Canada and the United States to Europe.

Allied merchant and amphibious shipping would be stretched to the limit to accommodate these requirements. The size of this ocean movement was testimony to the massive numbers of ships that had been produced in American and, to a lesser extent, British shipyards during the war. Besides the ships moving troops across the oceans, for Olympic the Navy would employ almost 1,400 amphibious ships and thousands of landing craft and amphibious tractors to carry the 14 Army and Marine divisions that would invade Kyushu in the largest invasion ever attempted.

On May 25, 1945, the Joint Chiefs of Staff issued the directive for Operation Olympic. Drawn up in Washington and Manila, the plans called for seven Army and three Marine divisions to make the assault landing against Kyushu. Two more Army divisions would form an afloat reserve–diversionary force, with another two divisions being landed as a follow-up force. The overall landing force would total some 340,000 troops under General Krueger, commanding the Sixth Army. His Army troops—half of the Army's divisions then in the Pacific—were withdrawn from combat on Luzon to rest, reequip, and train. The three Marine divisions, which had assaulted Iwo Jima earlier in the year, were already preparing for the invasion of Japan.

The Army's 11th Airborne Division was to be one of the follow-up divisions. It would come ashore and fight as infantry. So far in the Pacific War, MacArthur had used airborne troops only sparingly; several small parachute drops were made in New Guinea and on Luzon, and 2,050 troops of the 11th Airborne Division's 503rd Parachute Regiment were dropped onto Corregidor island in Manila Bay on February 16, 1945. That drop, made on Corregidor's golf course and parade field, was one of the most difficult parachute assaults of the war. The drop zones were small and littered with debris. There were steep cliffs rising from the sea, and the parachutists were fired at as they came down.

General MacArthur had received several proposals to use airborne troops in the Kyushu assault. Marshall was a strong believer in airborne assault operations, and with the war in Europe winding down, General Arnold recommended that the three U.S. parachute-glider divisions of the Allied Airborne Army be employed in the Pacific. He urged that airborne experts from Europe should meet with MacArthur "without delay." Within hours MacArthur responded: "It does not repeat not appear that there will be sufficient airdrome space to permit contemplation of extensive airborne operations during the campaign. . . ."

There was continued pressure from Washington to employ airborne troops in the Japanese invasion. Indeed, even the Joint War Plans Committee, on its own initiative, undertook a detailed study of Japan that indicated ". . . airborne units, particularly parachute elements, may be advantageously employed to facilitate the defeat of Japan." The study gave examples of specific targets for parachute and glider landings, and while pointing out that shipping such units to the Pacific was a problem and available airfield space would limit the use of gliders, planning "should still contemplate extensive employment of available airborne units. . . ." But MacArthur was adamant, and no airborne assaults were planned for Olympic-Coronet.

MacArthur would have 14 divisions at sea to assault Kyushu—more than 252,000 soldiers and 87,600 Marines.* His battle plan would land ten of these divisions and other combat units before and on X-Day, with the other four divisions to be offshore, ready to land as needed. The Kyushu assault force would be larger than the D-Day landings at Normandy, but comparisons between Olympic and Normandy had little meaning. The beaches of Normandy were a day's steaming from ports in southern England; for Olympic the divisions would sail from the Philippines, Okinawa, the Marianas, and Hawaii. For Coronet, two U.S. armored divisions would sail for Japan directly from the United States, a 30-day voyage.

The Fifth Fleet, under Admiral Raymond A. Spruance, would carry and protect the assault troops. The Third Fleet, under Admiral William F. Halsey, would bombard the Japanese home islands and, as necessary, provide close air support for the landings. Operating under Halsey would be a British

* See Appendix B, U.S. Forces for the Kyushu Assault.

force of at least five carriers and two fast battleships with their screening ships.

Meanwhile, from bases on Okinawa, Iwo Jima, and Luzon, General Kenney would send thousands of fighters and bombers (including four-engine B-24 Liberators) over Japan to support the landings, while he would deploy other planes over nearby areas of China, Formosa, and Korea to prevent the Japanese from sending reinforcements to the home islands. Finally, more than a thousand B-29s of the Eighth and Twentieth Air Forces—flying from Okinawa and the Marianas, respectively—would bombard Japanese cities and, if demanded by MacArthur, provide direct support to the invasion by pounding areas beyond his front lines on Kyushu.

MacArthur was confident that he had sufficient forces to invade Kyushu. His planners estimated that the Japanese would have 80,000 troops in southern Kyushu, but the buildup on the island had begun, and that estimate would soon be woefully wrong. MacArthur's only concern that he voiced to Marshall was about logistics. "With one exception it is believed that with a vigorous pooling of our Army and Navy interests throughout the Pacific the necessary service troops can be found to perform the minimum required functions. The exception is hospital beds. . . . Some 36,000 additional beds . . . will be required. . . ."

The November 1 landing on Kyushu was designated X-Day. MacArthur reportedly eschewed using the traditional D-Day label, a term that was now linked indelibly with the Normandy landings. In addition to the 14 divisions, he would have several smaller combat units available for the assault. If these forces were insufficient for the job, additional units earmarked for Coronet would be sent into Kyushu at the rate of three divisions per month. Planning for the invasion of Honshu would then be adjusted accordingly.

MacArthur's Downfall plan provided for Coronet to be an even larger assault on Honshu and the thrust to the Tokyo plain. On Y-Day, to distinguish it from Olympic's X-Day, MacArthur planned on 17 divisions for the initial Coronet landings, with another Army division afloat as a reserve force—close to a half million men for the largest amphibious assault ever conceived. All together, Downfall would be the most mammoth military operation of the war. And it would be commanded by a man who was himself a figure of larger-than-life proportions—General Douglas MacArthur. His invasion of Japan would raise him above all his rivals in America's military pantheon. For a man of infinite ambition, Downfall would be the ultimate military achievement and an overture to the ultimate political attainment, the presidency.

Two elaborate deception plans were worked out in support of Olympic and Coronet. The seeds of Operation Pastel, an effort to shield Olympic, were planted in 1944 when U.S. strategists were still considering an invasion of the southern China coast and Formosa. In plans drawn up in June 1944—known as "Operations Against Japan Subsequent to Formosa"—an invasion of Japan was to take place only after the China landings. But the rapid U.S. advances in the Pacific and the ineffectiveness of Chinese troops changed the basic Allied strategy. By mid-1945 the idea of a landing in China was only a memory.

At the strategic level, deception plans were being drafted by the Joint War Plans Committee, with the aid of the JCS's highly secret Joint Security Control unit, which managed large-scale deception activities. Joint Security Control, for example, was to acquire and ship to Okinawa 1,000 shoulder patches for a fictional airborne division. The planners, believing that the Japanese particularly feared parachute assaults, wanted to exploit that fear—although MacArthur had ruled out airborne operations in his plans for the real invasion of Japan.

The final Olympic deception plan, code-name Pastel II, was completed at MacArthur's Manila headquarters on July 30, 1945. The plan called for two fictitious landings, the first on the China coast, in the Chou-shan–Shanghai area, on October 1, a month before the real invasion of Kyushu, and a second on Shikoku Island on December 1. There were also to be elaborate deception tricks involving false glider and parachute operations during the actual assault on Kyushu.

After the cancellation of the *real* plans for landings on the China coast (Operation Longtom), Navy planners folded those into Pastel. The same planners, months before, had similarly recycled Operation Bluebird, a real planned attack on Formosa and the South China coast, into a fictional attack as a deception in the Okinawa invasion. The success of Bluebird apparently influenced the planners as they concocted deception ideas for Olympic and Coronet. Again, they would try to fool the Japanese with a fake landing on the China mainland.

Dissent came from Lieutenant Commander Douglas Fairbanks, Jr., the popular movie star, who was on the Navy deception staff. Fairbanks had firsthand experience in deception. He had led a PT-boat assault purporting to be an invasion force that drew German troops away from the actual landing sites in the invasion of southern France in August 1944. He argued, in vain, that the Japanese would be more alarmed by a faked landing on the Shantung coast, along the Yellow Sea.

While deception planners in the Pacific worked on Pastel, the Joint War Plans Committee in Washington, aided by Joint Security Control, was simultaneously and independently producing a master deception plan. This "General Directive for Deception Measures Against Japan"—given the code-name Broadaxe—was accepted by the Combined Chiefs of Staff on June 16, 1945. Broadaxe was designed to fool the Japanese into believing there would be no invasion of the heartland of Japan by staging false assaults on Formosa,

Hokkaido, and French Indochina, along with a thrust into Sumatra from India and an "advance into the Yellow Sea" to seize bases "for air and inland operations."

The separate creations of Pastel and Broadaxe generated bureaucratic embarrassment. All, however, was settled at a Washington meeting on June 27 between Nimitz's staff and the Joint Security Control. Essentially, the conferees acknowledged Broadaxe but stuck with the elements of Pastel. The Indochina and Sumatra ideas were politely set aside as not being in Nimitz's theater. The Joint Chiefs of Staff on July 9 accepted Pastel as the official deception plan but asked for more details. This resulted in the final plan, completed on July 30 and designated Pastel II.

Development of Coronet deception measures was difficult because the real invasion was six months further into the future than Olympic and planners faced a more complex mix of reality and fiction. To plan for the Coronet deception, they had to assume that Olympic's real operations had all succeeded and that the Japanese had reacted to the faked Chinese landings as expected. But they also had to assume that the Japanese, fooled by the Bluebird fakery in the Okinawa invasion and then by the similar Pastel fictions, would be fooled a third time by more faked landings.

Whether through deception or a lingering infatuation for landings on the China coast, the Navy in early 1945 was testing ways to land troops along a marshy section of the China coast. At least that was the belief of officers at the Pacific Amphibious Training Command in Coronado, California. Lieutenant (junior grade) Douglas Dies, an instructor, was told that the secret exercises in Grizzly Bay, north of San Francisco, were part of an "experimental amphibious landing" plan tied to the coming invasion of Japan. Experimental craft included ones that could skim across a marsh and deposit men on firm ground.

Army Air Forces officers involved in deception planning had gone along with the Navy-dominated Pastel concepts. But the airmen disagreed with Navy ideas about Coronet. While a supposed landing in Korea or China made sense for a Kyushu landing, the Air Forces officers argued, there seemed little point in such a move when the invasion target was Honshu. By then, all Japanese forces would be massed for defense of the home islands. Japanese strategists would have no reason to react to landings elsewhere.

The Air Forces dissenters came up with an audacious idea: a deception plan based on the very real feuding between MacArthur and Nimitz. The Air Forces plan called for faking "leapfrog" assaults from Kyushu against sites on both the northern and southern coasts of Honshu. The story would be put out that MacArthur wanted to use his previously highly publicized leapfrog tactics in New Guinea because he would be relying for support on land-based air forces from Kyushu rather than on Nimitz's carriers. But a Navy planner shot down the Air Forces idea, asserting that the leapfrogging would draw Japanese troops toward the actual invasion sites. As for the MacArthur-Nimitz controversy story, it was turned down because it could be "harmful to Allied morale." The original Coronet deception plan prevailed.

To some degree the deceptions and rumors of landings were successful. By April 1945, U.S. intercepts of diplomatic communications indicated that both the German ambassador to Japan and the Japanese military attaché in Stockholm had the same idea: Americans were planning to land in China. Early in June, Japanese intelligence officers in South China were getting reports of actions that seemed to be connected to anticipated Allied landings. Chinese-American guerrilla teams were reported in training in southern Fukien Province, and communist-led insurgents were said to be near Swatow, a port about 170 miles northwest of Hong Kong. But with the actual invasions of the home islands still months in the future, it was impossible to predict how the Japanese would react to the imaginary feints and thrusts of Pastel II and Coronet Deception.

Still another factor in planning for the invasion of Japan was the Soviet entry into the war. As secretly agreed to at the Yalta Conference in February 1945, the Soviet Union would enter the conflict against Japan within three months of Germany's surrender, and a massive Soviet buildup in Siberia had begun simultaneous with the German surrender. By August 1945 the Soviets had 1.5 million ground and air troops ready to strike Japan, including 80 divisions (smaller than their U.S. counterparts), 46 separate brigades, and more than 5,000 air force and naval aircraft. This massive force was commanded by Marshal of the Soviet Union Alexander M. Vasilevsky, who had directed the critical operations section of the Soviet General Staff in 1941–1942 and then had become Chief of the General Staff. Stalin rewarded his services by giving him the Far East command in July 1945. His orders were to invade Japanese-held Manchuria and Korea, capture the southern portion of Sakhalin, and land forces in the Kuril Islands in August. (Russia had traded the Kurils to Japan in exchange for Sakhalin in 1875; Japan took southern Sakhalin from Russia in 1905.)

While Soviet-American coordination in the Far East was minimal, in response to his discussions with President Truman, Stalin ordered Lieutenant-General Kuzma A. Derevyanko to Manila to serve as the Far Eastern military representative on MacArthur's staff. Some cooperation and coordination was needed in view of planned Soviet assaults on southern Sakhalin and the Kuril Islands. The Soviets were also planning to make incursions onto Hokkaido, the northernmost of the main Japanese islands. Detailed Soviet plans for the Far East invasions had been carefully drawn up, except that the landings for Hokkaido "existed in detail only in Stalin's mind. Those would have been put to paper after the conquest of Manchuria, Korea, and the Kurils," according to a distinguished Russian naval historian.

A mixed infantry-naval infantry (Marine) force was assembled on remote, isolated Kamchatka Peninsula, under General A.R. Grechko, to clear the Kuril Islands, while the 11th Guards Army on northern Sakhalin, under General L.G. Cheremisov, was to clear the Japanese from the southern portion of the island. The Soviet Pacific Fleet, numbering 2 cruisers, 11 destroyers, and 78 submarines plus lesser ships under Admiral I.S. Yumashev, would provide transport and support for these operations. The Soviet forces —with land-based air support—were expected to easily clear the Japanese defenders from those islands well in advance of Olympic, opening a northern Pacific sea route for U.S. shipping to carry war matériel to the Soviet Far East.

As early as April 1945, Admiral Nimitz had directed Admiral Halsey, commanding the Third Fleet, to prepare an operational plan for such operations. Subsequently, Task Force 49 was established under Rear Admiral Harold G. Martin, who met with Nimitz on Guam in early August 1945 and then steamed northward with five escort ("jeep") carriers, each with 24 F6F Hellcat fighters and 9 TBM Avenger bombers on board, plus a screen of destroyers and destroyer escorts. Upon arrival at Adak, Alaska, these ships would become part of Vice Admiral Frank Jack Fletcher's North Pacific Force, which had already been bombarding the northern Kuril Islands. In addition to the small carriers, Fletcher had 3 heavy and 2 scout cruisers, 24 destroyers, 3 destroyer escorts, and a dozen minesweepers. Supported by the carrier aircraft and land-based Army and Navy planes from Aleutian bases, Fletcher was to open and keep open the flow of cargo ships to Soviet Far Eastern ports.

Although the idea of an offensive against Japan from the north seemingly had been put to rest at the Sextant conference in November 1943, some U.S. and Canadian strategists still lobbied for it. High-ranking Canadian officers were particularly enthusiastic because they saw such an operation as a way to expand Canadian participation in the Pacific War. In May 1943, when U.S. forces recaptured Attu in the Aleutian Islands from the Japanese, a small team of Canadian "observers" accompanied the American troops—without the knowledge of the Minister of Defence or Prime Minister W.L. Mackenzie King. Outraged, King ruled out any Canadian participation in future U.S. operations unless President Roosevelt or Secretary of War Stimson made a formal request. When Stimson did make such a request, Canadian troops were added to the forces being assembled for the operation to retake Kiska, another Aleutian island, from the Japanese. The Allied troops stormed ashore on August 15, 1943, only to find that the Japanese had slipped away a month before.

Major General George R. Pearkes, Commanding in Chief of the Canadian Pacific Command, saw the recapture of Kiska as the first step "to Tokyo" and "the forerunner of larger expeditions from Pacific Command." Lieutenant General Kenneth Stuart, Chief of the Canadian General Staff, also hoped for a northern strategy and ordered a secret study—code-named Poppy—into the use of Canadian troops not only in the Aleutians but also on the mainland of Asia and elsewhere in the Pacific. By the summer of 1943 there were about 110,000 U.S. troops and 34,000 Canadian soldiers in Alaska and the Canadian Northwest. Eager Canadian war planners wanted to do something with those forces, as did Lieutenant General John L. DeWitt, head of the U.S. Western Defense Command.

DeWitt, apparently unaware that a northern strategy was already under discussion at the highest level, in August 1943 drew up a plan for the invasion of the Kurils. Admiral Nimitz opposed the plan, for he believed that there could not be any isolated action against the Kurils. In his view, a Kuril operation would have to be integrated with the major invasion of the home islands, and that invasion was far in the future.

Still, DeWitt's proposal was passed on to JCS planners, who decided it could not be carried out without Soviet entry into the Pacific War. But a Canadian division was included in the British Commonwealth force planned for the invasion of Honshu.

American planning for the assault on the main island of Honshu foresaw the possibility of Japanese resistance continuing into the fall of 1946. Beyond the 17 U.S. divisions and the three Commonwealth divisions, another 12 U.S. Army infantry divisions from Europe were to be sent into battle, as well as two or three more Commonwealth divisions, if they could be formed, equipped with American weapons, and transported to the Far East. The divisions that landed on Kyushu would be needed there for garrison duty and to repel Japanese counterattacks from the northern portion of the island.

MacArthur "would exercise personal command of the landing forces and direct the group operations on the mainland" in the Honshu operation. In all, MacArthur would have had more than 30 divisions ashore in Japan if the war went on into the fall of 1946, as envisioned under the "worst case" planning. By comparison, when the war in Europe ended, Eisenhower commanded 109 Allied divisions. Still, MacArthur would have a massive army to defeat the Japanese in what promised to be the bloodiest campaign of the war.

The military strategists' grand plans and grand deceptions, however, would be put to the supreme test only if their civilian Commander in Chief, former artillery captain Harry S. Truman, authorized the invasion of Japan. That decision had not yet been made. But when it was, for those who were preparing to wade ashore—the veterans as well as the green troops destined for the Pacific—the invasion would be the showdown, a last confrontation with a despised and fearsome enemy.

CHAPTER 7

THE ENEMY

The U.S. escort carrier *St. Lô* explodes in flames seconds after being hit by a kamikaze, one of the many suicide weapons the Japanese hurled against Allied forces.

In April 1944, General Douglas MacArthur's troops recaptured Hollandia, a settlement in Dutch New Guinea (now Kota Baru, Indonesia) that the Japanese had seized in April 1942. American forces killed 4,500 Japanese and took 663 prisoners. The number of soldiers who allowed themselves to be captured was somewhat high, but many were wounded or ill.

Also typical of the Pacific War was the tendency of American soldiers to search Japanese corpses for souvenirs. Although the practice was officially frowned on, occasionally the macabre searches turned up useful intelligence information. But no one was prepared for the two photographs that a GI found in the pocket of one Japanese body in Hollandia.

The photographs showed a Japanese soldier bringing a large sword down upon the neck of a man who knelt at the edge of a freshly dug hole. The photographs were turned over to intelligence officers, who showed them to New Guinea natives. They nodded at the photos and said that the beheading of captured Americans and Australians by Japanese troops was common. Natives then led investigators to graves containing bodies of American airmen. The heads of the bodies were missing.

Air Force Brigadier General Paul B. Wurtsmith personally inspected the graves, and news of the atrocities began moving up the chain of command. By mid-May 1944, copies of the photographs were in the hands of General Arnold and were then given to Secretary of War Stimson, who placed the photographs and reports about them in his safe. They were not revealed to the American public until May 1945, shortly after VE-Day, when U.S. officials feared a letdown in civilian support of the war.

But there was another concern among the planners and commanders of the forthcoming invasion of Japan. How would the Japanese treat prisoners of war already in camps? And would they even take prisoners in the battles on their home islands? Senior U.S. officials were well aware of intelligence reports that repeatedly recounted the torture and murder of Allied prisoners. Javanese natives near Aitape, where forces landed as part of the Hollandia operation in 1944, told of seeing a prisoner, believed to be an American, tied to a tree and questioned while being beaten with wooden clubs. The next morning, the witnesses said, the captive was beheaded "under great hilarity from the Japanese." Another intelligence report quoted a Christian missionary who said that "on numerous occasions [Japanese] military police had informed him that not one American airman would be permitted to live." A captured diary, believed to be written by a Japanese Navy warrant officer, contained this entry for December 14, 1943:

Three members of the crew of a B-24 that we shot down yesterday were discovered adrift on the sea. They were picked up as prisoners. One was an exceptionally tall fellow, and another was a clumsy fellow, just like a beer barrel. They had been in a lifeboat a day and a night. The third was rather nondescript in appearance and had a big bandage on his leg. He was probably shot by a machine gun. White men are certainly weaklings. These prisoners were placed in hastily built solitary cells. At night the prisoners were questioned by our defense force interrogators. I thought our sergeant's interpretation was rather good. He tried to scare them with a Japanese sword, but the young officer and noncommissioned officers would not reply as asked. Thereupon blows were struck on the officer's chin and that damned officer finally let out a scream. The beer-barreled radio technician answered quite freely. ... When I think that these guys took the lives of some of our men it rouses my anger; but when I see their pitiful plight and I think of myself in their position, I cannot remain angry long. Whatever the case may be I will not be taken prisoner. There is nothing more disloyal than that—I'd rather be eaten by a shark!

Another U.S. intelligence report quoted an intercepted radio message from a Japanese lieutenant to a colonel on April 3, 1944, regarding "conversation with the enemy who was shot." During questioning, according to the lieutenant, the prisoner, an Australian soldier, said, "Oh, my wound aches. Please give me water, please give me medicine." Then, the lieutenant went on, "when we gave him candy and coconut water from a canteen, he said, 'It is good,' and lost consciousness, so at last we shot him." During the Battle of Okinawa, at least four downed American airmen were beheaded; the fate of many others who bailed out around Okinawa was unknown, but presumably they were executed after capture.

Allied officials had been getting reports of Japanese atrocities since shortly after the attack on Pearl Harbor. To those who remembered what Japanese troops had done in China, the reports were appalling but not shocking. Particularly well known were the mass rapes and murders committed during the Japanese conquest of Nanking, then the capital of China under Chiang Kai-shek. As Japanese troops approached Nanking in December 1937, Chiang abandoned the city, leaving it open to its conquerors.

Because Westerners were in the city when it fell, the invaders' atrocities were well documented and extensively publicized as "the Rape of Nanking." The Japanese themselves even boasted of the barbarism rampant in Nanking. The *Japan Advertiser* told of two junior Japanese Army officers who were "in a friendly contest to see which of them will first fell 100 Chinese in

A Japanese officer beheads an Australian prisoner captured in the Dutch East Indies. The photograph outraged the American public, as it was first thought to show an American pilot being executed.

individual sword combat before the Japanese forces completely occupy Nan-king." A week later, the *Advertiser* reported that the goal had been increased to 150 Chinese after referees had not been able to pick a winner. Besides, one of the contestant's blades "was slightly damaged in the competition. He explained that this was the result of cutting a Chinese in half, helmet and all."

Prisoners in Nanking were shot to test new machine guns, were tied to posts and used as targets for bayonet practice, were decapitated by officers who also brought their heirloom samurai swords down upon the heads of prisoners in vain attempts to reenact legendary slashes that split a man in half. Other prisoners were buried neck-deep and killed under the hooves of horses, the tracks of tanks, and the bayonets of Japanese soldiers. Thou-sands of women and girls were raped on the street or taken to barracks and tied to beds, repeatedly raped by soldiers, and then killed.

"One poor woman was raped seven times," reported the American direc-tor of the Nanking Refugee Committee. "Another had her five months infant deliberately smothered by the brute to stop its crying while he abused her. . . . Vandalism and violence continue absolutely unchecked. Whole sections of the city are being systematically burned." By one authoritative estimate, 20,000 women were raped in and around the city, and more than 200,000 men were murdered.

Japan's "three-all" policy in China—"kill all, burn all, destroy all"—cost the lives of millions of Chinese. The population in occupied China plum-meted from 44 million to an estimated 25 million, and although millions fled to areas held by Chiang Kai-shek's forces, millions of others died from Japanese brutality and Japanese-inflicted starvation. Many Japanese looked upon Chinese as subhumans. To Japanese medical researchers performing hideous experiments, Chinese victims were *maruta*, "blocks of wood," not human beings. In the notorious Unit 731, Japan's major bacterial-warfare research organization, countless Chinese, Koreans, Mongolians, people from conquered Manchuria—as well as some U.S. prisoners—were treated, in the words of a Unit 731 worker, like "valuable laboratory animals." Some, infected with plague bacilli, were dissected as they lay dying so that their diseased organs could be used for new plague bacilli cultures.

While on duty in Central China, a Japanese Army surgeon said that he had tested anesthetics and performed practice amputations on healthy Chinese prisoners, then killed them. He also admitted shooting prisoners so that he could teach other surgeons how to remove bullets. Confessing long after the war, he said hundreds of other military doctors and nurses performed similar experiments. "Most have never recognized their crimes because it was 'justice' to kill and rape the Chinese and other Asians," he said. "It was all for the Emperor."

• • •

When Japan launched its war against the West in December 1941, it was generally believed that what had happened to Chinese and other Asians would not happen to Allied soldiers and civilians who fell into Japanese hands. All belligerents in World War II except for the Soviet Union had signed the 1929 Geneva Convention on humane treatment of prisoners of war. Unlike the other signatories, Japan had not ratified the convention. But the Japanese government formally told the Allies in February 1942 that it would adhere to it. By the time Japan made that announcement, Japanese troops already had tortured and killed Western prisoners.

To force the surrender of Fort Stanley in Hong Kong in December 1941, Japanese troops began torturing British and Chinese captives, cutting off ears and fingers, cutting out tongues, and gouging eyes before killing the victims by dismemberment. British and Chinese nurses were tied down on corpses and raped, then bayoneted to death. The captors allowed some witnesses to escape and report the atrocities. Fort Stanley surrendered.

In a similar terror tactic to induce surrender, a Japanese combat unit killed with bayonets 323 people in a Singapore hospital, including 230 patients, and let witnesses escape. At least 5,000 Chinese living in Singapore were rounded up and executed, many by bayonet and sword. Colonel Masanobu Tsuji, the architect of the Malaya campaign, a participant in the battle, and the author of a book about the fall of Singapore, glossed over the atrocities, writing, "The numerous and disgusting later breaches of military discipline must be considered in comparison with the far more numerous fine and noble actions on the battlefield. Beside them any discreditable actions will in time be swept aside into oblivion."

An Australian soldier, captured during the fighting in Singapore, lived through a botched beheading and survived to describe his ordeal at a war-crimes trial:

> I was told to sit down with my knees, legs, and feet projecting into the grave. My hands were tied behind my back. A small towel was tied over my eyes.... My shirt was unbuttoned and pulled back over my back, exposing the lower part of my neck. My head was bent forward, and after a few seconds I felt a heavy, dull-blow sensation on the back of my neck.

Pretending to be dead, he fell into the grave, which was then filled in. He was able to claw his way out, was recaptured and allowed to live, apparently as a curiosity. No one knew how many men captured by the Japanese did not live to tell grim stories of survival.

British Foreign Secretary Anthony Eden revealed the Japanese atrocities to Parliament, but Allied officials usually hesitated to make such revelations. They feared that disclosures of Japanese brutality, especially against prisoners of war, would not only lead to Japanese retaliation against other prisoners but would also inspire Allied soldiers to inflict their own retribution on the battlefield. Such behavior would deny the Allies their claim to moral superiority and could set off an endless spiral of revenge and counter-revenge.

The first authoritative reports of torture and murder of U.S. prisoners of war came in April 1943 when three American officers escaped from a prison camp at Davao in the Philippines. Filipino guerrillas led the escapees to a beach, where they were picked up by a U.S. submarine, which took them to Australia. At General MacArthur's headquarters they told about an ordeal that became known as the Bataan Death March.

On April 10, 1942, at Mariveles on the tip of the Bataan Peninsula, about 72,000 prisoners of war—10,000 of them Americans, the rest Filipino troops —were assembled, searched, and stripped of all belongings by their Japanese captors. Most of them were suffering from dysentery, malnutrition, and malaria. Japanese guards killed some men immediately because they had allegedly stolen Japanese money. Then, in groups of 500 to 1,000, the prisoners were marched along a dirt road, without food or water, on a journey that would kill thousands of them and end in a long captivity that would kill thousands more.

The Japanese had planned a road-and-rail journey: first a march to a railhead 60 miles away, then a 25-mile trip in boxcars, and finally an eight-mile trek to a partially built U.S. airfield that was to serve as a prison camp. The captors had not been prepared for ailing, starving men, and they had planned on transporting only about 40,000 prisoners. The Japanese were overwhelmed by having to deal with 72,000—an estimate; the real number will never be known. Despite the obvious need for change, the Japanese stuck to their original plan, and the Death March began. Ill and starving, many of the prisoners would have died from the rigors of the journey itself. But not only the sickly died. Countless victims were shot or were beaten to death on the march.

One survivor remembered that as he started out, his canteen was snatched away and emptied by a Japanese soldier. "...I bent over to pick up my canteen. But he turned around and hit me on the head with his rifle butt." A little later, the prisoner saw a sick U.S. soldier "wobbling along, uneasy on his feet." A Japanese soldier "grabbed this sick guy by the arm and ... flipped him out across the road." Several tanks rolled over his body until "his uniform was embedded in the cobblestone. The man disappeared, but his uniform had been pressed until it had become part of the ground."

Many horror stories were not told until survivors of the Death March were liberated. But the first reports in 1943 were horrifying enough. When MacArthur passed the information on to Washington, officials decided not to publicize the prisoners' stories, the first in a stream of atrocity reports from prison camps in the Philippines. President Roosevelt, wondering whether to release the reports, in September 1943 asked Stimson and Secretary of the Navy Frank Knox to have the Joint Chiefs of Staff make recommendations on how and when to inform the country about the abuse and murder of Americans held by the Japanese.

The President was particularly worried about the effect that disclosures would have on the mission of the *Gripsolm,* a Swedish ship chartered to exchange diplomats and other civilians held by belligerents. In early September the *Gripsolm* was en route to an exchange port with Japanese civilians who were to be repatriated. Also on board were food packages for Americans in Japanese hands.

"American officers who escaped from Japanese prison camps on Luzon have stated that they feel that conditions in such camps could scarcely be much worse and unless conditions are improved, few American prisoners will survive," said a report from General Marshall's office to Roosevelt. "They have emphasized the importance of getting Red Cross supplies to these prisoners and recommend that no action be taken which might interfere" with the mission of the *Gripsolm.* Roosevelt accepted the recommendation and ordered that the atrocity reports be suppressed until he personally authorized release. Even so, while virtually all Red Cross shipments reached Allied prisoners in German camps, hardly any Red Cross supplies ever reached prisoners held by the Japanese.

Many U.S. journalists had heard about the prison-camp horror stories, and while withholding publication under wartime voluntary censorship rules, they pressed for disclosure. The War Department finally gave in to the pressure and on January 27, 1944, announced that the Japanese had tortured, starved, or murdered thousands of U.S. and Filipino prisoners on a "march of death" after the fall of Bataan. A joint Army-Navy communiqué gave eyewitness reports. Men were killed because they begged for water. Men who stumbled out of line were clubbed, shot, or bayoneted to death.

The news intensified American loathing of the Japanese and, in an incalculable way, made both servicemen and civilians turn their hatred against the Japanese people rather than against their leaders. There was no Hitler to focus their hatred on. There were only "the Japs," a term used by American newspapers and wire services, by soldiers and sailors, and by U.S. officials from the President down.

President Roosevelt sought information on the Japanese from a Smithsonian anthropologist, Dr. Ales Hrdlicka, who explained that the Japanese were "as bad as they were" because their skulls were "some 2,000 years less developed than ours." Roosevelt and Hrdlicka wondered about the possibility of mating Japanese with Pacific islanders who were more docile.

Senator Theodore Bilbo of Mississippi, notorious for his hatred of black Americans, would tell MacArthur after the war, "Personally, if I had my way about it, I would sterilize every damn one of them so in one generation there would be no more Japs." Military leaders were no less intolerant.

General Arnold suggested that leaflets be dropped on Japan threatening to "annihilate the Japanese people." And Vice Admiral William Halsey at a press conference on Guadalcanal in November 1942, gave his formula for winning the war: "Kill Japs. Kill Japs. Keep on killing Japs."

Army psychologists found that 38 to 48 percent of soldiers agreed with the statement "I would really like to kill a Japanese soldier," compared to 5 to 9 percent who agreed to a statement about killing a German soldier. Many U.S. soldiers and Marines refused to take prisoners or care for enemy wounded. "After taking a position we routinely shot both the dead and wounded enemy troops in the head, to make sure they were dead," wrote Eugene B. Sledge, who fought on Peleliu and Okinawa. "Survival was hard enough . . . without taking chances being humane to men who fought so savagely."

American troops rationalized that since a Japanese did not willingly surrender, if he looked as if he were surrendering, he was undoubtedly faking. There were numerous stories of such trickery. On Kwajalein, a Japanese soldier emerged from a pillbox with upraised hands. "As five of our men went after him," a U.S. soldier said, "the Japs in the pillbox shot three of them. I saw them use this same ruse on several other occasions also." Other stories told of Japanese using a white flag to lure Americans into the open and then firing on them. Until late in the war, reluctance to take prisoners hampered U.S. psychological warfare efforts aimed at getting Japanese to give up by approaching U.S. lines while waving a surrender leaflet. In the popular 1943 movie *Gung Ho!,* about the Marine raid from submarines on Makin atoll in the Gilbert Islands, a group of Japanese are shown surrendering. As the Japanese approach the Marines, one bows, revealing a machine gun strapped to his back, which the others use to gun down their captors. Such scenes were often included in wartime films.

For Japanese propagandists, the Doolittle raid on Tokyo in April 1942 provided an opportunity to fan hatred of Americans. Military leaders focused their enmity on American fliers. The ex post facto law that authorized the trial and execution of three Doolittle fliers was extended to any other fliers who attacked Japan or Japanese-held territory.

For downed airmen, sometimes there was not even the semblance of a trial. In May 1945, for example, eight members of a B-29 crew were heinously treated in what postwar Japanese investigators called "the Human Vivisection Incident." Saburo Ienaga, a former professor at Tokyo University and a leading Japanese intellectual, reported after the war that the surgical "experiments" on conscious prisoners were arranged by Japanese military authorities and the director of external medicine at the respected Kyushu Imperial University.

The physician extracted a prisoner's lungs, then cut the lung artery and allowed the blood to flow into the thorax so that the man drowned in his own blood. He removed another prisoner's stomach and then pinched shut a larger artery to see how long the man would take to die with the blood flow to his heart shut off. In another operation, the doctor opened a conscious prisoner's skull and inserted a knife into the skull cavity. One experiment involved injecting seawater into prisoners' veins.

Not until after the war did Allied officials learn of the magnitude of Japanese atrocities against prisoners. Besides the vivisection horrors, there were many others. One of the worst centered on Wake Island, which fell to the Japanese in December 1941 after a valiant defense by the Marine garrison. In January 1942, about 800 of Wake's military prisoners were loaded onto a Japanese ship for transfer to a prison camp elsewhere in the Empire. While the ship was at sea, a Japanese officer arbitrarily selected five Americans and beheaded them. The bodies were mutilated and thrown overboard with the severed heads. Ninety-six U.S. civilian construction workers remained on Wake to work on Japanese projects. Two of them were beheaded for allegedly stealing food. Later, in October 1943, when the Japanese feared a U.S. invasion, the rest of the prisoners were killed. One was beheaded; the others were shot to death.

The murder of prisoners in anticipation of an invasion occurred again on Palawan, a large island of the Philippines where the Japanese kept a prisoner workforce of about 150 Americans. On December 14, 1944, when a U.S. force was sighted off the island, a Japanese officer told the prisoners to enter tunnels that served as air-raid shelters. Then he had his men throw buckets of either gasoline or kerosene into the tunnels and hurled in a lighted torch. "As screaming men ran from the shelter," said a report based on eyewitness accounts, "they were mowed down by machine guns and rifles." Others were bayoneted to death. Many died in the fiery tunnels. In the fire and smoke, five men managed to escape and were rescued by Filipino guerrillas. When Palawan was liberated in March 1945, the survivors told their story and showed the charred bodies of their comrades as evidence.

Postwar investigations and war-crimes-trial testimony revealed that the massacres of prisoners on Wake and Palawan were not aberrations. The Japanese military's attitude toward Allied prisoners was evolving toward condoned, vengeful murder. On March 17, 1945, a week after the massive B-29 firebomb raid on Tokyo, the vice war minister sent a message to commandants of prison camps: "Prisoners of war must be prevented by all means available from falling into enemy hands. . . . They should be kept alive to the last wherever their labor is needed."

Grayford C. Payne, who was a U.S. Army sergeant at the surrender of U.S. forces on Bataan in April 1942, survived the Death March and captivity in the Philippines. Transferred to Japan in August 1944, he was put in a camp at Hanawa, on northern Honshu. He and the 550 other prisoners, who worked in a nearby mine, expected to be killed when Japan was invaded. He remembered a note, posted for the prisoners, that read: "All prisoners of war will be shot" the moment the United States invaded Japan. "We'd seen people beheaded and bayoneted and shot," he remembered. "And we felt we hadn't survived just to be shot. We had a plan to grab the two machine guns—they could kill what they could—and then the rest of us would fight. We wouldn't just stand there and let them kill us."

Statistics reflected the ruthlessness of Japanese policy toward prisoners. Of 235,473 U.S. and British prisoners captured by Germans and Italians, four percent (9,348) died; of the 132,134 American, Australian, and British prisoners held by the Japanese, 27 percent (35,756) died.

In addition, Japan held an unknown number of Dutch, Indian, and native soldiers from conquered lands, along with tens of thousands of Allied civilians. By Japan's own records, the number of acknowledged captives exceeded 300,000. These did not include Chinese and Korean impressed workers and captives or Korean "comfort girls"—tens of thousands of involuntary prostitutes sent to Japanese Army brothels.

Japanese-held prisoners of war, in violation of the Geneva Convention, were put to work by their Japanese captors in mines, on docks, and at other jobs. The most notorious forced-labor project was the "Railroad of Death," a 265-mile military railway along the Kwae Noi (the "River Kwai" of Pierre Boulle's novel and the movie) into Burma from Thailand. The Japanese compelled about 270,000 Asians and 61,000 Allied prisoners—most of them Australian and British—to build the railway. Struggling through jungles and across gorges, the prisoners fought sickness and suffered under the torment of sadistic guards. Beatings, executions, malnutrition, and lack of medical care killed 12,568 of the prisoners of war and about 87,500 Asians.

Although much of the information about Japan's prisoners came out after the war, Allied officials knew during the war, from evidence and witnesses, that the Japanese were consistently torturing and killing prisoners. Intelligence officers, for example, found a handbook on interrogation techniques that authorized torture—"beating, kicking, and all conduct involving physical suffering"—when "all else fails." Another instruction said, "It is forbidden to make on-the-spot disposition of any officer among the prisoners of war." Asked to interpret this order, a Japanese prisoner told U.S. intelligence officers that "anything, including killing, may be done with prisoners of war below officer's rank."

When the U.S.-Filipino Army on Bataan surrendered, Hino Ashihei, a well-known Japanese war correspondent, was there. He wrote, "As I watch large numbers of the surrendered soldiers, I feel like I am watching filthy water running from the sewage of a nation which derives from impure origins and has lost its pride of race. Japanese soldiers look particularly beautiful, and I feel exceedingly proud of being Japanese." Those soldiers went on to commit what Westerners viewed as atrocities and Japanese saw as acceptable behavior, for their captives were enemies who had shamed themselves by being taken prisoner. By Japanese tradition, beheading was an acceptable form of execution.

Protests about barbaric behavior were about as likely to be made in wartime Japan as in wartime Germany. The military ruled the nation, although there was a semblance of democracy. The Imperial Rule Assistance Association (IRAA), the all-seeing management tool of the government, handled such matters as rationing and air-raid drills and enforced wartime regulations, which included bans on Western art and music. Women were told to stop wearing kimonos and getting permanent waves. They were expected to wear work pants gathered at the ankles. Many civilian men wore a kind of uniform, khaki caps and puttees.

Civilians were supposed to live by two guides, *The Cardinal Principles of Japanese Life,* which said that the mission of the Imperial Army was to conquer "those who refuse to conform to the august influence of the Emperor's virtues," and *The Way of the Subject,* which said that a desire for "individual freedom" was "unforgivable," for "all is related to the concerns of the State." One of the many slogans called the nation "A Hundred Million Hearts Beating as One!"

When, late in the war, the Army began drafting middle-aged and physically unfit men, it was as if the entire nation had become a battlefield and every civilian a soldier. With slogans such as The Sooner They Come, the Better and One Hundred Million Die Proudly, government propaganda operatives whipped up the people to repel, by whatever means possible, the invasion of their homeland.

U.S. soldiers were told that Japanese soldiers essentially lacked imagination and followed orders well. A U.S. Army guidebook distributed to American soldiers said:

> In combat the Japanese soldier is strong and hardy. On the offensive he is determined and willing to sustain sacrificial losses without flinching. When committed to an assault plan, Japanese troops adhere to it unremittingly even when severe casualties would dictate the need for abandonment or modification of the plan. The boldness and courage of the individual Japanese soldier are at their zenith when he is with his fellows, and when his group enjoys advantages of terrain or fire power. He is an expert at camouflage and delights in deceptions and ruses.

Japanese troops also had a guide. When Japan began the war against the Allies in December 1941, all officers and enlisted men going into combat in Malaya were given a 70-page booklet entitled *Read This Alone—And the War Can Be Won.* It gave the motivation for the war: to liberate the downtrodden people of Asia and "make men of them again." The war, it said, "is a struggle between races, and we must achieve the satisfaction of our just demands with no thought of leniency to Europeans, unless they be the Germans and the Italians."

THE ENEMY • 165

The booklet gave tips on how to avoid sunstroke and malaria and warned about poisonous fruit. The soldiers were to live so that they could die in combat. Each man was to write his will and send it home, along with a lock of hair and a nail clipping. In some Japanese units, soldiers cut off a dead comrade's hand and skinned it; then the flesh and bones were burned and, when possible, sent to the family of the deceased.

The booklet said:

> When you encounter the enemy after landing, regard yourself as the avenger come at last face to face with his father's murderer. . . . Here before you is the man whose death will lighten your heart of its burden of brooding anger. If you fail to destroy him utterly you can never rest at peace. And the first blow is the vital blow.
>
> Westerners—being very superior people, very effeminate, and very cowardly—have an intense dislike of fighting in the rain or the mist or at night. . . .
>
> You must demonstrate to the world the true worth of Japanese manhood. The implementation of the task of the Show Restoration [the Reign of Hirohito], which is to realize His Imperial Majesty's desire for peace in the Far East, and to set Asia free, rests squarely on your shoulders.

Twice in the booklet were the words of an old poem:

> Across the sea, corpses soaking in the water;
> Across the mountains, corpses heaped upon the grass.
> We shall die by the side of our lord.
> We shall never look back.

The Japanese soldier, fighting fiercely, dying willingly, confounded—and often frightened—U.S. troops. A dark, unfathomable acceptance of death drove the Japanese fighting man. After the Battle of Attu in the Aleutians in May 1943, when 2,500 Japanese soldiers fought almost to the last man, they were reported charging and shouting, in English, "Japanese drink blood like wine!" A poem was found on the body of one of the Japanese soldiers:

> I will become a deity with a smile in the heavy fog.
> I am only waiting for the day of death.

The Japanese warrior's code forbade surrender. Soldiers were told that they served the divine Emperor and, through him, were infused with the glory of a martial spirit. At death, their own spirits would journey to the Yasukuni Shrine, the patriots' memorial in Tokyo where the spirits of 2.5 million warriors dwelled. No Japanese soldier or sailor who had been taken prisoner could hope to have his spirit drift to the Yasukuni Shrine when he died. But men who died in battle and men who killed themselves for the Emperor would join the other heroic spirits of the shrine.

Japanese soldiers were expected to die rather than surrender. Lieutenant General Tokutaro Sakurai issued this order of the day in April 1944: "If your hands are broken, fight with your feet. If your hands and feet are broken, use your teeth. If there is no breath left in your body, fight with your spirit!" The die-for-the-Emperor code was implanted in every recruit. He was told that the last words of a dying soldier were expected to be "Long Live the Emperor!" (Actually, according to battlefield memories, it was usually "Mother!")

Asked why Japanese troops chose death over surrender, a senior Japanese staff officer said after the war, "When any man leaves Japan for foreign battlefields, he is not expected to return until the war is over. This is taught to the Japanese child, not at school, but from home life and the everyday life in the Japanese community. It has been the spirit of the Japanese from years ago. . . ."

The no-surrender code was not merely a quaint tradition. It was an order, clearly stated in the soldier's manual, *The Field Service Code:* "If alive, do not suffer the disgrace of becoming a prisoner; in death, do not leave behind a name soiled by misdeeds." The soldiers' families knew this well. Notes slipped into care packages sent to soldiers at the front typically said, "Please fight well and die a glorious death." Ogawa Masatsugu, an infantryman whose regiment fought in New Guinea, remembered that even in the despair of defeat, men were prepared to kill themselves rather than surrender. "Even those who tossed away their rifles never threw away their last grenade."

Japanese medics killed wounded men who might be captured. Men in units anticipating a tank attack grabbed explosives and burrowed into holes along the tanks' expected path. When a tank was rolling over the hole, the men detonated the explosives. Cornered soldiers with no hope of winning did not surrender. They mounted banzai charges and were cut to pieces as they took as many of the enemy with them as they could. For U.S. soldiers and Marines, it was a senseless, murderous tactic. A Marine veteran of Saipan remembered "yells and screams going on for hours." U.S. artillery and mortars fired in the direction of the din. Then

suddenly there is what sounded like a thousand people screaming all at once, as a horde of "mad men" broke out of the darkness before us. Screams of "Banzai" fill the air, Japanese officers leading the "devils from hell," their swords drawn and swishing in circles over their heads. Jap soldiers were following their leaders, firing their weapons at us and screaming "Banzai" as they charged toward us.

Our weapons open up. . . . Belt after belt of ammunition goes through that gun, the gunner swinging the barrel left and right. Even though Jap bodies build up in front of us, they still charged us, running over their comrades' fallen bodies. . . .

Bullets whiz around us, screams are deafening, the area reeks with death, and the smell of Japs and gunpowder permeate the air . . . and the only thought is to kill, kill, kill. . . .

As the battle for Saipan was ending on July 9, 1944, Japanese soldiers, extending the code to civilians, prevented women and children from surrendering. A Marine officer reported seeing "women, some carrying children, come out of the caves and start toward our lines. They'd be shot down by their own people." Many women and children made their way to steep seaside cliffs. "The women would come down and throw the children into the ocean and jump in."

The Marines summoned interpreters, who, using loudspeakers, pleaded with the civilians to surrender. Then, another Marine officer remembered,

the people drew closer together in a compact mass. It was still predominantly civilians, but several in uniform could be distinguished circling about in the throng and using civilians for protection. As they huddled closer, sounds of a weird singing chant carried up to us.

Suddenly a waving flag of the Rising Sun was unfurled. Movement grew more agitated; men started leaping into the sea, and the chanting gave way to startled cries, and with them the popping sound of detonating grenades. It was the handful of soldiers, determined to prevent the surrender or escape of their kinfolk, who tossed grenades into the milling throng of men, women, and children, and then dived into the sea from which escape was impossible. The exploding grenades cut the mob into patches of dead, dying, and wounded, and for the first time we actually saw water that ran red with human blood.

The mass murder and suicide of an estimated 10,000 civilians would seem an unlikely subject for lifting home-front morale. But Japanese propaganda officials seized on the Saipan deaths as proof that civilians possessed the same militant spirit as their soldiers. Japanese newspapers printed translations of *Time* magazine's description of the tragedy. A Tokyo Imperial University professor exulted that "our courage will be buoyed up by this one hundred times, one thousand times." The defeat on Saipan and the later defeat on Okinawa were called "great sacrifices prior to Japan's great victory." The victory presumably would come on the shores of the homeland, when U.S. invaders would be thrown back into the sea.

One of the weapons would be the kamikaze—suicide aircraft. After the formation of the first kamikaze units, Vice Admiral Matome Ugaki, the commander of the Fifth Air Fleet, wrote in his diary, "Oh, what a noble spirit this is! We are not afraid of a million enemies or a thousand carriers because our whole force shares the same spirit. . . . If the hundred million people set out for production and defense with this spirit now, nobody need worry about the future of the empire."

In May 1944, five suicide aircraft had flown to the U.S. airfield at Yontan on Okinawa. U.S. defenders shot down four planes. The fifth landed, and soldiers poured out, throwing hand grenades and incendiary weapons. Before they were mowed down, the Japanese destroyed seven aircraft, damaged 26, and set ablaze 70,000 gallons of fuel. The incident was a chilling reminder of what suicide troops could do on the ground in Japan, fighting invaders.

The successful use of kamikaze aircraft at Okinawa would inspire Japanese military leaders to send men out in other "special attack" weapons. "Special attack" came to mean "suicide," and Admiral Ugaki's admiration for these weapons evolved into official policy. The Supreme Council for the Direction of the War on January 18, 1945, decided to "concentrate on converting all armament production to special attack weapons of a few major types." These included one-way submarines, manned, high-speed small boats that exploded when they hit an enemy ship, human torpedoes, and human bombs and mines.

As on Saipan and Okinawa, not only soldiers but every man, woman, and child had to be ready to die. In cities, towns, and villages the Japanese government distributed *The People's Handbook of Resistance Combat.* "Should the enemy invade our mainland," the handbook said, "100 million of us, as the Special Attacking Forces, must exterminate them to protect our native soil and maintain our everlasting empire." A primer on guerrilla tactics, the handbook mustered civilians into a suicidal home-defense force whose weapons included rocks, sickles, kitchen knives, and sharpened bamboo spears.

The Japanese called the civilian forces Volunteer Home Defense Units. U.S. intelligence sometimes referred to them as "a Japanese *Volkssturm,*" the name of the German People's Army raised, by Hitler's decree, for a desperate last-ditch defense in the winter of 1944–1945. Members of the *Volkssturm* included boys of 16 and men of 60. A Washington intelligence briefing for Army planners in May 1945 estimated that the Japanese People's Army "will display considerable effectiveness as defensive units."

As U.S. intelligence officers focused on Kyushu for detailed invasion planning, they discovered that 125,000 members of Volunteer Home Defense Units, "composed largely of partially trained reservists," were augmenting Army and Navy units in southern Kyushu, with approximately 450,000 more volunteers in northern Kyushu. Appointments of major generals and lieutenant generals to hitherto unknown units indicated that the volunteer units were being organized into divisions and possibly even into corps. The volunteers were not merely scattered units. They were being deployed as major fighting forces.

"The brave talk about holding off the enemy with bamboo spears turned out not to be just rhetoric," educator Saburo Ienaga realized. "It was to be a martial virtue born of necessity."

• • •

Emperor Hirohito, as commander in chief of the Imperial Army and Navy, regularly received a Report to the Throne on the progress of the war. The January 1945 report, submitted by Admiral Koshiro Oikawa, chief of the Naval General Staff, and General Yoshijiro Umezu, chief of the General Staff, did not mention the suicide weapons, but free of flowery rhetoric, it gave a fairly objective view of the invasion that would almost surely come. "The war situation is now very grave," the document said, "and the fate of the nation is at stake." Landings might come as early as August, possibly on Kyushu, the southernmost of the major home islands, or on Shikoku, smallest of the home islands, which lies south of the main island of Honshu.

The report continued:

> No forecast as yet can be made as to the time, direction, or scale of the invasion of the Imperial homeland. However, the logical procedure would be to destroy our air and naval strength, advance air and sea bases, and demolish production and communication facilities in Japan, Manchuria, and China. These steps would crush our ability to wage war and cut off troop movements between the continent and Japan Proper. The enemy will prepare to concentrate and direct the needed land forces and then begin the invasion. . . . [W]e must be alert especially after this autumn.

Because "it is characteristic of Americans to hold human lives so dear," the report said, "it is necessary that we take advantage of this weakness, and inflict tremendous losses on the enemy, using all possible methods." Assuming U.S. landings in China, the Japanese planned a buildup on the mainland and attacks designed to inflict heavy losses, especially on Americans. Overwhelmingly outnumbered on the sea and in the sky, Japan's strategists saw their only hope was to fight on land "in bloody operations . . . to crush the enemy's fighting spirit."

After the surrender of Germany in May 1945, the Imperial General Staff's strategy centered on planning for an Allied invasion of Japan, expected to be accompanied by an American-backed offensive against Japanese forces in China and a British drive to regain lost territories in Southeast Asia. The Japanese believed that for the United States "the question of how to end the war hinges on the success of the battle against the Japanese mainland, the domestic situation, and the movements of Russia." Predictions of increased casualties were "contributing to decreased fighting morale," and Americans "are becoming doubtful about a prompt end to Pacific hostilities."

The Japanese planned to kill as many Americans as possible on the beach in "the decisive battle for the Japanese mainland." If U.S. troops were hurled back into the sea in the first assault, "it is inevitable that confidence in Truman and the military will be lost." America's partial demobilization and industrial reconversion, begun after the European victory, convinced Japanese military leaders that U.S. war weariness would help to build pressure for a negotiated end to the war.

Japan's grand strategy was determined by the Supreme Council for the Direction of the War, known as the Big Six: the premier, the foreign minister, the ministers of War and the Navy, and the chiefs of the Army and Navy general staffs. The Army and Navy chiefs told civilian Cabinet members little about the conduct of the war, claiming the need to protect military secrets. But when the council met on June 6, the Army came forth with a plan for the future direction of the war, a plan for the Decisive Battle.

As presented by Lieutenant General Torashiro Kawabe, the Army's vice chief of staff, the strategy for the Decisive Battle would be "altogether different" from the strategy that led to defeats at Iwo Jima, Saipan, and Okinawa. The main force of the Imperial Army was intact, he pointed out, and many aircraft and airfields were undamaged. The enemy "will be met at the point of landing by an overwhelming Japanese force, which will continue its attack until he is defeated and turned back," Kawabe said. Kamikaze planes would wipe out one-quarter of the invading forces at sea and another quarter during the attempted amphibious landing; the rest of the invaders would be annihilated at the beachhead.

Japanese strategists believed that a tactical victory at the beachhead would lead the Allies to call for a negotiated peace. But that issue was not raised at the all-day meeting. Premier Kantaro Suzuki accepted the plan. "There is only one way to win, and that is by determination," he told a Cabinet session the next day. "When the whole nation possesses this will, then we shall be able to achieve victory!" On June 8, the Army's fight-to-the-end plan was presented to the Emperor, who silently accepted it.

Convinced that invasion was imminent, the Imperial General Staff began analyzing probable U.S. invasion moves. Japanese intelligence work was, in some respects, highly effective. While little information about it survived the war, a December 1944 U.S. Army report on Japanese analysis of Allied communications revealed the depth of their efforts. The report's summary declared

> That the Japs have a very thorough knowledge of our activities and movements cannot be denied. They seem to obtain this information through call-sign analysis, visual means, the reading of American codes, spy reports, tactical intelligence, and from P.O.W. [prisoner of war] interrogation.

Major General Masakazu Amano, chief of the Army operations section at Imperial General Headquarters, once thought landings in China would be part of Allied strategy. Now he judged them to be "very slight." His other conclusions:

• The United States was urging the Soviet Union to attack Japan and might try to "gain a foothold in Korea at once in order to check any extensive Russian advance southward."

- Americans would find it "easy to effect operations to secure bases in outlying islands from which to obtain air control over western Japan."
- It also would be "easy to obtain air control over western Japan and isolate the home islands from the Asiatic continent."

As for the most probable invasion site, Amano selected Kyushu. "As the end of the Okinawa campaign approached," he later said, "an operation in southern Kyushu became all but inevitable. An operation against Cheju Island [off Korea] also became more probable with every passing day, and at the end of July, the feeling was that it might occur as early as the first of September."

But the focus was on Kyushu, which "would be important to the enemy as a means of securing bases and as an attrition campaign," Amano reasoned. "However, it would provide us with an eagerly sought opportunity to draw the enemy into a crucial battle and thereby weaken his morale or gain a substantial respite before the next operation." An invasion of Kyushu "would probably not come in September or October but two or three months later." Next, Amano believed, would come an invasion of Honshu and a drive on Tokyo, which "was regarded as indispensable for accomplishing the ultimate objective"—the conquest of Japan. The invasion of Honshu, he believed, "would not be attempted until the following spring."

The Imperial General Staff plunged into planning the defense of Kyushu, and Amano later said:

> we were absolutely sure of victory. It was the first and the only battle in which the main strength of the air, land, and sea forces were to be joined. The geographical advantages of the homeland were to be utilized to the highest degree, the enemy was to be crushed, and we were confident that the battle would prove to be the turning point in political maneuvering.

The U.S. Joint Chiefs of Staff ultimately decided on exactly what the Japanese had expected: an invasion of Kyushu in the fall of 1945 and an invasion of Honshu the following spring. It was a classic case of mirror thinking by rival strategists. Thus, the stage was set for the closing act of the war. An invasion force, bent on one objective—unconditional surrender—would face a defensive force that would not surrender except as part of a negotiated peace—by whatever means necessary, at whatever the cost.

CHAPTER 8

THE HORROR WEAPONS

Japanese troops, wearing gas masks, advance through the rubble of Shanghai during the 1937 invasion of China. Chinese investigators later charged that Japanese forces used poison gas and bacteriological weapons against the Chinese.

There was yet another, darker dimension to the forthcoming invasion of Japan. If the basic strategies of offense or defense proved unsuccessful, either side could summon up an unspeakable alternative—the use of horror weapons. Heavy American casualties on the beaches at Kyushu or Honshu undoubtedly would force U.S. military commanders to employ poison gas and biological weapons against the Japanese. And if the Japanese used these weapons against the invaders, American forces would retaliate.

The first U.S. amphibious landing in World War II to meet major opposition had been the assault on Tarawa Atoll in November 1943. The Marines who stormed ashore on what would be called "bloody Tarawa" lost almost 1,000 of their comrades killed and twice that number wounded in just over three days of savage fighting. These losses shocked the American public and led military commanders to consider the use of poison gas in future operations against the Japanese. Major General William N. Porter, chief of the Army's chemical-warfare service, a month after the Tarawa assault, wrote, "The initiative in gas warfare is of the greatest importance. We have an overwhelming advantage [over the Japanese] in the use of gas. Properly used gas could shorten the war in the Pacific and prevent loss of many American lives."

This was the core rationale for the use of chemical—and biological— weapons. They were perceived as a way for commanders to save the lives of their troops. And the option of chemical or gas warfare remained in the minds of U.S. military commanders and planners as Allied assaults moved closer and closer to the Japanese home islands.

Months before the scheduled invasion of Kyushu, U.S. forces in the Pacific had stockpiled thousands of tons of poison gas to use against the Japanese. And all was ready in the United States to produce hundreds of thousands of small bombs loaded with deadly anthrax germs, which cause ulcerations of the skin and eventual death. America's arsenal of horror weapons was extensive. So secret was U.S. work on these weapons that some of the wartime data is still classified. The Japanese Army was also prepared. (The Japanese effort is still largely unknown to the American public. After the war, U.S. occupation officials were determined to convert Japan into a Western-style democracy. To help Japan's image, they suppressed intelligence data about Japan's use of poison gas and germ warfare in China and experiments on human victims, among them Allied prisoners of war. U.S. officials also kept evidence of these activities from being introduced at war-crimes trials.)

At the time of the impending invasion, both American and Japanese commanders were contemplating the use of gas and germs, which would take a toll of human lives far greater than the weapons of conventional warfare.

The U.S. Army had long considered the use of chemical weapons, especially gases that would incapacitate or kill an enemy. Chemical and germ or biological weapons were already a part of American military history. In 1763, General Jeffrey Amherst, the British troop commander in the American colonies, sent smallpox-infected blankets to Indians who might support French interests. During the Civil War both sides poisoned wells, a tactic that had been practiced by armies throughout history.

Germany, with the world's largest and most varied chemical industry, was the first nation to use gas weapons in the 20th century. On April 22, 1915, a green vapor was seen moving toward the Allied lines at Ypres, Belgium. Seeking to break the stalemate of trench warfare, the Germans had released 168 tons of the chlorine gas from cylinders, which a light wind had carried over the French troops, leaving terrified soldiers blinded and dying. Two days later, on April 24, the Germans again used chlorine gas at Ypres. An estimated 5,000 Allied troops died and another 10,000 were injured in the two gas attacks.

Five months later, on September 25 and 27, the British responded with chlorine gas against the Germans at the Battle of Loos, Belgium. After that, gas was regularly used by both the Allies and the Germans. The French were the first to use true gas-filled artillery shells, in February 1916. The Germans introduced the more deadly phosgene gas in December 1915 and the even more toxic mustard gas in July 1917. But gas attacks failed to break the stalemate of battle. The effects of gas were too unpredictable, varying with wind, temperature, and humidity. And one's own troops had to move through the gassed area if the enemy pulled back. Of some 16 million battle deaths in the war, only 91,000 were caused by gas. U.S. troops on the Western Front suffered more than 25,000 casualties from German gas attacks and retaliated with their own gas weapons.

On the eve of World War II, the American public's perception of gas warfare was based on the experience of the Great War in Europe, 1914–1918. It was a vision of soldiers, blinded by gas and coughing, being led back from the front lines, their eyes bandaged; men in agony from the appalling mustard gas that inflamed and burned exposed parts of their bodies. Gas was a cruel and painful weapon in the public perception, although no less painful than a bullet, shrapnel, a bayonet, or a bomb that tore flesh and maimed as well as killed.

The U.S. Army's meager interest in chemical weapons after World War I focused on defending against toxic gases. From 1922 to 1937 the War Department forbade the manufacture of toxic agents in the United States. However, as war loomed in Asia and Europe in the late 1930s, there was a reawakening in the United States to the potential need for chemical-warfare capabilities. For a two-week period in 1937, the Army's Edgewood Arsenal, just north of Baltimore, Maryland, produced mustard gas to fill artillery shells. Large-scale production of toxic gases began at Edgewood in 1940. The congressional appropriations for the Army's chemical-warfare service jumped from approximately $2 million in 1940 to more than $60 million in 1941.

But few offensive chemical weapons were on hand when America entered World War II. There were gas-spraying devices for aircraft and 4.2-inch mortars for firing gas-filled projectiles. But only about 500 tons of toxic-gas mixtures were stored in American depots, less than the amount used in a single day in the major gas attacks of World War I.

The Army's Edgewood Arsenal and civilian laboratories accelerated research into toxic gases, and American factories quickly began producing toxic materials as well as weapons. The first plant was at Warners in New York State, which opened in April 1944. It initially produced 15 tons of cyanogen chloride per day, later increasing to 60 tons per day. Several additional plants also began to produce toxic gases, including phosgene and mustard gas, which had caused hundreds of thousands of casualties in World War I.

As chemical weapons were developed, remote places were needed to test them. In 1942 a chemical test area was set up in the desert wasteland of Utah, including part of the Dugway Valley, and at Fort Sibert in Alabama. Other chemical test areas—with more tropical conditions—were established at Bushnell, Florida, and San José Island in Panama. American toxic weapons were also tested on Brook Island in the Australian state of Queensland as well as at smaller test facilities in Canada and India.

Weapons intended to destroy tanks, planes, or even buildings could be tested against inanimate objects. But toxic gases were meant for human targets. Thus, volunteers—thousands of American and Australian servicemen—were exposed to various toxic gases. The exact number of men on whom gases were tested may never be known, but the U.S. Navy alone had at least 65,000 volunteers from the Great Lakes training station near Chicago for tests in various laboratories.

There were several joint Army-Navy research projects, and the Navy had a chemical-weapons test chamber at the Naval Research Laboratory in Washington, D.C., across the Potomac River from the suburb of Alexandria, a few miles from the Capitol. The chamber was 10 feet by 15 feet and 17 feet high.

Several men could be exposed to gases in the chamber for up to an hour to test the effectiveness of gas as well as protective clothing, masks, and ointments. The volunteers were tested using ordinary clothing as well as protective clothing, plus gas masks. Although the volunteers were carefully monitored and underwent medical examinations before and after tests, many suffered injuries. In Australia, volunteers, wearing normal clothing and gas masks, worked moving sandbags while exposed to gas in gas chambers. Many were hospitalized, often the skin around the scrotum and under the arms burned raw.

In the spring of 1944 among the many thousands of U.S. Army volunteers for chemical-weapons tests, the Army used 40 men identified as "Japanese"—apparently Japanese American, or Nisei—in an effort to determine if Asians responded to mustard gas differently from Caucasians. No difference was found. Significantly, the U.S. servicemen who volunteered for these tests did so out of a sense of duty and patriotism; no money was paid to them. Some of the volunteers, after being injured in the tests, again volunteered as soon as they were able to return to duty.

While many gases were being developed and tested, chemical munitions were being manufactured at a prodigious rate. By 1945 the U.S. Army had almost 5½ million chemical artillery shells, more than a million chemical bombs, and over 100,000 aircraft spray tanks. There were also some unconventional gas weapons. Glass bottles were filled with hydrogen cyanide for use as hand grenades. These gas grenades, which held about a pint of liquid, were intended as last-ditch weapons against tanks or for assaulting enemy bunkers. The grenades were discarded in 1944 because of the danger of breakage during shipment. Also, tests showed that the bottles did not always break against soft jungle underbrush and that they bounced off log bunkers.

Mustard-gas land mines were made from rectangular one-gallon tin cans, commonly used for varnish or syrup. The ten pounds of mustard in the can were detonated by a slow-burning fuse or electrical current, and the gas would spread over a considerable area. They were intended as booby traps or for contaminating fields, roads, or buildings. The Army procured and stored, but did not fill, almost two million such mines. By mid-1942, however, there were 25,000 filled land mines in Hawaii in addition to other chemical munitions. By April 1945 there were more than 43,000 such mines in Pacific stockpiles.

Some other chemicals were produced in large amounts but not used in specific weapons, including 20,000 tons of lewisite as well as 100 tons of nitrogen mustards, which were produced over four months "mainly to mislead German intelligence" away from actual U.S. chemical-weapons development. Also, thousands of tons of gas were produced for use mainly in tear-gas weapons. This massive American chemical arsenal was intended for a multifront war, supporting U.S. combat operations in Europe and the Mediterranean as well as the Pacific and Southwest Pacific areas. And, significantly, it included both offensive and defensive weapons.

What U.S. intelligence officials called "authoritative reports" of the Japanese using chemical weapons in China led President Roosevelt, on June 6, 1942, to declare that the United States would retaliate with the use of poison gas "if Japan persists in this inhuman form of warfare against China or against any other of the United Nations." The threat was similar to the one that British Prime Minister Winston Churchill had made earlier with respect to the Soviet-German front. On March 20, 1942, Churchill had told Joseph Stalin that he would "treat any use of this weapon of poison gas against Russia exactly as if it was directed against ourselves. I have been building up an immense store of gas bombs for discharge from aircraft, and we shall not hesitate to use these . . . from the moment that your armies and people are assaulted in this way." Churchill made public his warning in a radio broadcast on May 10, 1942. Thus, both Allied leaders had publicly threatened to use poison gas against their mutual enemies.

There was very real concern among the Allies that at some stage the Germans, who had initiated gas warfare in World War I, would resort to such weapons in World War II either to repel the Normandy invasion or in a last-ditch defense of their homeland. This did not happen, probably because of the fear of massive Allied retaliation. There was similar concern about the Japanese, and as the Pacific War advanced toward the Japanese home islands, massive amounts of chemical weapons were becoming available to U.S. military commanders. Meanwhile, plans were being drawn up for using these weapons in retaliation against Japanese gas attacks. In Washington the code-name used for such planning options was Project Sphinx, and several major studies were undertaken, mostly by the Army's planning staff, in the spring of 1945.

But retaliation was no longer being looked at as the only way that gas could be used; thought was being given to chemical weapons simply as effective offensive weapons. On May 29, 1945, General Marshall told Secretary of War Henry Stimson

> . . . of gas and the possibility of using it in a limited degree, say on the outlying islands where operations were now going on or were about to take place. [Marshall] spoke of the type of gas that might be employed. It did not need to be our newest and most potent—just drench them and sicken them so that the fight would be taken out of them—saturate an area, possibly with mustard, and just stand off. . . . The character of the weapon was no less humane than phosporous [sic] and flame throwers and need not be used against dense populations or civilians—merely against those last pockets of resistance which had to be wiped out but had no other military significance.

178 • CODE-NAME DOWNFALL

A subsequent Army study, which Marshall passed to Fleet Admiral Ernest King on June 14, addressed the fanatical Japanese resistance being encountered in the Pacific. The study stated: "Gas is the one single weapon hitherto unused which we can have readily available which assuredly can greatly decrease the cost in American lives and should materially shorten the war."

Meanwhile, at the tactical level, the Army was developing plans for using gas, usually labeled as weapons for "retaliation." The Army Air Forces plan of mid-1944 for the first 15 days of a retaliatory gas campaign in the Pacific called for the use of 86,000 aerial bombs of various sizes carrying either mustard gas or phosgene, plus 6,500 spray tanks for aircraft that would fly low over enemy troops and release mustard gas.

Against unprotected troops—or civilians—these weapons would have been devastating. Against protected troops they would have caused casualties and, equally important, forced defenders to fight in their gas masks and protective capes, greatly reducing their combat effectiveness. Thus far in the Pacific War no chemical weapons had been used by either side. But in an invasion of Japan, planners had every reason to fear there might be cause for both the Americans and the Japanese to resort to gas.

Toxic weapons were also considered for use against Japanese food crops. The Army's biological-weapons program had examined southern blight (*Sclerotium rolfsii*) to kill German potato and sugar-beet crops as well as certain Japanese crops. Army-sponsored research began in 1942 at the Department of Agriculture research station in Beltsville, Maryland, and was continued at the Army's research center at Camp Detrick, Maryland, from the fall of 1943. While the development of the toxic agent was successful, it was found that the principal Japanese crops—rice, cereal grains, and sweet potatoes—were all so blight-resistant that *Sclerotium rolfsii* would inflict little damage.

The Army Air Forces, seeking a way to mark targets in the jungle, got from the Chemical Warfare Service a compound that, when sprayed over an area, left an unmistakable mark because it discolored and then blighted all leafy vegetation it touched. Fliers also wanted a chemical to destroy food crops on Japanese-held islands in the Southwest Pacific. In 1944, Lieutenant General George C. Kenney had his planes spray crude oil and crank-case drainings on areas cultivated by the Japanese, but these substances were not very effective. Subsequently, 1,058 chemical compounds were examined at Camp Detrick for possible use against crops. Several were most promising, and a recommendation was made to the Army General Staff in May 1945 for tactical use of anti-crop agents against Japan.

Plans were outlined by the Army's Chemical Warfare Service for the destruction of almost eight million acres of cultivated land on the Japanese home islands—30 percent of the 1946 rice crop, a level of destruction certain to imperil Japan's ability to feed its people. This anti-crop effort would require a force of 1,500 aircraft, each flying 26 sorties. The chemical —2,4-dichlorophenoxyacetic acid—was to be sprayed or dropped into the water used to irrigate crops. The cost of the facilities to produce the chemical compound, the availability of raw materials, and the impact on other Army chemical-biological programs were also assessed.

Planning went so far that the War Department sought an opinion from the Army's judge advocate general, who stated that the use of chemicals to destroy crops "would not violate any rule of international law prohibiting poison gas, upon condition, however, that such chemicals do not produce poisonous effects upon enemy personnel, either from direct contact, or indirectly from ingestion of plants and vegetables which have been exposed thereto."

The Joint Staff Planning Committee of the Joint Chiefs of Staff reviewed the anti-crop proposals, and in May 1945 it was decided that the use of chemicals against Japanese crops would be tabled for restudy in January 1946, after the planned invasion of the home islands.

But the buildup of gas weapons kept pace with the Allied offensive moving closer to Japan. There were major toxic storage depots in Australia and Hawaii (where the weapons were handled by Italian prisoners of war as well as U.S. troops) and smaller depots on other islands. By mid-1945 depots were being prepared north of Manila and on Okinawa, with plans drawn up for storing some 7,500 tons of aerial toxic weapons on Luzon and 16,000 tons on Okinawa by November 1 in the event that they were needed in the invasion. The plans for Olympic called for another 8,500 tons of "ground toxic chemical warfare munitions" to be available afloat in merchant ships at Manila when the troops stormed ashore on Kyushu, ready to be sent to the front if needed.

As these plans were being drawn up, there was increasing concern about how many Americans were dying in Pacific battles. In May 1945, General Joseph Stilwell, soon to take command of the Tenth Army on Okinawa, wrote to General Marshall about the pending invasion of Japan. His suggestions concluded: "Consideration should be given to the use of gas. We are not bound in any way not to use it, and the stigma of using it on the civilian population can be avoided by restricting it to attack on military targets."

The American public was also becoming concerned about the high casualties in the Pacific. "You Can Cook Them with Gas," said the headline of an editorial in the *Chicago Tribune* on March 11, 1945, as U.S. troops were fighting on Luzon and Iwo Jima with heavy loss of life. The editorial declared that the charge that poison gas "is inhumane is both false and irrelevant. . . . The use of gas might save the lives of many hundreds of Americans and of some of the Japanese as well."

• • •

More terrible than the chemical weapons being sent to the Pacific were the deadly biological weapons, microscopic living organisms or large, toxic protein droplets developed from them that produced disease and death. As weapons, biological agents had several military advantages over chemical agents. Unlike chemicals, they are alive and can grow and multiply; a few bacteria introduced into food, drink, or body tissue can increase and spread rapidly. Dispatched to targets in shells and bombs, biological agents could be dispensed to contaminate food and water supplies or infect crops and other vegetation. Biological agents persist, from a matter of hours to many years (as is the duration of the anthrax organism), and are difficult to eliminate once an area is heavily contaminated. They usually infect through the respiratory tract or cause infections by entering the body through cuts or wounds. Compared to chemical agents, biological agents are far more difficult to detect and protect against.

U.S. biological-warfare efforts formally began in July 1941, inspired by concern that the Germans or Japanese might attack American troops with such weapons. That month the War Department called meetings with representatives of the Surgeon General, Army intelligence, and chemical-warfare staffs as well as the military-research community. Interest in biological weapons soon expanded beyond the Army to include the Navy, the National Academy of Sciences, and other federal agencies. At the instigation of Secretary of War Stimson, a Committee on Biological Warfare was established to combine the expertise of outstanding American authorities on human, animal, and plant pathology and bacteriology and to make a survey of the potential for biological warfare when the United States entered the European conflict.

In August 1941 the Army's Chemical Warfare Service established a biological research unit at the Edgewood Arsenal. Called the Medical Research Division, the new unit was to undertake preliminary planning "in conjunction with the medical aspects of chemical warfare, including bacteriology and immunization." In addition, liaison was to be established with the relevant activities in Canada and Britain, which was already engaged in the small-scale production of biological weapons.

While plans were developed to initiate biological weapons, attempts at defensive programs were hastily put into effect because of the fear that the Germans or Japanese might use such agents. Detection and defensive measures were initiated—from guarding water supplies to monitoring reported infections. Contracts were awarded to some 25 universities and foundations for research into biological warfare, and the well-known novelist John P. Marquand was appointed as director of intelligence and information for the program, although little information was ever released.

The Army's biological research, at first limited to studies and planning, entered a new phase in April 1943 when the Army began construction of a biological research center at Detrick Field, a small airport with a single hangar outside Frederick, Maryland, 40 miles northwest of Washington, D.C. The Army-Navy biological-warfare effort was growing rapidly. By mid-1945, Detrick—with two test facilities and a production plant—had a staff of some civilians and about 4,000 military personnel, one-quarter being Navy men and the remainder soldiers. A Navy biological research unit at the University of California worked closely with Detrick and other university laboratories.

Detrick and the entire biological-warfare program had strict security precautions, equaled only by those for the atomic bomb and code-breaking efforts. But many of the merchants in Frederick knew some of what was happening behind the high fences of Detrick because of the supplies ordered and the inevitable talk of soldiers in the town. And some services were required from the local hospital. There were 250 cases of accidental exposure to various biological agents at Detrick during the war, of which 60 were classified as proven infections. There were no related deaths. But had there been fatalities at Detrick, the Army and Navy "owned" their uniformed people; civilians working at Detrick had to sign an unusual consent form:

CONSENT FOR MEDICAL TREATMENT AND HOSPITALIZATION AND BURIAL IN THE EVENT OF DEATH

I, _____, a civilian employee of the War Department in the Chemical Warfare Service of the Army at Camp Detrick, Maryland, being aware of the hazards of my duties agree to the following as a condition of said employment:

1. In the event I become sick or disabled on or off the Post, I will immediately notify and report to the Post Surgeon and will consent to medical care, treatment and hospitalization exclusively by the Army.

2. In the event of death, I authorize the Commanding Officer at Camp Detrick, Maryland to make arrangements for and conduct the processing of my remains and to place them in a sealed casket which shall not thereafter be opened.

3. I authorize post-mortem examination of my remains to be made exclusively by proper Army representatives in their discretion.

I designate _____ as my emergency addressee.

_____ (SEAL)

(Date)

The principal aim of the U.S. biological programs was the defense of American troops, and there was particular concern about reported German development of botulism as a weapon. In response there was an urgent demand that Camp Detrick enter large-scale production of toxoids. The Surgeon General of the Army declared that mass inoculations of U.S. and

British troops with the toxoids to defend against botulism was not likely to provide them protection. Nevertheless, Detrick produced enough toxoids to inoculate more than 500,000 troops. The assault troops at Normandy carried syringes to inoculate themselves in case the Germans used biological weapons.

While protective measures against microorganisms were developed at Detrick, offensive biological weapons were also being spawned. A large number of biological agents were examined for possible use as weapons, among them plague *(Pasteurella pestis)*. The Navy looked into the possibility of plague as a weapon, employing against the Germans or Japanese the same "Black Death" that had killed at least one-quarter of Central Europe's population in the 1340s and many thousands more in Europe in the 1660s. By the spring of 1944 indications were that anthrax *(Bacillus anthraces)* was the agent that should be mass-produced as an offensive weapon. It was relatively easy to produce, infected all species of animals, and was highly toxic to humans, who faced a long convalescence—if they survived.

Simultaneous with the establishment of Detrick, two remote sites were acquired to test biological agents: Horn Island, with 2,000 acres of sand dunes some ten miles south of Biloxi, Mississippi, and Granite Peak, a prominence adjacent to the Dugway chemical test area in Utah. Horn Island had limited value because of a belated discovery: For two-thirds of the year the prevailing winds blew across the island toward the mainland. Granite Peak thus became the principal area for testing biological weapons on a variety of animals. Although anthrax agents were never disseminated within the United States, small quantities of anthrax were used at Granite Peak to test the longevity of the spores as ground contaminants, with inconclusive results. (A harmless anthrax simulant was tested in a variety of bomb sizes as well as in shotgun shells.)

To produce biological weapons the newly erected Vigo ordnance plant, six miles south of Terre Haute, Indiana, was taken over in May 1944. This top-secret complex included a theater, a laundry, an 85-bed hospital, dormitories, cafeterias, laboratories, incinerators, its own steam power plant, and refrigerator plants in addition to production lines. Although considered only as a pilot plant for biological agents, to demonstrate its capacity the Vigo plant continuously produced four percent anthrax slurry for filling four-pound aerial bombs at the rate of *500,000 bombs per month.*

In June–July 1945 production of the harmless anthrax simulant *Bacillus globiggi* was undertaken at the Vigo plant to test production procedures and bomb designs. Approximately 8,000 pounds of the agent were produced, proving the efficacy of the Vigo production line. Initially one million four-pound bomb casings were ordered. Half were to be filled with anthrax at Vigo and half set aside unfilled for possible British use.

The production of actual anthrax agents could have been undertaken at Vigo in the summer of 1945 and, barring technical problems or accidents, could have reached a maximum production rate of about 100 tons of bacteria per month. Vigo could probably have provided on the order of a million of the four-pound anthrax bombs by the time of the planned invasion of Kyushu in November 1945 and two or three times that number by the time of the March 1946 assault on Honshu. Biological weapons were still more arrows in the quiver of American forces approaching the Japanese home islands.

Few Americans knew of these biological-research efforts, which, like the atomic bomb, were kept secret from all but those immediately involved. And as in the development of the atomic bomb, a driving force in the development of biological weapons was the fear of what the enemy was doing. There is no record of serious opposition by the scientists involved in biological research to its use as a weapon—unlike the atomic bomb project. However, the President's Chief of Staff, Admiral Leahy, did express his abhorrence of such weapons to Roosevelt and, subsequently, to Truman. He participated in a spirited discussion of biological warfare in July 1944 as he and Roosevelt were at sea on board the heavy cruiser *Baltimore* en route to Honolulu for their meeting with MacArthur and Nimitz. In that meeting, in the President's cabin, some staffers present advocated destroying the Japanese rice crop with biological weapons. Leahy later wrote:

> Personally, I recoiled from the idea and said to Roosevelt, "Mr. President, this [using germs and poison] would violate every Christian ethic I have ever heard of and all of the known laws of war. It would be an attack on the noncombatant population of the enemy. The reaction can be foretold—if we use it, the enemy will use it."

"Roosevelt remained noncommittal throughout the discussion," Leahy added. But even as Leahy spoke, work was beginning in the Marianas to build airfields for B-29 "Superfortress" bombers to use "conventional" weapons to bomb and incinerate Japanese—civilians as well as military.

Somehow the use of chemical and, especially, biological weapons was considered more loathsome than high-explosive and incendiary bombs, even if they burned up portions of entire cities and inflicted horrible wounds. Captain Charles B. McVay, the commanding officer of the heavy cruiser *Indianapolis,* which carried Little Boy atomic bomb components to Saipan in July 1945, guessed that the wooden crate and metal cylinder being put aboard his ship at San Francisco contained biological weapons. When he saw his heavily guarded cargo and was told the two escorting Army officers were really medical officers and not artillerymen, as their insignia indicated, he declared: "I didn't think we were going to use B.W. in this war."

The Army officers said nothing.

· · ·

Germany did have a biological-weapons research program during the war, although such efforts were initially forbidden by Hitler. Still, the Germans lagged far behind their Far Eastern partner in the development of biological weapons. The extensive Japanese biological-warfare program had its origins in 1930 when Shiro Ishii, then a captain in the Army's medical service, returned to Japan from a European trip on which he became convinced that biological weapons were highly effective.

Japan, like other major nations, already had a chemical-warfare program. In the 1930s a poison-gas factory was established at Okunoshima in Hiroshima Prefecture, and poison gas was reportedly used in border fighting against the Soviets in Shanshi Province in 1939. Tanisuga Shizuo, a Japanese "gas soldier," recalled using poison gas in China in 1939. In his unit rifle squads carried two or three red canisters about eight inches long and two inches in diameter. After lighting the fuse, the canister was to be thrown. "If you threw with all your might, you could toss it maybe fifty meters [164 feet]," Shizuo later wrote.

His experience in using gas against the Chinese followed prescribed tactics:

> Once I got the command "Use Red Canister!" when I was at the front in China. I held up a piece of tissue paper and watched how it fluttered in the wind. I was glad to see conditions were favorable—the weather cloudy, wind blowing toward the other side. "Perfect," I thought. I shouted the order, "Take out the canisters!" I had the men put on their gas masks and fix bayonets, then ordered them to crouch down and wait. One after the other, I threw the canisters toward the enemy. I could see the white smoke come out, spreading across the ground. I ordered the men to charge into the village.

The Chinese soldiers and almost everyone else had already fled the village. But an old grandmother, Shizuo recalled, had failed to get away because of her bound feet. She was racked by coughing. She's not even dead yet, he thought. Shizuo described the gas as a "sneezing" gas. "It wasn't supposed to kill." But it was poison gas, and when Shizuo returned to Japan, he worked at a secret poison-gas plant.

By the time Japanese troops were fighting in China, a biological-warfare program was already under way. While an instructor of epidemiology at the Army Medical College in Tokyo from 1931 to 1936, Shiro Ishii strongly advocated a biological-weapons program. In this period he became famous for developing a water-purification filter that replaced the awkward boiling procedures and the use of chlorine. Reportedly, "to demonstrate the effectiveness of the 'Ishii filter,' Ishii urinated into, then drank from its output. Army and Navy chiefs attending Ishii's bizarre presentation were duly impressed." The device was adopted by the armed forces, and Emperor Hirohito was said to have also drunk from it when visiting a naval ship. (Undoubtedly, the Emperor did not sip filtered urine.)

Shortly after the Japanese Army took control of Manchuria in 1931–1932, the Army established a germ-warfare center in a factory outside the large city of Harbin. The center had the code-name Togo—honoring the Japanese admiral who defeated the Russians in the Battle of Tsushima in 1905. In the 1930s many Japanese military leaders considered Russia still the prime enemy of Japan.

By the mid-1930s the Togo secret biological-research facility had about 300 employees, of whom some 50 were scientists and physicians. The center was funded from a secret budget and commanded by Army officers. The facility was moved to a new, two-story building near the Harbin military hospital, and in mid-1936, Ishii arrived from Japan to take control of the biological-warfare effort. At about that time the facility was given the cover name Epidemic Prevention and Potable Water Supply Unit, and in 1941, the official designation Unit 731.

To the south, during the war with China that expanded in mid-1937, Ishii's unit gained favorable attention within the Army by providing water-filtration machines to help combat an epidemic of cholera among Japanese troops. This led to Ishii's specialists being assigned to most Japanese Army divisions. British historians have observed that Ishii's men "would have a presence in every battle zone, supplying water and dealing with epidemics. But when the time came they would also have an ideal training and the right tactical position to wage BW [biological warfare]. One of Ishii's dreams would come true—doctors in combat alongside the glorious infantry."

Under Ishii, the effort and size of the unit grew rapidly—from a staff of perhaps 1,000 military and civilian personnel when Ishii took command to some 3,000 scientists, technicians, and soldiers during the war. His organization quickly outgrew its Harbin facility and in 1938 was moved to a new complex at Pingfan, 15 miles south of Harbin. This was the world's first major biological-warfare installation. Over a two-year period about 150 buildings were constructed to house Unit 731, which rapidly became self-supporting, raising its own vegetables and livestock. Its complex included research and medical facilities, extensive production factories, animal kennels, power generators, a railroad siding, barracks, and dining halls, with a highly secure prison behind its surrounding walls. A school was also provided to train specialists for service in Army field units.

Scientists and technicians working in laboratories and production rooms were provided with rubberized protective suits and respirators. The officers assigned to Pingfan received dangerous service pay of an extra 60 yen ($25) per month, while enlisted men received additional food rations. The area around the sprawling Unit 731 facility—soon known as Togo—became one of the most affluent and modern villages in Manchuria.

Major branches of Unit 731 were subsequently established at Hailar, Hailun (also known as Botanko or Mutanchiang), Linkow (Rinkou), Songo, and smaller stations at other locations in the region. An expansive test area was provided for Unit 731's weapons at Anta, in the remote plains area of Manchuria. A seven-plane aviation detachment helped to test its biological weapons.

In 1940, Ishii was promoted to major general, and under his guidance Unit 731 explored ways to counter as well as to spread diseases. Biological defensive measures were important because the Japanese believed that the Soviets were using germs in their sabotage operations against Japanese activities in Manchuria. They also blamed Soviet-produced germs for the deaths from cholera of 6,000 Japanese soldiers in Shanghai and 2,000 Army horses killed by anthrax infections.

Unquestionably, however, Ishii's main efforts were in offensive biological warfare, especially deploying plague, cholera, and typhoid, and how to cause frostbite and gas gangrene among enemy troops. Researchers at Pingfan used men and women as involuntary test subjects, exposing them to unspeakable pain and suffering as they were injected with germs, fed infected foods, and bitten by rodents and fleas. The testing of frostbite and other types of cold exposure on human subjects was equally appalling. In some tests the victims were tied to stakes at prescribed distances from where bombs were detonated. Their heads and other parts of their bodies were covered so that only selected skin areas were exposed to explosions of germ-infected shrapnel. After being wounded, they were returned to Pingfan for monitoring until they died—or were killed.

The human beings used in Ishii's biological experiments are believed to have included some 3,000 Chinese, Koreans, and Manchurians. British sources contend that some of the American survivors of the 1942 Bataan Death March were also used in the experiments. This has never been confirmed or denied by official U.S. sources, although documentation once existed and U.S. officers conducted extensive interviews with members of Ishii's staff. Australian prisoners, Manchurian bandits, and Japanese petty criminals were also reported among the test victims. Those prisoners who survived the experiments were poisoned or machine-gunned when Soviet troops approached Pingfan in August 1945. Most of the bodies were then burned.

The mass production of biological agents was undertaken at Pingfan, which is reported to have had a productive capacity of eight tons of bacteria per month. A number of methods of spreading these biological agents were considered, among them unleashing hordes of infected rats or fleas on enemy armies, dropping them from aircraft or in special bombs. Standard bombs with metal casings could not be used because the explosive needed to shatter the casing would also kill the infected fleas. Ishii then conceived the idea of porcelain bombs, which were produced at a Unit 731 facility in Harbin. The 55-pound weapon carried fleas as well as oxygen to enable them to survive the high-altitude flight. When fuses detonated the bomb, it would shatter, spewing its deadly cargo of some 30,000 fleas, with the casing bursting into minuscule fragments, leaving no trace.

After more than 2,000 of these *Uji* bombs were tested, they were considered ready for operational use in 1944. Bombs carrying tetanus and anthrax bacilli were considered most appropriate for battlefield use, while typhoid and dysentery were thought more suitable for infecting troops in rear areas. A variation of the bomb was the "mother and daughter" concept, which could more accurately control the altitude of detonation of the *Uji* bomb. This weapon was in two parts: When the "mother" struck the ground, its radio link with the still airborne "daughter" was broken, and the ceramic bomb would explode, spreading its deadly fleas. A bomb with thin steel walls, called *Ha,* was also developed for releasing the anthrax bacilli. The *Ha* would shatter into thousands of pieces of shrapnel, each contaminated and estimated to have a 90 percent probability of causing death from an infected wound.

Several other types of bombs for delivering germs were considered and tested, as well as such "unconventional" means of delivery as dropping infected feathers. A Japanese Navy enlisted ordnance specialist, captured in February 1945, stated that a bacterial bomb, known as Mark 7, was developed from the Navy's 2.2-pound practice or smoke-signal bomb. He did not know details of the weapon but had heard that the bacteria might be carried in a "mold formation." On Kwajalein Atoll, American troops found references to a Mark 7 bomb with the notation "Bacteria disseminating bomb" and an indication that it was a 110-pound weapon. Still another reference—a notebook found on Kwajalein belonging to Lieutenant (junior grade) Akiraji Watanabe—noted a bacillus bomb for use against "cities, water reservoirs, animals, personnel." These and other references to different Mark 7 bacterial bombs indicated that the designation may have been a classification for biological weapons.

There was, however, no evidence that the bombs were in production. U.S. intelligence also recovered a secret order issued by the Navy Minister, Admiral Shigetaro Shimada, that "definitely connects the Jap Navy with Bacteriological Warfare." The order discussed the pay of employees working on "chemical agents" at various Navy facilities, defining "chemical agents" to include "Bacteriological Warfare agents."

Besides developing biological bombs, Ishii's Unit 731 produced devices for individual plague infection through fountain pens and pointed walking sticks and techniques for clandestinely poisoning drinking wells. The unit also developed a defoliation bacilli bomb that could destroy vegetation in an area of 20 square miles. Unit 731 experimented with (but discarded) artillery shells carrying gas as well as biological agents.

And in another research project, Unit 731 looked into using balloons to spread germs. This was especially significant because large balloons were

Lieutenant General Shiro Ishii, commanding officer of Unit 731, the secret Japanese biological warfare organization that performed lethal experiments on prisoners of war.

developed *and used* to attack the United States. During 1944–1945 the Japanese launched paper balloons carrying incendiary bombs to set fires in U.S. forests. The balloons were blown eastward from Japan at altitudes of 30,000 to 50,000 feet at speeds of 20 to 150 knots and reached the United States and Canada from three to five days after launching.

Remnants of incendiary balloons were first found in the northwestern United States in November 1944. By March 1945 there were confirmed reports of 100 per month crossing the North Pacific, but the numbers then declined, probably because the velocity of the winds across the North Pacific decreases as summer approaches. A total of some 9,300 of these incendiary balloons were launched, although only a few successfully made the 6,200-mile Pacific crossing to the northwestern United States. U.S. Army specialists were concerned that the balloons were, in fact, carrying germs, but none of Ishii's biological agents were used. Japanese proposals to load the balloons with germs were made by Ishii's Unit 731 in July 1944. One plan called for having the balloons drop the anthrax bacteria. Another would have spread cattle-plague viruses to destroy livestock or grain smut to devastate food crops. Ultimately, the balloon-germ ideas were vetoed by high-ranking Japanese officials, who feared that if Japan launched biological warfare against the United States, similar retaliation would be swift and massive.

The balloons that were sent did not contain germs—only incendiary bombs. The balloons looked so harmless that one South Dakota man carried a balloon bomb over rough roads in the trunk of his car. Another gave one to his children to use as a dollhouse. Witnesses in Wyoming reported a "phantom plane," and a woman in Colorado told an intelligence officer not to use her name in a report because her friends "think I'm having hallucinations."

The effects of the balloon warfare were essentially nil. But on May 5, 1945, Mrs. Elsie Mitchell and five children were killed. While fishing in Lake County, Oregon, they found a Japanese balloon bomb that detonated when they examined it. They were the only casualties of enemy action on the U.S. mainland during the war.

General Ishii's biological-warfare agents were repeatedly used in the war against China. Nanking was a Japanese center for bacteriological and chemical warfare research. In what had been a Chinese hospital, Japanese researchers bred disease-bearing fleas and lice, injected prisoners with snake venom, and tested poison gases on victims strapped in a chair in a chamber with an observation window.

On October 4, 1940, a lone Japanese plane circled over the town of Chühsien in Chekiang Province and scattered rice and wheat grains believed to be infected with fleas. A number of townspeople took ill, and 23 died of a plague-type illness. Three weeks later there was a release of infected wheat grain over the port of Ningpo, and 99 persons succumbed to plague. In a third incident, on November 4, 1941, a lone plane over Chengteh in Hunan Province released wheat and rice grains and pieces of paper and cotton that, upon scientific examination, appeared to have been infected. Plague also struck Chengteh. These were areas that had not experienced plague in many decades.

Several more strange flights of a single aircraft dropping material that was apparently infected were recorded over China. Traces of plague bacteria were found at some sites. Reports of these events in China led President Roosevelt and Prime Minister Churchill to threaten retaliation if biological weapons were employed against Allied forces. And it spurred on the efforts by American and British scientists to develop horror weapons and defenses against them.

It is difficult to ascertain precisely how far up in the Japanese high command there was knowledge of Ishii's diabolical research. The size of his budget, between 6 and 12 million yen per year (up to $5 million) and Ishii's promotion to lieutenant general in 1945 certainly brought Unit 731 and its activities to the attention of the highest military authorities. Also, a civilian bacteriologist working for the Japanese Army in Canton and an Army officer–pharmacist captured by American troops were able to name Ishii as head of the Japanese Army's biological research program.

When the war ended in August 1945, Ishii tried to erase all traces of Unit 731. Efforts were made to destroy all equipment, facilities, documents, and human test subjects, and Japanese personnel of the unit were given the highest priority for evacuation back to Japan before Soviet troops entered the area. These last arrangements also needed high-level approval. Ishii and several of his senior officers were interrogated by U.S. military investigators after the war. They were not brought to trial as war criminals, although some Pingfan officers captured in Manchuria by the Soviets were tried. Ishii came to the United States and lectured at Camp Detrick in 1948.

General Ishii and Unit 731 were ready to wage biological warfare from May 1944 onward. There were reports that the following month, as American troops assaulted Saipan in the Marianas, Ishii dispatched a 17-man team that was to land on Saipan and release plague-infected fleas. However, the ship carrying the specialists was said to have been torpedoed and sunk by a U.S. submarine. There was one survivor of the team.

What of the subsequent American thrusts in the Philippines, Iwo Jima, Okinawa, and the home islands? By 1944 senior Japanese officers appeared to doubt their ability to defend their own troops against gas or biological weapons while crediting U.S. forces with superior offensive weapons. Indeed, on July 15, 1944, Japanese commanders were directed not to use munitions, such as smoke shells, that could be mistaken for gas. "Every precaution must be taken not to give the enemy cause for a pretext to use gas," declared the Japanese high command. Troops going into Malaya in

February 1942 were told, "There is a possibility that the present enemy [the British], unlike the Chinese Army, may use gas."

The Japanese high command also rejected the use of chemical and biological weapons against U.S. forces in the Philippines, Iwo Jima, and Okinawa. But would they have rejected them on the beaches of Kyushu or Honshu? There is virtually no evidence on either side of the question—except the fact that the landings at Kyushu were to be resisted by all possible means—in a plan to increase the number of deaths among the Americans so there would be a negotiated end to the war. The sacrifice of thousands or millions of Japanese troops and even civilians would be readily accepted in these final battles. The use of horror weapons could have accomplished the goal of inflicting massive American casualties on the beaches, albeit at the cost of sacrificing many more Japanese.

Both sides had horror weapons of some kind available throughout the war. The Americans considered them a means to reduce casualties; the Japanese looked at them as a means to increase casualties—American. Thus far, their existence had led to mutual deterrence, but as the Pacific War approached its climax, the question that had to be asked was which side would use them first.

CHAPTER 9

"I HAVE TO DECIDE"

President Truman meets with Prime Minister Winston Churchill and Soviet dictator Joseph Stalin at Potsdam, where Truman learned of the successful test of the first atomic bomb at Alamogordo, New Mexico.

Victory in Europe in May 1945 brought an anticipation of peace in the United States. But on VE-Day Japanese soldiers were still fighting and killing Americans in the Philippines and on Okinawa. Japanese kamikaze aircraft were still crashing into American warships and transports. Japanese submarines were still going to sea. And an army of some four million men, plus untold millions of civilians, were preparing to die for their Emperor in a final defense of their homeland.

The Pacific War had yet to be won. But in Washington, congressmen urged military leaders to discharge European combat veterans and begin conversion to peacetime production. The Army, concerned over the "discharge itch," discovered that an overwhelming percentage of soldiers in Europe believed they would be going home within six months after VE-Day. "This 'Why Me?' kind of thinking is the greatest obstacle we face," an Army indoctrination paper said. "It is the source of Japan's last hope." The paper, a guide for discussions that junior officers were to have with their men, said: "The Japanese leaders know that they are lost, that their cause is hopeless except for one possibility: that our resolution will weaken and our attack lose its force."

Truman's military advisers began asking questions about surrender. Can unconditional surrender be modified? Will Japan suddenly give up because of Germany's surrender? If Japan's political leaders agree to a surrender, will the military decide to fight on? Secretary of War Stimson was suggesting that the United States change its war aim from unconditional surrender to "complete defeat and permanent destruction of the war making power of Japan." General Marshall endorsed the idea, urging that leaders stop talking about unconditional surrender without "giving any impression that we are growing soft."

Truman knew that the Soviets had agreed to enter the war against Japan within 90 days after VE-Day. But the State Department worried about the designs of the Soviet Union in Europe and the Pacific. Ambassador to Moscow Averell Harriman, a suave aristocrat with more than a touch of condescension toward the new President, warned Truman that the Soviets were launching a "barbarian invasion of Europe." Stimson and his Interim Committee wondered what the United States should tell Stalin about "S-1," his code for the atomic bomb. These problems, all entwined with the plan to invade Japan, ended up on the desk of Harry Truman, the Commander in

Chief, the man who had the final responsibility for finding a way to end what he called "the Jap War."

Among the most important sources of information that reached Truman were intelligence reports titled " 'Magic'—Diplomatic Summary." The Magic reports gave the President, along with a few high officials and military commanders, the ability to eavesdrop on diplomats of Japan and several other countries. This clandestine intelligence added immeasurably to Truman's education as Commander in Chief and provided him with invaluable insights into the thinking of Japanese leaders as they planned their endgame of the war.

Magic was the code-name for the efforts that in 1935 had cracked Japanese diplomatic codes generated by machine cipher. After the Japanese began to use a new code machine and cipher in March 1939, American cryptologists managed to replicate the machine, and the reading of the diplomatic codes continued. Subsequently, when Japanese naval and Army codes were cracked, products of those decrypts were added to the military section of the Magic summaries, which were circulated separately from the diplomatic summaries. Throughout World War II, Japan's political and military leaders did not know that a massive U.S. intelligence network was intercepting, decoding, and translating their most secret diplomatic and military messages. Nor were other countries aware that their diplomats' messages were also being read by U.S. intelligence and made part of the Magic summaries.

The summaries carried the maximum security label of the time: *Top Secret Ultra*. They were so secret that the few officials allowed to see them were told never to disclose what they read in Magic. A statement on the cover sheet of each summary warned: "No action is to be taken on information herein reported, regardless of temporary advantage, if such action might have the effect of revealing the existence of the source to the enemy." Release of the Magic summaries did not begin until the 1970s; many remained secret until 1993, and even those summaries still have censored pages.

Piecing together the flow of the intercepts, Truman and his advisers saw unmistakable signs that Japan, anticipating the U.S. invasion, was preparing for a *Götterdämmerung*. As Germany was about to fall, for example, the Japanese Army General Staff sent a message to the Japanese military attaché in Lisbon asking that the "battle of resistance" in Germany "be reported as fully as possible in order to furnish reference material for the decisive battle in our homeland and particularly for the training of special guard units and citizens' volunteer units. . . . In this way, we shall make firm our determination to defend the capital to the bitter end."

Magic was also intercepting the diplomatic traffic of neutral nations, gaining information from relatively objective eyewitnesses in Tokyo. An intercepted message from the Portuguese minister in Japan, for instance, said that "the fortification of coasts and mountains continues, giving the impression that this country, like Germany, is disposed to prosecute the war to its very end without the least probability of victory. . . . A national guard is being organized to fight as guerrillas against the invaders."

An intercepted dispatch from the Swiss minister in Tokyo said that Japan "is still hoping to escape [defeat] by prolonging the war long enough to exhaust [its] enemies. Many eagerly desire the landing of the Americans in Japan proper, since they think it would be the last chance to inflict upon the Americans a defeat serious enough to make them come to terms. These sentiments correspond quite well to those of the Germans before the landing in Normandy."

The intercepts showed that Japan was stepping up production in preparation for an expected "enemy landing on the homeland," with "number-one priority" given to "the materials needed to manufacture airplanes." Another summary carried a Japanese report on the stepping up of industrial production in northern China, Manchuria, and Korea. The move, the report said, was a way of "freeing ourselves from dependence on the resources of the South" and setting up "an organization to bring about continental self-sufficiency." That meant that if Japanese military forces were defeated in the home islands, they could evacuate and continue to fight in Manchuria.

One Japanese diplomat urged that German leaders and matériel be moved to French Indochina, Thailand, or Java so that Japan and Germany could "fight a joint war to the bitter end." But other Japanese diplomats advised against any association between Japan and a defeated Germany. The Japanese minister in Berne, for example, said that "any impression that Japan is following a policy with the Nazis to the bitter end should be avoided as far as possible. . . . No government-in-exile will be permitted in Japanese-controlled territory."

Baron Kantaro Suzuki, the aged admiral who became premier following the invasion of Okinawa in April 1945, had declared that Japan's only course was "to fight to the very end," even if it meant the death of "one hundred million" Japanese. The appointment of the 78-year-old Suzuki was approved by the Japanese Army only after he had promised senior Army officers that he would never surrender. Suzuki's minister of war showed what he thought of peace sentiments by ordering the arrest of 400 people suspected of harboring end-the-war opinions. Yet Suzuki allowed a potential peacemaker into his Cabinet.

Career diplomat Shigenori Togo accepted the post of foreign minister only after Suzuki promised to end the war if he determined that Japan could last for at least three more years. Togo, who favored Savile Row suits and Turkish cigarettes, was relatively worldly compared to the other members of the Cabinet. He had served in Moscow and in Berlin, where he met and married a German woman. A shrewd careerist, he preached peace while going along with war. When Tojo appointed him foreign minister in October 1941, he had insisted that Japan was not planning to go to war beyond

China. He quit the Tojo Cabinet in September 1942 over a bureaucratic issue, but he later would claim that it had been inspired by his yearning for peace.

Truman understood that Suzuki and Togo were playing a complex game. Magic intercepts revealed that the Japanese hoped to negotiate a separate peace with Chiang Kai-shek, allowing the transfer of more than a million soldiers from China and Formosa to the Decisive Battle on the beaches of the home islands, the final campaign that would bring the war to an honorable but cataclysmic end. At the same time, Foreign Minister Togo set in motion a "peace" plan in an effort to keep the Soviet Union out of the war and to entice Stalin into mediating a peace settlement. Naotake Sato, Japan's ambassador to the Soviet Union, told Tokyo that by acting as peacemakers, the Soviets "would achieve without effort an international position surpassing that of their allies, a point which will not escape the eagle-eyed Stalin." Togo believed that a Stalin-brokered peace settlement would be more favorable to Japan than the unconditional surrender demanded by the United States and Great Britain.

The germ of the idea seems to have come from a long, philosophic analysis of the world after VE-Day, transmitted to Togo on May 14 from Berne by Shonichi Kase, the Japanese minister to Switzerland. He suggested that "we work out a plan for changing the situation by diplomatic means." His target was the Soviet Union. The Americans, he said, "wishing to defeat Japan as quickly and at as small a cost as possible . . . desire to use the strength of the Soviet Union in the war against Japan. . . ." The key to Kase's plan was to split off the Soviets from the Americans and British by approaching "the Russians with a proposal for a general peace, asking for their help and offering them a considerable reward."

Soviet Foreign Affairs Commissar V.M. Molotov had announced in a terse statement on April 5, four days after U.S. troops invaded Okinawa, that the Soviet government would not renew its Neutrality Pact with Japan when it expired in April 1946. When Ambassador Sato asked him for clarification, the wily Molotov said that his government would continue to maintain its neutrality toward Japan until the scheduled expiration of the pact. And as the Soviets began to worry the Japanese about their future intentions, in Manila, Red Army Lieutenant-General Kuzma Derevyanko, moving toward those intentions, was discussing Soviet plans for the invasion of Manchuria with General MacArthur's intelligence staff.

Although the Soviets did not tell their American allies about the Japanese moves, Truman, through Magic, was informed of their attempts to woo the Soviets. Magic also allowed Truman to know something the Soviets did not know: that Japan had detailed knowledge of the Soviet buildup along the Manchurian border. Magic picked up the reports of Japanese diplomatic couriers traveling in the Soviet Union who had seen trainloads of Red Army troops and military supplies moving to the Soviet Manchurian frontier. Their messages, duly reported by Magic, added up to a massive movement of troops, vehicles, guns, aircraft, and horses. The military traffic taxed the Trans-Siberian Railway to its "maximum capacity," Ambassador Sato reported to Tokyo. "Construction of sidings and expansion of rail facilities were observed to be going on 'everywhere.'"

Couriers, hiding in places where they could spot trains, began 24-hour watches and saw "an average of 30 eastbound trains a day carrying military supplies and troops." Other couriers reported 195 eastbound military trains carrying 64,000 troops and construction and military equipment as well as about 500 tank cars believed to be "full of fuel oil and aviation gasoline."

Magic intercepts also showed that a clandestine radio transmitter had begun broadcasting anti-Japanese comments aimed at stirring up Russians in Manchuria. Harbin, the transportation hub of northern Manchuria, was known as the "Moscow of the Orient" because so many Russians lived there. The Japanese consul general in Harbin reported to Tokyo that he believed the broadcasts were part of a plan for a Soviet invasion of Manchuria on the pretext of protecting its Russian inhabitants. Alarmed by these signs of Soviet hostility, in a message to Japanese diplomats in Manchuria, Togo said, "We must maintain neutrality at all costs."

Because Sato's dispatches to Tokyo were often cast in dialogue form, the intercepts let Truman and other Magic readers literally eavesdrop on conversations between the ambassador and Molotov. Sato began a meeting on May 29 by saying, "I earnestly hope that no important change will take place in our present relations." Molotov, "extremely friendly and warm," changed the subject and said, "I would now like to ask your opinion as to how long the Pacific War will last."

"Japan follows Russia's example in her desire to end hostilities as quickly as possible," Sato replied. "The Pacific War, however, is a matter of life and death for Japan, and as a result of America's attitude, we have no choice but to continue the fight. May I inquire concerning the views of the Russian government, which is a neutral in this war?"

"Russia is not a belligerent," Molotov said. "We have had our fill of war in Europe, and our only desire is to obtain a guarantee of future peace. What do the Japanese leaders think of their chances in the Pacific War?"

"It has now become clearly impossible for Japan to submit," Sato said. "Japan is fighting for her very existence and must continue to fight."

The next day, Sato transmitted a pessimistic assessment of his meeting with Molotov. He made rare use of a special communications channel apparently available only to him in Moscow and top Foreign Office officials in Tokyo. He asked how far Japan was "willing to go in making concessions to Russia."

• • •

To give President Truman the most useful diplomatic information, the creators of the Magic summaries had to do more than translate Japanese words and phrases into English. There was always the problem of *haragei,* the Japanese art of saying one thing while meaning another. When a Japanese official publicly stated a desire to fight to the end, did he really mean it? "In the light of *haragei,*" wrote historian Robert J.C. Butow, "the efforts of a number of end-the-war advocates defy easy analysis. Because of its very ambiguity, a plea of *haragei* invites the suspicion that in questions of politics and diplomacy a conscious reliance upon this 'art of the bluff' may have constituted a purposeful deception predicated upon a desire to play both ends against the middle."

To American eavesdroppers, the observations of diplomats in Japan were vague and confusing. The German naval attaché in Tokyo heard rumors of Japanese interest in "capitulation even if the terms were hard, provided they were halfway honorable." There were diplomatic reports of "war weariness" among Japanese naval officers but no indications of such sentiments in the Army leadership.

American diplomats and intelligence operatives were also detecting Japanese negotiation feelers. Allen Dulles, the chief American intelligence representative in Switzerland, was talking to Commander Yoshiro Fujimura, a Japanese naval attaché in Berne, and a mysterious German who served as a purchasing agent for the Japanese Navy. Dulles, who had negotiated the surrender of German forces in Italy in April 1945, was seen by Fujimura as a likely conduit for talks. Although he never met with Dulles, he did send a flurry of cables to Japan seeking in vain to play a role as a conveyor of negotiation offers. Neither the United States nor Japan showed any serious interest in the efforts of Fujimura or the independent and similarly futile approaches by Japan's military attaché in Switzerland, who later killed himself.

In another diplomatic sortie, Matsutaro Inoune, counselor of the Japanese Embassy in Lisbon, approached Kurt Sell, a German journalist who was also an agent working for the American espionage agency, the Office of Strategic Services. Inoune, apparently aware of Sell's double role, asked him to find out from the American Embassy how the United States would react to a negotiated peace, since Japan would never accept unconditional surrender.

Lisbon was such a spy center that the Chinese minister there heard of Inoune's approach and reported it to his government in Chungking. That message was also intercepted. The Magic summary reported that Inoune was hoping for a negotiated peace; the terms were unimportant so long as the expression "unconditional surrender" was not used. Inoune said that the Japanese were convinced that within a few weeks all the wood-and-paper houses in Japan would be destroyed, but even that would not bring about unconditional surrender. If necessary, he said, the Japanese would fight on in China for years.

Whatever the truth of Japanese interest in negotiations, President Truman believed he had to be inflexible about unconditional surrender, a war aim that had almost total popular and congressional support. The first test of the doctrine had come when Italy surrendered on September 8, 1943. The surrender had been unconditional, but it had been preceded by complicated negotiations with representatives of Marshal Pietro Badoglio, Chief of the Italian General Staff and Italian head of state since the overthrow of Benito Mussolini two months earlier.

Two aspects of Italy's surrender foreshadowed questions that could arise in a Japanese surrender. What happens to the military forces when politicians surrender? And what happens to the ruling monarch? Italian Army units in Italy and abroad had been left on their own at the surrender. Most of the one million Italian soldiers in Italy, demoralized and cut adrift by their high command, were easily disarmed by 400,000 German troops. Another 900,000 Italian soldiers were scattered throughout Europe. Germans also disarmed those units, except for a division in Greece. Those Italians resisted, and more than 9,600 died fighting Germans. Did that last-ditch stand in Greece foreshadow what could happen if Japanese troops in Manchuria fought on after surrender? Fanatical Japanese had continued to fight after the capture of Okinawa and other islands, and after the Philippines were liberated. And there was the very real possibility of at least guerrilla resistance after the capitulation of Japan, whatever the terms of surrender.

Accompanied by King Emmanuel and the Italian Cabinet, Badoglio fled from Rome to Brindisi in southern Italy and proclaimed it the capital of the new Italy. The Allies' surrender terms, however, called for the installation of a democratic government. In June 1944, following the Allied liberation of Rome, the king abdicated, Badoglio stepped down, and Italy began forging a democratic nation. But would Emperor Hirohito step down after surrender? Or would he flee from Tokyo and, like King Emmanuel, proclaim a new imperial capital?

Some planners feared that a public peace proposal from Japan could have an impact on U.S. opinion. "War weariness in the United States," a JCS memo said, "might then lead to some public demand for acceptance of a Japanese offer designed to prevent both invasion of the home islands and our prosecution of the war to a point which would destroy Japanese capacity to start a new war." To thwart such a Japanese move, the memo suggested, the United States should reaffirm its unwavering demand for unconditional surrender.

Japan's soldiers, unlike those of other warring nations, lived by a no-surrender code. During the European War, military units on both sides had surrendered when their commanders found the situation hopeless. But no organized Japanese military unit of any size had yet surrendered in the Pacific War. Soldiers fought under orders that said, "Do not live in shame as a prisoner. Die, and leave no ignominious crime behind you!"

In his VE-Day statement President Truman had, in fact, slightly modified the implication of unconditional surrender. Stimson had urged the change, as had Navy Secretary James Forrestal and Joseph C. Grew, U.S. Ambassador to Japan when Pearl Harbor was attacked and now Acting Secretary of State. What had been "unconditional surrender" became in Truman's statement "unconditional surrender of the armed forces." And that, Truman said, meant "the termination of the influence of the military leaders who brought Japan to the present brink of disaster." It also meant "provision for the return of soldiers and sailors to their families, their farms, and their jobs." Unconditional surrender, he concluded, "does not mean extermination or enslavement of the Japanese people."

A report on surrender policy, prepared by JCS planners at Stimson's request, said in early June that the Japanese were basing "their protracted resistance . . . upon the hope of achieving a conditional surrender. Presumably, only the conviction that their position is hopeless will persuade them to give up their holdings in Asia. Probably it will take Russian entry into the war, coupled with a landing, or imminent threat of landing, on Japan proper by us, to convince them of the hopelessness of their position." A second study, issued a few days later, urged "a public declaration of war aims, in effect giving definition to 'unconditional' surrender."

Truman, preparing for a Big Three meeting in Germany with Churchill and Stalin, was far more interested in the reality of Soviet participation in the Pacific War than in theories about unconditional surrender. "Our military experts," he later wrote, "had estimated that an invasion of Japan would cost at least five hundred thousand American casualties even if the Japanese forces then in Asia were held on the Chinese mainland." Without the Red Army on that mainland, he realized, the casualties would be immensely larger. He also observed, "Russia's entry into the war would mean the saving of hundreds of thousands of American casualties," a figure he shortly increased to "at least five hundred thousand."

Truman sent Harry Hopkins, an old hand at special missions, to Moscow, telling him that the United States needed to get "as early a date as possible on Russia's entry into the war against Japan." On May 28, 1945, Hopkins cabled Truman to report that Stalin had said that the Red Army "will be properly deployed on the Manchurian positions by August 8th. . . . He left no doubt in our mind that he intends to attack during August."

The news from Hopkins reassured Truman, who now had firsthand confirmation that the Red Army soon would be fighting Japanese soldiers. But if Truman saw Soviet entry as a way to save American lives in the final assault on Japan, was an invasion really necessary? Advisers gave him conflicting counsel. Admirals Leahy and King still insisted that blockade and bombing could bring eventual victory without a costly invasion. General Arnold, of course, believed his bombers alone could bring about Japan's capitulation. General Marshall, backed by MacArthur, said that the war could be ended only by an invasion of Japan and a simultaneous Red Army invasion of Manchuria.

Still, the U.S. war effort was clearly shutting down. The Army, 8.3 million strong on VE-Day, was being substantially reduced through demobilization spurred by Congress. Men were to be discharged under a point system: one point for each month of service, one for each month overseas, and five for each of several specified decorations and for participation in an officially recognized battle. A father got 12 points for each child under 18, up to three children. A total of 85 points would make a man a potential civilian.

The Army said there would be no discharges for "men possessing special skills required in the war against Japan" or men who had to be shipped to the Pacific "so swiftly that no opportunity is provided for replacing" them. The "special skills" exemption caught many airmen, for the Army Air Forces declared two-thirds of its military specialties as essential. And many of the men in the "so swiftly" category were black soldiers—the pick-and-shovel GIs who would build the port facilities and air bases needed for the invasion of Japan.

Black troops, who in late stages of the war went overseas in combat units, would not be among the invaders of Japan. Walter White, head of the National Association for the Advancement of Colored People, had complained to President Roosevelt about the Army's treatment of black troops, focusing on a division serving under MacArthur—the 93rd Infantry. MacArthur, attacking White as "a troublemaker and a menace to the war effort," said the 93rd was inferior to other divisions "except in the matter of motor maintenance," with poor morale—"as evidenced by courts martials, homosexual activities, selfmaiming, alleged discrimination, etcetera." MacArthur said his decision to order the division to a rear area was "not, repeat not influenced in the slightest degree by race or color. . . ." The 93rd would not be included in MacArthur's order of battle for the invasion of Japan.

Demobilization meant little to men in the Pacific War. The Navy and Marine Corps were not cutting back, and the Army said no one could be released until another man could take his place. Men in the Pacific knew they would not get home until Japan was conquered, mile by bloody mile. And those who had survived amphibious landings and kamikaze attacks now wondered what their chances were for surviving the final landing, the final kamikaze attack.

The war in Europe, from the invasion of Normandy on June 6, 1944, to the German surrender 11 months later, had cost 135,576 American lives. Military planners expected the war against Japan to be almost as long—until the fall of 1946—and bloodier, whatever military strategy was pursued. In the conflicting counsel offered by Truman's top commanders, that was the one constant: answers to his questions about how many American lives would be lost.

To Truman, most generals and admirals were "just like horses with blinders on. They can't see beyond the ends of their noses, most of them." But, he quickly added, "General Marshall was an exception to every rule that ever was." The new President trusted Marshall, and his frequent talks with the general, along with repeated visits to the White House Map Room, enabled Truman to grasp the military complexities of the Pacific War. But he knew that he alone would have to make the final decisions about how that war was won.

The European War had been a war of familiar places, an air and land war across France and into Germany, a war with British and Soviet allies. The Pacific War had been an American war with little help from the Allies— except for the Australians. It was a war on, over, and beneath the vast Pacific Ocean, a war of soldiers and Marines dying on islands that Americans had never heard of until they saw the headlines of their morning newspapers and read about the invasion of still another Pacific atoll. It was a remote, complicated war. The supply lines from the United States to the Pacific War were two to three times as long as the U.S. supply lines to Europe, and without the kind of large forward base that Britain had provided.

The Japanese Empire encompassed, in land area, a territory larger than that of the continental United States. And besides the Japanese troops in the home islands there were troops in China, Korea, Malaya, Thailand, Singapore, Indochina, Burma, and Manchuria, along with remnants of garrisons in the Dutch East Indies and New Guinea. Even after an invasion of the home islands, American forces might face a lengthy war of attrition. And the war might end not with a VJ-Day but with a long, frustrating series of skirmishes with Japanese holdouts in widely scattered outposts. China might well make a separate peace, leaving a formidable Japanese force living off the land there and refusing to surrender.

Japan in early 1945 had about four million men under arms; the United States had about 1.5 million men in the Pacific. And the United States stood nearly alone. For a final assault on Japan, there was little likelihood of much help from European Allies, with one exception—the Soviet Union.

In the strategies that Army and Navy planners were drawing up for the invasion of Japan, the Soviet Union was a key participant despite the problems the United States had had with this truculent ally throughout the war. In fact, the Soviets often treated American servicemen more as agents of a foreign power than as allies. When B-29s bombing Manchuria made emergency landings on Soviet airfields in 1944–1945, for example, the crews were interrogated and interned for more than a month before being released to American officials at the Iranian border. At Stalin's orders, the B-29s were minutely examined, copied by the Tupolev design bureau, and subsequently mass-produced in the Soviet Union with the designation Tu-4.

The only major military cooperation between the two nations had been a shuttle-bombing operation, code-named Frantic, in which U.S. aircraft took off from bases in England and Italy, attacked German targets in Eastern and Central Europe, and flew on to land at air bases in the Ukraine. There U.S.-Soviet teams serviced the aircraft, which flew back to their home bases, striking other targets along the way. The operation, which began in June 1944, soon broke down and was abandoned. The United States hoped that a similar operation could be resumed in Siberia so that U.S. bombers could strike Japanese targets. But the Soviets refused to authorize such an operation, and the venture officially ended in June 1945. Stalin's promise to enter the war against Japan had reassured Truman, but there was no guarantee that the Soviets would not pursue their own agenda independent of, or even in conflict with, America's plans for the invasion.

On June 14, Admiral Leahy sent a memo to the Chiefs of Staff saying that the President wanted to meet with them on June 18 "to discuss details of our campaign against Japan." Truman, Leahy said, "expects at this meeting to be thoroughly informed of our intentions and prospects in preparation for his discussions with Churchill and Stalin." He also wanted specific information, as listed by Leahy:

• The number of men of the Army and ships of the Navy that will be necessary to defeat Japan
• An estimate of the time required and an estimate of the losses in killed and wounded that will result from an invasion of Japan proper
• An estimate of the time and the losses that will result from an effort to defeat Japan by isolation, blockade, and bombardment by sea and air forces
• Exactly what we want the Russians to do
• What useful contribution, if any, could be made by other Allied nations

"It is his intention," Leahy wrote, "to make his decisions on the campaign with the purpose of economizing to the maximum extent possible in the loss of American lives.

"Economy in the use of time and in money cost is comparatively unimportant."

The Joint Chiefs moved swiftly to prepare a major briefing for the President. Major General John E. Hull, chief of the Army's Operations Division, saw the heart of what Truman wanted, telling Brigadier General George Lincoln that "the President is very much perturbed over the losses on Okinawa." Hull suggested that Lincoln get for Marshall all the casualty information he could find, not only on Okinawa but also on Iwo Jima, Leyte, Luzon, and "overall figures on MacArthur's operations to date."

To get these figures, a priority message went out on June 16 from Marshall to MacArthur: "Request by 17 June (Washington [time]) the estimate you are using for planning purposes of battle casualties in OLYMPIC up to D + 90." MacArthur promptly sent these casualty numbers—expectations of dead, wounded, and missing—for 30-day increments from the landing, at the time referred to as D for D-Day.

$$D \text{ to } D + 30: 50,800$$
$$D + 30 \text{ to } D + 60: 27,150$$
$$D + 60 \text{ to } D + 90: 17,100$$

"The foregoing," he said, "are estimated total battle casualties from which estimated return to duty numbers are deducted. Not included in the foregoing are non battle casualties which are estimated at 4200 for each 30 day period."

Marshall was not satisfied. A few hours before the scheduled June 18 briefing, he sent another message to MacArthur:

> The President is very much concerned as to the number of casualties we will receive in the OLYMPIC operation. This will be discussed with the President about 3:30 PM today Washington time. Is the estimate given in your [message] of 50,800 for the period of D to D + 30 based on plans for medical installations to be established or is it your best estimate of the casualties you anticipate from the operational viewpoint. Please rush answer.

MacArthur apparently only now appreciated the extreme importance that the casualty rates would play in Truman's decision about the invasion. In his long reply, he backpedaled from his original estimate, saying it had been

> a routine report . . . for medical and replacement planning purposes. . . . The estimate is purely academic and routine and was made for planning alone. It had not come to my prior attention. I do not anticipate such a high rate of loss. I believe the operation presents less hazards of excessive loss than any other that has been suggested and that its decisive effect will eventually save lives by eliminating wasteful operations of a nondecisive character. I regard the operation as the most economical one in effort and lives that is possible. In this respect it must be remembered that the several preceding months will involve practically no losses in ground troops and that sooner or later a decisive ground attack must be made. The hazard and loss will be greatly lessened if an attack is launched from Siberia sufficiently ahead of our target date to commit the enemy to major combat. I most earnestly recommend no change in OLYMPIC. Additional subsidiary attacks will simply build up our final total casualties.

MacArthur, like Truman, realized the importance of Soviet action, and his final sentence indicated that he seemed to fear that Truman's concern over casualties might imperil the invasion itself.

Two other documents pertaining to the casualty estimates were prepared

Tending the dead and wounded during the assault on Iwo Jima. Scenes like this pervaded Truman's thoughts as he authorized the invasion of Japan and considered the use of the atomic bomb.

for Truman. One put the casualties as high as 220,000; the other said casualties would be closer to those suffered in the invasion of Luzon, 31,000. It was a remarkable discrepancy, and exactly what Truman believed would depend on which of the two briefing papers prepared for him he actually relied on.

Both top-secret documents were entitled "Memorandum for the President, Subject: Campaign against Japan." The first one, dated June 15, 1945, and subtitled "Details of the Campaign against Japan," was prepared by the Joint War Plans Committee, which, in a covering memo, recommended "that the enclosed memorandum be presented to the President at his conference with the Joint Chiefs of Staff," scheduled for June 18. The covering memo went on to say that the committee "has assumed that the questions brought up by the President will be answered and discussed orally at the conference, and that the purpose of the memorandum is for the President to have available an aide memoire which he could examine at his convenience and possibly use at the forthcoming tripartite conferences [a reference to the Potsdam Conference]." The second document, also subtitled "Details of the Campaign against Japan" but originating with the Joint Chiefs of Staff, was dated July 11—five days before the Potsdam Conference, which most of the Joint Chiefs attended.

The two documents were almost identical as they went through sections labeled *Strategy, Presently planned campaign, Forces required for presently planned campaign.* Then came the section labeled *Casualties.*

The June memorandum said:

> *Casualties.* The cost in casualties of the main operations against Japan are [*sic*] not subject to accurate estimate. The scale of Japanese resistance in the past has not been predictable. Casualty expectancy rates based on experience in the Pacific vary greatly from the short bloody battle of Tarawa to the unopposed landing at Lingayen [Luzon]. It would be difficult to predict whether Jap resistance on Kyushu would more closely resemble the fighting on Okinawa or whether it would parallel the battle of Leyte. Certain general conclusions can, however, be reached. The highest casualty rate occurs during the assault phase of an amphibious operation; casualties in land warfare are a function of the length of the campaign and of the scale of opposition encountered. Naval casualties can be expected to vary directly with the number of amphibious operations involved and with the length of the campaign. Casualties can be kept to a minimum, then, by terminating the war at the earliest possible time by means of the fewest possible assault operations and by conducting land campaigns only in decisive areas. The presently planned campaign, which involves two assault operations followed by land campaigns in the Japanese homeland, is in conformity with this principle. Further, the extent of the objective area gives us an opportunity to effect surprise as to the points of landing and, once ashore, to profit by our superiority in mobility and mechanized power through maneuver. Should it be decided to follow the southern Kyushu operation by another operation such as against northern Kyushu in order to exploit bombardment and blockade, and should this bring about capitulation of the Japanese, the casualties should be less than for the presently planned campaign. We consider that at this time it would be a pure gamble that the Japanese would admit defeat under such conditions. If they do not, invasion of the Tokyo Plain might still be required with resultant increased total casualties.

The best estimate of casualties for these possible sequences of operations follows. For the reasons stated above, it is admittedly only an "educated guess."

The July memorandum, which would be the basis for Pacific War strategy discussion at Potsdam, had a drastically different prediction about casualties. And instead of preceding the estimates with a long, thoughtful explanation of how the estimates were made, the memorandum merely said:

	KILLED IN ACTION	WOUNDED IN ACTION	MISSING IN ACTION	TOTAL
Southern Kyushu, followed by Tokyo Plain, to mid-1946	40,000	150,000	3,500	193,500
Southern Kyushu; Northwestern Kyushu	25,000	105,000	2,500	132,500
Southern Kyushu; Northwestern Kyushu; Tokyo Plain	46,000	170,000	4,000	220,000

Casualties. Our casualty experience in the Pacific war has been so diverse as to throw serious doubt on the validity of any quantitative estimate of casualties for future operations. The following data indicate results of experience.

Then it gave this table:

CAMPAIGN	U.S. CASUALTIES KILLED, WOUNDED, MISSING	JAP CASUALTIES KILLED AND PRISONERS (NOT INCLUDING WOUNDED)	RATIO U.S. TO JAP
Leyte	17,000	78,000	1:4.6
Luzon	31,000	156,000	1:5.0
Iwo Jima	20,000	25,000	1:1.25
Okinawa	39,000 (ground) 7,700 (Navy)*	119,000 (not a complete count)	1:3
Normandy (1st 30 days)	42,000		

After the table, still under the *Casualties* heading, there were these paragraphs:

The record of General MacArthur's operations from 1 March 1944 through 1 May 1945 shows 13,742 U.S. killed compared to 310,165 Japanese killed, or a

---

* This is the first time Navy casualties are mentioned. At Okinawa, over 4,900 Navy men were killed and almost that many wounded. Off Kyushu, the casualties would have been higher—probably much higher.

ratio of 22 to 1. During this same period the total U.S. casualties, killed, wounded and missing, were 63,510 or a ratio of approximately 5 to 1.

The nature of the objective area in Kyushu gives maneuver room for land and sea operations. For these and other reasons it is probable that the cost in ground force casualties for the first 30 days of the Kyushu operation will be on the order of that for Luzon. Naval casualties will probably be at about the same rate as for Okinawa.

A paraphrase of General MacArthur's comments on the Kyushu operation (taken almost verbatim from his message to Marshall) followed, repeating his recommendation that "no change in the operation" be made for the invasion of southern Kyushu. It also advocated adherence to the plan to invade Honshu and the Tokyo Plain.

The difference between the two casualty tables was astonishing. The first used broad experience and objective criteria as its guide. The second blatantly reflected MacArthur's view of casualties as merely a U.S.-to-Japanese kill ratio. The table also gratuitously included a reference to D-Day casualties at Normandy—a reflection of one of MacArthur's perennial criticisms: Allied conduct of the European War. The second memo also showed that MacArthur—or at least MacArthuresque thinking—had already taken over the paper-pushing aspect of invasion.

Of the many sets of numbers and arguments that would be presented to the President, the most honest were those that MacArthur gave in response to Marshall's original message of June 16. In that response, MacArthur estimated that in the landing and three months of fighting on Kyushu, 94,250 men would be killed or wounded in battle, and another 12,600 would be felled by disease and accidents—a casualty total of 106,850.

The June 15 Joint War Plans Committee memo offered three scenarios and three sets of casualty estimates. If the Olympic-Coronet plan went according to schedule, there would be two landings, which were expected to result in a total of 193,500 battle casualties. If, as some planners believed, the Kyushu invasion ended the war, then the battle casualty count would be 132,500. The worst-case scenario envisioned *three* major amphibious assaults, and the estimated consequence of this triple invasion was 220,000 battle casualties. To all of these figures must be added the nonbattle casualties of accidents and disease. In that case, total casualties, in the triple-invasion scenario, would exceed 250,000 and were climbing toward 500,000.

The July JWPC memorandum, prepared for the Potsdam Conference, switched the casualty issue. Instead of presenting estimates of future casualties, the memorandum introduced two entirely different concepts: actual U.S. and Japanese casualties in four different campaigns and a gratuitous comparison of MacArthur's performance with that of the U.S. commanders in other theaters. MacArthur appeared to be a battlefield genius, killing or wounding 22 Japanese for every American killed or wounded, while elsewhere in the Pacific and in Europe other U.S. commanders were achieving only a 5:1 casualty ratio. The ratio argument apparently was prepared merely to soothe Truman into believing in MacArthur; it did not answer Truman's question about casualties.

That question haunted Truman as he considered the next moves in the war against Japan. As he saw it, he could authorize the invasion or order the use of the atomic bomb, which, he knew, was nearing reality. And if the bomb failed or was delayed, then invasion was still an option. The casualty estimates from his military advisers would profoundly influence his decision. Simply put, low estimates would give MacArthur and Marshall the invasion they and other Army leaders wanted. High estimates would make the invasion a far less attractive alternative to the bomb.

Navy leaders, mindful of the heavy toll kamikazes took on their ships at Leyte and Okinawa, tended toward pessimistic forecasts about the invasion. Leahy foresaw Okinawa-size casualty lists. Nimitz, in a memo to King, had said, "We must be prepared to accept heavy casualties whenever we invade Japan. Our previous successes against ill-fed and poorly supplied units, cut down by our overpowering naval and air action, should not be used as the sole basis of estimating the type of resistance we will meet in the Japanese homeland where the enemy lines of communication will be short and the enemy supplies more adequate."

Truman had stated his bomb-or-invade view in his diary on June 17: "I have to decide Japanese strategy—shall we invade Japan proper or shall we bomb and blockade?" He seemed to have been referring to conventional aerial bombardment, but he also had to make a decision about S-1, the code-name for the atomic bomb, which, of course, he did not mention in his diary. On June 16, the science panel of the all-civilian Interim Committee, headed by Stimson, had discussed a proposal to demonstrate the atomic bomb to intimidate the Japanese with its awesome power. But such a trial was totally impractical. There was some concern, albeit minor, that the bomb would simply not function properly. More significant was the possibility that if a suitable, uninhabited site could be found on the home islands, the Japanese would move Allied prisoners of war there. A test at a remote Pacific island would have been difficult to handle and would have taken a long time to arrange, especially since Japanese observers somehow would have to be transported to the site. Also, if the Japanese knew the time and location of the test, they could have attempted to shoot down the B-29 carrying the bomb—for, after all, there was a war going on, with fighting on Okinawa and in the Philippines. Any demonstration would, of course, require willing Japanese participation, an unknown factor. And any attempt at a demonstration would have required a level of U.S.-Japanese communications that was inconceivable in wartime. And, finally, if the Japanese did agree to witness a demonstration, they would probably spend weeks or months debating what they had seen. The Interim Committee's recommendation on the use of the atomic bomb said, ". . . we recognize our obligation to our nation to use the weapons to help save American lives in the Japanese war. . . . We can propose no technical demonstration likely to bring an end to the war; we see no acceptable alternative to direct military use."

Monday, June 18 began for Truman with a meeting of the Senate and House leaders at the White House. Routine appointments followed every 15 minutes or half hour throughout the morning and early afternoon. At 2:30 he pinned a Distinguished Service Medal on the chest of General of the Army Eisenhower, who would be the guest of honor at a White House dinner that night.

At 3:30, Truman presided over the Japanese strategy meeting that he had requested through Admiral Leahy. Attending were Leahy, Marshall, King, Stimson, Navy Secretary James Forrestal, Assistant Secretary of War John J. McCloy, Lieutenant General Ira C. Eaker (representing the ailing General Arnold), and Brigadier General A.J. McFarland, secretary of the JCS. Stimson, who was also ailing, had sent McCloy as his representative but decided at the last minute to leave his sickbed and attend what he knew was an important meeting.

Marshall opened the meeting by saying, according to the edited minutes, that "the present situation . . . was practically identical with the situation which had existed in connection with the operations against Normandy." He then read, "as an expression of his views," a memorandum prepared by the Joint Chiefs of Staff for the President that strongly urged that the invasion of Kyushu proceed as planned. "General MacArthur and Admiral Nimitz are in agreement" with the plan, the memo said. A November landing was vital, Marshall said. "If we delay much after the beginning of November the weather situation in the succeeding months may be such that the invasion of Japan, and hence the end of the war, will be delayed for up to six months."

As for the Asiatic mainland, he said, "Our objective should be to get the Russians to deal with the Japs in Manchuria (and Korea, if necessary) and to vitalize the Chinese to a point where, with assistance of American air power and some supplies, they can mop up their own country." When he turned to casualties, Marshall used the "Ratio U.S. to Jap" table and the low MacArthur estimates that would be incorporated in the July 11 JCS memorandum.

"It is a grim fact," Marshall told the President, "that there is not an easy, bloodless way to victory in war, and it is the thankless task of the leaders to maintain their firm outward front which holds the resolution of their subordinates. It was this basic difficulty with the Prime Minister [Churchill] which clouded and hampered all our preparations for the cross-channel operation now demonstrated as having been essential to victory in Europe."

The invasion of Japan, he continued, "would be difficult but not more so than the assault in Normandy." The original minutes quoted Marshall as saying that everyone going to the Pacific "should be filled with the determination to see the plan through." This was later edited to read "should be indoctrinated with a firm determination to see it through." (There were several penciled-in changes in the original minutes. A second, smooth copy was prepared, and it became the official minutes.)

Another editing slightly changed Marshall's urging about going on to Tokyo. He had said the preparations must begin at once because "they cannot be arranged for later." Once started, however, he added, "they can always be stopped if necessary." In the edited version, "necessary" was changed to "desired."

Admiral Leahy said that the President was "interested in knowing what the price in casualties for Kyushu would be and whether or not that price could be paid." Leahy also wanted to know how many troops would be used on Kyushu. (Stricken from the minutes was what had been the rest of Leahy's sentence: "with a view to determining therefrom the number of casualties which might be expected.") Leahy "pointed out that the troops on Okinawa had lost 35 percent in casualties." Leahy apparently based his figure on the casualties as then known. The final American toll for Okinawa was 7,613 killed and 31,807 wounded, a total Army-Marine-Navy casualty toll ashore of 39,420. The assault force numbered about 100,000. So the actual casualty rate was over 39 percent.

Admiral King assured Leahy that Kyushu would be different from Okinawa because the only way to attack Okinawa was by "a straight frontal attack against a highly fortified position," while on Kyushu "landings would be made on three fronts simultaneously and there would be much more room for maneuver. It was his opinion that a realistic casualty figure for Kyushu would lie somewhere between the number experienced by General MacArthur in the operations on Luzon and the Okinawa casualties," or approximately 40,000 casualties.

Marshall said that the total assault troops for the Kyushu campaign were 766,700. Marshall was being uncharacteristically disingenuous, for he had to know that he was exaggerating the number of men who would actually land and engage the Japanese defenders in combat. Fourteen divisions were assigned to the invasion of southern Kyushu. The Army and Marine combat troops making the landings totaled 340,600.

Marshall had just heard from MacArthur himself that the "total force involved" was estimated as 681,000, with "one half engaged the first 15 days" for the landings, almost exactly the 340,600 figure. Using Leahy's 35 percent estimate on MacArthur's 681,000 would mean that 238,350 Americans would be killed or wounded in battle. Using Marshall's 766,700 figure, the theoretical casualty estimate would be that much higher. No one pursued this arithmetic at the meeting, although the impression may have been left that American casualties might reach more than a quarter of a million.

How did Marshall get that 766,700 figure, the number that threw casualty calculations into confusion? He probably began with the total Sixth Army forces committed to the invasion:

Army: 3 corps, 11 divisions	253,000
Marines: 1 corps, 3 divisions	87,600
Combat total	340,600
Service and support troops	218,360
Navy forces going ashore	15,770
Total Sixth Army	574,730

The service and support troops were assigned to post-landing work that included unloading supplies and building bases and airfields. The Navy forces included men who would come ashore during the assault—communications specialists, men to unload cargo, and medical personnel to support the Marines. All of these men would come under enemy fire but were not assault troops.

To inflate the "total force involved" further, Marshall could have added in MacArthur's Far East Air Forces (FEAF), whose personnel totaled 131,800, including Marine air units assigned to the FEAF. This would bring Marshall's total up to 706,530. To that he could have added more than 42,000 men of the B-29 bomber groups in the Marianas and the support personnel who operated the bases, unloaded the freighters and tankers, and ran the post exchanges. These men, although contributing to the invasion, could hardly be included in the invasion force.

But Marshall was a very determined man. He knew that Japan had to be beaten soon or a "war weariness" would set in and lead America to seek peace through negotiations. He was convinced that the invasion was the only way to end the war. He had violated his own moral principles in contemplating the use of poison gas against the Japanese. Now, at a meeting where the President would decide whether or not to authorize an invasion, Marshall was counting every soldier, sailor, Marine, and airman that he could muster to give Truman the assurance he needed. He realized that the new President was greatly influenced by Leahy, who did not believe the invasion was necessary. And so Marshall used rhetoric—his "grim fact . . . thankless task" speech, his exaggerated numbers—to win the battle for Truman's assent.

When the President asked Marshall whether Japanese troops would be able to reinforce Kyushu, the minutes recorded that "Marshall said that it was expected that all communications with Kyushu would be destroyed." Truman then asked Eaker's view of an invasion "as an air man." Eaker said he agreed with Marshall and had just received a similar endorsement of the plan from General Arnold. The minutes quoted him as saying, "Those who advocated the use against Japan of air power alone overlooked the very impressive fact that air casualties are always much heavier when the air [*sic*] faces the enemy alone and that these casualties never fail to drop as soon as the ground forces come in. Present air casualties are averaging 2 percent per mission, about 30 percent per month." Eaker said, "Delay favored only the enemy."

Truman then turned to Stimson, who said he saw no other choice and added that he was "personally acquainted with the terrain between Tokyo and Osaka and it was not, in his opinion, suited for a war of movement." (This sentence was edited out of the official minutes.)

Stimson, who "still hoped for some fruitful accomplishment through other means" than invasion, said he believed there was "a large submerged class in Japan who do not favor the present war." But he felt that members of this class "would fight and fight tenaciously if attacked on their own ground." He wanted to do something "to arouse them and to develop any possible influence they might have before it became necessary to come to grips with them." (Stimson's original statement, according to the unedited minutes, was: "He felt sure that this submerged class would fight and fight tenaciously if attacked on the ground. He was concerned that something should be done ... before it came to grips on the ground." Most likely, Stimson did not wish to imply that he was making a distinction between bombing and invasion. Thus, "on the ground" was changed to "on their own ground" in the official minutes.)

Truman wondered aloud "if the invasion of Japan by white men would not have the effect of more closely uniting the Japanese." Stimson said he thought "there was every prospect of this."

Forrestal, asked his opinion by Truman, said that "even if we wished to besiege Japan for a year or a year and a half, the capture of Kyushu would still be essential."

Leahy raised the issue of modifying the demand for unconditional surrender. The minutes recorded that "he feared no menace from Japan in the foreseeable future, even if we were unsuccessful in forcing unconditional surrender. What he did fear was that our insistence on unconditional surrender would result only in making the Japanese desperate and thereby result in large casualties." (In the official minutes this became "thereby increase our casualty lists.") He "did not think such a result was necessary" (changed to "this was at all necessary").

Truman said he wanted "to know definitely how far we could afford to go in this operation." He "hoped that there was a possibility of preventing an Okinawa from one end of Japan to the other."

The briefing used a map that showed the probable disposition of Japanese forces in November 1945. According to the map, when the invasion of Kyushu was launched, the home islands would be defended by an estimated 1,690,000 Japanese soldiers and 2,000 aircraft. Notations on the map showed another 1,650,000 troops and 625 aircraft in Manchuria and China. The

214 • CODE-NAME DOWNFALL

rest of Japan's ground forces—1,625,000 men—were shown deployed in divisions scattered from Korea to New Guinea. There was no mention in the minutes of how these other Japanese forces would be dealt with or at what cost in American lives.

Evasion or confusion over casualty estimates persistently haunt documents about the proposed invasion. Furthermore, casualty estimates in comparison with other wartime operations were extremely speculative. The invasion of Japan was actually two invasions, two massive amphibious landings, each larger and more complex than D-Day at Normandy. And fighting in Japan would almost certainly go on much longer than it had on Okinawa. Truman himself would later use the figure 250,000 in recalling what he had been told about casualties. That figure does not appear in records of the crucial June 18 meeting. But if that was his impression, it was a somber prospect. Even so, he endorsed the Joint Chiefs plan. There would be an invasion of Japan, and the first landings would be made on the beaches of Kyushu on November 1.

The atomic bomb, usually referred to by the code-name S-1, was not mentioned until after Truman made his decision. As the meeting was ending, Truman turned to McCloy and said, "McCloy, you didn't express yourself, and nobody gets out of this room without standing up and being counted. Do you think I have any reasonable alternative to the decision which has just been made?"

McCloy looked at Stimson, who told him, "Say what you feel about it."

"Well, I do think you've got an alternative," McCloy said. "And I think it's an alternative that ought to be explored and that, really, we ought to have our heads examined if we don't explore some other method by which we can terminate this war than just by another conventional attack and landing."

McCloy suggested that the United States attempt to communicate with the Japanese—without using the term "unconditional surrender." He would tell them that they would be permitted to choose their own form of government, including retention of the Emperor.

"Well, that's what I've been thinking about," Truman said (by McCloy's recollection). "I wonder if you could put that down and give it to the Secretary of State and see what we can do from that."

Emboldened, McCloy took up another subject. As he later remembered this moment, he said, "I raised the question whether we oughtn't to tell them that we had the bomb and that we would drop the bomb. Well, as soon as I mentioned the word 'bomb'—the atomic bomb—even in that select circle—it was sort of a shock. You didn't mention the bomb out loud; it was like mentioning Skull and Bones in polite society at Yale. It just wasn't done."

But McCloy pressed on. "I think our moral position would be better if we gave them specific warning of the bomb," he told Truman. There was immediate dissent. He remembered some of the words:

"We don't know that it will go off."

"Suppose it doesn't go off."

"Our prestige will be greatly marred."

By McCloy's recollection, amid a general buzz of dissent, Truman told him, "You send your memorandum to the State Department, and we'll consider this and explore this." McCloy also remembered a feeling about "the point of view of the soldiers and sailors that were present: They were all anxious to employ their own forces for the conclusion of the war."

The bomb, as McCloy observed, was on one strategic track. The invasion was on another. S-1, then untested and of still unknown worth, might be an important weapon. The invasion, as real as blood and Okinawa and Normandy, was a known option. Truman, "clear on the situation" as he ended the meeting, said he was "quite sure that the Joint Chiefs of Staff should proceed with the Kyushu operation." He had made his decision about the invasion. There could not be a decision about the bomb because there was no bomb.

That night, after the White House reception and dinner honoring Eisenhower, Truman wrote one of his "Dear Bess" letters to Mrs. Truman, who was spending the summer at their home in Independence, Missouri. "Eisenhower's party was a grand success," he wrote. "I pinned a medal on him in the afternoon. He is a nice fellow and a good man. He's done a whale of job. They are running him for President, which is O.K. with me. I'd turn it over to him now if I could."

There was a third alternative for Truman: a negotiated end of the war. The suggestion came from former President Herbert Hoover, who wrote a long memo in which he said he believed he had a way to save "the lives of 500,000 to 1,000,000 American boys"—an estimate that he did not give a source for. Circulated among JCS planners as a top-secret paper, the Hoover memo gave new impetus to sentiments for avoiding an invasion and modifying the principle of unconditional surrender.

The conditions of surrender, Hoover said, should be restricted to the abolition of the Japanese "military caste," with criminal trials for Japanese officers charged with "violation of the rules of war and human conduct." Hoover also called for the ceding to the Allies of Japanese-held islands in the Pacific and restoration of Manchuria to China, which would receive reparations in the form of all Japanese property in China. "Beyond this point," Hoover said, "there can be no American objectives that are worth the expenditure of 500,000 to 1,000,000 American lives." A fight to the end, he believed, would mean not only high casualties but would also extend the war for at least 18 months and "prostrate the United States to a point where the Americans can spare no aid to recovery of other nations."

He urged that the United States and Britain (with China, "if possible") issue a proclamation that would state that the Allies "have no desire to destroy either the Japanese people or their government, or to interfere in the Japanese way of life. . . ." Hoover would allow Japan to keep Korea and Formosa and would not demand reparations or indemnities except for the forfeiture of Japanese property in China. A peace negotiated along the lines he recommended, Hoover said, would "stop Russian expansion in the Asian and Pacific areas." Japan "would not be likely to go Communist" and could "make economic recovery . . . to the advance of all free nations."

"If we fight Japan to the bitter end," Hoover said, "there would be (as in Germany) no group left who are capable of establishing government and order. We will be confronted with establishing a military government in which China, Russia and France will demand participation with all the dangers that that involves."

Strategists in the office of the Joint Chiefs, ordered by Marshall to analyze Hoover's proposal, dismissed it point by point, beginning with the casualty estimate, which was judged "entirely too high." As for Japanese acceptance of any surrender terms, the analysis concluded, "Presumably, only the conviction that their position is completely hopeless will persuade them to give up their holdings in Asia. Probably it will take Russian entry into the war, coupled with a landing, or imminent threat of landing, on Japan proper by us, to convince them of the hopelessness of their position."

The circulation of Hoover's memo was among the bits of business Truman completed in anticipation of his meeting with Churchill and Stalin in Potsdam, a suburb of devastated Berlin. Churchill, who enjoyed picking codenames, suggested calling the conference Terminal. It was prophetic. The votes of a British general election would be counted during the conference, and Churchill, who was present when Terminal opened on July 17, would shortly be voted out of office. He was replaced by Clement R. Attlee as Britain's Prime Minister.

Although the conference was devoted primarily to the geopolitics of postwar Europe, the Combined Chiefs of Staff, meeting simultaneously in Potsdam, focused on strategy for ending the Pacific War. "For the purpose of planning production and the allocation," the Chiefs decided, "the planning date for the end of organized resistance by Japan should be 15 November 1946 and this date should be adjusted periodically to conform to the courses of the war."

That was what Truman and his nation faced in July 1945—an invasion of Japan and 16 more months of war.

CHAPTER 10

"LAND THE LANDING FORCE!"

Japanese women practicing to use
bamboo spears to kill invaders.
Death was preferable to surrender.

Tokyo in April 1945 was a smoldering black wasteland. During March and early April, U.S. B-29 Superfortress bombers had dropped thousands of tons of incendiary bombs, creating infernos that had leveled a third of the city. More than 100,000 people had died, many of them in their flaming wood-and-paper houses. Hospitals were filled with the wounded and dying. At least a million people were wandering through the ashes in search of a place to live. But in the War Ministry the mimeograph machines were still grinding, and the propaganda experts were still producing patriotic slogans and songs to rally the Japanese people to the defense of their homeland.

On April 20, from the headquarters of the Imperial Japanese Army came

THE DECREE OF THE HOMELAND DECISIVE BATTLE

1. The object of the homeland operation is to force the enemy into the decisive battle and to win the battle to secure the Empire's eternal presence. . . . We shall throw everything conceivable, material and spiritual, into the battle and annihilate the enemy landing force by fierce and bold offensive attacks.

2. The result of the decisive battle in the homeland will directly relate to the fate of the Empire. Thus all soldiers should pray for the eternal existence of our nation and give their all to accomplishing the object of the operation . . . including the principle to repay the Emperor by their own death. . . .

3. Every soldier should fight to the last moment believing the final victory. All the forces should trust each other to cope with every obstacle and keep the iron solidarity. Our people should fight to the last person to repel the enemy force. . . .

4. Our divine land is indestructible and the Imperial Armed Forces should fight the righteous war of self-existence and self-defense. Thus every soldier should believe in the absolute victory of the Imperial Armed Forces and devote the ultimate effort to gain the eternal existence of the Imperial Nation.

5. The battlefield will be the eternally existing Imperial land. Our ancestors' land is the place where our eternal race will live. . . .

6. The circumstances of normal life and emotions tend to reduce the intrepid spirit for the decisive battle. Thus, every commander should use firm control without hesitation. . . .

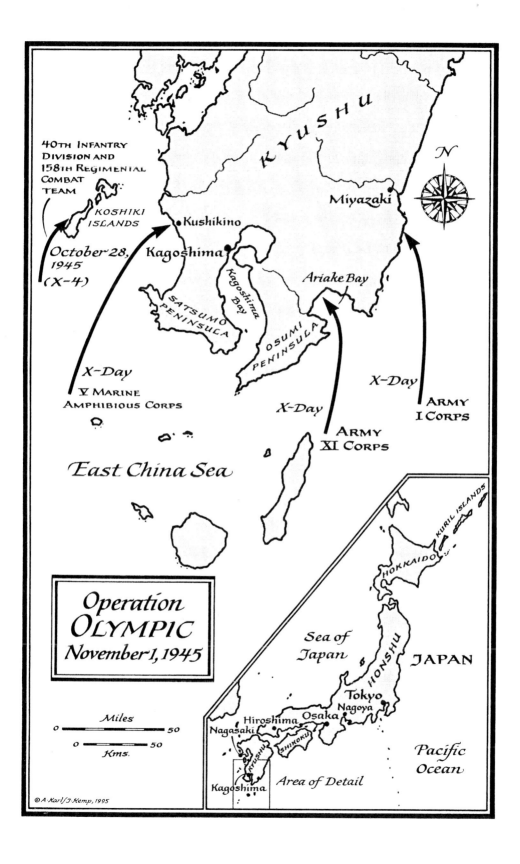

40TH INFANTRY
DIVISION AND
158TH REGIMENTAL
COMBAT
TEAM

KOSHIKI
ISLANDS

October 28,
1945
(X-4)

KYUSHU

Miyazaki

N

• Kushikino

Kagoshima

Ariake Bay

Kagoshima Bay

SATSUMO PENINSULA

OSUMI PENINSULA

X-Day

**V MARINE
AMPHIBIOUS CORPS**

X-Day

**ARMY
XI CORPS**

X-Day

**ARMY
I CORPS**

East China Sea

Operation
OLYMPIC
November 1, 1945

Miles	
0	50

Kms.	
0	50

© A. Karl / J. Kemp, 1995

KURIL ISLANDS

HOKKAIDO

HONSHU

JAPAN

*Sea of
Japan*

Tokyo
Nagoya
Osaka
Hiroshima
Nagasaki

SHIKOKU
KYUSHU

Kagoshima

Area of Detail

*Pacific
Ocean*

220 • CODE-NAME DOWNFALL

In the Regulations of Battle, the decree said that soldiers should be "the shield to our Emperor." They should be men "not afraid of death, believing the hope of reviving seven times to reward the nation, as well as delighting to become the foundation of the immortal Empire. . . .

"During the decisive battle the sick and wounded shall not be evacuated to the rear" but would somehow keep on fighting and "annihilating the enemy force." There would be no retreat. Men were to stand and die. Other regulations ordered:

- Nursing and tending to comrades is not allowed.
- Units shall not retreat.
- Every unit of the operational force should be a fighting unit. Even the rear, logistic, and medical units shall be prepared for fighting.
- Soldiers without weapons shall take the arms from dead enemy soldiers.
- Wounded soldiers and patients shall accompany troops during the march and participate in the decisive battle. Dropping out shall not be permitted.

Commanders were told to expect not only American artillery and air bombardment but also "attacks by tanks, flamethrowers, and gas." This reference to possible American use of poison gas was followed by an ominous order to use "countermeasures"—apparently retaliatory poison gas.

"It is expected that the enemy might conduct these tactics," the decree warned: "that our civilians—women, old persons, and children—will be forced to march ahead of them to prevent our soldiers from shooting at the enemy. On this occasion, our soldiers should consider that the victory of the Empire is much more important than our own lives and not hesitate to destroy the enemy."

As for civilians, according to the slogans that spread through Japan after the "Decree of the Homeland Decisive Battle," every man, woman, and child was expected to fight to the death. People were told to sing a song entitled "One Hundred Million Souls for the Emperor." With the Decisive Battle would come "the Honorable Death of a Hundred Million," who were also sometimes called "One Hundred Million Bullets of Fire."

Some zealots advocated involuntary sacrifices. In June 1945, for example, a senior officer in Osaka said, "Due to the nationwide food shortage and the imminent invasion of the home islands, it will be necessary to kill all the infirm old people, the very young, and the sick. We cannot allow Japan to perish because of them."

When U.S. invasion planners looked at Japan, they saw an archipelago of four major islands. Northernmost Hokkaido, a cold, bleak island that was a source of Japan's fish, coal, and timber, was strategic only in terms of its proximity to Soviet territory—the northern portion of Sakhalin Island. To the south, across a narrow strait, was Honshu, the largest, most populous island and, as the site of Tokyo, the heart of Japan and the ultimate target of invasion and conquest. But a Honshu-only assault was ruled out as too costly. Shikoku, the smallest and least defended island, was tempting, but it lacked sizable harbors, and as the Normandy landing had shown, only a major harbor could satisfy the logistic demands of mammoth invasion forces.

Finally, there was Kyushu, about twice the size of Massachusetts, with a population of some ten million. The southernmost of the home islands, Kyushu had two peninsulas that seemed to form the head of a dragon. Its mouth was Kagoshima Bay, its fiery tongue Sakurajima, the active volcano in the bay. In the shadow of the volcano was Kagoshima, a city with a fine harbor, into which would pour the men and matériel in preparation for the final assault on Honshu and Tokyo.

Kyushu, said a Shinto myth, was the wellspring of the Japanese people, the island where the gods walked, became mortal, and begat the divine Japanese race. But if U.S. strategists also saw Kyushu as the gateway to the conquest of Japan, so did Japan's defense strategists. In a "Report to the Throne" on January 19, 1945, the Imperial General Headquarters predicted "the final assault on the Homeland in the fall of 1945 at the earliest." The question was where. While Japanese troops were fighting on Okinawa in the spring of 1945, Major Eizo Hori, an intelligence officer on the Imperial General Staff, was given an assignment: to predict the probable sites for U.S. landings in Japan.

Throughout the war Hori had shown a remarkable talent for anticipating U.S. operations. He made his predictions by trying to think like his principal enemy, General Douglas MacArthur. Hori's forecasts were so accurate that fellow officers called him "MacArthur's staff officer." When his superiors, for instance, believed that MacArthur would thrust toward Japan after American forces took Saipan in June 1944, Hori insisted, correctly, that he would invade the Philippines.

Hori analyzed U.S. B-29 flights over Japan, determined which ones were probably for reconnaissance, and deduced that Kyushu was getting a great deal of attention. Then, after walking Kyushu beaches, he picked Ariake Bay (now Shibushi Bay) on the southwestern coast of the island as a likely invasion site. He knew that weather would play a role. Landings early in the fall risked typhoons, which were unlikely after October. Freezing or near-freezing weather came in December and January, when U.S. troops would be fighting on southern Kyushu. But at least they would be dry, for rain was rare, and the rice fields would be drained. Taking all this into consideration, Hori decided on late October as the probable date. U.S. planners would pick November 1 for the Kyushu landings.

Hori's reasoning was welcome news to Japanese defenders, who desperately needed as much time as possible. Preparations for repelling the expected landings were far behind schedule. There were tunnels to dig, hidden kamikaze airstrips to prepare, and thousands of kamikaze aircraft, boats, and submarines to produce.

In January 1945 the Japanese high command, convinced that the homeland itself soon would become a battlefield, had ordered a strengthening of Japan's defense perimeter, which included Iwo Jima, Formosa, Okinawa, the Shanghai area, and Korea's southern coasts. Japanese troops in the Philippines, although far beyond the inner perimeter, were to contribute by fighting a delaying action. The longer the Philippines and the outer ring held, the more time Japan's defenders would have to fortify the home islands. When the order was issued to hold the inner perimeter, Iwo Jima had been under bombardment for more than two months and was an obvious target. The invasion came on February 19, and the 21,000 defenders fought nearly to the last man. Their deaths, like those of their comrades in the Philippines, bought the first installment of time for building Japan's defenses.

Next was the turn of Okinawa, which American troops invaded on April 1. By then the Imperial General Staff had nearly completed a new homeland defense plan—called *Ketsu-go*. The plan divided the home islands into seven *Ketsu* defense sectors, concentrating most forces in *Ketsu* No. 3, the Yokohama-Tokyo region of Honshu, and *Ketsu* No. 6, Kyushu.

U.S. decrypts of Japanese communications indicated the rapidly growing strength of the Japanese forces in the home islands and, especially, the buildup on Kyushu. Near the end of April, U.S. intelligence analysts realized that Japan was preparing for invasion and that Japanese defense planners considered Kyushu the prime invasion site. Analysts noted that new combat formations were being organized on the home islands and that the flow of reinforcements to outlying garrisons had ceased. "Troops guarding the close approaches to Japan," said a U.S. intelligence report, "are dying in place in desperate delaying actions. . . ." Troops were being sent from Manchuria to Japan "to provide strength for final defense of the Empire."

The report estimated that there were 84,200 Japanese troops in southern Kyushu; only about 25,000 were rated as first-line combat troops. By November 1945, the U.S. intelligence analysts believed, two more infantry divisions, more naval ground units, and other additional forces would bring the overall total of defenders in southern Kyushu to between 95,000 and 115,000. Another 144,500 troops, including one infantry division, were believed to be in northern Kyushu.

The tempo of *Ketsu-go* was stepping up. Japan was rapidly assembling troops at potential invasion sites, mobilizing civilians, transforming the nation into a fortress. Imperial General Headquarters split Japan into two army districts, each with a general army headquarters. By the time General Marshall briefed President Truman on the invasion plans on June 18, U.S. intelligence wrongly estimated that there were 350,000 Japanese troops on Kyushu. In reality, from May 1 to late July, the Japanese forces on Kyushu grew to 14 divisions, 7 mixed brigades, and 3 tank brigades—an increase to almost 600,000 troops, significantly more than U.S. intelligence estimates. Although most of the forces were in northern Kyushu, some 125,000 were in the south, and there was a possibility that more were coming into the area.

General MacArthur's intelligence (G-2) staff had estimated in April that the Japanese could increase the Kyushu force by one or two divisions by X-Day but that this would have no appreciable effect on the U.S. battle plan. On July 29, however, came a report that was more a warning than an estimate:

> a. The rate and probable continuity of Japanese reinforcements into the Kyushu area are changing that tactical and strategical situation sharply.
>
> At least six (6) additional major units have been picked up in June/July; it is obvious that they are coming in from adjacent areas over lines of communication, that have apparently not been seriously affected by air strikes.
>
> There is a strong likelihood that additional major units will enter the area before target date; we are engaged in a race against time by which the ratio of attack-effort vis-a-vis defense capacity is perilously balanced.

This MacArthur G-2 estimate concluded with an ominous statement: "Unless the use of these [Japanese land and sea] routes [to Kyushu] is restricted by air and/or naval action . . . enemy forces in Southern Kyushu may be still further augmented until our planned local superiority is overcome, and the Japanese will enjoy complete freedom of action in organizing the area and in completing their preparations for defense."

The Japanese buildup so worried General Marshall that, in an "eyes only" message to MacArthur, he wondered about "possible alternative objectives" to Olympic. The three possible alternative landing sites he mentioned were *on Honshu:* Sendai, a large city about 180 miles north of Tokyo; Ominato, a small town on Mutsu Bay on the northern tip of Honshu; and—amazingly —Tokyo itself.

As usual, Marshall handled MacArthur cautiously, and he was well aware of MacArthur's disdain of Magic and other intelligence that did not originate with his own G-2 staff, led by Major General Charles A. Willoughby, who had been with MacArthur since the start of the war. MacArthur was so concerned with controlling intelligence himself that he had even barred the Office of Strategic Services from operating in his command.

Marshall noted the large buildup of "suicide planes" and a shift of Japanese forces "to a point where the defensive capabilities in Northern Honshu and Hokkaido appear to be extraordinarily weak." Although he wondered whether the Japanese somehow might be deceiving U.S. intelligence, he still mentioned the possible change in Olympic and asked MacArthur for "your personal estimate of the Japanese intentions and capabilities."

MacArthur replied immediately, dismissing the massing of Japanese aircraft as "greatly exaggerated" [*sic*] and reminiscent of a similar "erroneous estimate" prior to the Luzon invasion. "As to the movement of ground forces," he said, "the Japanese are reported as trying to concentrate in the few areas in which landings can be effected from Tokyo southward, and it is possible that some strength may have been drawn from the areas of northern Honshu. I do not, repeat not, credit, however, the heavy strengths reported to you in southern Kyushu." Whatever was there, he said, would be taken out by U.S. air power.

"In my opinion," he continued,

> there should not, repeat not, be the slightest thought of changing the Olympic operation. . . . The plan is sound and will be successful. An attack directly into Tokyo or to the northward thereof would have to be made without the benefit of land based aviation . . . and for that reason alone would be fraught with the greatest danger. I seriously doubt the advisability of a direct attack into Tokyo without the installation of heavy air force closer than Okinawa. Only a limited study has been made of the Sendai and Ominato areas. . . .
>
> Throughout the Southwest Pacific campaigns, as we have neared an operation intelligence has invariably pointed to greatly increased enemy forces. Without exception, this buildup has been found to be erroneous. . . .

MacArthur's stance personified him. He had absolute confidence in his own battle plan and little confidence in any information that came from Magic or Ultra, the code-name for intercepted Japanese military communications. Willoughby had recently reported that U.S. air forces were not doing enough to stop Japanese reinforcements from reaching southern Kyushu. But when MacArthur wanted to refute Ultra's penetration of Japanese Army movements in his message to Marshall, he proclaimed his faith in air power's ability to knock out the Japanese reinforcements coming to Kyushu.

MacArthur disliked Ultra because in some of his southwestern Pacific operations it had proved him wrong in *his* estimates of Japanese strengths and intentions. Also, through 1943, the main source of Ultra in the Pacific was Japanese naval codes, which were deciphered and distributed by the U.S. Navy, MacArthur's nemesis.

Japan was, in fact, systematically mobilizing a vast manpower pool—in addition to its military force—of 13.3 million males aged 15 to 59. Women were also being recruited as so-called volunteers to serve as ammunition carriers and untrained battlefield nurses. Three types of home-defense units were being formed:

• Special Guard Forces, made up mostly of men who had some previous military training. They were attached to major units primarily for such noncombat duties as fortification building, transport, and "casualty clearing" on the battlefield. But, as the Decisive Battle order said, everyone would be expected to fight. On Okinawa, such units, lacking uniforms but armed with makeshift weapons, fought U.S. troops.

• Independent Companies, consisting of reservists drawn from civilian life and used principally as labor troops until called to combat.

• Civilian Volunteer Corps, a mobilization not of volunteers but of all boys and men 15 to 60 and all girls and women 17 to 40 except for those exempted as unfit or needed to care for dependents. The corps was formed in June 1945 with the stated mission of "concentration on munitions and food production and the preparation for conversion to combat units in case of emergency." Conversion to combat did not necessarily mean that the volunteers would fight; in combat status they would be under Army control and could be assigned to combat. They wore whatever uniform they could find. On the right sleeve at the shoulder was a white cloth with the word *Combat* stitched on it.

These civilians, many of them eager schoolchildren, were trained with hand grenades, swords, halberds, fire hooks, and bamboo spears. Their training manual was a hastily printed, crudely illustrated *People's Handbook of Resistance Combat,* which showed them how to make a Molotov cocktail (called a "flame bottle" by the Japanese) and hurl it at a U.S. tank. They were also told to rush the tank with a satchel charge of explosives or, if they did not have explosives, climb a hill and push rocks down on the tank. Those who managed to get a rifle were expected to rely on sketches that showed how to shoot down a parachutist or fire from behind a bush. Lacking a rifle, they were to fight hand to hand, as succinctly described in three lessons:

1. With a sword or spear, neither swing vertically nor horizontally, but always thrust tall Yankees in their belly.
2. With a sickle, hatchet, heavy kitchen knife, or fireman's hook, attack from behind.
3. Scuffle: Make full use of judo and karate. Kick in the testicles. Strike in the pit of the stomach.

A 15-year-old girl later said a teacher told her to use an awl as a weapon. "You must aim at the enemy's abdomen, understand? The abdomen!" the teacher instructed. "If you don't kill at least one enemy soldier, you don't deserve to die."

The instructions to the Civilian Volunteer Corps members revealed that behind the patriotic rhetoric of the "Decree of the Homeland Decisive Battle" was a dark, suicidal reality. In other cultures, irregular units would be considered guerrillas. But Japanese civilians were not merely required to fight; they were to die fighting. "Should the enemy invade our mainland," said the *People's Handbook,* "100 million of us, as the *Tokko,* or Special

Attack Forces [the euphemistic term for suicide warriors], must exterminate them to protect our native soil and to maintain our everlasting Empire."

"We did not have enough equipment, ammunition, weapons," a former Japanese naval officer recalled. "Only one thing remained: the people's spirit against invasion was very high. The people in the home islands knew that the people of Okinawa had lost their lives for their country, and they would do the same." People in Kyushu, he said, hoped to kill ten Americans before they themselves died.

In August 1945, a new U.S. intelligence report, based primarily on Ultra decrypts and analyses, said that the Japanese already in 1945 had formed 31 new divisions and converted existing ground units into 14 additional divisions. Senior U.S. officers planning the invasion also knew about the mobilization of civilians and they had been told that "the operation will be opposed not only by the available organized military forces of the Empire, but also by a fanatically hostile population."

Suicide weapons now were standard equipment in the Japanese arsenal. By midsummer of 1945, some 8,000 kamikaze aircraft had been produced, mostly by converting fighters, bombers, trainers, and reconnaissance aircraft. Another 2,500 were to be built by September. The rocket-powered, piloted bomb called *Ohka* (Cherry Blossom) or Baka was also in full production. Japanese aircraft factories had produced 755 of the Bakas through March 1945, and many were sent against the U.S. invasion fleet off Okinawa. An improved Model 22 had an extended range to permit the launch aircraft to release the suicider at a greater distance from defending U.S. warships. They were to be mass-produced in underground factories, and more advanced models were being designed.

The Navy's secret suicide weapon was the *Kaiten,* a manned torpedo. The standard 24-inch diameter Type 93 "Long Lance" torpedo was cut in half and a cockpit section inserted for a pilot and control panel. Launched by a submarine, the Kaiten sped toward a ship at 40 knots and could propel itself for an hour and outrun any U.S. warship. If the Kaiten missed a target, it sank with its pilot. Kaitens were lashed to a submarine's deck, and the pilots could enter while the submarine was underwater. First used in November 1944, Kaitens did not yet have an impressive record. One sank a U.S. tanker in the Caroline Islands, and another sank a destroyer escort off Okinawa. But they were also being produced as quickly as possible, and hundreds of Kaiten pilots were being trained.

Hiroshi Iwai, at the age of 14, enlisted in naval aviation. "There were so few planes for training that there could not be any training," he remembered. So he was told he would be trained as a Kaiten pilot. Kaitens being built then were partially made of plywood. They had a range of about three miles and could submerge to a depth of about 15 feet. About half of the training class died because the Kaitens failed or because the students dove them too deep. The survivors of Iwai's class, in the summer of 1945, were being prepared for missions to repel the invasion.

Beyond the Kaitens, the Japanese Navy was also producing hundreds of five-man midget submarines. Known as the *Koryu* Type D, these submersibles had an underwater endurance of 40 minutes at 16 knots and 50 hours at 2.5 knots and were armed with two torpedoes. However, because of a shortage of torpedoes, some were being fitted with explosive charges for use in a suicide role. The Navy planned to have 540 of these midget submarines in service by the fall of 1945, with a production rate of 180 units per month from ten shipyards.

A more advanced midget submarine, the *Kairyu* type, was also beginning construction, with 740 units planned to be in service by the fall of 1945. These two-man craft were also armed with either two torpedoes or a (suicide) explosive charge. Production of these submarines was slowed by American air raids that destroyed component-producing facilities and prevented shipyards from working effectively. But by early August some 360 midget submarines had been completed. Hundreds more were on the building ways.

The Navy was also training men to become human mines, known as *Fukuryu,* "hiders." Clad in a diving suit and breathing from oxygen tanks, a Fukuryu carried an explosive charge, which was mounted on a stick with a contact fuse. He was to swim up to landing craft and strike it with the stick-bomb. As part of the defense buildup, 650-man Fukuryu battalions were being organized and trained with dummy mines, which they were to release or carry to their targets. The Navy hoped to have 4,000 men trained and equipped for this suicide force before the invasion began. U.S. intelligence also believed that the Japanese had acquired rocket technology from their German allies and might unveil V-1 missiles during the invasion.

The Japanese knew exactly what beaches the invaders would head for when the order "Land the landing force!" was given. Not only was there Major Hori's analysis; there were also the American bombs and leaflets falling from the skies over Kyushu's principal city, Kagoshima. "Time Is Pressing!!" said the urgent Japanese headline on a leaflet that showed the face of a clock. Each hour was symbolized as an American victory; on each conquest was a Japanese flag hanging limply from a broken flagstaff. Spaced around the clock face were Guadalcanal, Attu, Bougainville, Tarawa, the Marshalls, the Admiralty Islands, New Guinea, Saipan, Guam, the Philippines.

The minute hand pointed to the penultimate conquest, Okinawa, and the hour hand was on Japan itself. It was five minutes to midnight. Those who dared pick up a leaflet knew the message at a glance: Between Okinawa and the main island of Honshu, between five minutes to midnight and midnight, was Kyushu.

And now the minute hand was getting closer to Kyushu.

Kagoshima lay deep within Kagoshima Bay. A direct invasion into the bay would be suicidal, for two peninsulas, the jaws of the Kyushu dragon head, enclosed its narrow opening. An invasion force would have to thread its way through that opening, then run a 50-mile gauntlet between the jaws.

To seize Kagoshima, the invaders had to reach it overland from the north and west. Therefore the Olympic invasion plan called for three landings, two on the eastern coast of Osumi Peninsula, which formed the upper jaw of the Kyushu dragon, and one on the Satsuma Peninsula, the lower jaw. From the invasion sites American forces would fight their way inland and link up beyond the northern shores of Kagoshima Bay. They were then to advance northward to a line extending from Sendai, a city of about 240,000 near the west coast, to Tsuno, a small town on the eastern coast, just above Saito. This was the Saito-Tsuno line, the boundary that set the high-water mark for the American advance. The line signified Olympic's basic mission —the securing of southern Kyushu to use it for air attacks and for the construction of bases to support the invasion of Honshu and the march on Tokyo.

In July, feigned and real preliminaries for Olympic began. Some U.S. soldiers and airmen worked on the props and scenarios for the complex deception plan, Pastel II. And Admiral Halsey's Third Fleet—17 aircraft carriers, 8 fast battleships, 20 cruisers, 75 destroyers—started pounding the Japanese coast and battering Japanese air and naval forces, especially targeting the waters between Kyushu and Honshu. On July 10 the carrier planes struck Tokyo, with virtually no fighter opposition or anti-aircraft fire. Vice Admiral John (Big Jack) Shafroth led three battleships and two heavy cruisers, with their destroyer escorts, to within 29,000 yards of the coast of northern Honshu. The warships came in so close that the Japanese could see them. The Third Fleet was to continue this first phase of Olympic preparation from July 28 (X-95) to October 23 (X-8).

Leaflets and radio propaganda scripts were being prepared for the first act of deception: indications that the invasion site was the Shanghai area of the Chinese coast, perhaps Chusan (now Zhoushan) Island south of Shanghai. For months there had been expectation of American landings. A real landing, however, would put U.S. forces in the middle of a brewing civil war. Communist troops, not Chiang Kai-shek's men, controlled practically all the north and central coast areas not occupied by the Japanese. Magic eavesdroppers listened in on the French ambassador in Chungking and picked up his report that potential conflict between the two Chinas "is becoming more and more significant as the possibility of an American landing on the Asiatic continent approaches." The deception plan had the

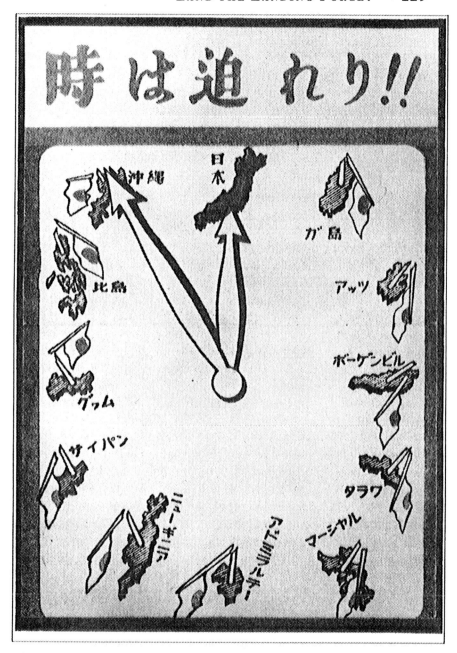

The message of this American propaganda leaflet dropped over southern Japan was clear: Time is running out. The Japanese had been defeated in a succession of island assaults, and now the Allied juggernaut was about to invade Japan.

advantage of avoiding that conflict while still exploiting rumors about landings.

The leaflets, which were to begin dropping in the Shanghai area in August, carried messages designed to weaken Japanese morale and strengthen Chinese resolve. They would not say that an invasion was imminent, but Japanese intelligence officers would draw that inference. Next would come reconnaissance flights over the area, then bombing and strafing missions. British warships would attack Hong Kong and Canton on September 18 (X-45) and September 28 (X-35). Radio broadcasts would warn Chinese fishermen and crews of junks to stay out of the waters north of Formosa beginning on September 15. Men would even be landed on Chinese beaches, according to Pastel plans, which did not specify exactly where and how the "beach penetration parties" would be landed and withdrawn.

Meanwhile, around September 7, the Shanghai-Chusan operation would be called off. Word of its cancellation would be passed in "covert" ways, although simulated radio traffic would continue to appear to focus on Shanghai. Long "book messages," which were often radioed after high-level decisions were made, would be transmitted just as word leaked that Washington officials had decided to cancel the Shanghai landings. The communist-Chiang conflict would provide a realistic basis for the purported cancellation. The idea was to confuse Japanese intelligence, which would have to analyze the lack of signs of an invasion (no shore bombardment, no rising of guerrillas) with the signs of a possible invasion (the overflights and the radio traffic).

The Western news media would be fed fake stories. Production figures for nonexistent gliders would be announced, along with mention of areas in the United States being used for airborne training. It would be said that a "large number of selected Chinese" were heading from the United States to the Pacific "to be used as interpreters, some being especially trained in government and municipal administration." The deception was designed to keep as many Japanese forces as possible on the Chinese mainland. Later would come leaks to the Western media indicating that the target for an invasion of Japan was Shikoku and that December 1 was the likely day for launching the assault.

Whatever might have been the results of Pastel's deceptions, the only way to pin down the nearly three million Japanese troops in Manchuria and China—so they could not play a role in the U.S. invasion of the home islands—was the entry of the Soviet Union into the war. And when that occurred would depend on Stalin's timetable.

For the men of MacArthur's Sixth Army, the invasion became inevitable on July 1, when the Eighth Army took over the Luzon campaign so that the Sixth Army could regroup, reequip, and train for Olympic. Organized fighting had ceased on Luzon, although the remnants of a Japanese army still held out in the mountains. As the Sixth Army got ready on Luzon for its final campaign, the Marines rehearsed landings at their bases in Hawaii and the Marianas.

The invasion armada, which would be the largest ever to put to sea, began to assemble at ports throughout the Pacific. All together, the plan called for a total of 1,371 transport, cargo, landing and evacuation ships with a capacity to carry 539,290 men and 61,190 tanks and vehicles.

Several LSTs were fitted out as miniature "aircraft carriers" to launch and recover Piper Cubs, popularly known as grasshoppers, to spot fire for artillery after the guns went ashore. Twenty-one LSTs would carry thousands of units of blood and mobile blood-distribution units. They, along with four evacuation transports, would carry the wounded out of the beachhead area to major hospitals on Okinawa and Luzon or transfer them at sea to white-painted hospital ships that would stay far offshore. The hospital ships would be as vulnerable to kamikaze attack as any warship. Ordinarily, medical personnel did not carry arms. But a training document for the invasion noted that they would be trained and armed because Japan would not recognize any invader as a noncombatant.

The total carrying capacity of the assault fleet indicated, but did not define, the actual size of the ground forces that would be sent into Kyushu. The original planning by MacArthur's and Krueger's headquarters called for the Sixth Army to land 337,000 soldiers and 87,000 Marines in the assault and the immediate follow-on operations of the assault. Those numbers, however, would periodically change as the planning progressed, as Army and Marine unit organizations were changed, and as additional troops were assigned to the corps and army commands that would participate in the landings.

General MacArthur, in his message to Marshall on casualties for President Truman's June 18 invasion meeting, used 681,000 as the "total force involved," with "one-half engaged the first 15 days and the entire strength thereafter." But his authorized postwar description of invasion plans, while discussing manpower in the broad Army terms of corps and divisions, did not produce an overall total, although enemy units were described in specific numbers. MacArthur's chief of engineers, for planning purposes, used 549,503 as the total "force to be landed"—including the engineers to build airfields and port facilities, Army Air Forces personnel to fly and maintain many hundreds of aircraft, and men to garrison the southern half of Kyushu, to operate military prison camps, and to provide services and military government for the captured Japanese civilian population. But this figure did not include the three divisions of Marines, since they would be providing for their own engineering needs.

A planning document, which listed Sixth Army invasion units down to scout dog platoons, gave the total, including the three Marine divisions (59,898 men), as 382,937. To this was then added 49,382 medical, quartermaster, and other service troops, 18,970 men assigned to military government tasks, and 35,857 men from the Far East Air Forces. When all of these numbers were added up, the total was 487,146, far from the figures that MacArthur gave to Marshall or the ones used by his chief of engineers. But his 681,000 figure could easily have been obtained by adding the men of the Navy and Army Air Forces supporting the invasion.

While this massive force was being assembled, in August, on Ie Shima, four miles off Okinawa, some B-24s were ordered to begin practicing low, slow flying. "We would drop some flaps, reduce power, and slow down to about 90 knots," Arlo Roth, a B-24 Liberator copilot, would later remember. "At the time my understanding was that we would be carrying paratroopers for the invasion of Japan. It would seem to be more logical for us to carry equipment." But the B-24s were not being refitted to carry paratroopers. They apparently had been secretly selected by Pastel deception planners for the next phase of the operation, which would begin on Halloween, the night of X-1, when aircraft were to drop equipment for airborne units on airstrips behind each of the landing beaches. MacArthur had ruled that there would be no airborne drops in the invasion. The plan was for the Japanese to find the parachutes and the equipment and draw the false conclusion that parachutists were floating down from the night sky. This, planners thought, would keep some Japanese forces away from the landing beaches.

Okinawa, one of the actual staging areas of the invasion, was also the center of deception activities. Around August 20 transports containing unassembled gliders were to fly into Okinawa. These real gliders would be assembled, and six glider pilots would begin training other pilots. At or near military airfields on Okinawa, 100 fake gliders would be assembled. A fictional airborne corps and division headquarters would be formed, and troops would begin wearing shoulder patches for the imaginary airborne unit. At the time of the invasion, Japanese forces were expected to be on the watch for nonexistent gliders.

By the time the preinvasion air and naval bombardment of Kyushu began, U.S. planners believed, Pastel tricks would probably no longer fool the Japanese. Between October 18 and 24, Admiral Halsey's Third Fleet would focus on aircraft, airfields, and shipping between Honshu and Shikoku and Kyushu. On October 24 two of his carrier groups would join the Fifth Fleet, under the command of Admiral Raymond A. Spruance, the first time since early 1942 that the two admirals would be at sea fighting together.

Beginning on October 24 (X-8), battleships, cruisers, and destroyers would begin bombarding the landing beaches, trying to knock out the elaborate Japanese coastal defenses. The effectiveness of shore bombardment had long been debated. Some—but rarely all—coastal defense positions were destroyed in the various naval bombardments in the Pacific amphibious assaults. Still, *some* were destroyed. And bombardments immediately prior to the landings invariably forced the defenders to cower in their bunkers, generally preventing them from firing on the landing craft.

Among the 13 old battleships moving in to pound the landing sites with 16-inch and 14-inch guns would be seven resurrected veterans of the Japanese attack on Pearl Harbor—the *Nevada,* which had been torpedoed and hit by five 500-pound bombs; the *California,* struck by two torpedoes and a bomb; the *West Virginia,* hit by at least three and perhaps seven torpedoes; and the *Tennessee, Maryland,* and *Pennsylvania,* all three hit but only slightly damaged.

The Olympic plan called for MacArthur's Far East Air Forces, under General George C. Kenney, to cut off northern Kyushu from the invasion area to the south. Kenney's fighters and bombers were to take out the railroads and the paralleling *Kokudo,* or national highway, a two-lane gravel road that ran along the coasts and linked the island's cities. The railroad seemed to be particularly vulnerable, for its tracks ran across bridges and through tunnels. The highway and railroad network had so far remained solid enough for tens of thousands of defenders to pass to the south. Completely wiping out the transportation system might have been tempting, but the attackers were going to need to move, and the Kokudo was their best hope.

On October 27 (X-5), elements of the 40th Infantry Division and the 158th Regimental Combat Team were to begin landing on small islands lying off the west coast of Kyushu. These units probably would have met little opposition because the Japanese planned to throw nearly all they had into a fierce shore defense of Kyushu itself. Japanese strategists had predicted that the Americans would precede the invasion with a seizure of the offshore islands, for that was what the same Sixth Army had done in Leyte Gulf prior to the invasion of Leyte and what the Marines had done at Okinawa.

The Olympic invasion plan called for taking only the southern part of Kyushu, an area of about 3,000 square miles, where the massive airfields would be built to support operations against Honshu and the subsequent Coronet invasion in March 1946. Mountainous Kyushu had few places where such airfields could be built or a large invasion force could land. But military geographers found four: the Kagoshima strip, from the island's principal city westward to the East China Sea; the coastal plain sweeping up from Ariake Bay; plains radiating out from Kanoya, a town near the eastern shore of Kagoshima Bay; and the long coastal strip that ran northward from Miyazaki, a port on the southeast coast. Looking at a map, planners could see where they wanted the assault forces to land. What they could not see was what lay under the ground.

In 1943, Donald Belcher, a young civil engineer teaching at Purdue University, wrote a letter to General MacArthur saying that he had a way to interpret soil conditions by looking at aerial photographs. MacArthur passed the letter on to his chief engineer, Major General Hugh J. Casey, who had also been with him since Bataan. Casey, a tough, exacting combat engineer, had built fortifications to defend the Philippines and had blown up bridges in the American retreat down the Bataan peninsula. Once, to get the water depth at a potential landing site in New Guinea, he had taken soundings from a native canoe. He had been with MacArthur in New Guinea and in the liberation of the Philippines. When MacArthur began planning for Olympic, Casey was a key aide.

To verify Belcher's claim, Casey had tested him with an aerial photograph of an area whose soil was known, and when he found that Belcher could indeed perceive soil properties, he helped him set up an Engineer Intelligence Division (EID) at Casey's headquarters. The division, which resembled a college geology faculty more than a military unit, was headed by a lieutenant colonel who was a professor of paleontology in civilian life.

As planning for Olympic got under way, a group under John A. Wolfe, a geologist, began looking at what the soil of Kyushu held in store for an infantryman or a squadron of warplanes and prepared a report. One day, as Wolfe told it, a colonel from the planning staff came into the EID office and slapped a map on the desk of Professor William Putnam. "I want to send 20,000 men onto this beach in the first wave," he said. "They told me to come and see you."

The map showed a beach, 20 miles long and 600 feet wide, backed by a 350-foot cliff. Astonished, Putnam called the colonel a murderer and asked whether they taught cadets at West Point to read maps. He pointed to the contours on the map. "That's a cliff," he said. "C-L-I-F-F." The colonel stalked off, but it would be the strategists, not the geologists, who would decide where the X-Day landings would be.

To a geologist, southern Kyushu, with its volcanic soil, was similar to Batangas Province on Luzon. EID specialists studied Batangas on the ground and from aerial photographs, then compared their findings to aerial photographs of Kyushu. In both places, old roads tended to lie one to eight feet below ground level, sometimes with ditches on both sides, making it difficult for vehicles to pull off the road. In Batangas, Japanese defenders had burrowed into the high banks, making them into ambush sites. On Kyushu, they would undoubtedly do the same.

In both places there were terraced croplands with stone embankments. For men who wanted to dig in suddenly, the EID report said, "Hasty entrenchment [would be] difficult because of hard, shallow soil over consolidated ash." On Kyushu, slopes were steep and cliffs "abundant." Ravines were deep and steep, and "high natural or artificial banks" blocked the heads of ravines to vehicles.

Ariake Bay, wide-mouthed with about two miles of shore, had a deep, sweeping beach. Wolfe would later write:

It is the only place on the island where an army with mechanized equipment could land and maneuver easily. The Japanese knew this as well as we did. They had gun emplacement in the hills on both sides of the mouth of the bay, capable of covering the entire landing area. Photographs showed entrances to a network of tunnels a short distance inland, where troops could remain fairly safe during the pre-invasion bombardment, then emerge and attack the landing forces.

The amount of construction planned on Kyushu was staggering. When MacArthur first sketched the airfield needs on Kyushu, he had told Casey there would be 31 air groups. By the time the invasion plans were completed, the number of air groups had grown to 51. Casey would have to build runways and hardstands for the aircraft and pipeline networks that would provide the airfields with 400,000 gallons of aviation gasoline a day and get regular gasoline to the 71,857 jeeps, trucks, tanks, bulldozers, staff cars, and other vehicles that were to be landed. There would also be anti-freeze for the vehicles and winter clothing for the troops. For the first time in Pacific fighting, men would be going into battle in cold weather. Sixth Army planners ordered that the soldiers get instructions about frostbite before they embarked.

Casey's engineers, along with Navy Seabees, were to build as many as 500 miles of roads, most of them in trackless ravines. Plans called for garrison bases to rise near each invasion site, along with hospitals with a total of 42,750 beds. The largest base, at Kushikino on the west shore of the island, was to support 400,000 men; Shibushi, 185,000 men; Miyazaki, 135,000. The engineers were to build warehouses covering 7.8 million square feet and camps that could accommodate 475,000 replacements, prisoners of war, and internees.

Because southern Kyushu had few good harbors, Casey said that floating piers would have to be built after X-Day at two of the landing sites. He also wanted Kagoshima, which would have been pummeled by bombers for months, quickly rehabilitated so that its volcano-shadowed harbor could unload more than 7,000 tons of cargo a day. The shattered single-track railroad into Kagoshima would have to be rebuilt, along with its many blocked tunnels.

Among the troops who were to land on Kyushu were Casey's engineer demolition experts, whose job would be the blowing up of underground fortifications and the clearing out of caves. The engineers would first hurl phosphorous grenades to startle and blind the Japanese inside the caves. They next threw in satchel charges with delayed fuses and dummy fuses to thwart attempts to pull out the right fuse in the 10 to 15 seconds the cave fighters had to live. To wipe out underground forts, they would lay pipe and pump in a mixture of gasoline and fuel oil, then seal ventilators by lowering aerial bombs into the shafts, timing the bombs to explode when the fuel ignited. The training of all the invasion force was methodical and thorough. It lacked only the chaos and terror of an actual assault. And the ferocity of the Japanese defending their homeland.

The first troops to land on Kyushu on November 1 were to be the veterans of the Army's 40th Infantry Division, who had taken the Kerama island chain off Okinawa to launch that invasion. Their maps and terrain models showed their objective as Koshiki Retto, two islands off the southwestern tip of Kyushu. The islands were to serve as sites for an emergency anchorage and radar stations. The maps also showed the code-name motif of Olympic: The beaches were all named after cars or car parts. The Koshiki Retto's eastern shore was marked off in landing beaches that were named alphabetically, from north to south, Brakedrum, Cylinder, Dashboard, Gearshift, Headlight, Hubcap, Mudguard, Rumbleseat, Sparkplug, and Toolbox. The only western landing beach was Windshield.

The tip of Kyushu was divided into five beach zones—Town Car, Station Wagon, Limousine, Roadster, and Taxicab—and the beaches were alphabetically named, starting with Austin, Buick, Cadillac, Chevrolet, Chrysler, and Cord on the eastern shore, going around the tip with DeSoto, Dusenberg, Essex, Ford, and Franklin, then into Kagoshima Bay, divided into Delivery Wagon and Convertible beach zones and subdivided into Graham Page, Hudson, Hupmobile, LaSalle, Lincoln, Locomobile, Maxwell, Mercedes, Moon, Nash, Oldsmobile, and Overland. The beaches on the western coast were Packard, Plymouth, Pontiac, Red, Rolls-Royce, Saxon, Star, Studebaker, Stutz, Winton, and Zephyr.

No one expected that landings on any of these beaches would be unopposed, as had happened on some other island assaults. The Japanese intended to start their defense at sea, sending kamikaze aircraft and Bakas out to the invasion fleet as it approached the X-Day beaches. Submarines carrying Kaitens would try to fire their human torpedoes as the fleet massed between Okinawa and Kyushu. Hundreds of Kaitens would go to sea. Conventional submarines—Japan still had 60—would take suicidal chances to score a kill, as would the midget submarines, which were not suicide weapons but probably would have been used that way in the Decisive Battle. Other midget submarines were to be stored in well-camouflaged shoreside caves and tunnels, from which they were to be launched on rails for one-way raids on the invasion fleet.

The suicide planes would probably have held back until the invasion fleet was 20 or 30 miles from shore. The suicide attacks would then begin, intensifying around X-Day, when the fleet was taking up stations for the invasion. Japanese defense strategists, basing their optimism on magnified reports of kamikaze and Baka successes in the Philippines and Okinawa, estimated that "special attackers" would take out 30 to 50 percent of the invasion fleet. Captain Rikihei Inoguchi, an air staff officer, was more guarded. He estimated that in the Philippines only one of every six kamikaze planes hit a target; at Okinawa, the rate was one in nine. Off Kyushui, against intense U.S. fighter opposition, he expected a hit score of around one in ten.

One hundred and forty Japanese Navy reconnaisance planes and some Army planes were to fly surveillance missions night and day along a 600-mile radius of the home islands. If they spotted an invasion fleet, the attacks would be held back until the enemy was within easier striking distance for the thousands of kamikaze aircraft hidden on scattered airfields. Plans were to have 10,500 kamikaze aircraft ready for massive attacks by early fall. At the end of June, 8,000 had been prepared for battle.

Aircraft production was dropping to near zero due to relentless U.S. air attacks. Fuel supplies were low, without hope of replenishment. But Japanese intentions were clear. On July 13, Imperial General Headquarters ordered, "United States convoys carrying invasion troops will be destroyed mainly by special attack [suicide] tactics" and stated Japan's *Ketsu* policy:

> The total air strength of the Army and Navy, under a unified command, will annihilate United States forces at sea in the initial stage of their operations to invade the Homeland. Air defense and antisubmarine operations in the Homeland will be strengthened.

In the summer of 1945, airmen already felt the chill of the Decisive Battle. Their motto, Kiyochi Aikawa remembered, was Seven Times Die. No airman could expect to last through more than seven missions. Aikawa, a bomber navigator, was training fliers that summer. They could train only at night because they risked being shot down by day. For them—"the expendables"—the odds dropped down to "die six times." When the time came, their prime target would be the troop transports and assault-craft launching ships of the invasion fleet. Plans were to expend *all* of the 10,500 aircraft in a ten-day-and-night orgy of attacks.

Japan's 19 surviving destroyers, hidden among the islands, would attempt to speed toward the invasion beaches. They would sail to die, carrying on the suicidal tradition of the battleship *Yamato*. Closer in, and probably during the landings, suicide boats would strike. Roaring out of hiding places as landing craft neared shore, the explosives-laden boats would aim at any craft carrying troops. The Navy's *Shinyo* carried 550 pounds of explosives in its bow; the Army's *Renraku-tei* carried two 240-pound depth charges set to explode six seconds after release.

Finally, there would be the usual underwater obstacles designed to rip open or hang up landing craft. And there would be rows of Fukuryu in their diving gear 30 feet or so beneath the water. The outermost row of the suicide frogmen would hover near rows of mines anchored to the bottom.

As the craft neared the mines, the Fukuryu divers would release them, many of them to die in the subsequent explosions; survivors would carry mines to craft that passed nearby. Closer to shore there would be three rows of divers, arrayed so that they were about 60 feet apart. If there had been time to build them, there would also be Fukuryu lairs, underwater "foxholes" made of reinforced concrete with steel doors. As many as 18 divers could be stationed in each underwater foxhole. Just one Fukuryu could take out a landing craft carrying a score or more Americans.

By early August, Ultra was reporting the massing of 560,000 Japanese troops on Kyushu, including 370,000 Army ground troops. Augmenting these military regulars were some 575,000 home-defense forces—125,000 of them in southern Kyushu. The original Olympic plan had anticipated about 450,000 defenders. Under amphibious-warfare doctrine, the assault force should outnumber the defenders by a 3:1 ratio. As Japanese divisions poured into Kyushu, MacArthur's G-2 said that "the end is not in sight. . . . If this deployment is not checked it may grow to a point where we attack on a ratio of one (1) to one (1) which is not the recipe for victory."

Lieutenant General Isamu Yokoyama, commander of the Sixteenth Area Army, was head of the defense of *Ketsu* Area No. 6, Kyushu and adjacent islands. He had deployed his 15 divisions (one an anti-aircraft division) into coastal defense forces and reserve forces that would be "utilized as an assault group to be rushed to the areas where the main enemy effort was being directed."

Yokoyama, who had fought in Manchuria and China, expected that air and naval suicide units would so maul the landing craft that the invasion would be blunted. His artillery, deeply dug into coastal cliffs and hills, would have been gridded and ranged. Guns that survived U.S. coastal bombardment would be able to fire on any square yard of beach quickly, with no need for aiming calculations. The Japanese battle plan called for the surviving artillery to withdraw as the U.S. troops landed. But they would be met by defenders dug into pillboxes and bunkers. The beach, bristling with barbed wire and concrete obstacles, would be strewn with land mines and dotted with machine-gun emplacements and "spider holes," the Japanese version of foxholes.

The artillery would come into play again in support of counterattack forces held back from the beaches. Lacking air support and literally under the guns of offshore warships, the Japanese planned to "confuse the battle lines," sending coastal infantry troops forward into close-quarter fighting. The Japanese expected that the invaders and defenders would form such a beachhead melee that U.S. air power and firepower would be withheld, lest Americans be killed by friendly fire.

The Americans would be landing on three heavily defended beaches:

• The assault on the west coast would be by the V Marine Amphibious Corps (2nd, 3rd, and 5th Marine Divisions). This force was to land on the western shore of the Satsuma Peninsula—the Roadster Beach Zone, with Pontiac to Zephyr beaches encompassing a large bay. The Marines would confront about 52,000 Japanese troops as they attempted to land, move on through hilly, cave-riddled country, and take Kagoshima.

• The I Corps (25th, 33rd, and 41st Infantry Divisions) would land near Miyazaki on Town Car Beach Zone, the longest stretch of invasion shore—about 14 miles from Austin to Cord. The soldiers were to head inland through a gauntlet of cliffs pocked with caves. They were to seize airfields and block Japanese forces heading south. They would face about 61,000 Japanese coastal defense and backup forces.

• The XI Corps (1st Cavalry, 43rd Infantry, and Americal Divisions) would land at the head of Ariake Bay south of Shibushi. They were to take the airfield near Shibushi and head northwest to link up with I Corps. They would be opposed by about 55,000 Japanese troops and 21 coastal guns planned for the mountains flanking the landing beach.

Once the landings had begun, General Yokoyama planned to move troop and tank reserves during the night against one of the beaches, his strategy calling for his own Decisive Battle—a focus of much of his forces on the Shibushi invasion area. His hope was that his beach defenders would have pinned down the invaders through the night. Then, on X + 1, he would fall upon them with four divisions and three tank brigades. In mass attacks—furious banzai charges—the tanks would be used as artillery.

If several troop-filled transports could be sunk, if the Americans on one beach could be annihilated, then Japanese strategists believed that the bloodshed would bring America to the negotiating table. "One punch, then talk" was the way one retired Japanese naval officer put it. But whatever the statesmen might do, the invasion would have taken place. Two or three beaches would have been seized, and Kyushu would have become what U.S. planners wanted it to be: a springboard for the assault on Tokyo. If the Japanese annihilation plan had produced another Iwo Jima, another Okinawa, then that was the cost of victory. And if unconditional surrender did not come, Operation Downfall would proceed as planned with an invasion of Honshu, where the ferocity of Japanese resistance would be far greater and the cost of victory even higher.

CHAPTER 11

OBJECTIVE: TOKYO

Koryu midget submarines, each manned by a crew of five and armed with two torpedoes, were being made ready to attack U.S. troop ships as they approached Japan.

U.S. military planners had to look far into the future when they developed the invasion plan for Honshu, the heart of the Japanese Empire. For Coronet to proceed, they had to assume that Olympic had succeeded. They also had to assume that certain events had occurred during the Kyushu assaults. For example, a planning document for Coronet said that the Kyushu invasion "may prompt the Jap Naval High Command to launch 'all out' surface suicide attacks against the Kyushu Task Forces." If this had happened, Japan's few surviving warships undoubtedly would have been destroyed by the time of the Coronet landings.

The two invasions were distinctly different. While the Olympic landings would conquer homeland territory, its concept was similar to the other amphibious operations in the Pacific: seize land, build bases, and push on to the next objective. Coronet, which Marshall had seen as the "decisive operation" against Japan, was unique. There was nothing beyond Coronet. It was the ultimate goal.

The islands were also vastly different. Kyushu, mountainous and isolated, had no focal point and was viewed as hardly more than real estate for the building of airfields and a fleet anchorage. On Kyushu, Japanese troops would be killed, captured—if any surrendered—or driven northward as far as the Saito-Tsuno line and not pursued. Honshu, the setting for the jewel of Tokyo, was much larger than Kyushu, and there would be no line drawn there. In an extended struggle, all of Honshu and all of its defenders had to be conquered.

The Kyushu invasion had employed troops who had fought in the Pacific. For Honshu, troops from Europe would be needed. To carry out the redeployment, which the War Department called "the greatest transportation problem that has ever been undertaken in war," some troops and supplies would be shipped 14,000 miles from Europe to Manila by way of the Panama Canal. Others would land at East Coast ports, take trains across the country, and ship out from San Francisco to Manila, a 6,700-mile voyage. The luckier troops heading for the Pacific would get furloughs and specialized training in the United States before heading back to war.

In choosing the date for Coronet, planners tried to find the time of most favorable weather, as they had done in setting November 1 as X-Day for Olympic. Although that date meant that the troops would have to fight in cold weather, the typhoon and rainy season would be over. But invasion

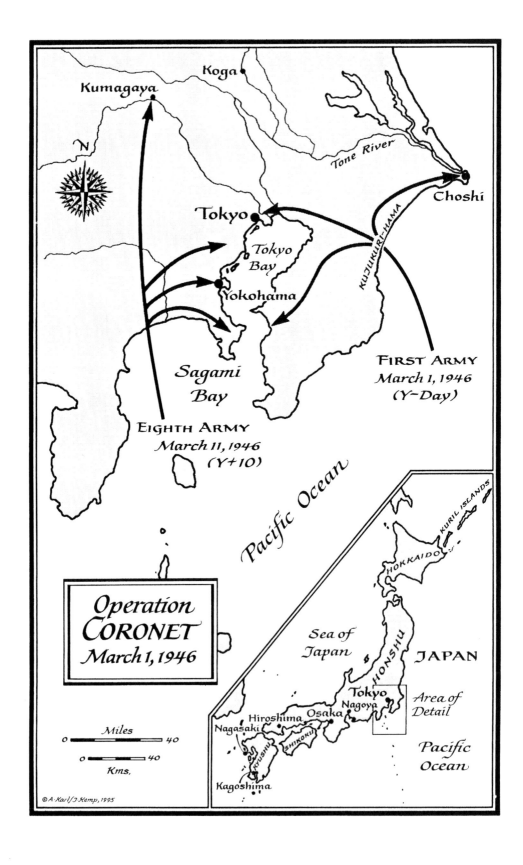

Koga

Kumagaya

N

Tone River

Tokyo

Choshi

KUJIUKIRI-HAMA

Tokyo
Bay

Yokohama

FIRST ARMY
March 1, 1946
(Y–Day)

Sagami
Bay

EIGHTH ARMY
March 11, 1946
(Y+10)

Pacific Ocean

Operation
CORONET
March 1, 1946

Miles
0   40

0   40
Kms.

© A. Karl / J. Kemp, 1995

KURIL ISLANDS

HOKKAIDO

Sea of
Japan

HONSHU

JAPAN

Tokyo
Nagoya

Area of
Detail

Hiroshima   Osaka
Nagasaki

SHIKOKU

Pacific
Ocean

KYUSHU

Kagoshima

planners could not predict the weather for X-Day. However, it would be a factor in the buildup. In August 1945, part of the Kyushu invasion fleet was already assembling at Okinawa, and the ships were still there on October 9, when Typhoon Louise, one of the most powerful storms ever recorded, roared across the island. Driven by 100-knot winds with frequent 120-knot gusts, waves towered 30 to 35 feet. Winds, seas, and rain pounded the Okinawa anchorage. Ships slammed into each other. Crews abandoned foundering ships to struggle ashore in tossing boats. They sought shelter in caves, tombs, and ditches.

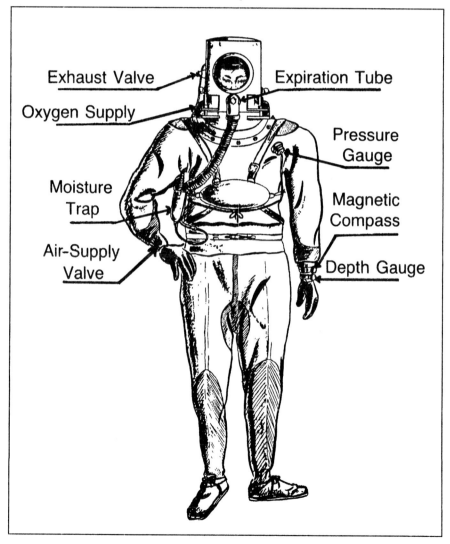

Fukuryu guerrillas, human mines, were trained to swim out and blow up landing craft with hand-held explosives.

What Typhoon Louise did to the cargo ship *Flagler* was typical. The *Flagler,* which had been assigned to the invasion force, dragged anchor. With her engines running she was still blown ashore, where she smashed into the grounded *LST 826,* another invasion ship. At bases on shore, winds ripped away 50 to 95 percent of the tents, tossed around Quonset huts and aircraft, destroyed or severely damaged about 80 percent of the buildings on Okinawa, and wiped out most food and medical stocks. In all, 12 ships were sunk, and 222 ships, landing craft, and barges were grounded, 32 of them damaged beyond repair by their crews. At least 36 men were killed, 47 more were reported missing, and about 100 were seriously injured.

So large was the Olympic invasion fleet that Typhoon Louise hardly put a dent in it. The storm probably would have set back the invasion schedule by about two weeks at most. But if a storm struck Okinawa as the "slow tow" was being assembled—gasoline barges, freighters bearing deck cargo, and other slow-moving shipping—damage to vital supplies would be considerable and could cause a delay of 30 to 45 days. And if a typhoon had struck Kyushu and swept through the troop-filled amphibious craft on or about X-Day, Japan could have hailed another "Divine Wind."

There was little chance of typhoons interfering with the March 1946 invasion of Honshu; the typhoon season was past. What some planners did fear was heavy seas, which did not need a typhoon's winds to swamp a landing craft or drown invaders. Except in rare times of very low surf, said an American specialist on waves and beaches, an attempt to land on the beaches of Honshu "would have been an amphibious disaster." One of the objectives was Katakai, near the midpoint of the curving 50 miles of Kujukuri-Hama, a cliff-backed beach called the Dover of Japan. The surf usually hit the sloping beach high and strong, smashing into the numerous breakwaters thrusting from the shore. Cliffs 100 to 130 feet high rose from the beach, and the area had long been known as a prime habitat for sharks.

The planning for Coronet was more tentative than the planning for Olym-pic. On May 25, 1945, when the Joint Chiefs approved Olympic, they avoided a similar directive for detailed planning of Coronet—"this much-dreaded operation," as the official JCS history called it. "To a large extent," the history said, "Coronet would be a follow-up of Olympic, using some of the same forces, and planning could proceed without a final directive from the JCS to the theater commanders. Finally, hopes were strong that by the time Olympic was launched the situation might have changed" and Coronet would not be necessary.

In the briefing paper prepared for the meeting with President Truman on June 18, the Joint Chiefs said that the Kyushu invasion "may well prove to be the decisive operation which will terminate the war." Less than a month later, a revision of that document said, "It may well be that Japanese capitulation will be forced by this invasion." Whatever the language, the JCS kept hoping that an assault on Honshu could be avoided.

The possibility of "a sudden collapse or surrender" also appealed to the Joint Chiefs. They so strongly believed this might happen that on June 8 they ordered Admiral Nimitz and General MacArthur to make plans "to effect an entry into Japan proper for occupational purposes." But when Nimitz produced a plan calling for "Prompt emergency naval occupation of Tokyo," MacArthur strenuously objected, saying in a message to General Marshall that "it would be psychologically offensive to ground and air forces of the Pacific theater to be relegated from their proper missions at the hour of victory for which they have paid the highest price in blood during the last three and one-half years."

Marshall, responding to MacArthur, agreed that only the Army "can provide sufficient military force to seize and secure the key areas and disarm the Jap forces." But he added that there could be "no hiatus period," because if the naval and air bombardment stopped on the day of surrender, "the Jap authorities might well recover from the initial shock and individual commanders choose to organize key areas and fight to the finish."

That was the greatest fear of American military leaders, a fight to the finish. Assuming that the Japanese strategy on Kyushu had succeeded, tens of thousands of Americans would have died—drowned at sea in transports sunk by suicide torpedoes and kamikaze aircraft, killed in landing craft blown up by human mines on X-Day, slaughtered on the beach by Japanese gloriously dying in banzai charges, ambushed by civilians bearing explosive charges.

But a high death toll on Kyushu would not stop the American invasion any more than high death tolls had stopped the invasions of Tarawa, Iwo Jima, and Okinawa. Southern Kyushu would still be taken, and American demands for total victory and unconditional surrender would be strengthened, not weakened. Perhaps humiliation for Truman and MacArthur would have come in the wake of a disaster at Kyushu, but a public demand for a negotiated end of the war would be far less likely. The Japanese had hoped that the Decisive Battle would produce calls for negotiation. Far more likely would be calls for vengeance.

Nor would the cost of defending Kyushu have inspired a Japanese attempt at negotiations. Even if Japan had expended most of its kamikaze aircraft and had lost the remnants of the Imperial Japanese Navy at Kyushu, there would still be millions of soldiers—and tens of millions of civilians—ready to fight and die on Honshu.

There had been a provisional U.S. plan to land troops on northern Honshu in Mutsu Bay. Marshall had hinted at the plan when, concerned about the Japanese buildup on Kyushu, in a worried message to MacArthur, he mentioned Ominato on Mutsu Bay as an alternative. There were five airfields in the Mutsu area and potential sites for about 15 more. U.S. planes taking off from northern Honshu would have to fly only about 400 miles to Tokyo; from Kyushu the distance was about 600 miles.

To assault northern Honshu, the invasion force would have to win control of the Tsugaru Strait, which separates Honshu from the long, curving O-Shima Peninsula of Hokkaido to the north. American troops would have landed near Hachinohe and the Shimokita Peninsula, which reaches out toward Hokkaido and encompasses much of Mutsu Bay. Other forces would land on the shores along both sides of the strait and knock out coast defenses. Intelligence estimates put Japanese strength around Mutsu at about 100,000 men. U.S. planners believed that the Japanese might at first see the landings as a diversion and delay the sending of reinforcements to the area.

American forces probably would have suffered far fewer casualties in lightly defended northern Honshu. But the time for battle and building in that cold land was short. By December, frozen ground would have stopped much of the construction work, and persistent bad weather would have curtailed flights from the newly won and newly built airfields. Most of all, northern Honshu was not Tokyo, and U.S. strategists believed that somehow, someday, Tokyo would have to be taken.

Tokyo sprawls out from the vast Kanto (Tokyo) Plain and spreads across the upper reaches of Tokyo Bay. The Kanto Plain, the largest lowland in Japan, is about 120 miles deep and 80 to 110 miles wide, stretching from the shores of the Pacific, through Tokyo, to a mountain barrier, dominated by Mount Fuji. Low, scattered hills and terraced farmland rise from the flat terrain. One-sixth of Japan's population lived on the plain, most of them in Tokyo, Yokohama, and more than 80 other cities, until the bombings and evacuations in the spring and summer of 1945.

The Coronet plan exploited the Kanto Plain, using it as a stage for a classic pincer movement, with U.S. forces landing southeast and southwest of Tokyo and closing in on the city. The plain was also seen as an ideal battleground for American tanks, and the Honshu invasion would employ the first U.S. armored divisions used in the Pacific War.

General MacArthur declared that he "would exercise personal command of the landing forces and direct the group operations on the mainland." He would be in command of some 575,000 soldiers and Marines, by far the largest invasion force ever assembled. The Tokyo Bay area would be battered by the most powerful and sustained preinvasion bombardment of the war. For 180 days the bay defenses would be hit by the usual naval bombardment and air strikes, augmented by rocket-firing craft and American versions of the German V-1 "buzz bomb." Chemical defoliants would be sprayed by aircraft 1,000 to 5,000 yards inland to uncover fortifications hidden beneath trees. Then the exposed defense complexes and troop concentrations would be pounded by bombs and shells.

Army planners expected to encounter beachhead fortifications so formidable that a special weapon was being developed for the landings. It was the T-92, a 240-mm howitzer—the largest U.S. Army field gun—mounted on a modified Pershing tank chassis. The 240-mm shell, which weighed 360 pounds, could penetrate five feet of reinforced concrete before exploding. The Army had ordered 216 T-92s and in 1945 had begun training crews for them in the United States.

In the summer of 1945 1st Lieutenant Paul I. Andrews, of the 784th Armored Field Artillery Battalion, at Fort Bragg, North Carolina, was learning to operate the T-92. One night a man in his company went to the public library in nearby Fayetteville and brought back a grade-school geography book. Andrews and his men, over coffee in the mess hall, looked up Japan. On a map of Honshu, the lowlands were in green, and higher elevations were indicated by other colors. There was a green stretch from one beach, marked "Kujukuri," to Tokyo.

Andrews suddenly knew that he and his battalion's T-92s would be landing on that beach in not too many months. He wondered how a 69-ton monster would manage to travel across rice paddies, even dry rice paddies. "Logistics and coordination were what bothered me," he later recalled. "We ran out of ammunition in Italy. We didn't take out the bunkers in Normandy. We ran out of gas going up through France."

He could console himself with the knowledge that a 240-mm howitzer was an awesome weapon. As he figured out, one B-29 flying out of Tinian could deliver an 18,000-pound bombload every two days. A 240, firing at a sustained rate of a round every two minutes, could deliver the same amount of explosives in one hour and 40 minutes. The howitzer, which had a range of about 14 miles, was to land with the assault forces and fire point-blank to take out beachhead fortifications.

By the time of the Honshu landings, the skies over Japan would be dark with Twining and Doolittle's B-29s, Kenney's B-24s and B-32s, hordes of fighters and light and medium bombers, and Halsey's 1,000 carrier planes as well as Marine aircraft. The U.S. air armada, meeting little meaningful opposition, would have pounded every Japanese city, every town, every crossroad, every rail line, every storage facility, and every other target that air intelligence could identify as having any military value.

In September 1945, the bomb drop was expected to reach 100,000 tons. In January 1946, as part of the pre-Coronet bombardment, 170,000 tons of bombs were to fall on Japanese targets. Then, in March, as Coronet was to begin, 220,000 tons of bombs would be dropped. Thus, in March alone, U.S. bombers would drop about one-quarter of the total bomb tonnage dropped on Germany in all of 1944.

On Y-Day, March 1, 1946, the U.S. First Army, commanded by General Courtney H. Hodges, would storm the Kujukuri-Hama shore south of Katakai and split into three elements. The spearhead would advance 50 miles across the plain to the eastern edge of Tokyo. A second element would move southwestward to take the eastern shore of Tokyo Bay, and the third would move northward to seize the mouth of the Tone River, which would become an unloading point and harbor for small craft.

Then, ten days after Y-Day, the Eighth Army, under Lieutenant General Robert L. Eichelberger, was to land on beaches at the head of Sagami Bay, southwest of the narrow mouth of Tokyo Bay, about 35 miles from Emperor Hirohito's palace. Three elements would move eastward to take the western shore of Tokyo Bay, including Yokohama, and begin a western encirclement of Tokyo. A fourth element, an armored force, would roll northward past Tokyo to seize the Kumagaya-Koga area and block Japanese reinforcements by cutting north-south routes.

Coronet Deception planning for the Honshu invasion involved several fictitious assaults and feints. A story would be put out that before invading Honshu the United States wanted to tighten the naval blockade of Japan and step up the bombing of Japanese cities. That strategy called for the capture of land on the southeastern coast of Korea to prevent Japanese shipping from crossing the Korea Strait, and the goal of the invasion of Shikoku was to acquire additional airfields for fighters and bombers.

The elaborate hoax would begin around November 1, 1945—just when the Olympic invasion was to be launched. Korean guerrilla bands, making their way from Chinese territory held by Chiang Kai-shek, would slip over the border into Korea and begin transmitting weather reports. They would also blow up rail bridges and perform other acts of sabotage. All this was to convince the Japanese that an invasion of Korea was imminent.

Sometime in April 1946 news would leak in America about the departure from West Coast ports of Korean-American interpreters and civil government officers trained to administer U.S.-occupied Korea. Red Cross officials in Washington, Chungking, and Kunming would be told to have people ready for transport to Korea. An officer on the staff of the commanding general of U.S. forces in China would go into Japanese-held territory, presumably on an inspection trip. He would lose detailed plans for the Korean landings in hopes a Japanese spy eventually would acquire them, perhaps from a Chinese double agent.

The Army would name a commander for the fake Korea landing. Men of certain divisions in training would be shown models of the Korean coast and movies about Korea. There would also be drops of leaflets and fake airborne supplies and seemingly discarded parachutes. Around December 1, reconnaissance planes would swoop over the Korean Strait. Submarines would appear off the coast and, through fake radio messages and props simulating rubber-raft landings, would appear to be putting commandos and spies ashore.

To intensify the realism of the Shikoku landing, a commander of that invasion force was also to be named. His divisions, training in the Philippines and on Okinawa, would be told that they were to land in Shikoku. The division on Okinawa would be given amphibious training using the names of Shikoku sites. Japanese prisoners of war at a nearby camp would witness this training, and if it could be arranged smoothly, a couple of the prisoners would be allowed to escape. The divisions in training would also be given fictitious numbers in deceptive radio transmissions.

Many of the deception plans implied that U.S. intelligence officers not only believed that GIs would talk to outsiders about the landings but also that there were in the Philippines and on Okinawa Japanese spies who could make reports to Tokyo. Presumably, the intelligence officers also believed that the escaped prisoners would be able to make contact with Japanese spies on Okinawa.

Around January 1, 1946, planes of the U.S. Far East Air Forces would fly over Shikoku and drop packets containing parachutes and damaged supplies, which would appear to have been abandoned by men who had been clandestinely dropped on Shikoku. For the next few weeks there would be muffled blasts off the beaches of Shikoku—the explosions of time-delay bombs left on rubber rafts by U.S. Navy ships sailing close to shore. Jittery Japanese defenders were expected to believe that the explosions were caused by the typical preinvasion work of Navy Underwater Demolition Teams clearing mines and underwater obstacles. Adding to the realism were leaflets that planes would drop on Shikoku warning civilians to avoid airfields and beaches beginning on March 1, the actual day when Honshu was to be invaded.

At camps in the Philippines, the Marianas, and Oahu, officers of Army and Marine divisions assigned to the Honshu landings would study models of that island and of Shikoku. Troops would see movies of cities on the Inland Sea, which separates southern Honshu from Shikoku. In Manila, an Army truck would have a minor accident. Maps and documents would spill to the street, and soldiers would frantically gather them up, trying to hide the Shikoku names on the map. Army experts on civil government and airfield construction would get briefings on Shikoku.

The Coronet Deception plan was to be carried on well beyond Y-Day. While U.S. troops were fighting on Honshu, attempts would be made to induce the Japanese to believe that a landing on Hokkaido was imminent. Strategically, U.S. deceivers hoped that the Hokkaido hoax would keep Japanese troops on that island from going to the aid of their comrades on Honshu.

Confusion over possible northern moves would begin when some U.S. divisions destined for Coronet were embarked from Seattle, Washington, and sent northward with the report that they were en route to the Aleutian Islands. Japanese strategists had long believed that U.S. troops, possibly in concert with Canadian forces, would use the Aleutians as steppingstones for an assault on Hokkaido. Fictitious bases would be readied in the Aleutians, where radio traffic would build up and be sustained to indicate that the divisions were training there for winter fighting. Radio traffic also would lead the Japanese to believe that a Canadian division would be part of an Aleutians-to-Hokkaido invasion.

If Stalin had kept his promise to enter the Pacific War in the late summer of 1945, Soviet troops by early 1946 would have consolidated positions in Manchuria and taken over most or all of Korea, southern Sakhalin Island, and the Kurils. They would also be preparing for an amphibious-airborne assault on Hokkaido; such an invasion was definitely planned by Stalin. Had the war given the Soviets time to land on Hokkaido, the result most likely would have been a Japan divided into U.S. and Soviet occupation zones, a Korea entirely occupied by the Red Army, and a China even more rapidly taken over by Soviet-aided communists.

Early in 1946 U.S. reconnaissance flights would have begun over Hokkaido and northern Honshu. Fast-spreading dyes would be dropped on the waters off Hokkaido, and garrisons there would have had puzzling and disturbing stains to contemplate on their beaches. What did this mean? What kind of chemical weapon was this?

In the Kurils, U.S. submarines would land shore parties to capture prisoners and perhaps place agents, actions that would show defenders their vulnerability and add the Kurils to the list of possible invasion sites. Planes would drop leaflets warning fishermen in the Kurils and Hokkaido to avoid specified waters. Radio broadcasts to Hokkaido would also warn civilians to stay away from certain shore areas.

U.S. intelligence officers knew that the Japanese had broken some low-level codes used by U.S. Army Air Forces and U.S. Navy aviation units. In a compromised code, they would send messages about the building of rocket launchers in the Aleutians. Japanese intelligence, aware of German V-1 and V-2 characteristics, would probably assume that the most likely targets were in northern Japan.

Seven days before Y-Day, a large force would sail into Sendai Bay and begin bombarding and bombing defenses. Closer in, deception units would sweep mines and simulate the destruction of underwater obstacles with time bombs sent into shore in unmanned rubber boats. Ships would lay smoke, set off pyrotechnics, and jam shore radar. They would also send frequent long messages that Japanese radio-traffic analysts would interpret as orders for an invasion of Sendai Bay. The performance off Sendai Bay was to be the opening scene in a complex invasion drama of many scenes and many acts of deception. Even Y-Day itself was partially false, for there were to be two Y-Days, one on March 1 and the other, known as Y + 10, ten days later.

The most complex scenario would come on Y-Day itself, when both real and fictional assaults were planned. On Y-Day, General MacArthur would be offshore, personally directing the operation. As a courtesy, he could conceivably be on an Australian warship, part of the British Commonwealth contribution to the invasion fleet. For practical reasons, however, a U.S. cruiser or command ship would provide better communications and space for staff officers than would an Australian ship.

By MacArthur's personal orders, only American troops would go ashore for the climactic invasion of the war. And all of the assault troops would be white.

The initial landings would be made by the First Army under General Hodges. The question of having the First Army's black troops in the invasion had arisen in May 1945, when MacArthur had been asked whether he intended to deploy newly integrated First Army divisions. He had said he would. But those divisions did not appear in his invasion order of battle.

Landing craft would carry a corps of three infantry divisions—more than 75,000 men—through the Kujukuri-Hama surf near Katakai. At the same time, some 30 miles north, two more divisions would hit the beach at Ioka, a town at the northern end of the Kujukuri-Hama. These troops were to capture a nearby airfield and take the port of Choshi.

Meanwhile, at Kashima, a town about 50 miles northeast of Tokyo, a third force would move as if to launch an invasion there, presumably drawing Japanese reinforcements northward. Then, on Y + 5, this same phantom invasion fleet would appear off Sendai, about 180 miles north of Tokyo. Minesweepers would clear mines, and warships would begin a typical preinvasion bombardment. The fleet would make a feint as if to launch a landing. Instead, a First Army division would come ashore at Katakai.

The real-and-fake invasion scheme would continue until Y + 10 in a pattern that was to "simulate by radio and radar deception the northward, rather than the actual southward, movement" of the main attack force—the phantom fleet that had staged the fake assaults. Now, on Y + 10, this force would make the major landing of the invasion, an assault on Sagami Bay. That operation—a second, separate invasion larger than the first—would be the mission of the Eighth Army under General Eichelberger. It would begin with the landing of a corps of three divisions in an arc of beaches centering on Oiso, at the head of the bay. If that beachhead held, on Y + 10 would also come a corps consisting of the 13th and 20th Armored Divisions. In the following days, other reinforcing troops would pour onto the beachhead. They would all be Americans. British, Canadian, French, and Australian troops, said MacArthur's report on the anticipated invasion, "would be employed in case Japanese resistance should continue even after the heart of their Homeland was in American hands."

In mid-April, U.S. planners hoped that about half a million American troops would be ready for the final phase of the final battle, the taking of Tokyo. Forces would close on the city from the east and west while a third force pushed northward from Sagami Bay, along the edge of the Kanto Plain. Elements of that force were also to hold a front extending from Kumagaya to Koga, hoping to bottle up Japanese troops and keep them from reaching Tokyo.

That was the American invasion plan. The Japanese defense plan had anticipated much of it.

No matter what might have happened at Kyushu, Japan still had surprises for invaders of Honshu. At Yokosuka, south of Yokohama on the western shore of Tokyo Bay, Korean slave laborers had carved a three-level warren of tunnels, one more than a mile long. Here Japanese workers assembled Baka suicide attack planes and rocket-powered J8M *Shusui* (Swinging Sword) interceptors. The rocket-powered Bakas were originally designed to be carried aloft and released as the mother aircraft neared target. The Yokosuka Bakas would have been placed on hidden ground launchers and fired directly against the invasion landing craft.

A prototype of the Shusui interceptor was tested on July 7, 1945. On takeoff it dropped its wheels, flew as fast as 560 miles per hour for about five and a half minutes, then glided back to earth and landed on a grass strip like a glider. Although not designed as a suicide craft, it would have been used as a kamikaze against invaders.

The underground assembly plant was beneath the Yokosuka naval base, where midget submarines were also being built. Many of these would have been mounted on rails in shoreside tunnels and launched directly into the sea to seek out troop-filled transports. In the 20 miles of tunnels under the base were living quarters for several hundred workers and sailors, a two-level command center, arsenals, gunnery and navigation schools, and a 100-bed hospital. The Yokosuka labyrinth was an elaborate version of the countless caverns and hideaways where Japanese troops, with their food, ammunition, fuel, and other supplies, would await the Decisive Battle on Honshu.

For the defense of Honshu, every aircraft, submarine, and surface ship was a potential kamikaze weapon. Takeshi Maeda, who had torpedoed the *West Virginia* during the attack on Pearl Harbor and fought in the Battle of Midway, was awaiting the invasion at Katori Air Base near Kujukuri-Hama. He, like all Japanese pilots, was now a kamikaze warrior. When the invaders came, he believed, every Japanese plane would be sacrificed in a final suicidal assault. The chosen targets, as at Kyushu, would be troop-carrying transports at sea and, at the beaches, landing craft.

"The Kanto Plain," said a U.S. intelligence assessment, "is the most heavily fortified area in Japan. . . . The number of guns reported to be in the Kanto Plain area, as of 15 April 1945, was approximately 320 coast defense, 165 dual purpose, 575 antiaircraft, and 935 automatic weapons." Another intelligence report estimated that the plain would be defended by about 366,000 Japanese troops and 500,000 armed members of Civilian Volunteer Units and

Special Guard Units. In an assessment of Japanese defense strategy, the latter report said that "manpower will be exceedingly cheap." Likely invasion beaches "will be defended by substantial concentrations of reservists stiffened by a leavening of regular troops" because the Japanese defenders "will strive to conserve [their] best troops for employment in less costly inland defense. . . ."

A Japanese army—about 100,000 men—was deployed at each of the landing areas selected by the Coronet planners. As on Kyushu, on Honshu the Japanese chose one beach for maximum defense and maximum killing of Americans. That beach was Kujukuri-Hama, and also as on Kyushu, highly expendable coastal-combat divisions would be among the "exceedingly cheap" manpower thrown at the invaders. U.S. air and sea power would mean little on the beaches, for the coastal troops would be "merging all lines into an interlocking and continuously fluid struggle in which American air, artillery, and naval gunfire would be seriously hampered in choice of targets."

Even with control of the air and sea, U.S. ships would be in peril from Japanese suicide planes. Of all the Japanese forces committed to the Decisive Battle, the pilots were the warriors expected to die. Naval officers and crewmen without ships had similar suicidal expectations. About 25,000 "naval ground units" were assigned to combat on Honshu; the Japanese Navy also supplied 10,000 men for anti-aircraft defense around Tokyo Bay and another 4,000 men for guard force units.

Japan's major defensive force beyond the beaches would be the Tokyo Defense Army, formed in late June 1945. Its core consisted of three infantry brigades and two engineer battalions whose dual mission would be the destruction of bridges that U.S. troops wanted to cross and the rebuilding of bridges and roads destroyed by U.S. bombings. As soon as the battles for the beachheads had ended, tank and artillery units and two or three infantry divisions would make their way to Tokyo for a last-ditch defense. The Decisive Battle would be elusive and never-ending, a battle in motion, drawing more and more Americans into fight-to-the-death engagements until the climactic struggle for Tokyo.

Tokyo, which had been largely destroyed by March and April bombings, would have been pulverized by the time of Coronet. But desperate men defending their capital will fight in rubble and make the invaders bleed for every foot of smoldering ruin. Berlin, 80 percent of its dwellings destroyed by Allied bombing and surrounded by the Red Army, had seemed doomed to immediate collapse by April 1945. But Hitler demanded a fight to the death. There was no surrender until May 2, after Hitler was dead.

The battle for Tokyo would be as ferocious as the *Götterdämmerung* for Berlin but not as climactic. For Japanese military leaders were prepared to fight on when Tokyo fell. In the mountain town of Matsushiro, about 100 miles northwest of Tokyo, thousands of Koreans, forced to labor for Japan, were working day and night to finish a gigantic secret project: an underground shelter, carved, mostly by hand tools, into a rocky mountain. The underground redoubt, which had more than eight miles of tunnels, covered 84,200 square feet. It would be known as the Matsushiro Underground Imperial Headquarters, and from here the Imperial Army, government ministries, and Emperor Hirohito would continue the Decisive Battle. Elsewhere in Japan the military planned to fight a furtive war, using underground fortifications stocked with supplies that would last a year. Civilians were expected to fight with spears and kitchen knives, killing any American they could find.

In June 1945, General MacArthur had been characteristically optimistic about the potential success of Operation Downfall. However, by August his staff had learned enough about Japanese defense plans to wonder about the cost. By then, too, senior officers in Manila and in Washington would have known that the Army's redeployment program, the key to getting European veterans to Coronet, was a disaster.

As early as March 1945, General Marshall, Admiral Halsey, and Admiral Nimitz separately conducted off-the-record conversations with influential Washington journalists. They were told to spread the word that there would not be any large-scale demobilization of U.S. troops in Europe when the war there ended. When VE-Day came, however, so did demobilization. While no men in either the Navy or the Army Air Forces could expect to go home from the Pacific until the war ended, tens of thousands of veterans of the European War, demobilized under the Army's point system, were beginning their peacetime lives. Tokyo Rose was not just mouthing propaganda when she told sailors and GIs in the Pacific that they were losing their jobs and their girlfriends to able-bodied men in new civilian suits.

The Navy theoretically kept men aboard ships for no more than 18 months, but in the Pacific in 1945 that policy was an empty promise. The Eighth Air Force in the European theater had sent bomber air crews home after they completed 25 combat missions; when Lieutenant General Doolittle took over the Eighth, he increased that to 35, and when he led the Eighth to the Pacific in the summer of 1945, no one expected that Doolittle would give anyone a respite from the relentless air war.

Typical was the experience of Whitmal W. Hill, who had been a ground crewman in the Eighth Air Force's 91st Heavy Bomb Group in England since September 1942. He had accumulated more than 100 points, well over the 85 that was earning foot soldiers a one-way ticket home. When he sailed back to the United States on board the *Queen Elizabeth* in late June 1945, he expected to be discharged. But after 30-day furloughs, he and others from his group were sent to Drew Field, Florida, marched to the base theater, and told that they were heading for the Pacific. William T. Clark, a

B-17 navigator transferred to Drew Field at about the same time, remembers a mutinous vow that men were making at Drew Field: "Two guys ain't going to the Pacific—me and the man they send to get me."

In the summer of 1945 Staff Sergeant Raymond E. Logan, on Leyte, was told that his outfit, the 304th Signal Operations Battalion, was being shipped to Okinawa in preparation for the invasion. Most of the men had worked for Northwestern Bell, with some from Pennsylvania Bell and Southern Bell. Many of them had been in the Pacific since 1942. "We knew the road home lay through Tokyo," he remembered. "We just accepted it."

Although it was patently unfair, a Gallup Poll showed that 70 percent of the American public supported the point system. What the public did not know was that demobilization was undermining the redeployment of troops from Europe to the Pacific. Combat veterans were going home by the tens of thousands, and green troops were replacing them. Many Army units that had won the war in Europe were empty shells by July 1945, and those units, filled with untested troops, were to be a significant part of the forces assembling for the final campaign against Japan.

In typical units selected for redeployment, combat veterans were being replaced by green troops at an alarming rate. A tank destroyer battalion, for instance, lost 50 percent of its men. An ordnance company reported in August that 73 percent of its men had been in the company less than a month. A radio intelligence company was about to fall apart, for 95 percent of its men had enough points to go home. One division of about 25,000 men was anticipating a loss of 11,000 enlisted men and 600 officers.

"A large proportion of the men lost," said an Army report, were specialists and noncommissioned officers. Newcomers "usually were greatly inferior in training, experience, and leadership to the men whom they replaced." Also lost was the venerable military concept of cohesion—the shoulder-to-shoulder stability that holds a fighting unit together. Violation of this concept, said the report, "would mean loss of lives and battle efficiency. The period of redeployment training was all too brief to permit of molding into a team a unit which had lost most of its key specialists and from one-third to three-fourths of its officers and men," the report continued. There was no question that the large number of untested troops would have greatly increased American casualties in the battle for Honshu.

The training being given to Pacific-bound men included such standards as care and maintenance of arms, the use of camouflage, and information about malaria and other Pacific health problems. Also covered were Japanese tactics and weapons and identification of Japanese planes and equipment. But something else had been added: "the offensive employment of toxic gases." As part of the secret Project Sphinx, troops were to be taught how to use poison gas for the "reduction of Japanese cave fortifications."

By the time of the Honshu invasion, poison gas would have been readily available in the forward areas and relatively easy to employ through bombs, aircraft sprayers, and long-range artillery. However, the anthrax being produced near Terre Haute, Indiana, would not be used because it was too difficult to handle. Gas weapons could not be used while U.S. troops were locked in combat on the beaches. But even if one of the beachheads were lost, the American offensive would continue, and the use of gas would have been considered as a way to reduce American casualties.

Americans who survived the beachheads would be pressed by the Japanese into defiles or valleys, natural funnels for the creation of deep, narrow fronts. Frontline Japanese troops, backing up their expendable coastal-combat comrades, hoped to hold the mouths of these funnels and prevent the Americans from fighting the tank-led battles they preferred. These Japanese tactics would make the rear echelons of their massed troops prime targets for gas attacks.

U.S. war planners had examined the possibility of using gas bombs on Japanese cities, and that plan could have been adapted quickly for tactical use against massed Japanese troops. "Had gas warfare been inaugurated during 1945," said an unpublished, still partially classified Army history,

> Japan would have suffered materially from U.S. Air Forces, particularly from bombers based on Saipan. Plans for gas warfare called for one rate of expenditure during the "initial" stage of gas operations and for a reduced rate during a "normal" phase. During the initial phase, from G [Gas] Day to G plus 15, the bombers would have operated strategically against Japan proper and tactically against other targets. During this period 150 percent of normal aircraft sorties would have been flown and 75 percent of the bomb load would have consisted of toxic bombs.

President Roosevelt had promised that gas would not be used except in retaliation, but no such promise was made by President Truman. By the time of the Honshu invasion, the extent of Japanese gas- and germ-warfare work would probably have been known at least by senior U.S. officials and possibly by the American public. The Red Army, in its drive into Manchuria, would have discovered the headquarters of Unit 731, and news of that discovery would probably have reached U.S. intelligence. Or the Soviets, for propaganda purposes, most likely would have revealed the horrors of Unit 731. By whatever means this news was made public, it would have given Truman solid ground for authorizing the use of gas.

The Soviet discovery and destruction of Unit 731 would not have eliminated Japan's ability to retaliate against the use of gas. Several laboratories in Japan had been experimenting with biological weapons. Anthrax, easily produced and transported, might have been the weapon of choice for retaliation, however feeble such efforts would be. Assuming that the Japanese would not have the resources to deliver gas or germs by aircraft or artillery, the only realistic means for using anthrax-type plagues against American troops would have been by suicide attacks.

Most germ-infected banzai attackers would have been mowed down. But their bodies would become bacteriological booby traps. Even though U.S. troops would have landed with protective clothing and gas masks, the use of germ warfare weeks after the landings would have been effective. On D-Day in Normandy and in other landings, U.S. troops had discarded their cumbersome protective equipment soon after they had discovered the absence of gas on the beaches. In all probability they would have done the same after X-Day and Y-Day.

Still another idea was put forward in the final days of the Japanese Empire. This was the use of submarine-launched aircraft to disperse germs over the western United States. As late as August 1945 the Japanese still had three large, aircraft-carrying submarines—the *I-14*, which could carry two float-planes, and the *I-400* and *I-401*, which could each accommodate four float-planes. Earlier in the war, the submarine *I-25* had twice flown off an aircraft that dropped incendiary bombs on forests in the Pacific Northwest. The bombing caused no damage, but the flights proved the feasibility of aircraft strikes against the United States.

The *I-400* submarine carriers, the largest submarines built by any nation during the war, were originally designed for launching air attacks against New York and other American cities. Now, under a more diabolical plan, the submarines would carry out a mission given the code-name Cherry Blossoms at Night.

These submarines, taking some 30 days or more for the transit, were to come within a dozen miles or so of the coast of California. They would surface at night, their floatplanes' wings would be spread, and the planes would be catapulted into the night sky. They would spread their cargo of plague-infected fleas over West Coast cities on one-way kamikaze missions. One target date for the attack, cited by Japanese officials, was September 22, 1945, a little more than a month before the planned American landing on Kyushu.

If not at Kyushu, then certainly at Honshu, the American casualty rate would have forced U.S. military commanders to employ horror weapons and prepare their troops for retaliatory horror. And there was yet another weapon of mass destruction waiting in the wings: the atomic bomb. General Marshall, musing about the cost of the invasion, would say, "Even an ill-equipped force can cost terrible loss to a landing party. . . . We knew that the Japanese were determined and fanatical . . . and we would have to extermi-nate them, almost man by man. So we thought the bomb would be a won-derful weapon as a protection and preparation for landings. . . ."

CHAPTER 12

GROPING TOWARD SURRENDER

The *Enola Gay* returning to its base on Tinian after dropping the atomic bomb on Hiroshima.

There was no invasion. But if atomic bombs had not been dropped on Hiroshima and Nagasaki—an escalation of the systematic gutting of Japanese cities by B-29s—then Operation Downfall would have proceeded. And almost certainly any available atomic bombs would have become awesome tactical weapons in the invasions of Kyushu and Honshu.

First mention of the possible use of tactical atomic bombs was not directly linked to the Downfall invasion plans. At the Los Alamos laboratory, the secret New Mexico facility where the atomic bombs were designed and built, three scientists suggested a bizarre use of the weapon: to blind enemy soldiers on the battlefield. In a memorandum written on July 17, 1945, after the successful test of the bomb, the scientists noted that a man ten miles away from the test tower had been awakened by the intense light and then, looking at a lessening light, "was blind several hours after the explosion."

The scientists' idea was to get enemy troops to look at the flash by having the bomb-carrying plane accompanied by one that would first drop on a parachute an attention-attracting device, such as a powerful light or siren. Hearing or seeing the device, the enemy troops would instinctively look up "during the instant of detonation," blinding themselves. The scientists believed that "nobody within a radius of five miles could look directly at the gadget [the Los Alamos nickname for the bomb] and retain his eyesight." There was no indication that the scientists' idea went anywhere beyond the memo, which was written to Navy Captain William S. (Deke) Parsons, a weapons expert at Los Alamos.

Atomic bombs were not mentioned in plans for the invasion of Japan, for few planners knew about the top-secret Manhattan Project. One of the planners aware of the atomic bomb, Rear Admiral Richard L. Conolly, did not give the untested bomb any thought while he was working on the naval aspects of the Kyushu invasion. When he heard about the Hiroshima bombing, he later said, he wanted "six of these things" for the Kyushu landings, hoping "to put one on either side of each landing, before the troops landed."

Major General Leslie R. Groves, director of the Manhattan Project, also saw a battlefield role for the bomb. In a memo to General Marshall on July 30, 1945, Groves said that an atomic bomb "dropped on enemy lines" would "wipe out his resistance over an area 2000 feet in diameter; to paralyze it over an area a mile in diameter; and to impede it seriously over an area five miles in diameter." Troops in slit trenches within 800 feet of the blast would be killed, he said, while troops in caves a mile away would probably emerge unscathed.

Groves warned that U.S. troops would need protective glasses and would have to be at least six miles away from the detonation. He estimated that if the bomb was exploded 1,800 feet above a battlefield, U.S. troops and tanks could "move through the area immediately, preferably by motor [vehicle] but on foot if desired."

Groves had asked J. Robert Oppenheimer, chief scientist at Los Alamos, "whether we could develop something that would be useful in the event of an invasion of Japan to help the troops that would be faced with an entrenched and determined enemy." Oppenheimer told Groves that the Fat Man bomb could be modified for possible tactical use.

The thinking of Conolly, Groves, and Oppenheimer might have resulted in an extraordinary scenario. While U.S. invasion forces headed inland from the beaches, atomic bombs would be dropped on Japanese troop concentrations, and American infantrymen would advance through the ground-zero blast zone. Groves envisioned the use of the bombs in a huge aerial bombardment—large-scale but still tactical—without paying much heed to radiation dangers. An assistant, Colonel L.E. Seeman, did. He suggested the creation of "monitoring teams" for atomic-bombed battlefields, soldiers who would go into the blast area and check it for radiation before the main body of troops was allowed into the area.

Marshall later speculated about the tactical use of atomic bombs. He believed that at least nine atomic bombs could have been used in the invasion, three in support of each of the three U.S. corps in the Kyushu assault. One would be dropped, before the landing, on the stretch of shore assigned to each corps; a second would be targeted on Japanese forces inland from the beaches, and a third would be dropped on enemy reinforcements "that might try to come through the mountains" in northern Kyushu.

Marshall's view of tactical nuclear warfare looks naive—or even criminal—today because he ignored the danger of radiation to U.S. troops. But little was known about radiation effects in an age when shoe stores routinely used X-ray machines as an aid for fitting customers. Atomic bombs were not used as tactical weapons, but they were dropped over Hiroshima and Nagasaki. Radiation injuries in the two bombed cities, said an *Encyclopaedia Britannica* account published in 1947, were "similar to the results of severe X-ray overexposure. . . . No harmful amounts of persistent radioactivity were found in either of the two cities." In reality, death rates soared for months after the bombs were dropped, and later studies attributed the deaths of thousands to radiation effects.

Was the use of weapons of such enormous destructive power justified in the attempt to end the war and save American lives? Or was it a senseless slaughter inflicted upon a nation already on the brink of surrender? The answers to these questions can only be found in the complex actions and events of the final weeks of the war.

On Sunday, July 15, President Truman arrived in Babelsberg, a suburb of Berlin near Potsdam, where he, Prime Minister Churchill, and Generalissimo Stalin were to confer on the future of Europe and ending of the Pacific War. Truman was staying in a yellow lakeside villa that had been promptly named the Little White House. The conference was delayed a day to await Stalin, who had suffered a slight, unpublicized heart attack. On Monday, Truman took advantage of the delay for a motor tour through the rubble of Berlin. "In that two-hour drive," he later wrote, "I saw evidence of a great world tragedy, and I was thankful that the United States had been spared the unbelievable devastation of this war."

Soon after he returned to the Little White House, Secretary of War Stimson handed him a cable: OPERATED ON THIS MORNING. DIAGNOSIS NOT YET COMPLETE BUT RESULTS SEEM SATISFACTORY AND ALREADY EXCEED EXPECTATIONS. . . . Later came the details. At a desolate Army bombing range near Alamogordo, New Mexico, a Fat Man atomic bomb was detonated at 5:29 that morning atop a steel tower 100 feet above a spot in the sand and sagebrush designated as Ground Zero.

"For a brief period," Groves wrote in his subsequent report, "there was a lighting effect within a radius of 20 miles equal to several suns in midday; a huge ball of fire was formed which lasted for several seconds. This ball mushroomed and rose to a height of over 10,000 feet before it dimmed." Groves estimated the energy generated by the bomb to be more than that of 15,000 to 20,000 tons of TNT.

The light from the test explosion, code-named Trinity, was seen clearly about 180 miles away. The sound was heard about 100 miles away. Windows broke in Gallup, New Mexico, 235 miles away. "A crater from which all vegetation had vanished, with a diameter of 1,200 feet and a slight slope toward the center, was formed," Groves's report continued. "In the center was a shallow bowl 130 feet in diameter and 6 feet in depth. . . . The steel from the tower was evaporated."

In smoldering Tokyo, Emperor Hirohito was also seeking to end the war, but he believed that "unconditional surrender" meant that he would be dethroned and his dynasty ended. Ever since January 1945, when the U.S. Sixth Army landed on Luzon in the second phase of the invasion of the Philippines, Hirohito had been thinking seriously about a negotiated end to the war. He confided his thoughts to his closest advisers—Marquis Koichi Kido, the lord privy seal, and Prince Fumimaro Konoye, an aristocratic politician.

Kido, a teenager when he met the younger Hirohito, was known as one of the prince's "big brothers." He became secretary to the lord privy seal in 1930 and in 1940 became lord privy seal, the chief civilian adviser to the Emperor. Long disillusioned about the war, Kido confided to his diary as early as January 6, 1944, that Japan was economically beaten and that it would certainly lose the war. He used his considerable influence to bring the Emperor to the same conclusion.

Konoye had been a close friend of the Emperor's since they were boys. He was premier in 1937, when Japan formally launched its war against China, and again in 1940–1941, when Japan planned the attacks on Pearl Harbor and on British and Dutch territories. He had been replaced in October 1941 by General Hideki Tojo, who, often caricatured, was personified as America's enemy. Konoye became the titular leader of what was known as the Peace Faction, a small group of Japanese diplomats and General Staff officers who in 1944 began making cautious moves to feel out sentiments in Japan for ending the war through negotiations.

Kido had helped to orchestrate the resignation of Tojo, who left office on July 18, 1944, after Saipan fell. Some Japanese politicians saw a chance to end the war at that time, but the most influential among them decided that the war should go on, saying that the military must be given more time to fail. Tojo had been succeeded by Kuniake Koiso, a former Army general who was governor-general of Korea. Koiso saw himself as an interim premier, but he still hoped for military victories, and he wanted a voice in running the war.

Previous civilian premiers had been excluded from discussions of military strategy. As premier, Koiso changed this by reconstituting the Supreme Council for the Direction of the War, which consisted of himself, the foreign minister, the ministers of War and the Navy, and the chiefs of staff of the Army and Navy. Although the "Big Six" did, with the Emperor, form the power base of the Japanese government, the military chiefs continued to make decisions on their own, usually in secret.

When Hirohito first raised the idea of negotiations in January 1945, Kido bided his time. Not until April 1945, with Americans on Okinawa, with much of Tokyo a smoking wasteland, with B-29 bombers battering Japanese cities at will, did Kido campaign for the appointment of Baron Kantaro Suzuki as premier. He had a military background, which would satisfy the pro-war faction, a malleable personality, which pleased Kido, and skill in the practice of *baragei,* that Japanese ability to not say what you mean.

Suzuki was well known in Japan as a survivor of the kind of military coup that Kido now saw as a possibility if he pushed peace efforts too far too fast. In February 1936 groups of young officers, in an abortive plot to take over what they saw as a weak government, assassinated the lord privy seal, attempted to kill the premier, and severely wounded Suzuki, then the grand chamberlain, chief aide to the Emperor. Emperor Hirohito, with his palace ringed by loyal troops, made a rare intervention into civil affairs and declared the officers in unlawful rebellion, providing the moral authority to put down the mutiny. Some leaders were allowed to commit suicide; others were executed.

Kido—and presumably Hirohito—wanted Suzuki to take the first delicate steps toward peace. Suzuki later said he had been "given to understand," without any direct word from the Emperor, that he was to end the war by somehow bringing about peace. But the "peace" premier launched his administration by proclaiming that Japan's "one hundred million" people, as shields to the Emperor during an invasion, should be prepared to fight and die.

Kido, directing the Emperor's search for a way to end the war, worked with a loose coalition of diplomats, politicians, and a few military officers. The chief operative on the diplomatic front was Foreign Minister Shigenori Togo, who believed that the path to negotiations was through the Soviet Union.

The Magic intercepts of Japanese diplomatic communications gave President Truman and his principal advisers a view of Togo's moves. They began on June 1 with a message, marked "absolutely secret," to Japan's ambassador to the Soviet Union, Naotake Sato. Togo told Sato that he had assigned a veteran politician and diplomat, Koki Hirota, to begin talking directly to Jacob A. Malik, the Soviet Union's ambassador to Japan. Hirota, a former foreign minister and ambassador to Moscow, had been premier from March 1936 to February 1937. Togo did not say whether he had informed Hirota about the Japanese courier reports on Soviet troop movements toward the Manchurian border.

Malik, like most diplomats, had moved out of the ruins of Tokyo. Hirota called on him at the Gora Hotel, in the nearby mountains, on June 3 and told him that Japan "hopes to maintain the security of Asia" and believed this had to be based "on cooperation with Russia." Malik invited Hirota to meet him the following night. At dinner on June 4, Hirota proposed a new treaty between the two countries—"over a rather long period, say 20 or 30 years." At their next meeting, on June 14, Hirota said that Japan was "quite willing to consider" putting questions about Manchuria and China on the table, along with the possibility of supplying the Soviet Union with commodities from Japanese-conquered lands to the south.

Malik remained noncommittal. Then Hirota made an amazing—and desperate—offer: a Soviet-Japan alliance in the Pacific. "Japan will increase her naval strength in the future," Hirota told Malik, "and that, together with the Russian Army, would make a force unequalled in the world." Hirota proposed that the Soviet Union supply Japan with oil in return for rubber, tin, lead, tungsten, and other commodities from the conquered lands. Malik said that the Soviet Union had no oil to spare but that he would study the proposal.

In Tokyo, meanwhile, military leaders were making moves of their own. The Army called a June 6 meeting of the Supreme Council for the Direction of the War to discuss "the Fundamental Policy to be Followed Henceforth in the Conduct of the War." Their path to peace was across a battlefield. Proclaiming plans for the "Decisive Battle," the Army leaders said they would hold off any move toward negotiations until their troops had massacred the invaders and forced them to plead for peace.

Premier Suzuki, to the chagrin of Togo and his peace seekers, backed the Army. The next day, presenting the council's decision to the full Cabinet for rubber-stamp approval, he said, "There is only one way to win, and that is by determination. When the whole nation possesses this will, then we shall be able to achieve victory!" Suzuki also informed the Cabinet that to defend the homeland against the invaders, civilians would strap explosives on themselves and throw themselves under enemy tanks and that kamikaze pilots would fly against approaching enemy ships even in training planes.

The Army, meanwhile, issued to all troops in Japan a pamphlet, "Quick Way to Learn Tactics for the Battle of the Homeland," which told the soldiers that the strategy against the invaders would be attack, not passive defense. The key to victory, the pamphlet said, was what the Japanese formally called "body-attack combat tactics"—suicidal banzai charges and death-to-the-last-man orders.

An alleged peacemaker advocating suicidal war, Suzuki later tried to explain what looked like duplicity: "On the one hand, I had to carry out to the best of my ability the mission given me by the Emperor, to arrange for the conclusion of the War, whereas if anyone heard of this, I naturally would have been attacked and probably killed by people opposed to such a policy."

On June 8 the Army plan for continuing the war was presented to the Emperor in a solemn rite—*gozen kaigin,* "a conference in the Imperial Presence." Such conferences occurred only during extreme crises in foreign affairs, and traditionally the Emperor did not speak but endowed the conference with his "august mind" and "indisputable dignity." Although *gozen kaigin* was supposed to be rare, the Emperor called another on June 22 (coincidentally, the day that U.S. commanders announced the conquest of Okinawa). Speaking with the usual imperial ambiguity, Hirohito told the Supreme Council that while all steps should be taken for defense of the homeland, there should also be an effort to negotiate an end to the war. When General Yoshijiro Umezu, Chief of the Army General Staff, suggested that not all of the Army might support negotiations, Hirohito directly asked him whether he personally opposed the idea, Umezu said he did not.

Foreign Minister Togo, given vague assent by the Emperor, authorized Sato in Moscow to say that if the Soviets were able to mediate a peace, Japan would withdraw her troops from Manchuria and make the region a neutral nation, with sovereignty guaranteed by Japan and the Soviet Union. Japan would also renounce fisheries rights in disputed waters in exchange for Soviet oil. Sato had little faith in such talk. But Togo curtly told Sato, "Your opinions notwithstanding, please carry out my orders."

In an "extremely urgent" message to Sato on July 11, Togo said, "We are now secretly giving consideration to the termination of the war because of the pressing situation which confronts Japan both at home and abroad." He instructed Sato to speak directly with Foreign Affairs Commissar Vyacheslav M. Molotov. "You should not confine yourself to the objective of a rapprochement between Russia and Japan," Togo said, "but should also sound him out on the extent to which it is possible to make use of Russia in ending the war." Sato was also to tell Molotov that "Japan—as a proposal for ending the war and because of her concern for the establishment and maintenance of lasting peace—has absolutely no idea of annexing or holding territories which she occupied during the war."

Togo followed this with a "very urgent" message to Sato telling him to immediately relay the following to Molotov:

> His Majesty the Emperor, mindful of the fact that the present war daily brings greater evil and sacrifice upon the peoples of all belligerent powers, desires from his heart that it may be quickly terminated. But so long as England and the United States insist upon unconditional surrender the Japanese Empire has no alternative but to fight on with all its strength for the honor and the existence of the Motherland. His Majesty is deeply reluctant to have any further blood lost among the people on both sides, and it is his desire for the welfare of humanity to restore peace with all possible speed. . . .

The statement went on to say that the Emperor wanted to send Prince Konoye to Moscow as a special envoy. Konoye would bear an imperial message and would be given the power to negotiate issues that had been brought up in the Hirota-Malik talks.

Sato responded by bluntly telling Togo, "There is no hope" that the Soviets would be interested. "I send this message," he said, "in the belief that it is my first responsibility to prevent the harboring of illusions which are at variance with reality. I beg your indulgence." Later, he added, "I kneel in veneration before the exalted solicitude of His Majesty for the restoration of peace. . . ."

In still another message that followed, Sato elaborated: "If the Japanese Empire is really faced with the necessity of terminating the war, we must first of all make up our own minds to do so. Unless we make up our own minds, there is absolutely no point in sounding out the views of the Soviet Government. . . ." Since the Soviets insisted upon the unconditional surrender of Germany, he said, "it will obviously be extremely difficult to obtain Russia's support for any proposal concerning negotiation of a peace treaty."

Unable to meet with Molotov, who was about to leave for the Potsdam Conference, Sato talked to his vice commissar, Alexander Lozovsky, like Molotov a crafty old Bolshevik. Sato asked that a confidential letter to Molotov be given to him before he left. Lozovsky agreed to do so. The days passed without any response to the frustrated Sato from Lozovsky or anyone else in the Kremlin.

At Potsdam, on July 17, President Truman met Stalin for the first time. Stalin, accompanied by Molotov and an interpreter, paid a visit to the Little White House around 11 A.M. As Truman told it, he issued an impromptu invitation for lunch, and Stalin accepted. During their informal talk through interpreters, Stalin said that the Soviet Union would be ready to enter the Pacific War in about the middle of August. Truman summed it up in a letter to his wife, Bess: "I've gotten what I came for—Stalin goes to war with no strings on it."

That same day, in Tokyo, Togo sent a fateful message to Sato: "If today, when we are still maintaining our strength, the Anglo-Americans were to have regard for Japan's honor and existence, they could save humanity by bringing the war to an end. If, however, they insist unrelentingly upon unconditional surrender, the Japanese are unanimous in their resolve to wage a thorough-going war." This message, also intercepted by American code breakers, showed that even a peace seeker like Togo still harbored fight-to-the-death sentiments about unconditional surrender to the United States while at the same time offering major concessions to the Soviet Union.

Whatever the motive, Togo's quixotic attempt to stave off defeat by enlisting Soviet help ended on July 18 when the Soviet government formally turned down Prince Konoye's proposed mission. Earlier, Stalin had revealed the Japanese offer to Truman, who, of course, already knew about it through the Magic code breakers.

After learning details of the success of the Alamogordo test, Truman met with his principal advisers on July 22—Stimson, Byrnes, Leahy, King, Marshall, and Arnold. It was apparently at this meeting, Truman wrote, that "I asked General Marshall what it would cost in lives to land on the Tokyo plain and other places in Japan. It was his opinion that such an invasion would cost at a minimum one-quarter of a million casualties, and might cost as much as a million, on the American side alone, with an equal number of the enemy. The other military and naval men present agreed. . . ." In reality, Arnold opposed the bomb, pointing out to Truman and his advisers that Japan could be bombed into submission by B-29 attacks with incendiary bombs.

"But none of the other military men—especially General Marshall—concurred with General Arnold," Margaret Truman later wrote in an insightful biography of her father. "Anyway, my father saw that conventional bombing, even if it worked—and no one doubted that it might take months, even a year—would cause more Japanese deaths than the use of one or two atomic bombs." Marshall's latest estimate of casualties added to Truman's growing conviction about the need to use the bomb.

Truman told Churchill about the successful detonation of the atomic bomb shortly after he received details of the Alamogordo test, but he held back on giving the information to Stalin until July 24. When he "casually mentioned to Stalin that we had a new weapon of unusual destructive force," Stalin "showed no special interest," Truman later wrote.

The Soviet Union had initiated its own atomic bomb project in late 1942, by which time the Soviet leadership was aware of nuclear research in the United States as well as in Germany. Throughout the war, the Soviet government was well informed about the Anglo-American program to build the atomic bomb, with several spies in Britain and the United States—some at the Los Alamos laboratory where the bomb was developed—providing a steady flow of information about designs and progress.

As Truman's principal civilian adviser, Stimson was still preoccupied with finding a possible alternative to a final assault on Japan. In his view, the best way to get the Japanese to capitulate was somehow to let them know that the Emperor would be allowed to stay on his throne. As he said in his diary, "In order to save us from a score of bloody Iwo Jimas and Okinawas," the United States needed to make use of Emperor Hirohito, "the only source of authority in Japan under the Japanese theory of State."

Stimson had laid the foundation for his concept in a memorandum he had given the President in Washington on July 2, as Truman was preparing for the Potsdam Conference. Although only Stimson's name was on the memo, he had written it after discussions with Secretary of the Navy James Forrestal and Under Secretary of State Joseph C. Grew, a former U.S. ambassador to Japan, who was regarded—especially by himself—as the government's authority on the Japanese psyche.

Stimson had begun his memo by drawing on his own recollections of Japan, which he had visited on several occasions. As he recalled the terrain, it "would be susceptible to a last ditch defense such as has been made on Iwo Jima and Okinawa" and would be "much more unfavorable with regard to tank maneuvering than either the Philippines or Germany."

He continued:

> If we once land on one of the main islands and begin a forceful occupation of Japan, we shall probably have cast the die of last ditch resistance. The Japanese are highly patriotic and certainly susceptible to calls for fanatical

resistance to repel an invasion. Once started in actual invasion, we shall in my opinion have to go through with an even more bitter finish fight than in Germany. We shall incur losses incident to such a war and we shall have to leave the Japanese islands even more thoroughly destroyed than was the case with Germany.

Stimson believed that invasion was so potentially bloody that the United States should search for "any alternative" that "will secure for us the equivalent of an unconditional surrender." So he suggested "our giving them a warning of what is to come and a definite opportunity to capitulate." Japan, he believed, "has the mental intelligence" to "recognize the folly of a fight to the finish and to accept the proffer of what will amount to an unconditional surrender."

The warning, Stimson said, should not only describe the catastrophe in store for Japan but also stress the Allied determination "to destroy permanently all authority and influence of those who have deceived and misled their country into embarking on world conquest." But he wanted the warning to state that "we do not exclude a constitutional monarchy under her present dynasty."

Stimson took his argument to the new Secretary of State, James Byrnes, who opposed any concession to Japan, primarily for reasons of domestic politics. Polls were showing that Americans viewed Hirohito as a war criminal. Byrnes had already won the backing of a predecessor, Cordell Hull, who had been Secretary of State in December 1941. Hull well remembered Pearl Harbor. He had been waiting in Washington to meet with the Emperor's envoys while Japanese warplanes were attacking Pearl Harbor. Hull saw any attempt to preserve the Emperor as "appeasement"—a particularly nasty word in those days—and a guarantee of "continuance . . . of the feudal privileges of a ruling caste under the Emperor."

But Stimson's search for "any alternative" to an invasion of Japan was still alive, and the words of the memo he had written back on July 2 were evolving into what would become the Potsdam Proclamation.

On July 26, American radio stations beamed the proclamation to Tokyo in words that Truman hoped would end the war: "We—the President of the United States, the President of the National Government of the Republic of China, and the Prime Minister of Great Britain, representing the hundreds of millions of our countrymen, have conferred and agree that Japan shall be given an opportunity to end this war," it began. (Stalin, as head of an officially neutral nation, was excluded.) The proclamation—Truman called it "our ultimatum"—warned that unless Japan surrendered, Allied military forces "are poised to strike the final blows upon Japan."

Many of Stimson's points appeared in the proclamation—permission to maintain industries, access to raw materials, "participation in world trade relations"—and even some of his words (eliminate the "authority and influence of those who have deceived and misled" Japan) were there. But the concession he wanted the most, preservation of the institution of the Emperor, did not appear. The only discernible alteration in the principle of unconditional surrender was a call for Japan "to proclaim now the unconditional surrender of all Japanese armed forces," a distinction expected to appeal to Japan's civilian officials.

To some Japanese, it indeed did. In Tokyo, Togo's Foreign Ministry colleagues saw the proclamation as acceptable. So did Shonichi Kase, the Japanese minister to Switzerland. Reporting on the proclamation, he said in a Magic-intercepted message, ". . . it seems to me that this Proclamation provides a basis on which we can carry on our national life. . . . I definitely have the impression" that unconditional surrender "is meant to refer to the Japanese Army and not to the Japanese people or Japanese Government. . . ." The Allies' offer to Japan, he said, was better than what was demanded of Germany, which "has been handled as a country without a ruler or a government. . . ."

Togo, however, clung to his hope of peace through Moscow. He told Ambassador Sato in Moscow that he realized that the time was short "before the enemy lands on the Japanese mainland." But rather than respond to the countries that issued the proclamation, Togo chose to "seek the good offices of the Russians in ending the war." He ordered Sato, in "accordance with the Imperial Will," to "persuade the Soviet Government to accept the mission of our Special Envoy [Prince Konoye]. His Majesty, the Emperor, is most profoundly concerned about the matter and has been following developments with the keenest interest."

The Emperor at this point was aloof from the debate over how to respond to the proclamation. The military faction of the council, led by the War Minister, General Korechika Anami, wanted to publish the proclamation, along with the military's objections to its provisions. Togo did not want to publish it at all until the government had decided its position. Finally, the ministers reached a compromise. The proclamation would be published, with unacknowledged deletions of some statements that the military did not like, but the newspapers—all government controlled—were not to give the document prominence or comment on it.

At a press conference on July 28, Premier Suzuki dismissed the proclamation as a "thing of no great value" and said that the government would *mokusatsu* it. What that word meant depended on which dictionary one preferred. Japanese apologists for Suzuki defined it by its root meaning: *moku*, "to be silent," and *satsu*, "to kill." But it could also be translated as an idiom that means "treat with silent contempt." Suzuki went on to say that Japan would keep fighting until the war was won. No matter what *mokusatsu* might mean, there was nothing ambiguous about the decision to keep fighting on.

U.S. diplomats interpreted *mokusatsu* as "unworthy of public notice." As

Stimson later wrote, "In the face of this rejection, we could only proceed to demonstrate that the ultimatum had meant exactly what it had stated, that if the Japanese continued the war, 'the full application of our military power, backed by our resolve, will mean the inevitable and complete destruction of the Japanese armed forces and just as inevitably the utter devastation of the Japanese homeland.' For such a purpose, the atomic bomb was an eminently suitable weapon." Stimson had found the alternative to an invasion that he had been searching for—and the most powerful warning imaginable.

If Stimson saw the bomb as a weapon of terror, Marshall saw it as a tactical weapon that could be used in support of the invasion. Both men advocated its use. But, typically, Truman's view was simple and straightforward. He saw the bomb as a way to end the war, although no one could be certain that it would do so or even that it would work.

On July 24, the day that Truman told Stalin about the bomb, General Carl A. Spaatz, commander of the Strategic Air Forces in the Pacific, received— via Groves in Washington and Marshall and Stimson in Potsdam—an order authorizing the atomic bomb unit on Tinian, the 509th Composite Group of the Twentieth Air Force, to "deliver its first special bomb as soon as weather will permit visual bombing after about 3 August 1945 on one of the targets: Hiroshima, Kokura, Niigata, and Nagasaki. Additional bombs will be delivered on the above targets as soon as made ready. . . ." Truman, undoubtedly shown the order, did not formally acknowledge it by initialing or signing it. But, in response to a July 30 message from Washington asking for a "statement for release by you," he did scrawl a cryptic note that said, "Release when ready but not sooner than August 2. HST."

Early on August 6, the B-29 *Enola Gay* took off from Tinian carrying an atomic bomb. The pilot, Colonel Paul W. Tibbets, aware that B-29 crewmen were being tortured and executed by the Japanese, carried in the knee pocket of his flying suit a box containing 12 cyanide capsules, one for each member of his crew. The *Enola Gay* flew to Hiroshima, on southern Honshu. The city was the headquarters for the Second Army and had a garrison of some 25,000 troops. It was the main port of the shipment of men and supplies between Honshu and Kyushu, the expected first target of the American invasion. When the *Enola Gay* dropped the bomb on Hiroshima, it detonated 1,900 feet above the city. The bomb's force was the equivalent to 15,000 tons of TNT. The city was instantly destroyed, and at least 140,000 people were killed or would be dead by the end of the year.

That same day, President Truman was at sea, returning from the Potsdam Conference on board the heavy cruiser *Augusta*. While he was eating lunch with members of the crew, Captain Frank Graham, the watch officer in the Advance Map Room, entered the mess and handed the President a message from Stimson, who had flown back to the United States: "Big Bomb dropped on Hiroshima August 5 at 7:15 P.M. Washington time. First reports indicate complete success which was even more conspicuous than earlier test."

While Truman told applauding *Augusta* sailors about "the dropping of a powerful new bomb," in Washington the White House released a statement describing the bomb ("more than 2,000 times the blast power of the British 'grand slam' which was the largest bomb ever yet used in the history of warfare") and the work that produced the bomb ("the greatest achievement of organized science in history"). Then the statement, although aimed at an American audience, spoke directly to the Japanese people:

> It was to spare the Japanese people from utter destruction that the ultimatum of July 26 was issued at Potsdam. Their leaders promptly rejected that ultimatum. If they do not now accept our terms, they may expect a rain of ruin from the air, the like of which has never been seen on this earth. . . .

Not until early evening on August 6 (Tokyo time) did word reach Tokyo that an "entirely new-type bomb" had been dropped by "a small number of enemy planes." (A weather plane had preceded the bomb-carrying *Enola Gay*, which had been accompanied by two other B-29s, an instrumented observation plane and a photo plane.) At dawn on August 7 an incredible damage assessment was sent from Hiroshima to Army headquarters in Tokyo: "The whole city of Hiroshima was destroyed instantly by a single bomb." Yoshio Nishina, a physicist who had been working on nuclear-weapon research, told the vice chief of the Army General Staff that what had been dropped on Hiroshima was probably an atomic bomb.

Nishina had been a key figure in Japan's effort to produce atomic weapons. By August 1945, that effort had failed, and the two major atomic-research projects had halted. Nishina's Army-sponsored Riken laboratory in Tokyo had been destroyed in a B-29 raid in April 1945, and Navy-sponsored work apparently continued, although at a minuscule level. Earlier scientists had told senior Navy officers there was not enough time to produce a weapon for use in the war. In that case, Navy officials told the scientists, it could be used in the next war.

But evidence that Japan was still seriously contemplating atomic bomb research until the end of the war had literally surfaced in May 1945 when the German submarine *U-234* surrendered to American warships off the U.S. Atlantic coast. The American prize crew that boarded the U-boat discovered that the *U-234* had been carrying two Japanese officers and 1,232 pounds of uranium, labeled for delivery to the Japanese Army. The submarine was en route to Japan when Germany surrendered, and all U-boats were ordered to surface and head for the nearest Allied port. The prize crew took the *U-234* and brought her into the Navy Yard at Portsmouth, New

Hampshire, where the captain told interrogators that soon after news of the surrender the two Japanese officers had killed themselves. They had been given burial at sea.

If Japan had succeeded in developing a nuclear weapon, there is little doubt that it would have been used against the Allies. Indeed, when Captain Minoru Genda, one of Japan's leading naval aviators, was later asked about such use, he replied, "Why wouldn't we have?"

The destruction of Hiroshima sent Japanese leaders, both civilian and military, into a frenzy of activity. Togo informed Emperor Hirohito about the atomic bomb and urged that Japan end the war at once. To do so, the Supreme Council for the Direction of the War would have to be assembled. But the military members of the council evaded Premier Suzuki's summons.

Ambassador Sato, again ordered by Togo to press the Soviets for an answer, on August 8 had an 8 P.M. appointment with Molotov. Inexplicably Molotov moved it up to 5 P.M. (11 P.M. Tokyo time). As Sato, speaking in Russian, welcomed Molotov back from Potsdam, Molotov impatiently interrupted. He said he had "a notification" to present to the Japanese government. Sato sat down, and Molotov read a declaration of war, effective August 9.

By Soviet reckoning, August 9 was two hours away—1 A.M. on August 9, Tokyo time. At 1 A.M. Red Army troops and planes crossed the border into Manchuria in surprise attacks, not preceded by artillery or air bombardment. In a massive display of Soviet might, these assaults involved more than 1.5 million men and over 5,500 tanks and self-propelled guns. Japan's vaunted Kwantung Army, drained of men and weapons for various island battles and the Decisive Battle of the homeland, was routed by massive air and ground attacks.

The Soviet battle plan, which Stalin had personally supervised, poured troops into Manchuria from three sides. Other forces struck from Outer Mongolia and across the Gobi Desert into China, which had given permission for the passage of Red Army troops to Manchuria. Then, in a double strike at Korea, Red Army columns pressed southward to Wonsan, and an amphibious task force from Vladivostok landed troops along the coast. Airborne troops were parachuted at several strategic points as part of the Soviet assault. The Soviet Pacific Fleet and the Northern Pacific Flotilla—more than 400 warships and small craft—sailed into the Sea of Japan to support assaults on Korea and the Kuril Islands.

One of its principal cities had been all but obliterated by an atomic bomb, and with the massive Soviet military incursions into Japanese-held territory, all hopes ended for a negotiated settlement with the Soviets. Still, Japan refused to surrender.

· · ·

In the aftermath of the destruction of Hiroshima, leaflets rained down on other Japanese cities, revealing Japan's desperate plight to any citizens who dared pick them up. "Your future lies in your own hands," said one with a drawing of the Goddess of Mercy. "You can choose between a useless death for many of your forces or a peace with honor." Downfall's troops and supplies continued to be assembled in massive numbers on Okinawa, on Luzon, on Guam, and in Hawaii. The assault ships were moving to advance bases. Warships of Admiral William F. Halsey's Third Fleet were bombarding the coast of Hokkaido, and his carrier planes were smashing airfields north of Tokyo. General of the Army Douglas MacArthur, a national hero with an eye on the White House, was ready to lead invasions that would dwarf the D-Day exploits of General of the Army Dwight D. Eisenhower, his rival for fame and possibly even the presidency.

President Truman had expected the Japanese government to surrender after Hiroshima was destroyed. No such communication came, and conventional bombing attacks continued. On August 7 a 131-plane B-29 strike was flown against Tokyo, and a large B-29 incendiary raid against Yawata on August 8, followed by more bombing as well as mining missions. Truman later described his next move: "An order was issued to General Spaatz to continue operations as planned unless otherwise instructed." A second atomic bomb would be dropped.

At 8 A.M. on Thursday, August 9, Foreign Minister Togo went to Suzuki's home and demanded that the premier call an immediate meeting of the Supreme Council. Suzuki agreed. Togo next called on Admiral Mitsumasa Yonai, the Navy Minister, who reluctantly conceded that Japan must surrender, putting a senior military man on Togo's side. Yonai had briefly served as premier in 1940 and had been forced to resign because he opposed an alliance with Germany and Italy.

Rumors were sweeping through official circles that an atomic bomb would soon drop on Tokyo. The rumor stemmed from the false answers given by 1st Lieutenant Marcus McDilda when he was beaten and interrogated. McDilda, who had bailed out of a B-29 shot down over Osaka on August 8, knew nothing about atomic bomb targets. But he told his captors that atomic bombs would fall on Kyoto and Tokyo "in the next few days." In fact, General Spaatz had favored dropping the third bomb on Tokyo, but it was not on the approved target list, and little of value remained in the burned-out capital.

Suzuki prudently chose an air-raid shelter as the place for a meeting of the Supreme Council at 10 A.M. on August 9. He told the five other members of the Big Six that the war must end. "I believe that we have no alternative but to accept the Potsdam Proclamation," he said, "and I would now like to hear your opinions."

For long moments no one said a word. Then Admiral Yonai spoke out. "Do we accept the enemy ultimatum unconditionally? Do we propose conditions?" he asked. "If so, we had better discuss them here and now."

Now the others spoke, Suzuki and Togo joining Yonai in accepting the proclamation with one proviso: that the Emperor be preserved. General Anami, General Umezu, the Chief of the Army Staff, and Admiral Soemu Toyoda, the Chief of the Naval General Staff, agreed but wanted more: no occupation of Japan or hardly more than a token occupation; no war-crimes trials (which had been an Allied principle since the beginning of the war); and disarming and demobilization of Japanese troops under supervision of their own officers.

As if in response to these patently impossible demands, word came of the atomic bombing of Nagasaki. Again a B-29 had taken off from Tinian in the early morning carrying an atomic bomb. Named *Bockscar,* the bomber headed for the Japanese city of Kokura—site of an arsenal and Army base on the island of Kyushu—with another atomic bomb. Clouds and smoke swathed the city, and anti-aircraft bursts erupted around the plane. The pilot and weapons officer opted for the alternate Kyushu city on their target list: Nagasaki. Their atomic bomb detonated 1,650 feet above the port city with a force equivalent to 21,000 tons of TNT. Hemmed in by hills around the impact point, the explosion caused less damage than the Hiroshima bomb. Still, in the instant of explosion thousands died; by the end of the year an estimated 70,000 who had been at Nagasaki were dead.

The news of the Nagasaki bombing seemed to have had little effect on the "Big Six" debate in Tokyo. Admiral Toyoda had earlier believed that the atomic bomb dropped on Hiroshima was the only one available because of the scarcity of critical nuclear materials, a belief that might have been based on his knowledge of the Japanese Navy's atomic bomb program. But now another bomb had devastated another city. The question of how many more bombs existed was certainly on everyone's mind.

Suzuki adjourned the deadlocked council and called for a full Cabinet meeting at 2:30 P.M. at his official residence. Again Anami demanded the Decisive Battle. "That we will inflict severe losses on the enemy when he invades Japan is certain," he said, "and it is by no means impossible that we may be able to reverse the situation in our favor, pulling victory out of defeat. . . . Our men simply will not lay down their arms. . . ."

Ominously, Genki Abe, Minister of Home Affairs, recalled the 1936 Army mutiny in which Suzuki had been shot. Abe said he could not guarantee civil obedience if Japan surrendered. He supported the military. Other ministers took sides. Debate droned on. Finally, Suzuki recessed the meeting. By unbreakable tradition, a decision of the Cabinet must be unanimous. If that was impossible, the Cabinet must fall. But in this supreme crisis Suzuki could not allow that to happen. He and Togo went to the palace and asked the Emperor to immediately call another *gozen kaigin.*

At 11:30 on the night of August 9, 11 government officials filed down a narrow stairway into the hot, humid bomb shelter of the Emperor of Japan. It was 60 feet below the Imperial Library, a one-story structure that stood amid the fountains, the gardens, and the ruins of palace buildings destroyed in the May 25–26 air raid. The bomb shelter's conference room, 18 by 30 feet, was poorly ventilated. Its arched ceiling, supported by steel beams, and its dark, wood-paneled walls added to the gloom that enveloped the men. They took their seats at two long cloth-covered tables, five on one side, six on the other, and awaited the Emperor. Seven of the officials wore uniforms, and four wore formal morning dress, a display of the preponderance of the military in Japan's leadership.

Shortly before midnight, Emperor Hirohito entered, accompanied by an aide. The officials stood and bowed, their eyes turned away from him as he sat in a straight-backed chair before a sixfold gilded screen. Hirohito, a sad-eyed man of 44, was garbed as a field marshal, but his uniform was ill fitting because no tailor's hands could touch his Imperial person.

Baron Suzuki, sweating heavily in the stifling heat of the shelter, began the meeting by asking the chief Cabinet secretary to read the Potsdam Procla-

A depiction of the meeting of Japan's Supreme Council for the Direction of the War in the presence of the Emperor Hirohito on August 9, 1945. Even after the destruction of Hiroshima and Nagasaki, some military leaders refused unconditional surrender and mounted an unsuccessful coup.

mation aloud. The Japanese had received the text by radio *thirteen days before,* at 6 A.M. on July 27 (Tokyo time), and the Big Six had been debating it ever since. Then Suzuki reviewed the events leading up to the present meeting. One by one, the ministers reiterated their arguments, Anami again passionately vowing a glorious defense of the homeland in the Decisive Battle. Togo recommended acceptance provided the Allies gave assurance that the Imperial system would be preserved.

At 2 A.M. on August 10, after all had spoken, Suzuki stood and did something no premier had ever done. He asked for a decision from the Emperor. It was an amazing request, never before made in modern Japanese history. Suzuki was asking for an Imperial command—the Voice of the Crane. According to an old saying, the crane, revered in Japanese tradition, can be heard even when he flies unseen.

Hirohito now spoke. He said he did not believe that his nation could continue to fight a war despite what the military claimed about the Decisive Battle. "But the time has come to bear the unbearable," he concluded. ". . . I give my sanction to the proposal to accept the Allied proclamation on the basis outlined by the Foreign Minister."

Suzuki, hoping to maintain the momentum of this epochal event, called an immediate Cabinet meeting back at his official residence to legalize the action of the Emperor and to draft a response to the Allies. At 7 A.M. the Foreign Ministry transmitted a message to the American, British, and Soviet governments through Sweden and Switzerland:

> The Japanese government are ready to accept the terms enumerated in the Joint Declaration which was issued at Potsdam on July 26th . . . with the understanding that the said declaration does not comprise any demand which prejudices the prerogatives of His Majesty as a Sovereign Ruler.

In Washington, President Truman learned of the acceptance soon after monitors picked up the transmission at 7:33 A.M. on August 10. He called a 9 o'clock meeting of Stimson, Forrestal, Byrnes, and Leahy. At that session, Stimson restated his belief that the Emperor should be allowed to stay. Leahy agreed. Byrnes still opposed any retreat from unconditional surrender. Forrestal suggested that the U.S. reply could show a willingness to accept while still defining the terms that reflected the Potsdam Proclamation.

The officials soon agreed to a reply demanding that "the authority of the Emperor and the Japanese Government to rule the state shall be subject to the Supreme Commander of the Allied Powers who will take such steps as he deems proper to effectuate the surrender terms." Other demands were the immediate release of all Allied prisoners, establishment of a government "by the freely expressed will of the Japanese people," occupation by Allied forces, and the signing of the surrender by the Emperor along with "the Japanese High Command."

The reply was transmitted to London at 3:45 P.M., and at the request of the British, the Emperor was asked only to "authorize" the signing. Chiang Kai-shek endorsed the reply. The Soviets were also sent the reply. On August 11 the completed message, accepted by the four Allied governments, was handed by Byrnes to the Swiss chargé d'affaires and transmitted to Tokyo.

When news of the Japanese note was broadcast to U.S. forces, General Spaatz, head of U.S. Strategic Air Forces in the Pacific, ordered a halt to city bombing by B-29s because he feared it might complicate negotiations. This order led American journalists in the Marianas to assume that a cease-fire had gone into effect. The next day, Truman, believing that any B-29 strikes would be a public indication that moves toward peace were faltering, halted all strategic bombing, a directive extended on August 12 to General George Kenney's fighters and bombers as well. But with no further moves toward peace by the Japanese, on August 14 all U.S. air commanders were told to resume bombing.

In America, most people believed that peace had come. On August 11, the *New York Times* summed up the mood in the headline "GI's in Pacific Go Wild With Joy; 'Let 'Em Keep Emperor,' They Say." In the Philippines, Staff Sergeant Raymond E. Logan, the ex-telephone man waiting to invade Japan, heard about the atomic bomb and expected that the war would end right away. "Then came the news of some holdup because of the status of the Emperor," he recalled. "I still remember guys yelling at the top of their voices, 'Let them keep the son-of-a-bitch!' "

Meanwhile, in Tokyo, General Anami heard grumblings among Army officers. He asked the secret police—the dreaded *Kempei Tai*—to investigate the reports. He remained uncommitted to those officers talking about rebellion and ordered acceptance of the surrender. On August 10, however, Tokyo radio stations had broadcast an Anami statement that rang with defiance: "We have but one choice: we must fight on until we win the sacred war to preserve our national polity. We must fight on, even if we have to chew grass and eat earth and live in fields—for in our death there is a chance of our country's survival. . . ." Supposedly, the statement was not authorized. But Anami apparently made no move to correct it, for the statement was published in the morning newspapers of August 11. Accompanying that statement was one from the Cabinet saying that the nation was "facing a situation that is as bad as it can be." A reader could see between the lines that the government was in a crisis that it had chosen not to describe.

For three hours on the night of August 13, Umezu and Toyoda argued with Togo, saying nothing new as they prolonged the war. Then there appeared, like a wraith, Vice Admiral Takijiro Onishi, creator of the kamikazes, known euphemistically as the special attack forces. Tears in his eyes, he said,

"Let us formulate a plan for certain victory. . . . If we are prepared to sacrifice 20 million Japanese lives in a special attack effort, victory is ours!" That broke up the meeting.

By August 13 (Washington time) surrender had not happened, and the invasion was still on Marshall's mind. "We had 100,000 people killed in Tokyo in one night," he once said, referring to the March 1945 attack by B-29s, "and it had seemingly no effect whatsoever." Now, after two even more devastating attacks and no surrender, it was conceivable that more atomic bombs would have been used.

That same day, Lieutenant General John E. Hull, chief of the Army's Operations and Plans Division, telephoned Colonel Seeman of the Manhattan Project. Hull, like Marshall, was not a product of West Point. He had gone from college into the Army as a reserve lieutenant in World War I, had become a strategist early in his career, and was recognized as a tough-minded intellectual who could look beyond rules and regulations to new ideas.

With an intuitive grasp of Marshall's thinking, Hull told Seeman, "What General Marshall wants to know is the status of the development of these bombs now so we can determine how to use them. General Marshall feels we should consider now whether or not dropping them as originally planned [against cities] or [if] these we have should be held back for use in direct support of major operations"—the invasion of Japan.

Seeman said that there was "a good chance" that there would be seven bombs ready for use by October 31. Hull and Seeman discussed the bomb-production schedule. Then Hull went back to talking about the tactical use of atomic bombs and discussed one possibility: "You plan to land on a certain beach. Beyond which, you know, there is a good road communication or maybe a division or two of Japanese troops. . . . I am thinking about neutralizing a division or a communication center or something so that it would facilitate the movement ashore of troops."

Hull ended the conversation with a request that Seeman ask Groves what he thought about a change in the planned use of the bombs. After two bombs, the "psychological effect is lost," Hull said, almost certainly reflecting Marshall's thoughts. Marshall was, in fact, looking beyond the bombings of Hiroshima and Nagasaki. If those atomic bombs did not convince Japanese leaders to surrender, then the invasion was inevitable. And the next available bombs should be reserved to support the Downfall landings.

Atomic bombs of the Fat Man or plutonium type were already in production. The first had been tested at Alamogordo in July; the second had been available on Tinian on August 1 and was dropped on Nagasaki. The third could have been available on Tinian by late August. Possibly three more would have been ready in September, and the production rate was expected to increase to seven or more per month by December 1945. The Little Boy uranium bombs were more difficult to produce. The first was dropped on Hiroshima, and a second would have been ready by the end of the year. This bomb-production schedule could have put numerous atomic bombs in General MacArthur's invasion arsenal. Groves's principal deputy, Brigadier General Kenneth D. Nichols, later recalled that "if the landings actually took place, we might supply fifteen atomic bombs to support the troops."

On the morning of August 14 the B-29s returned to Japan's cities, dropping five million leaflets. An Imperial Chamberlain handed Kido one of the leaflets. "These American planes are not dropping bombs on you today," the leaflets said. "American planes are dropping these leaflets instead because the Japanese government has offered to surrender and every Japanese has a right to know the terms of the offer. . . ." On the leaflets were the full texts of the Japanese acceptance of surrender and the American reply. The secret of the surrender, which the government had kept from the Japanese public, was out. "One look," Kido later said, "caused me to be stricken with consternation. . . . If the leaflets should fall into the hands of the troops and enrage them, a military coup d'état would become inevitable. . . ."

In fact, a military coup was under way. General Anami had learned about it soon after having an early breakfast with Field Marshal Shunroku Hata, commander of the Second General Army. Hata, just back from Hiroshima, told Anami about the horrors he had seen, then mentioned that people who were below ground had survived. Be sure to tell that to the Emperor, Anami said. It might change his decision about seeking surrender.

Anami went to the War Ministry, which buzzed with talk of the coup. A hard-drinking man and a fearless leader in combat, Anami lived by the samurai code and probably had been more content fighting the Americans in New Guinea than he was sitting behind a desk in Tokyo. Anami knew that younger officers were planning a desperate coup. If Anami were to give his support to the plot, much of the Japanese Army—an army of several million, scattered across the Empire—would almost certainly rise against the Cabinet, while claiming allegiance to an Emperor duped by cowardly civilians. Suzuki and Kido were marked for assassination, and Anami knew that if he resigned from the Cabinet, it would fall. Without a Cabinet, Japan would be ruled in its death throes by only the military leaders, and he would get his wish for the Decisive Battle.

At the Imperial Library on the Palace grounds, Kido showed the leaflet to the Emperor and urged him to hold another *gozen kaigin*. Hirohito agreed, and Kido met with Suzuki, who called for a meeting of the Cabinet at 10:30, again in the air-raid shelter. Circumstance was changing so fast that Kido ruled that the usual court attire of frock coat or cutaway would not be necessary for the civilians.

As before, Togo's military opponents presented their cases, each apologizing for "the unfavorable turn of events which must be a disappointment to Your Majesty" and each calling for the Decisive Battle and death before dishonor. Of the military men, only Yonai, the Navy Minister, remained on Togo's side.

Then the Emperor spoke: "I have listened carefully to all of the arguments. . . . I have studied the terms of the Allied reply, and I have come to the conclusion that they represent a virtually complete acknowledgment of our position as we outlined in the note dispatched a few days ago. In short, I consider the reply to be acceptable." He was weeping.

Hirohito knew, he said, "how difficult it will be for the officers and men of the Army and Navy to submit to being disarmed," and he spoke of his sorrow for all who had died in the war "on the battlefield or in the homeland." He vaguely mentioned the possibility of "my faithful ministers" being "punished as war criminals."

Many of the men in the room were also weeping as Hirohito concluded: "As the people of Japan are unaware of the present situation," he said, "I know they will be deeply shocked when they hear of our decision. . . . I desire the Cabinet to prepare as soon as possible an Imperial Rescript announcing the termination of the war." He would read the rescript—a proclamation of the gravest import—on the radio. For the first time in history, the Emperor's subjects would hear the Voice of the Crane. Sobbing men slipped to the floor and knelt as Hirohito turned and left the room.

Immediately the Cabinet met at Suzuki's residence to ratify the Emperor's wishes (officially and traditionally *not* a decision) and draft the rescript. During a break in the meeting, Anami slipped into an anteroom and met with his brother-in-law, Lieutenant Colonel Masahiko Takeshita, a leader of the planned coup. Takeshita had with him a blueprint for the plot, a document headed "Employment of Troops—Second Plan." Earlier, he had thought he had the support of Anami and of Chief of Staff Umezu. Now Takeshita bluntly asked Anami to support the coup passively, by resigning and thus bringing down the Cabinet.

Anami looked hard at Takeshita and refused. Takeshita stalked out of the room. By Anami's code, he would not report Takeshita's mutiny.

Although most people in America now believed the war had ended, it was not officially over, and the wait was getting on Truman's nerves. Washington wits were asking, "Do you think Japan's surrender will shorten the war?"

In Tokyo, the struggle between those who wanted peace and those who would fight on was reaching a crisis point. Kido and other aides to the Emperor were hectically arranging for a historic event—the broadcast of an Imperial address. Directors of the Japan Broadcasting Corporation (NHK) were told that Hirohito wanted to read an Imperial Rescript on the radio.

The NHK men were astonished. Never had the people heard the Voice of the Crane, the divine voice of the Emperor.

Kido and Hiroshi Shimomura, director of the Cabinet Information Bureau, decided that since the Emperor was not an accomplished speaker, it would be better for him to record his speech than to give it live. NHK sent a recording team to the Palace complex on the afternoon of August 14.

Meanwhile, Major Hidemasa Koga, a staff officer in the Imperial Guards Division and son-in-law of former Premier Hideki Tojo, was meeting with several other officers at Guards headquarters. He had just asked his wife, Makie, whether she had preserved his fingernail clippings and a lock of his hair. Makie knew that this was the traditional question of a Japanese soldier going off to battle.

Far more soldiers than usual patrolled the grounds of the Imperial Palace that day. Instead of one battalion, there were two battalions of the Imperial Guards Division on duty. The second battalion, led by Colonel Toyojiro Haga, a regimental commander, arrived around noon. Prince Konoye, the former premier, recently named as a prospective emissary to Moscow, called on Kido. "I am afraid of what may be happening at the Imperial Guards Division," he said, and told him of coup rumors. Kido shrugged off the report, insisting that the rumors were unfounded. He went on with his work, arranging for the Emperor's speech.

The Cabinet, haggling over language of the rescript, kept the recording team waiting in a room near Kido's office. Around 8 P.M., copyists finally got the scrawled, heavily edited copy of the rescript and began transcribing it into classic calligraphy. Changes kept coming in. The copyists, much to their aesthetic abhorrence, had to make corrections on tiny pieces of paper and paste them in. Shamefaced, they presented a smudged and patched rescript to Suzuki, who took it to the Emperor for his signature.

The regular 9 P.M. Japanese radio news had the usual announcements from Imperial Army Headquarters. Then a voice said that an important broadcast would be made at noon the next day, August 15. Meanwhile, the premier's office mimeographed copies of the final text of the rescript and sent them to newspapers, with the orders that the text not be published until after the noon broadcast by the Emperor. The same newspapers got pronouncements from Imperial Japanese Army headquarters: The Army was in revolt against a cowardly government. One editor made up two front pages, the first with the surrender story, the second with the Army revolt story, and waited to see which side would win.

At 11 P.M. the Emperor left his living quarters in the Imperial Library, entered a car, and was driven the short distance through the gardens to the blacked-out Household Ministry building. In the audience hall on the second floor the NHK technicians bowed to the Emperor. Hirohito, looking uncomfortable and perplexed, stepped before the microphone. "How loudly should I speak?" he asked. Hesitatingly, an engineer respectfully suggested that he speak in an ordinary voice. The Emperor began:

> To our good and loyal subjects: After pondering deeply the general trends of the world and the actual conditions obtaining in Our Empire today, We have decided to effect a settlement of the present situation. . . . Let the entire nation continue as one family from generation to generation, ever firm in its faith in the imperishability of its sacred land. . . .

When he finished, he asked, "Was it all right?" The chief engineer stuttered a reply: "There were no technical errors, but a few words were not entirely clear."

The Emperor read the rescript again, tears in his eyes and soon in the eyes of all in the room. "I am quite willing to make a third," he said. He was told that another reading would not be needed. All bowed as he left the room.

Each reading took two records to complete. The technicians picked the first recording as the one for the noon broadcast, but they kept all four records, putting them in metal cases and then in khaki bags. The technicians, like everyone else in the Palace, had heard rumors of a coup, and it was decided to remain in the Palace with them. A chamberlain placed the records in a safe in a small office used by a member of the Empress's retinue—a room normally off-limits to men. Then he hid the safe by placing a pile of papers in front of it.

The coup got off to a bloody start when, in the early hours of August 15, Major Kenji Hatanaka, a fiery-eyed zealot, and Army Air Force Captain Shigetaro Uehara burst into the office of Lieutenant General Takeshi Mori, commander of the Imperial Guards Division, located on the northern side of the Palace grounds. Hatanaka fatally shot and slashed Mori, and Uehara beheaded another officer who happened to be there. Hatanaka then affixed Mori's private seal to a false order directing the Imperial Guards to occupy the Palace and its grounds, sever communications with the Imperial Palace except through division headquarters, and occupy NHK and prohibit all broadcasts. Major Koga, meanwhile, tried in vain to recruit other officers, hoping to get the Eastern District Army, deployed to defend Tokyo and the Kanto Plain, into the plot.

At the Palace, soldiers supporting the coup, with bayonets affixed to their rifles, rounded up the radio technicians and imprisoned them in a barracks. The soldiers wore white bands across their chests to distinguish themselves from guards loyal to the Palace. The white-banded troops stormed the Palace and began cutting telephone wires with fire hatchets. They disarmed the Palace police and had them remove their uniforms.

Major Koga, hoping to find and destroy what he thought was a single record of the Emperor's message, ordered a radio technician to find it. The technician, unfamiliar with the Palace, led several soldiers into the labyrinth. They roamed Palace buildings, kicking in doors, flinging contents of chests onto the polished floors, and threatening the aged chamberlains. Kido grabbed up secret documents, tore them into pieces, and flushed them down a toilet. Machine-gun fire was heard, but no casualties were reported. The Emperor, told of the attempted coup by a chamberlain, remained in his quarters.

Lieutenant Colonel Takeshita, meanwhile, tried again to bring Anami into the plot. But Anami once more declined and said he was about to commit *seppuku,* ritualized suicide. Several hours later, with Takeshita in the room, Anami knelt on a mat and, facing toward the Palace, drove an heirloom dagger into his stomach and drew it across his waist. He then removed the knife and thrust it into his neck. As he lingered, Takeshita pushed the knife deeper into Anami's neck until, finally, he died.

Another, separate plot was beginning in Yokohama, west of Tokyo. Captain Takeo Sasaki, commander of the Yokohama Guards, had been seething with plans for vengeance. He believed that his unit "has no such word as 'surrender' in its vocabulary. Japan must fight! It has the men and the will to fight—why should it surrender? There is still a huge Japanese army on the Chinese mainland, and Japan still holds 350,000 Allied prisoners of war. Why should Japan surrender?"

He could do nothing about prisoners. So he tried to mobilize a battalion of men and lead them to Tokyo to kill Premier Suzuki. When his company commanders demanded a higher authority for his order, Sasaki rounded up a band of 29 soldiers, five students, and two members of the Yokohama Youth Corps. Armed with swords, rifles, pistols, and two machine guns, they called themselves the National Kamikaze Corps. They climbed into cars and trucks and headed for Tokyo, about 25 miles away.

When they reached Tokyo, Sasaki and his men drove to Suzuki's official residence and raked it with machine-gun fire, but Suzuki was not there. Later, they set fire to Suzuki's private home. Seven uniformed members of the secret police swooped down on Kido's home. One of his guards was wounded in a firefight. The raiders retreated and were never heard of again.

Elsewhere in Tokyo, rebellious soldiers swarmed into the NHK building, rounded up 60 employees, locked them in a studio, and demanded assistance to go on the air with their appeal to the nation to fight on. An executive slipped out of the building and tried to get word to the Palace. If the soldiers held the building, there would be no broadcast of the Voice of the Crane.

Shortly before 5 A.M. on August 15, Major Hatanaka walked into Studio 2, put a pistol to the head of Morio Tateno, an announcer, and said he was taking over the 5 o'clock news show. Tateno refused to let him near the microphone. Hatanaka, who had just killed an Army general, cocked his pistol but, impressed by Tateno's courage, lowered the gun. An engineer, meanwhile, had disconnected the building from the broadcasting tower.

If Hatanaka had spoken into a microphone, his words would have gone nowhere.

In Washington, on the morning of August 14, Commodore James K. Vardaman, President Truman's naval aide, told him that a coded telegram from Tokyo had been received in Berne. "It turned out that it was not an answer to our message at all," Truman later wrote, "and the wait continued." Finally, at 3 o'clock, Secretary of State Byrnes told Truman that another coded message was being received in Berne. At 3:55 he learned that the message was: "Japan had surrendered!"

In Tokyo, however, the war was not over. The Emperor had not spoken. The Army coup still simmered. And Japanese troops were fighting fiercely, if futilely, against Soviet assaults in Manchuria, Korea, Sakhalin, and the Kuril Islands. The Japanese held Manchuria with the 440,000 men of the Kwantung Army, a force so powerful that it was nearly a government unto itself. About 140,000 men of the Kwantung Army were stationed in seven heavily fortified areas along the Manchurian-Soviet border. In Inner Mongolia were another 280,000 Japanese troops, with about 100,000 more on southern Sakhalin and in the Kurils. The Soviet forces that had attacked on August 9 quickly crushed the Japanese strong points, surged into the heartland of Manchuria, and destroyed the Kwantung Army.

On August 13, as Soviet troops approached Pingfan in Manchuria, headquarters of infamous Unit 731, Lieutenant General Shiro Ishii ordered all buildings, equipment, documents, and human test subjects to be destroyed. Hundreds of prisoners used in germ and frostbite tests were gassed by poisonous chemicals thrown into their cells. Manchurian and Chinese laborers were machine-gunned. Attempts were then made to burn the bodies, but there were too many of them. Japanese engineer troops were called in to aid with the destruction of the facility.

The more than 2,000 personnel in Unit 731 were issued vials of poison, for Ishii expected them to take their own lives (as well as those of family members in nearby Togo village). But, dissuaded by his research chief, Major General Hitoshi Kikuchi, Ishii obtained high priority for passage of his people back to Japan. Some of Ishii's senior people, however, were captured and later tried in the Soviet Union for war crimes.

When Red Army soldiers took Mukden in Manchuria, they also liberated a prisoner-of-war camp, freeing more than 3,000 Allied servicemen who had thought they were about to be killed by their captors. Like prisoners being held in Japan, they believed that if war came close to their camp, the guards would murder them.

There can be little doubt that the Allied prisoners held in Japan would be killed. A Japanese directive sent out earlier described "the methods":

(a) *Whether they are destroyed individually or in groups, or however it is done, with mass bombing, or poisonous smoke, poisons, drowning, decapitation, or what, dispose of them as the situation dictates.*

(b) *In any case it is the aim not to allow the escape of a single one, to annihilate them all, and not to leave any traces.* [Emphasis in original.]

There were some 100,000 Allied prisoners of war held within Japanese territory—perhaps 70,000 in Japan. Their probable fate left little to the imagination.

On Sakhalin, the Soviets, who occupied the northern portion of the island, crossed the border on August 9 and defeated a combined force of Japanese soldiers and civilians. As Red Army units were rolling over Japanese defenders, on August 12, Soviet amphibious forces landed at two points on the western coast of Sakhalin. On August 17, Imperial General Headquarters issued a curious order to the Japanese on Sakhalin and the Kurils: "Hostilities with the enemy will cease. However, self-defense actions will be permitted under unavoidable circumstances."

At daybreak on August 18, Soviet troops began landing on Shumshu, the northernmost of the Kuril Islands, just off the tip of the Kamchatka Peninsula. As Japanese tanks and infantry headed for battle on the beach, they received a cease-fire order, and a battle was averted. On Sakhalin, however, when more Red Army troops landed, Japanese trying to surrender were shot, and fighting broke out again. Off the western coast, between Sakhalin and Hokkaido, submarines, apparently Soviet, torpedoed a ship carrying Japanese refugees; another ship was sunk and a third damaged. Not until August 24 did the Japanese troops begin disarming and the isolated war in those cold, bleak islands finally end.

The momentum and resources of the Soviet Army that had captured Sakhalin and the Kurils were next to have been turned toward an assault on Hokkaido. Although amphibious operations were the most complex of the war, the short distances involved, the available Soviet ships and small craft, and the state of the Japanese defenders would have enabled the Soviets to at least have gotten a foothold on northern Hokkaido. They would have suffered heavy casualties, however, because Hokkaido, as a home island, was much better defended than Sakhalin and the Kurils. But Soviet troops would have been in Japan proper.

At the Imperial Palace loyal troops rounded up the mutineers at dawn on August 15 and liberated those held prisoner. In separate cars using different routes, the NHK engineers brought the Emperor's records to the radio station, hid one set in an underground studio, and prepared to play the other. At 7:21 A.M., Tateno went on the air and, without recounting the adventures of the night before, announced, "His Majesty the Emperor has issued a Rescript. It will be broadcast at noon today. Let us all respectfully listen to the voice of the Emperor. . . . Power will be specially transmitted to those districts where it is not usually available during daylight hours. Receivers should be prepared and ready at all railroad stations, postal departments, and offices both government and private. The broadcast will take place at twelve o'clock noon today."

At noon, groups of people gathered to listen to the Emperor. As his voice was heard, "the response of the listeners was practically uniform throughout the whole nation," wrote Kazuo Kawai, editor of the *Nippon Times*. "In virtually every group, someone—generally a woman—broke out in a gasping sob. Then the men, who with contorted features had been trying to stay their tears, also quickly broke down. Within a few minutes almost everyone was weeping unabashedly as a wave of emotion engulfed the populace. It was a sudden mass hysteria on a national scale. . . ."

In his speech, the Emperor presented a highly self-serving view of the war. "Indeed," he said, "we declared war on America and Britain out of Our sincere desire to ensure Japan's self preservation and the stabilization of East Asia, it being far from Our thought either to infringe upon the sovereignty of other nations or to embark upon territorial aggrandizement."

The "war situation," he continued, "has developed not necessarily to Japan's advantage, while the general trends of the world have turned against her interest. Moreover, the enemy has begun to employ a new and most cruel bomb, the power of which to do damage is indeed incalculable, taking the toll of many innocent lives. . . . However, it is according to the dictate of time and fate that We have resolved to pave the way for a grand peace for all the generations to come by enduring the unendurable and suffering what is insufferable."

In the long and solemn speech he never used the word "defeat" or "surrender."

Nor were those words in the vocabulary of countless Japanese soldiers, sailors, and airmen. Twenty miles from Tokyo, at the huge Atsugi naval air station, where thousands of kamikaze pilots were being trained, Captain Yasuna Kozono, commander of the 302nd Air Group, led an insurrection. He and other pilots flew over Atsugi and Tokyo, scattering hastily printed leaflets that urged Japanese to fight on and defy the "traitors around the throne." Kozono threatened to attack the Allied fleet as it steamed into Tokyo Bay, led by the battleship *Missouri*. Although the Atsugi mutineers did not resort to hostile acts, they refused to obey orders from superior officers.

Foreign Minister Togo had become so concerned that on August 15 he sent a warning to the Allies about the situation. "Disarming of the Japanese forces," Togo's message said, would be "a most delicate task," so he suggested that "the most effective method would be that under the command of His Majesty the Emperor, the Japanese forces are allowed to disarm themselves and surrender arms of their own accord. . . ." The message's wording appeared to the Allies to be a brazen attempt to have Japanese officials supervise the disarming of Japanese troops. Togo also called the Allies' attention to The Hague Convention, which, he cited, would allow his surrendering officers to continue "to wear swords." (Hirohito did not specifically command the Japanese military "to lay down their arms" until September 2.)

On August 17, some 200 to 400 soldiers at the Army air signal training center at Mito boarded a train to Tokyo. There they took over Ueno Park and the Imperial Museum of Art, threatening to attack the government. Pilots, meanwhile, kept threatening to make kamikaze attacks on U.S. warships when they began entering Tokyo Bay.

Prince Toichiro Takamatsu, brother of the Emperor and a captain in the Navy, telephoned Atsugi on August 19 in a personal appeal to Captain Kozono and his rebellious followers. His intervention did not end their defiance. On August 21 the extremists seized several aircraft and flew them to Army airfields in an effort to gain support for their simmering insurrection. They failed, but not until August 25 did they surrender.

Japanese Army and Navy officers loyal to the wishes of the Emperor disarmed their troops, drained fuel from aircraft, and forced the Mito mutineers—at the cost of several lives—to leave the capital. On Atago Hill, half a mile from the Palace, armed civilians defied authorities for several days; finally joining hands, they blew themselves up with grenades. Throughout Japan, for many days, small groups of civilians as well as soldiers refused to accept the surrender.

Major Hatanaka ended his mutiny standing outside the Palace gates, trying to hand out leaflets that called on civilians to "join with us to fight for the preservation of our country and the elimination of the traitors around the Emperor. . . ." No one took the leaflets. Hatanaka shot himself in the head. A fellow conspirator, who had sat on a horse passing out the leaflets, dismounted, stabbed himself in the stomach with his sword, then shot himself in the head. Around the same time, in an Army office, Major Koga drew his sword and committed *seppuku*.

In the days that followed, at least eight generals killed themselves, as did Vice Admiral Onishi, the man who had founded the kamikazes and stirred the Divine Wind, and Vice Admiral Matome Ugaki, commander of the Fifth Air Fleet on Kyushu. Late on the afternoon of August 15, Ugaki drank a farewell cup of sake with his staff and drove to Oita airfield, where 11 Suisei D4Y dive bombers were lined up, engines roaring. Before the planes stood 22 young men, each wearing a white headband emblazoned with a red rising sun.

Ugaki climbed onto a platform and, gazing down on them, asked, "Will all of you go with me?"

"Yes, sir!" they shouted, raising their right hands in the air.

"Many thanks to all of you," he said. He climbed down from the stand, got into his plane, and took off. The other planes followed him into the sky.

Aloft, he sent back a message: ". . . I am going to proceed to Okinawa, where our men lost their lives like cherry blossoms, and ram into the arrogant American ships, displaying the real spirit of a Japanese warrior."

None of the planes reached the American ships off Okinawa. All of them were lost at sea. Ugaki and the men who perished with him had found their Decisive Battle.

The war ended in a formal surrender ceremony on the deck of the battle-ship *Missouri,* anchored in Tokyo Bay amid an armada of U.S. and Allied warships. On the morning of September 2, American, Allied, and, lastly, Japanese officials came aboard the *Missouri.* Hundreds of news journalists and photographers crowded the decks of the battleship, along with more than a thousand American sailors.

General MacArthur presided over the brief, solemn ceremony. He wore khaki shirt and slacks, the shirt open at the neck, without medals or ribbons, as did most of the Allied officers at the surrender. It was the uniform they had worn to fight the war. A baize-covered *Missouri* mess table was in the center of the deck adjacent to the No. 2 16-inch gun turret. On it were the leather-bound surrender documents.

Newly appointed Foreign Minister Mamoru Shigemitsu, who was to sign the surrender documents for the Emperor, limped toward the table, leaning heavily on a cane. He had lost his left leg to a grenade thrown by a Korean nationalist in Shanghai. Shigemitsu wore a top hat, tails, and striped trousers. He took off his gloves and silk hat, sat down, dropped his cane, picked it up, fiddled with his hat and gloves, and seemed to be looking for a pen. "Sutherland," MacArthur snapped to his chief of staff, "show him where to sign." One of Shigemitsu's aides handed him a pen and he signed.

Admiral Halsey later said that when he saw Shigemitsu delaying, "I wanted to slap him and tell him, 'Sign, damn you! Sign!' " MacArthur responded, "Why didn't you?"

Then General Yoshijiro Umezu, who had so vigorously opposed the surrender, stepped forward to sign for the Imperial General Staff. He wore a uniform but no sword. He did his job briskly, not even sitting down.

General MacArthur came next, using several pens to sign the surrender for the United Nations. Admiral Nimitz signed as the U.S. representative. Nimitz was accompanied to the table by Admiral Halsey, Third Fleet commander, and Rear Admiral Forrest Sherman, his plans officer. The Fifth Fleet commander, Admiral Raymond Spruance, was on his flagship, the battleship *New Jersey,* off Okinawa: Nimitz's biographer speculated about the reason why he was not invited to the ceremony: ". . . possibly because [Nimitz] wanted there to be somebody to take command of the Pacific Fleet in the event the Japanese treacherously attacked the *Missouri* in Tokyo Bay and killed the officers aboard her." And Halsey kept the carriers at sea until after the surrender, apparently fearing a kamikaze attack on them.

Nimitz was followed by the representatives of China, Great Britain, the Soviet Union, Australia, Canada, France, the Netherlands, and New Zealand. As the brief ceremony was concluded, hundreds of carrier aircraft and waves of B-29s flew overhead.

Meanwhile, ashore, thousands of U.S. soldiers, sailors, and Marines were taking over Japanese facilities, caring for liberated Allied prisoners of war, and disarming the Japanese Army. There had been no Operation Downfall, but they had landed in Japan—without a shot being fired.

EPILOGUE

"WHOSE SON WILL DIE . . . ?"

The billboard at the entrance to the Oak Ridge atomic development center. With the surrender of Japan on August 14, 1945, countless thousands of American —and Japanese—lives had been saved.

Some postwar historians have challenged President Truman's decision to use the atomic bomb to shorten the war and save American lives. They claim that the Allies could have ended the war by negotiating with the Japanese. Others contend dropping the bomb was patent racism and that atomic bombs would never have been dropped on the Germans. Still others have called the dropping of the bomb a cynical demonstration of U.S. power—making Hiroshima and Nagasaki not the last targets of World War II but rather the first targets of the Cold War.

In reality, anyone who closely and dispassionately examines the last weeks of the war would have to conclude that Truman was looking for ways to end the conflict honorably and at the lowest possible cost in American *and Japanese* lives. He had seen the Magic summaries that revealed the Japanese turning to the Soviet Union, not the United States, in a search not for peace but for negotiations. Because secrecy still shrouded the Magic decryptions for decades after the war, neither Truman nor any other U.S. decision maker could include Magic disclosures in his postwar memoirs. Indeed, not even the U.S. Strategic Bombing Survey, looking into the causes of Japan's defeat, had access to code-breaking intelligence. As for the use of the atomic bomb as an implied threat to the Soviet Union, geopolitics may have been on the minds of some of Truman's advisers, but the war and American lives were on his mind. Preparations for the massive amphibious assault on Japan were under way, and Truman went to Potsdam in July seeking assurance that Stalin would enter the war against Japan. Then Truman learned on July 16 that the atomic bomb would work, and he ordered it used. It was a weapon, and it *might* end the war without an invasion.

But as the events in Japan on the night of August 14–15 clearly show, the atomic bomb had not yet ended the war. Even with Hiroshima and Nagasaki destroyed and a "rain of ruin" threatened, many senior Japanese Army and Navy officers still wanted the Decisive Battle. Had the military coup succeeded, the war would have gone on, the Decisive Battle would have been fought, and hundreds of thousands of American and Japanese lives would have been lost.

How many lives? That is another question raised by the critics of Truman. They seize, for example, on Truman's recollection that General Marshall had told him an invasion of Japan "would cost at a minimum one-quarter of a million casualties, and might cost as much as a million, on the American side alone, with an equal number of the enemy." Secretary of War Stimson made a similar estimate in his postwar memoirs. These numbers were intentionally exaggerated, critics argue, to justify the dropping of the bomb. Searching for sources for those numbers, they cite the estimates that General MacArthur submitted to General Marshall for the crucial June 18 White House meeting at which President Truman approved plans for Downfall. MacArthur's figures were well below Truman's recollection of Marshall's estimates.

For whatever reason, MacArthur's figures were unrealistic. But far more important is what MacArthur's own intelligence officers discovered after the war. From interrogations of high-ranking Japanese staff officers, MacArthur's G-2 staff reported,

> The strategists at Imperial General Headquarters believed that, if they could succeed in inflicting unacceptable losses on the United States in the Kyushu operation, convince the American people of the huge sacrifices involved in an amphibious invasion of Japan, and make them aware of the determined fighting spirit of the Japanese army and civilian population, they might be able to postpone, if not escape altogether, a crucial battle in the Kanto [Tokyo] area. In this way, they hoped to gain time and grasp an opportunity which would lead to the termination of hostility on more favorable terms than those which unconditional surrender offered.

As Olympic neared, two U.S. Army agencies made independent estimates of invasion casualties. The Philadelphia Quartermaster Depot—which procured everything from combat boots to medals for the Army—ordered more than 370,000 Purple Hearts for award to the wounded and the families of those killed in the final battles for Japan.

At the same time, on Luzon, the Sixth Army's medical staff estimated that casualties from the Kyushu assault and subsequent fighting to secure the southern half of the island would cost 394,000 Americans dead, wounded, and missing. At Okinawa—in a battle that proffered many similarities to the fighting on Kyushu—the Tenth Army suffered 7,613 soldiers and Marines killed and missing, and 31,807 wounded. Using that same 1:4 ratio for the Kyushu battles, the Sixth Army could expect some 98,500 dead and 295,500 wounded.

Also using Okinawa as a model, where 4,907 U.S. Navy men were killed aboard ships and 4,824 wounded, the Kyushu assault in the face of heavy air and undersea kamikaze attacks could have similarly inflicted ten times the number of naval casualties—on the order of 49,000 Navy men killed and 48,000 injured.

Thus, a reasonable casualty estimate of the Kyushu assault—based on medical staff estimates and not influenced by the politics of MacArthur's headquarters or Washington—could have been on the order of 147,500 dead and 343,000 wounded. While these numbers are of a different magnitude than those developed by MacArthur's headquarters for President Truman's meeting with the Joint Chiefs of Staff, the estimates were developed by medical specialists experienced in battle, men who had to be ready with whole blood and plasma, medical personnel, and evacuation spaces on ships. Even allowing a contingency margin, the Sixth Army's estimates must be taken seriously. Kyushu would have been the bloodiest invasion in history. And it could have been surpassed by the assault of Honshu, which was planned to follow if the Japanese did not surrender by the spring of 1946.

The summons to the Decisive Battle was not just a patriotic shout. It was a strategy. But there was no Decisive Battle. Just as the atomic bomb gave Truman an alternative to invasion, it gave the Emperor an alternative way to end the war. By citing the "new and most cruel bomb," he could tell his people that they must surrender.

Had the invasion occurred, there could be no doubt that it would have launched the bloodiest battles of the war. Thousands of young American men and perhaps millions of Japanese soldiers and civilians would have died. Terror weapons—poison gas, possibly germ warfare, and perhaps crop-destroying chemicals—could have scarred the land and made the end of the war an Armageddon even worse than the devastation caused by two atomic bombs. A third atomic bomb was ready before the end of August. It probably would have been dropped on another Japanese city. And from what is now known about Marshall's thinking on the tactical use of atomic bombs, the plans for Operation Downfall would have been modified to include their use in support of the landings. The devastation of Japan could have been total.

In those final, desperate days in Tokyo, War Minister Anami could have stopped the surrender process and put Japan on the road toward ultimate catastrophe. There is no doubt that if Anami had let his samurai heart rule him, he could have rallied the Japanese military to his lost cause and fought on. And what of the millions of Japanese troops in Manchuria, China, Korea, Burma, and elsewhere in Asia? If their comrades in the homeland were fighting to the death, it seems likely that they would have done the same.

As memory of the war faded, the American fears of carnage on the beaches of Kyushu and Honshu were forgotten, and the focus of history turned to the decision to drop the bomb. Was it truly a decision motivated by a desire to save lives? At Oak Ridge, Tennessee, where components for the atomic bomb were produced, there was a billboard that showed American soldiers dying on a battlefield. "Whose son will die in the last minute of the war?" a headline on the billboard asked. That question drove the decision to drop the bomb.

But what had been in 1945 an act of war against an enemy was viewed

294 • CODE-NAME DOWNFALL

decades later as an act against humanity. And if in 1945 Truman saw the bomb as an alternative to a bloody invasion, his critics would claim there was a much more humane alternative: negotiations. It was a view, however, that ignores indelible realities. The Japanese had used negotiations in 1941 to mask the attack on Pearl Harbor. If Japanese leaders had wanted to negotiate in 1945, Foreign Minister Togo could have chosen to negotiate with the United States through a neutral nation rather than with the Soviet Union. Morever, as Magic intercepts revealed to American leaders, even that vain attempt at negotiations was tinged with treachery, through Togo's suggestion of a Japanese-Soviet military alliance.

The Potsdam Proclamation was not accepted by the Japanese. The atomic bomb dropped on Hiroshima did not produce a surrender. Not until the dropping of the second bomb on Nagasaki and the Soviet invasion of Japanese-held territory did the Big Six begin to seriously contemplate surrender. Still, they demanded unacceptable terms. The Emperor's broadcast, which finally ended the war, was not made until six days after that. And every day that surrender was delayed the death toll rose. Rebellious Army and Navy officers attacked and killed other Japanese, calling for continued resistance. Allied prisoners of war and civilian internees died throughout the vast Japanese Empire. More civilian internees died. Captured American B-29 crewmen were tortured, multilated, and executed.

The Japanese people were permitted no thoughts of surrender. And among the military leadership in the final days of the war, death was more principled than surrender in any form. General Anami chose personal death rather than the death of his nation. So did the leaders of the mutiny he did nothing to stop. Their lives belonged to tradition, to the Emperor, to Japan. Had they been commanded to do so, the Decisive Battle would have been fought tenaciously by the Japanese on the beaches of Kyushu and possibly even Honshu. There can be little doubt that, even without the atomic bomb, the United States would have won the war—but at the cost of tens of thousands of American lives and possibly millions of Japanese lives. President Truman's decision to use the bomb ended the war and saved those lives.

AFTERWORD

THE PLAN TO POISON JAPAN

The atomic bomb that devastated
Hiroshima (below) caused the death
of 140,000 within a year; the Nagasaki
bomb killed 70,000. A poison gas attack
might have killed up to five million.

The planned U.S. amphibious assault on the Japanese home islands and the supporting air bombardment could well have killed more Japanese—military and civilian—than did the atomic bombs dropped on Hiroshima and Nagasaki. (In addition, tens of thousands if not hundreds of thousands of U.S. soldiers, sailors, and Marines would have been killed in such an assault, and thousands more maimed and wounded.)

In Washington, as the invasion of the Japanese home islands was being planned, a group of U.S. Army chemical warfare officers proposed a devastating launch of the assault: A massive, preemptive attack with poison gas against twenty-five Japanese cities, among them Hiroshima and Nagasaki. *It was predicted that up to five million Japanese would die in the gas attacks.*

While writing this book the authors had periodically seen references to proposals for a massive gas offensive against Japan. Our inquiries usually were met with shrugged shoulders or blank stares. The Army had a massive chemical weapons program in World War II, but there was virtually nothing in the available files on attacking the home islands with poison gas. Then, a reference was found to an Army proposal that had been formally put forward for such an attack. The authors immediately requested the document under the Freedom of Information Act (FOIA), legislation that forces the government to release to the public those documents that by any logic should no longer be classified (except when intelligence means and sources would be revealed).

But the FOIA process could take months, especially when—as in this instance—both Department of Defense agencies and the Department of State were involved. Thus, the first edition of our book, entitled, *Code-name Downfall* was published without our having had access to the document. So it was after publication of the book before the long-suppressed report was made available to us: *Preemptive poison-gas attack: A Study of the Possible Use of Toxic Gas in Operation Olympic.*

The U.S. Army officers who wrote the 30-page top secret report saw a preemptive gas attack as the best way to launch the forthcoming invasion. U.S. aircraft would drop 56,683 tons of poison-gas bombs in the first fifteen days in the "initial gas blitz" on Japan. Another 23,935 tons of gas bombs would be dropped every additional month that the war went on or until all targets were destroyed. On the ground, when the invasion began in November 1945, U.S. Army artillery would fire about 1,400 tons of gas shells every thirty days.

Army planners envisioned a stockpile of 144,762 tons of gas munitions available in the Western Pacific when the invasion started. The gas would be dispensed from the air either by bombs or low-level spraying; on the ground, gas-filled mortar and artillery shells would be used. During the next seventy-five days an additional 9,356 tons would be sent to the war zone for this aerial and artillery bombardment of Japan.

Contrary to U.S. declared policy, first stated by President Roosevelt, the poison-gas document laid out plans for the *preemptive* use of gas in the invasion. It recommended, for example, that the U.S. Joint Chiefs of Staff issue "a policy at once directing the use of toxic gas on both strategic and tactical targets in support of Operation Olympic," code name for the November 1945 invasion of Kyushu.

Use of poison gas was to start fifteen days before the landings—beginning with the drenching of much of Tokyo with gas. Twenty-four additional target cities were selected, including Hiroshima, Nagasaki, Yokohama, Osaka, Kobe, Nagoya, and Kyoto.

Three officers of the U.S. Army's Chemical Warfare Service wrote the study and on June 9, 1945, submitted it to the chief of the Chemical Warfare Service, Major General William N. Porter, who approved the document. On June 14, other documents show, Fleet Admiral King received a secret report on poison gas from General Marshall. President Truman, who had taken office the previous April 12, had announced that he would carry on Roosevelt's war policies, including a demand for the unconditional surrender of Japan. But Truman had not publicly spoken about the use of poison gas.

The timing of the discussion between King and Marshall strongly suggests that poison gas was discussed at the June 18 meeting in the White House about Operation Downfall. The minutes of that meeting refer to undisclosed topics. One of the topics was later revealed to be the atomic bomb. The poison-gas documents indicate that another topic was the massive use of poison gas. On June 21, according to one of the documents, orders went out to step up production of several types of poison gas to bring stockpiles up to the massive amounts urged in the study.

The Army planners had chosen fifty "profitable urban and industrial targets" in Japan, with the twenty-five cities listed as "especially suitable for gas attacks." The report further declared, "Gas attacks of the size and intensity recommended on these 250 square miles of urban population might easily kill 5,000,000 people and injure that many more."

The largest poison-gas raid would be on Tokyo because an "attack of this size against an urban city of large population should be used to initiate gas warfare." The planners targeted 17.5 square miles directly north of the Imperial Palace and west of the Sumida River. In that area were 948,000 people. Within two miles of the target area were another 776,000 people; they would probably be in the path of wind-carried gas. Ironically, the size of the targeted area was almost exactly the same size as the area of Tokyo burned out by the firebombing on the night of March 9-10, 1945. (The chemical warfare planners made no reference to previous bombing damage to cities on the target list.)

The plan was to launch the gas attack on Tokyo at eight o'clock in the morning, when the greatest number of people would be concentrated in the city. Bombers would drop either 21,680 gas bombs weighing 500 pounds or 5,420 bombs weighing 1,000 pounds, depending upon the availability of the bombs. All of the bombs would be filled with a gas known as phosgene.

Phosgene or carbonyl chloride—known in the Army by the symbol CG—was a vapor unless it was under slight pressure, as in a sealed cylinder or artillery shell. The vapor dissipates into the air in a few minutes and is thus a non-persistent gas. When inhaled, phosgene damages the capillaries in the lungs, allowing watery fluid to seep into the air cells. Small doses cause slight injuries, from which the patient eventually recovers; large amounts flood the lungs and the victim dies of a lack of oxygen. (CG caused more than 80 percent of all chemical fatalities in World War I.)

During the subsequent attacks on other Japanese targets—both by U.S. aircraft and artillery—three types of gas would be used in addition to phosgene. Hydrogen cyanide, designated AC by the Army, interferes with normal processes of the respiratory center of the nervous system; if present in more than a small concentration it quickly kills.

Cyanogen chloride, a colorless liquid called CK by the Army, gives off a vapor that was about twice as dense as air and which irritated the eyes and nasal passages. When air containing a high concentration of CK is inhaled, the compound quickly paralyzes the nervous system and kills. If a low concentration is inhaled, the reaction is not as rapid, but the compound can accumulate in the body to a lethal concentration. (This gas was to be used in flame throwers as a substitute for fire against caves and pill boxes.)

Mustard gas is an oily brown liquid that evaporated slowly, giving off a vapor five times heavier than air. Mustard gas is highly persistent and is almost odorless although in high concentrations it smells like garlic or mustard—hence its name. It mainly attacks the skin, soaking through clothes and causing painful blisters. However, the inhalation of the gas injures the respiratory tract and causes poisoning in other tracts and passages, although symptoms of such poisoning can be delayed for hours or even weeks before manifesting themselves.

Mustard gas would be used against Yawata and the nearby cities of Tobata, Wakamatsu, and Kokura, a highly industrialized area. "Liquid mustard," the report said, "is readily absorbed by wood which is impracticable to decontaminate. Since most Japanese cities are congested predominantly with structures which are low and wooden, an attack on a city with a sufficient number of bombs filled with mustard, will probably greatly impair the war effort in that area."

The objective of that attack was to "hamper operations and produce mustard gas vapor casualties" among the 279,200 people in the gas attack zones. "Refresher attacks" would be launched every six days until the first frost.

In direct support of the invasion of Kyushu in November 1945, cyanogen chloride bombs would be dropped on Japanese army units around Kagoshima, the chief city on Kyushu, although it was probable that raids on reserve troops would "produce large numbers of casualties among the unprotected urban population of Kagoshima." Gas attacks, the report continued, "should be coordinated with the softening up bombardment of the beaches prior to landing."

The U.S. plan was based on extremely detailed analyses of city layouts, even giving concern to the width of streets and the location of parks. Discussing one of the gas-attack zones in Yokohama, for example, the report said: "Zone 1 covers the center of the city proper, a triangular area congested with residential and mercantile structures. This is the most densely populated region in the city. Dense clusters of low residences, broken only by narrow streets, extend inward. The northern and western parts of this district are covered with cheap native shops and theatres. There are no large factories in this zone and comparatively few household shops."

Army planners believed that Japanese officials would not evacuate cities even after the first wave of poison-gas attacks because of the strain that mass evacuation would place on the transportation system and because workers must remain to keep factories operating.

The selection of targets was based on the thesis that "most Japanese cities of over 100,000 population are located on or very near the coast, a fact of significance for gas attack because it aids identification and exposes them to daily land-sea winds. . . ." There are few open spaces in most Japanese cities. There are a number of parks in Tokyo but few elsewhere." Noting that about 70 to 80 percent of the roofs in typical cities are tiled and the rest are sheet metal, the report said that both types "are easily penetrated by gas bombs."

Cities were "studied in considerable detail for the purpose of preparing gas zone maps." Each city was divided into several zones, depending upon the density of population. The greater the concentration of people, the better the zone as a gas target.

The disclosure of the Army gas-attack study raises new questions about U.S. war policy in the summer of 1945. Until this document came to light, U.S. wartime policy had supposedly called for the use of poison gas only in retaliation. To preserve the appearance of that policy, in 1947 U.S. Army officials directed that the report be altered when it was downgraded from top secret to the next lower classification, secret. The original document was to be retyped and the word *retaliatory* frequently inserted to make it agree with announced U.S. wartime policy.

A paragraph on policy originally stated: "The use of gas may disrupt national life in Japan if used aggressively and freely for fifteen days prior to Operation Olympic. The advantage of initiating the use of this weapon is so great in comparison to giving the Japanese the initiative in the matter that we stand to profit greatly by the sudden full-scale use of this weapon." This paragraph was crossed out, apparently sometime in 1947, and the following was written in by hand: "The retaliatory use of gas may disrupt national life in Japan."

While most previously known documents discussing the U.S. use of poison gas in the war addressed tactical operations, the newly disclosed report of June 1945 raised the killing of enemy civilians to a level far beyond anything seen in the World War II.

By comparison, the German bomber *blitz* of London in 1940-1941 killed 40,503 men, women, and children; Allied bombing killed about 45,000 in Hamburg, Germany, in July 1943, and 135,000 in Dresden in February 1945; the firebombing of Tokyo in March 1945 killed more than 83,000 and the two atomic bombs dropped on Hiroshima and Nagasaki killed in total about 200,000 people.

The U.S. Army gas attack plan was begun "to determine whether or not gas should be used" in the invasion and "if so, when its use should be initiated." The recommendations in the document were based on large-scale tests at the Dugway Proving Ground in the state on Utah and San Jose Island off Panama.

Much of the thinking behind the study had come from a meeting of Army planners on October 12, 1944, when General Porter, as head of the Chemical Warfare Service, estimated that an attack "on a congested city area" would produce ten percent casualties—an "impact never yet attained in this war by air attack or robot bombs." (This referred to the German V-1 and V-2 missiles that had begun raining down on London in the summer of 1944.) The United States had ample evidence that Japan had used gas against China, and this could have been cited as a reason for American use of gas against Japan.

The poison-gas documents show that high-ranking U.S. military officers were prepared to go to any length to defeat Japan. The atomic bomb's killing power is dwarfed in comparison to the potential of a massive poison-gas attack on twenty-five Japanese cities. This, then, was the atmosphere in decision-making circles as the atomic bomb became a reality. Not only could the bomb possibly eliminate the need for an invasion costly in American lives; it also shelved plans for poison-gas attacks that would have killed millions of Japanese civilians.

THOMAS B. ALLEN

NORMAN POLMAR

APPENDIX A

JAPANESE DEFENSIVE FORCES

When the Joint Chiefs of Staff briefed President Truman on June 18, 1945, they showed him a map with the current U.S. intelligence estimates of what Japanese strength would be on November 1, 1945, the date scheduled for the invasion of Kyushu. These were the numbers and locations on the JCS map.

The number of troops estimated in the home islands was low, but paramilitary forces were not included. The number of aircraft available to the Japanese was low, with some 8,000 suicide planes and several hundred others in the home islands in the summer of 1945.

Location	Troops	Aircraft
Honshu Island*	1,230,000	1,600
Shikoku Island*	110,000	100
Kyushu Island*	350,000	300
Hokkaido Island*	180,000	200
Kuril Islands	90,000	50
Manchuria	750,000	400
North China	425,000	100
Central and East China	365,000	100
Canton–Hong Kong	110,000	25
Korea	250,000	200
Karafuto (Southern Sakhalin Island)	40,000	50
Bonin Islands	20,000	
Ryukyu Islands†	90,000	
Formosa	190,000	50
Mariana and Caroline Islands	100,000	
Bismarck and Solomon Islands	80,000	
Northern Indochina	75,000	
Southern Indochina	25,000	
Thailand	125,000	
Malaya	80,000	25
New Guinea area	125,000	
Java	40,000	25
Borneo	20,000	
Sumatra	75,000	25
Andaman Islands	20,000	
Totals	4,965,000	3,250

* Japanese home islands.
† Other than U.S.-occupied Okinawa.

APPENDIX B

U.S. FORCES FOR THE

KYUSHU ASSAULT

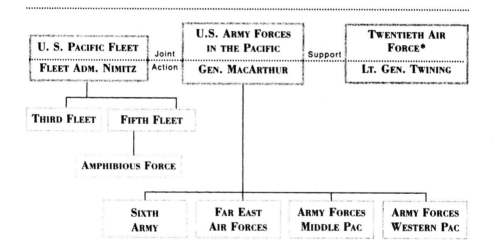

OPERATION OLYMPIC

SIXTH ARMY (Gen. Walter Krueger)

Beyond the assault forces listed below (252,150 Army troops and 87,643 Marines), the Sixth Army included 40,377 service troops, 177,983 support troops, and 15,772 naval personnel (beach parties, communications personnel, etc.).

---

* Under the direction of the Army Strategic Air Force Pacific; Nimitz and MacArthur reported to the Joint Chiefs of Staff. MacArthur's organization charts showed the Twentieth Air Force but not the Eighth (under Lt. Gen. Doolittle), while Nimitz's documents showed both.

Although no divisions were being moved from Europe to the Pacific for the Olympic landings, 32,900 ground troops (mostly engineers), 75,900 service forces, and 48,000 Army Air Forces personnel were being transferred directly to MacArthur's command; see Appendix D.

NAKAKOSHIKI URA AND KOSHIKI RETTO (X-4)

40th Infantry Division + 158th Regimental Combat Team

KUSHIKINO

V Marine Amphibious Corps
  2nd Marine Division
  3rd Marine Division
  5th Marine Division

ARIAKE BAY

XI Corps
  Americal Division (Infantry)
  1st Cavalry Division
  43rd Infantry Division

MIYAZAKI

I Corps
  25th Infantry Division
  33rd Infantry Division
  41st Infantry Division

AFLOAT RESERVE; DIVERSIONARY THREAT AT SHIKOKU (X-2 to X-Day)

IX Corps
  81st Infantry Division
  98th Infantry Division

FOLLOW-UP FORCES

11th Airborne Division
77th Infantry Division

NAVAL FORCES

Initially, the Third Fleet would continue to carry out air and surface strikes against Japan in support of the Kyushu operation, concentrating on airfields.

The Fifth Fleet would include the British carrier force and, as assigned, anti-submarine and logistics groups. The Fifth Fleet would have the amphibious ships, covering and supporting forces, minesweepers, and support ships in addition to a wing of flying boats and their tenders. The Seventh Fleet would be assigned ships and missions as appropriate by Admiral Nimitz and other commanders. Only warships and amphibious ships are indicated below; several hundred minesweepers and auxiliary ships would also participate in Olympic.

THIRD FLEET (Adm. William F. Halsey)
fast carrier task force
14	CV	fast aircraft carriers (approx. 100 aircraft each)
6	CVL	light aircraft carriers (approx. 35 aircraft each)
9	BB	fast battleships (16-inch guns)
2	CB	large cruisers (12-inch guns)
7	CA	heavy cruisers (8-inch guns)
12	CL	light cruisers (6-inch guns)
5	CLAA	anti-aircraft cruisers (5-inch guns)
75	DD	destroyers

FIFTH FLEET (Adm. Raymond A. Spruance)
amphibious support forces
12	CVE	escort aircraft carriers (28–32 aircraft each)
11	OBB	old battleships (12-, 14-, 16-inch guns)
10	CA	heavy cruisers (8-inch guns)
15	CL	light cruisers (6-inch guns)
36	DD	destroyers
6	DE	destroyer escorts

attack forces (to protect amphibious ships)
10	CVE	escort aircraft carriers (28–32 aircraft each)
81	DD	destroyers
122	DE	destroyer escorts

follow-up forces (to protect follow-up amphibious ships)
16	DD	destroyers
48	DE	destroyer escorts

hunter-killer groups (offensive anti-submarine forces)
4	CVE	escort aircraft carriers (28–32 aircraft each)
24	DE	destroyer escorts

logistics group (to protect oilers and ammunition ships)
10	CVE	escort aircraft carriers (28–32 aircraft each)
1	CL	light cruiser
12	DD	destroyers
42	DE	destroyer escorts

*amphibious forces**

95	AKA	attack cargo ships (23,750 troops)
17	AP	troop transports (34,000 troops)
210	APA	attack transports (273,000 troops)
68	APD	destroyer transports (10,290 troops)
4	APH	evacuation transports (3,200 troops)
16	LSD	dock landing ships (3,840 troops)
400	LSM	medium landing ships (20,000 troops)
555	LST	tank landing ships (166,500 troops)
6	LSV	vehicle landing ships (4,800 troops)

SEVENTH FLEET (Adm. Thomas C. Kinkaid)
Forces as assigned.

SOURCES: *MacArthur Reports,* Vol. I; various Operation Olympic staff studies of Headquarters, U.S. Army Forces in the Pacific, and Headquarters, U.S. Pacific Fleet, especially Commander in Chief, Pacific Fleet, "Operation Plan No. 10–45, Central Pacific Area: Olympic," 8 Aug. 1945.

* Aggregate troop capacity indicated; total capacity for amphibious force was 539,380 troops.

APPENDIX C

U.S. FORCES FOR THE

HONSHU ASSAULT

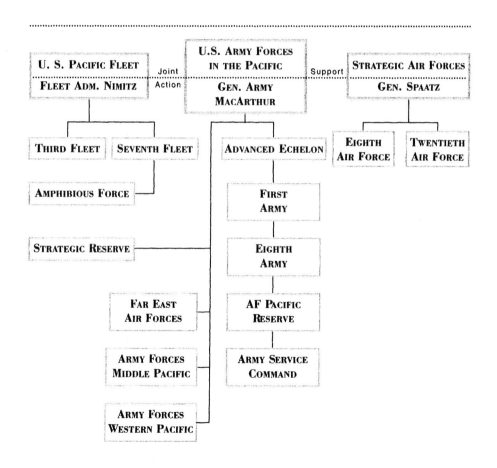

OPERATION CORONET

ARMY GROUP (Gen. MacArthur)

FIRST ARMY (Gen. Courtney H. Hodges)*
  III Marine Amphibious Corps
    1st Marine Division
    4th Marine Division
    + 6th Marine Division on Day Y + 5
  XXIV Corps
    7th Infantry Division
    27th Infantry Division
    + 96th Infantry Division on Day Y + 5

EIGHTH ARMY (Lt. Gen. Robert L. Eichelberger)
  X Corps
    24th Infantry Division
    31st Infantry Division
    + 37th Infantry Division on Day Y + 5
  XIII Corps landing on Day Y + 10
    13th Armored Division*
    20th Armored Division*
  XIV Corps
    6th Infantry Division
    32nd Infantry Division
    + 38th Infantry Division on Day Y + 5
  Army Forces Pacific Reserve
    97th Infantry Division*

FOLLOW-ON ECHELONS

The Army's redeployment plan provided for six infantry divisions to be transferred from Europe to serve as follow-on forces for the campaign on Honshu, to be formed into two corps:
  First Army: 5th, 44th, and 86th Infantry Divisions
  Eighth Army: 4th, 8th, and 87th Infantry Divisions

Another corps consisting of the 2nd, 28th, and 35th Infantry Divisions from Europe was to serve as the Army Forces Pacific reserve, and a corps with the 91st, 95th, and 104th would form a strategic reserve in the Philippines. On Day Y + 35 the 11th Airborne Division as well as the strategic reserve corps (three divisions) would be available for combat on Honshu.

* Transferred from the European Theater.

(The 86th and 97th Divisions were originally intended for the Pacific but were sent to Europe instead because of losses in the Battle of the Bulge. These were the only divisions from Europe to reach the Pacific before the Japanese surrender.)

Including the above reserves, with redeployments from Europe, some four divisions per month would be available for combat on Honshu from about April 1, 1946.

A breakdown of the Army forces being transferred to the Pacific from Europe, both directly and through the United States, is in Appendix D.

FOURTH ARMY (Lt. Gen. Alexander McC. Patch)*

The Fourth Army headquarters, at Fort Sam Houston, Texas, was preparing for operations in the Pacific when the war ended. It was intended to send the command staff to the Pacific if required for continued operations on Honshu.

FOREIGN TROOPS

X Corps Headquarters (Lt. Gen. Sir Charles F. Kneightley)
3rd British Division
6th Canadian Division
10th Australian Division

The Commonwealth Corps was to have formed an afloat reserve for the Honshu assault. The British intended to provide two follow-up divisions on about Day Y + 40.

---

* General Patch commanded the Seventh Army in Europe from March 1944 to May 1945.

APPENDIX D

REDEPLOYMENT OF U.S. FORCES

FROM EUROPE

In the spring of 1945 the U.S. Joint Chiefs of Staff developed a plan for the movement of troops from the European theater to the Pacific, as indicated in the following table.

PURPOSE	STRENGTH	OPERATIONAL READINESS
Direct from Europe to the Pacific		
Army Air Forces for Olympic	48,000	Sept. 1945–Nov. 1945
Army Ground Forces for Olympic	32,900	Sept. 1945–Nov. 1945
Army Service Forces for Olympic	75,900	Sept. 1945–Nov. 1945
Army Air Forces for Coronet	30,000	Dec. 1945
Army Ground Forces for Coronet*	66,000	Dec. 1945–Jan. 1946
Army Service Forces for Coronet	72,900	Nov. 1945–Jan. 1946
5 divisions for Pacific garrisons	70,200	Nov. 1945–Dec. 1945
Total	395,900	
From Europe Through the United States to the Pacific		
Army Air Forces for Coronet	63,000	Oct. 1945–Mar. 1946
Army Ground Forces for Coronet	263,600	Oct. 1945–Apr. 1946
Army Service Forces for Coronet	75,900	Sept. 1945–Nov. 1945
Army Air Forces for B-29 Groups†	75,200	to USA in Sept. 1945
Total	477,700	

* The 13th and 20th Armored Divisions and supporting troops.
† Eighth Air Force, to operate from Okinawa.

Originating in the United States to the Pacific

Army Air Forces for B-29 Groups

   (including 75,200 from Europe)   102,500   Aug. 1945–Apr. 1946

Army attrition replacements   5 percent of overseas strength at the

                                         start of each quarter

Rotation replacements   36,000 per month

Returning from Europe to Remain in the United States

Hospital patients   75,000 first quarter after V-E Day

Demobilization and retention in

   strategic reserve   2,180,000 to begin at the end of first

                                          quarter of redeployment and to be

                                          completed between $13\frac{1}{2}$ and $17\frac{1}{2}$

                                          months after V-E Day

---

SOURCE: Joint Chiefs of Staff, "Factors Underlying the Strategic Deployment of U.S. Forces Following Defeat of Germany," JCS 521/13, 29 Mar. 1945; and Robert W. Coakley and Richard M. Leighton, *Global Logistics and Strategy 1943–1945*.

NOTES

PROLOGUE

12 *Strike back at Japan:* Lt. Gen. Henry H. Arnold, USA, Memorandum of White House meeting, 4 Jan. 1942, as cited in James Doolittle, *I Could Never Be So Lucky Again*; however, the subject is not mentioned in Arnold's memorandum of the conference.

13 *Preliminary plans:* Lt. Gen. Henry H. Arnold, USA, Memorandum of White House meeting, 28 Jan. 1942.

13 *Discussions with Roosevelt and Churchill:* Lt. Gen. Henry H. Arnold, USA, Memorandum of White House meeting, 4 Jan. 1942.

13 *North African invasion:* A Navy escort (jeep) aircraft carrier did fly off 76 Army P-40F Warhawk fighter planes in the Nov. 1942 invasion of French North Africa, but no Army bomber aircraft were flown from carriers.

13 *Low talking to King:* Doolittle, 233.

14 *Meeting with Arnold:* In his autobiography, Gen. Arnold contends that it was King who came to see him; evidence is that it was Duncan and Low; see H.H. Arnold, *Global Mission*, 298.

15 *Secrecy of operation:* Ernest King and Walter Muir Whitehill, *Fleet Admiral King: A Naval Record*, 376.

16 *Doolittle brief to his pilots:* Doolittle, 270.

16 *Japanese picket detection:* Doolittle, 273–274.

18 *Doolittle after crashing in China:* Doolittle, 13.

18 *Fate of captured fliers:* Doolittle, 459.

19 *Estimate of Chinese killed:* Doolittle, 551.

19 *Base of Doolittle raiders:* A War Department communiqué of 20 Apr. 1943 identified the USS *Hornet* as the base of the raiders. It also provided the first public details of the mission and listed the fliers.

CHAPTER 1

22 *The first American:* A most detailed and well-written study of Pacific war planning is Edward S. Miller, *War Plan Orange: The U.S. Strategy to Defeat Japan, 1897–1945.*

23 *Bases in the Philippines:* Lt. Col. Henry G. Morgan, Jr., USA, *Planning the Defeat of Japan: A Study of Total War Strategy* (Washington, D.C.: Office of the Chief of Military History [n.d.]) [monograph], 12.

24 *MacArthur's viewpoint:* Gen. Douglas MacArthur, USA (Ret.), letter to Capt. Bonner Fellars, USA, 1 June 1939 (MacArthur Archives).

25 *Flunking midshipmen offered Marine commissions:* Ronald H. Spector, *Eagle Against the Sun*, 24.

25 *Lejeune on "true mission":* Col. Allan R. Millett, USMC (Ret.), *Semper Fidelis*, 285.

25 *Ellis inspired by War Plan Orange:* Millett, 325.

25 *Ellis plans for the Pacific:* Maj. Earl H. Ellis, USMC, "Advanced Base Operations in Micronesia," Operations Plan 712-H (Marine Corps Schools, Quantico, Va.). Robert Debs Heinl, Jr., the dean of Marine historians, hailed Ellis's "brilliant imagination," which "made

him a leader among the [amphibious] thinkers of the prewar period. . . ." (Heinl, *Soldiers of the Sea: The U.S. Marine Corps, 1775–1962*, 256.)

25 *Ellis on need for Marines:* Ellis, *op. cit.*

27 *Ellis's behavior:* Dirk Anthony Ballendorf, "Earl Hancock Ellis: A Final Assessment," *Marine Corps Gazette*, 84.

27 *Death of Ellis:* Ballendorf, 84.

27 *Fate of Chief Pharmacist Zembsch:* In a strange twist of fate, Zembsch arrived back in Yokohama on Aug. 14, 1923, and was hospitalized, apparently because of the strain of his mission. He was said to have been recovering when, at about noon on Sept. 1, 1923, the great Kanto earthquake completely destroyed the hospital, burying him beneath tons of debris.

28 *1929 War Plan:* "Navy Basic Plan—ORANGE, WPL-13," 1 Mar. 1929.

28 *Embick's proposal:* Memorandum from Brig. Gen. S.D. Embick, USA, for Commanding General Philippine Department, "Military Policy of U.S. in the Philippine Islands," 19 Apr. 1933.

28 *Richardson on war plans:* George C. Dyer, *On the Treadmill to Pearl Harbor*, 255. Adm. Richardson was Commander in Chief U.S. Fleet from Jan. 1940 to Feb. 1941.

29 *Japan's political position:* Japan felt an affinity for the similar aggressive policies of Nazi Germany, and on Nov. 25, 1936, the two countries signed the Anti-Comintern Pact. The pact was aimed at the international communism sponsored by the Soviet Union and pledged the safeguarding of "common interests" against threats by the Soviet Union. The Tripartite Pact signed with Germany and Italy on Sept. 27, 1940, was a full military-political alliance.

29 *In September 1938:* Letter from the Major General Commandant of the Marine Corps (Maj. Gen. Thomas Holcomb) to Chief of Naval Operations (Adm. Harold R. Stark), "Surveys of Midway, Johnston and Wake Islands by a Marine officer," 21 Sept. 1938.

30 *Views given to Hull:* Dyer, 385.

31 *Roosevelt on deterrence effect of fleet:* Dyer, 427.

32 *Higgins boat:* Quoted in Frank O. Hough et al., *Pearl Harbor to Guadalcanal*, 27.

33 *Information about Higgins:* Stephen E. Ambrose, *D-Day June 6, 1944: The Climactic Battle of World War II*, 45–46.

33 *Marine landing craft:* Lt. Gen. H.M. Smith, USMC (Ret.), *Coral and Brass*, 95.

33 *Pictures in rest rooms:* Ambrose, 46. Higgins's aircraft venture was less successful. His Higgins Aircraft Co. was "one of the AAF's more expensive failures." The aircraft plant, erected at a cost of more than $23 million, produced only two C-46 Commando transport aircraft before the end of the war; contracts for 498 more planes were canceled. (See Wesley Frank Craven and James Lea Cate, *Men and Planes*, 316.)

33 *"Did more to win the war . . .":* Smith, 72; *Eisenhower on Higgins:* Ambrose, 45.

34 *Importance of LSTs:* Winston Churchill, *Closing the Ring*, 514.

34 *Design of the LST:* James L. Mooney, *Dictionary of American Naval Fighting Ships*, vol. VII, 569.

35 *Tojo and war preparations:* Courtney Browne, *Tojo: The Last Banzai*, 108.

36 *Attack on Taranto:* The Swordfish attack planes sank two Italian battleships and damaged a third.

37 *Direction of Japanese fleet:* "The President Faces War," in Paul Stillwell (ed.), *Air Raid: Pearl Harbor!*, 114. The source is "Reminiscences of Frances Perkins," vol. VIII (1955), 35–98, Oral History Collection of Columbia University. Perkins was Secretary of Labor at the time.

37 *Pearl Harbor attack timing:* The time difference between Washington and Pearl Harbor then was 7½ hours.

39 *Book for Japanese soldiers:* Masanobu Tsuji, *Singapore: The Japanese Version*, 301. *Read This Alone—And the War Can Be Won* (also called *Read This and the War Is Won*) was prepared for soldiers participating in the Far East campaign. Its contents ranged from battlefield exhortations to tips on how to avoid sunstroke.

Chapter 2

41 *Tell Nimitz about his selection:* E.B. Potter, *Nimitz*, 6.

41 *Nimitz reaction to destruction of fleet:* H. Arthur Lamar, "Replacing the Commander in Chief," in Paul Stillwell (ed.), *Air Raid: Pearl Harbor!*, 258–259.

44 *Nimitz-Kimmel meeting:* E.B. Potter, *Nimitz,* 17, 19.

44 *U.S. code-breaking efforts:* These efforts are described in Edward J. Drea, *MacArthur's ULTRA: Codebreaking and the War against Japan, 1942–1945,* and Ronald Lewin, *The American Magic: Codes, Ciphers and the Defeat of Japan*; both are outstanding works.

44 *Coral Sea losses:* The USS *Lexington* and *Saratoga* had been converted during construction from battle cruisers. The only larger carrier completed during the war was the Japanese *Shinano,* converted while under construction from a *Yamato*-class battle cruiser. She was sunk by a U.S. submarine before becoming operational.

46 *Admiral Leahy:* A former Chief of Naval Operations (1937–1939), Leahy was subsequently appointed by Roosevelt to serve as governor of Puerto Rico and then American ambassador to Vichy France.

46 *JCS composition:* As initially constituted the JCS included Adm. King as Commander in Chief U.S. Fleet and Adm. Harold R. Stark, the Chief of Naval Operations. In March 1942, King assumed the latter post while remaining CinC U.S. Fleet (with Stark being sent to England as U.S. naval commander in Europe, a form of purgatory as his punishment for the Pearl Harbor debacle).

46 *"My God, man . . .":* Forrest C. Pogue, *George C. Marshall: Ordeal and Hope, 1939–1943,* 93.

47 *"I was accused . . .":* Pogue, 97.

47 *Marshall suggests Leahy:* Pogue, 299–300.

47 *"Pig-headed Dutchman":* Adm. William D. Leahy, USN, *I Was There,* 97, 136.

47 *Information on King:* Vice Adm. Charles Wellborn, "The Fog of War," in Stillwell, 97; Lewin, 116. When a White House aide, Navy Capt. John McCrea, later asked King about the "sons of bitches" remark, King replied, "I didn't say that, but I would have if I had thought of it." McCrea's account is from an interview with Robert Greenhalgh Albion for his book *Makers of Naval Policy 1798–1947* (Annapolis, Md.: Naval Institute Press, 1980), 393.

47 *Marshall-King relationship:* Pogue, 372.

48 *Arnold and air power:* Kent Roberts Greenfield, *American Strategy in World War II: A Reconsideration,* 88–90.

48 *Marshall and Arnold:* Pogue, 84, 290–291.

48 *Arnold on use of air power:* Ronald Spector, *Eagle Against the Sun,* 206–207. *Reichsmarschall* Hermann Göring was head of the German Air Force.

48 *Pacific command:* Message from Roosevelt to Churchill, Mar. 9, 1942, and from Churchill to Roosevelt, Mar. 17, 1942; see also Winston S. Churchill, *The Hinge of Fate,* 197–198.

49 *Establishing two theaters:* Grace Person Hayes, *The History of the Joint Chiefs of Staff in World War II,* 96–101.

49 *MacArthur's $500,000:* Michael Schaller, *Douglas MacArthur: The Far Eastern General,* 59–61. The transaction was first revealed by historian Carol M. Petillo, "Douglas MacArthur and Manuel Quezon: A Note on an Imperial Bond," *Pacific Historical Review,* Feb. 1979, 107–117; see also Petillo, *Douglas MacArthur: The Philippine Years* (Bloomington: Indiana University Press, 1981), 208–212.

50 *MacArthur, Quezon ordered to leave:* Schaller, 60–61.

50 *Johnson's report:* Schaller, 65. Johnson, who had told his Texas constituents in 1941 that if war came he "would be in the front line," volunteered for active duty soon after the Japanese attack on Pearl Harbor. He spent four months inspecting shipyards and war plants and then went to the Southwest Pacific. He was a passenger in a B-26 Marauder attacked by Japanese fighters, which shot down the plane carrying the two other officers on his survey team. Johnson was unscathed, and MacArthur awarded him the Silver Star for the flight. On July 9, 1942, Roosevelt ordered all members of Congress in the armed forces to return to Congress. Of eight then on active duty, four resigned from Congress and remained in the armed forces; Johnson was one of those who returned to Congress.

51 *The assault force:* The aircraft carriers were the *Enterprise, Saratoga,* and *Wasp.* At the time, the Navy had one other carrier in the Pacific, the *Hornet*; the *Ranger,* unsuitable for Pacific operations, was in the Atlantic.

52 *Americal Division:* The only U.S. division with a name rather than number. The term "Americal" was derived from *Ameri*can and New *Cal*edonia, the division having been activated

at New Caledonia in May 1942. (In 1954 the Americal Division was redesignated as the 23rd Infantry Division.)

54 *MacArthur to Eichelberger:* William Manchester, *American Caesar,* 325.

54 *Halsey's command:* Nimitz's Pacific Ocean Areas command was subdivided into north, central, and south subcommands.

54 *". . . but not reckless":* James M. Merrill, *A Sailor's Admiral,* 25.

55 *Halsey and MacArthur:* Fleet Adm. William F. Halsey, USN, and Lt. Comdr. J. Bryan III, USNR, *Admiral Halsey's Story,* 154–155.

56 *British opposition to Pacific campaigns:* Hayes, 281.

58 *Pyle aboard transport.* Ernie Pyle, *The Last Chapter,* 95.

58 *Amphibious tractors:* LVT indicated Landing Vehicle Tracked, i.e., Donald Roebling's vehicles.

59 *Landing craft:* LVT(A) = Landing Vehicle, Tracked (Armored); LCVP = Landing Craft, Vehicles and Personnel; and LCM = Landing Craft, Mechanized.

59 *Pyle in landing craft:* Pyle, 100.

61 *The Kwajalein operation:* Adm. Spruance letter to J.A. Isley, 14 Jan. 1949 (Princeton University Library).

64 *Smith-versus-Smith controversy:* Smith was made Commander Fleet Marine Force Pacific, the administrative commander of all Marines in the Pacific.

66 *MacArthur's intelligence estimates:* MacArthur and to a lesser degree his air commander, Lt. Gen. George C. Kenney, often refused to accept Ultra (code-breaking) intelligence, especially when it was in conflict with their preconceived views. This attitude was due, in part, to Navy Ultra being the principal source of communications intelligence in the Pacific from the spring of 1942 until early 1944.

67 *"The fighting in the ridges . . .":* Eugene B. Sledge, "Peleliu 1944: Why Did We Go There?" U.S. Naval Institute *Proceedings,* Sept. 1994, 74.

68 *Navy support to MacArthur:* Numerous amphibious ships and landing craft in this and other Pacific operations were manned by Coast Guard personnel, that service being part of the Navy during the war.

69 *Kamikaze attack:* James J. Fahey, *Pacific War Diary,* 87, 88, 92.

72 *Holland Smith's fear of casualties:* Lt. Gen. Howland M. Smith, USMC (Ret.), and Percy Finch, *Coral and Brass,* 253.

Chapter 3

76 *Air power philosophy:* Gen. Giulio Douhet, *Command of the Air,* 32.

76 *Independent air force:* Douhet, 33.

76 *Attack enemy cities:* Douhet, 98.

76 *"The Bomber will always get through . . .":* "Simon Urges Europe to Ban Use of Force," *The New York Times* (Nov. 11, 1932), 1. Sir John Simon was the British Foreign Secretary.

77 *Norden bombsight:* U.S. Strategic Bombing Survey, *The United States Strategic Bombing Survey: Summary Report,* 5. See also Wesley Frank Craven and James Lea Cate, *Plans and Early Operations, January 1939 to August 1942,* 38–39.

78 *Reliance on carrier aircraft:* Combined Planning Staff [JCS], "Appreciation and Plan for the Defeat of Japan," 8 Aug. 1943 (National Archives).

78 *Plans for bombing Japan:* In reality, 106,800 tons of bombs were dropped on the Japanese home islands through Aug. 1945. Of these, 147,000 were dropped by B-29s, 6,800 tons by Navy carrier-based planes, and 7,000 tons by other AAF aircraft. In contrast, 1,360,000 tons of bombs were dropped on Germany by U.S. and British aircraft during five years of the air assault on Germany—which did not surrender under that aerial onslaught.

79 *Flying Tigers:* The Flying Tigers were highly popularized by the press and by fighter pilot Robert Lee Scott in his book *God Is My Co-Pilot* (1943), made into a movie by the same name in 1945 starring Dennis Morgan and Raymond Massey. Scott, not a Flying Tiger, retired as a brigadier general, having scored 13 aerial kills against the Japanese.

79 *Marshall on China problems:* Herbert Feis, *The China Tangle,* 60.

80 *Chennault's plan for the "collapse of Japan":* Barbara W. Tuchman, *Stilwell and the American Experience in China, 1911–45,* 337.

80 *Marshall's reaction:* Tuchman, 338.

80 *Arnold's reaction:* Gen. of the Air Force H.H. Arnold, USAF, *Global Mission,* 413.

80 *Chennault's plan:* Wesley Frank Craven and John Lea Cate, *The Pacific—Matterhorn to Nagasaki, June 1944 to August 1945,* 14–15. Chennault was ably assisted in these efforts by his public relations officer, journalist Joseph Alsop.

80 *Matterhorn's development:* Craven and Cate, *The Pacific,* 22 *passim.*

81 *Yawata bombing:* Craven and Cate, *The Pacific,* 101.

82 *Reconnaissance flight over Tokyo:* Gen. Curtis E. LeMay, USAF (Ret.), and Bill Yenne, *Superfortress,* 118

84 *"You've got to kill people...":* Gen. Thomas Powers, USAF (Ret.), "Nuclear Winter and Nuclear Strategy," *Atlantic,* Nov. 1984, 60.

84 *Norstad's advice:* Gen. Curtis E. LeMay, USAF (Ret.), with MacKinlay Kantor, *Mission with LeMay,* 347.

84 *Japanese cities:* LeMay and Kantor, *op. cit.*

85 *Dugway mock-ups:* "Salt Lake Telegram Runs Column," *The Sand Blast* [Dugway Army Proving Ground], 24 Aug. 1945, 8; this is a reprint of the story "Dugway Mystery Depot to Continue Test Work" that was originally published in the *Salt Lake Telegram.*

85 *Napalm bombs:* Brooks E. Kleber and Dale Birdsell, *The Chemical Warfare Service: Chemicals in Combat,* 159–163, 624–630.

86 *"The Great Tokyo Air Raid":* Don Oberdorfer, "Tokyo Recalls 1945 'Rain of Fire' With Sadness, Little Anger," *Washington Post* (Mar. 10, 1975), A20.

86 *LeMay on slaughtering civilians:* LeMay and Kantor, 384.

87 *LeMay's firebomb raids:* Craven and Cates, *The Pacific,* 638.

88 *Bombing the Imperial Palace:* Brig. Gen. Paul W. Tibbets, USAF (Ret.), *The Tibbets Story,* 192–193.

90 *Civilian casualties:* LeMay and Yenne, 125.

90 *Training crews for B-29s:* During June–July 1945, 2,118 four-engine B-17s and B-24s of Doolittle's Eighth Air Force were flown from Britain to the United States; the planes were junked and most of their crews trained to fly B-29s.

91 *Eisenhower-Spaatz controversy:* Stephen E Ambrose, *D-Day,* 94–96.

91 *Twining relieving LeMay:* Maj. Gen. Haywood S. Hansell, Jr., USAF, *Strategic Air War Against Japan,* 70.

92 *The Tiger Force:* The British bomber force would require some 90,000 men—air crews, maintenance men, construction troops, cooks, and others on Okinawa.

92 *Soviet cooperation:* The B-29 missions against Japan would have also benefited from weather reporting from Siberia; according to LeMay, "We received meager quantities of information [from the Soviets] from time to time, offered most grudgingly, but we could never depend on it" (*Mission with LeMay,* 343). The AAF and Navy both had some weather-reporting stations in China and Mongolia.

93 *Army missile plans:* Max Rosenberg, *The Air Force and the National Guided Missile Program, 1944–1950,* 9.

93 *Roosevelt approving the bat project:* Leo P. Brophy et al., *The Chemical Warfare Service: From Laboratory to Field,* 188.

93 *Bat mission description:* Brophy, *op. cit* See also Robert Sherrod, *History of Marine Corps Aviation in World War II,* 129.

94 *Volcano attacks:* War Department General Staff, Military Intelligence Service, Research Unit, "The Bombing of Japanese Volcanos for the Purpose of Causing Eruptions," Project No. 1804, 23 Mar. 1945 (National Archives).

CHAPTER 4

96 *Battle slogan:* 32nd Army Battle Instructions, 15 Feb. 1945, in Commander in Chief Pacific-Pacific Ocean Areas, Bulletin 122-45, Translations and Interrogations No. 30, 1 June 1945 (Marine Corps Historical Center).

97 *Strength of Okinawa defenders:* The 66,600 Army personnel included 5,000 Okinawans, mostly regular conscripts, integrated into regular Japanese units. Defenders' data from Maj.

Chas. S. Nichols, Jr., USMC, and Henry I. Shaw, Jr., *Okinawa: Victory in the Pacific*, 302–304, and Benis M. Frank and Henry I. Shaw, Jr., *Victory and Occupation*, 41–50.

97 *Attitudes of Okinawans:* Saburo Ienaga, *The Pacific War*, 291.

100 *Orders of Akamatsu:* Ienaga, 185.

101 *Description of landing:* Ernie Pyle, *The Last Chapter*, 103.

101 *Attitude of kamikaze pilots:* Rear Adm. Toshiyuki Yokoi, "Kamikazes and the Okinawa Campaign," U.S. Naval Institute *Proceedings*, May 1954, 510.

101 *Dedication of kamikaze pilots:* Rikihei Inoguchi et al., *The Divine Wind*, 84.

102 *Kamikaze pilot's letter:* Translated into English on tape available at the Peace Museum for Special Air Force Attack Pilots, Chiran, Kyushu.

102 *Adventures of the* Defense: Action Report of *Defense* (AM 317), 15 Apr. 1945; Rear Adm. Samuel Eliot Morison, USNR (Ret.), *Victory in the Pacific 1945*, 184.

104 *Attack on* Laffey: Morison, 235.

104 *Strain of kamikaze attacks:* Ronald H. Spector, *Eagle Against the Sun*, 539.

104 *Role of kamikazes:* General Headquarters, Far East Command, Military Intelligence Section, Historical Division, "Interrogations of Japanese Officials on World War II," interrogation of Capt. Rikihei Inoguchi, IJN, Mar. 7, 1947 (Center of Military History).

106 *The last night on the* Yamato: Russell Spurr, *A Curious Way to Die: The Kamikaze Mission of the Battleship* Yamato, *April 1945*, 125.

106 *Sinking of the* Yamato: Ens. Mitsuru Yoshida, IJN, "The End of the *Yamato*," U.S. Naval Institute *Proceedings*, Feb. 1952, 124.

107 *Why the* Yamato *died:* Capt. Tameichi Hara, IJN, et al., *Japanese Destroyer Captain*, 278.

107 *Turner's prognosis:* Morison, 215–216, and E.B. Potter, *Nimitz*, 372. Morison says the Turner message was "jocular," and Potter says it was sent "playfully." Nimitz, however, was serious. The message is not mentioned in the stilted biography by Vice Adm. George Carroll Dyer, USN (Ret.), *The Amphibians Came to Conquer: The Story of Admiral Richmond Kelly Turner*, vol. II (Washington, D.C.: U.S. Naval History Division, 1972); Turner was promoted to full admiral in May 1945.

108 *Conditions for generals in the field:* Isshi Kamichi, *Okinawa senshi* [The Battle for Okinawa], cited in Ienaga, 191.

108 *Description of fighting:* Maj. Gen. Wilburt S. Brown, USMC, oral history, Marine Corps Historical Center, 214–215.

109 *Suicide of Japanese generals:* Frank and Shaw, 367. The account of the generals' death is from a prisoner-of-war interrogation in the history of the Army's 7th Infantry Division.

CHAPTER 5

112 *Rumor "swept through the corridors":* Harry S. Truman, *Year of Decisions*, 11.

112 *Watson died on the* Quincy: Truman, 2.

112 *"His eyes were sunken . . .":* Truman, 2.

113 *"Once Germany was finally defeated":* Keith Eubank, *Summit at Teheran*, 258.

113 *No such staff talks ever materialized:* Eubank, 297.

113 *Conditions in Chiang's army:* Grace Person Hayes, *The History of the Joint Chiefs of Staff in World War II: The War Against Japan*, 647; Christopher Thorne, *The Far Eastern War*, 258.

114 *The Three Demands:* Barbara W. Tuchman, *Stilwell and the American Experience in China, 1911–45*, 313.

114 *Soviet diplomats tell of firefights:* Herbert Feis, *The China Tangle*, 86.

114 *"Civil war" warning:* Feis, 89, quoting dispatch from U.S. Embassy, Chungking, 14 Oct. 1943.

115 *Roosevelt sent Wallace to China:* Feis, 145.

115 *Background on MacArthur:* William Manchester, *American Caesar*, 308; Michael Schaller, *Douglas MacArthur: The Far Eastern General*, 80–84.

116 *MacArthur-Miller correspondence:* Schaller, 83; Manchester, 362–363.

117 *Roosevelt seeking Wallace replacement:* David McCullough, *Truman*, 299.

117 *Roosevelt-Hannegan phone call:* McCullough, 314.

117 *"Hoping for a funeral":* McCullough, 299.

117 *Not "to give a damn":* McCullough, 323.

118 *Navy "had no interest...":* Manchester, 566–567.

118 *"Use of China as a base...":* Thomas Buell, *Master of Sea Power,* 440. King's beliefs are in a scathing letter to Nimitz. King, Buell says, was "enraged at Nimitz's defection" at the Hawaii conference.

118 *"Steal the food...":* Manchester, 368.

118 *"Well, Douglas...":* Manchester, 370.

119 *"Ike and Doug" as campaigners:* Ray Tucker, "Elections," in *Encyclopaedia Britannica, 10 Eventful Years,* Vol. 2, 200.

119 *Japanese offensive:* Tuchman, 508.

119 *"This theater is written off...":* Stilwell's diary, quoted by Feis, 196.

119 *Kept out of sight:* Tuchman, 507.

119 *Marshall letters to Dewey:* Ronald H. Spector (ed.), *Listening to the Enemy,* ix–x; Ronald Lewin, *The American Magic,* 3–11. The letters were so secret that they were not declassified until 1979. Col. Clarke, later promoted to brigadier general, became deputy chief of the Military Intelligence Service and was a key dispenser of Magic summaries to the President and a handful of senior officials.

120 *Martin's promise:* Joe Martin (as told to Robert J. Donovan), *My First Fifty Years in Politics* (New York: McGraw-Hill, 1960), 100–101; quoted in McCullough, 291.

120 *Had not met Stettinius:* McCullough, 333.

120 *Knew nothing about commitments:* Martin J. Sherwin, *A World Destroyed,* 147.

120 *Concerns about Roosevelt's health:* Diane Shaver Clemens, *Yalta,* 103; McCullough, 295, 323–324. The reports on Roosevelt's failing health are mentioned in *Affectionately, F.D.R. A Son's Story of a Lonely Man,* written by James Roosevelt and Sidney Shallett (New York: Harcourt, Brace, 1959), 351–352.

120 *"Would in all probability be the next President":* McCullough, 295, quoting the recollection of George E. Allen, secretary of the Democratic National Committee.

120 *"Too damned old":* Merle Miller, *Plain Speaking,* 205. The story is told by Truman in this "oral biography." In it Truman also says that he and Marshall first met in World War I when Truman was a captain and Marshall a colonel.

121 *Stimson-Truman conversation:* McCullough, 289; from records of telephone conversation, June 17, 1943, in the Truman Library.

121 *"Truman is a nuisance":* Stimson diaries, Mar. 13, 1944.

121 *Roosevelt words to Congress, to Truman:* Truman, 3–4.

121 *Concessions to Stalin:* Clemens, 310.

122 *Truman had sessions with Roosevelt:* McCullough, 339.

122 *Physician's remarks on Roosevelt:* "Clinical Notes," Oral History Interview by Rexford Tugwell, Roosevelt Library.

122 *Stimson "statement left me puzzled":* Truman, 10. Truman actually had some knowledge of the project as early as July 15, 1943, when he wrote to a friend about construction of a plant near Hanford, Washington, "to make a terrific explosion for a secret weapon that will be a wonder."

122 *State Department briefing:* Truman, 14–17.

122 *Truman on Map Room:* Truman, 50–51.

123 *Map showing invasion plans:* The map, then in the possession of the National Geographic Society, was shown to one of the authors. *National Geographic* magazine maps were also used by military planners, including MacArthur's staff. One was used by Maj. Gen. Leslie Groves to select possible targets for the first atomic bombs, and another was marked up by planners laying out the postwar occupation zones in Berlin.

124 *Harriman on Truman:* Truman, 72.

124 *Information on Manhattan Project:* Sherwin, 42; Richard Rhodes, *The Making of the Atomic Bomb,* 369.

125 *"Perfecting an explosive...":* Truman, 11.

125 *Note from Stimson:* Sherwin, 162.

125 *Stimson tells Truman about the bomb:* Manhattan Engineer District Records, Record Group 77, National Archives; Stimson "Memo discussed with the President," Apr. 25, 1945, Rhodes, 625–626.

125 *Leahy on bomb:* "The damn thing" quote appears in Cabell Phillips, *The Truman Presidency* (New York: Macmillan, 1966), 54. Leahy does not use that quote in his own account; the rest of the Leahy words here come from Leahy, *I Was There,* 441.

126 *Marshall on "great impatience":* From Marshall's address to the Academy of Political Sciences, New York City, Apr. 4, 1945.

126 *King's fear about "pressure at home":* Charles F. Brower IV; "Sophisticated Strategist," 321–322.

126 *"Unconditional surrender":* Public Papers of the Presidents of the United States, Harry S. Truman, Apr. 16, 1945, 2.

126 *JCS on unconditional surrender:* Joint Intelligence Committee report, JIC 268/1, "Unconditional Surrender of Japan," 25 Apr. 1945 (National Archives).

127 *"Mad as a wet hen":* Truman, 206.

127 *"Victory is only half over":* Truman, 207.

127 *"Possibility of a general letdown":* Brower, 326.

CHAPTER 6

129 *First invasion planning:* Grace Person Hayes, *The History of the Joint Chiefs of Staff in World War II,* 367; JCS, Joint War Plans Committee, "A Strategic Plan for the Defeat of Japan," 28 Apr. 1943.

129 *Strategy for the defeat of Japan:* JCS, JWPC, "A Strategic Plan for the Defeat of Japan," 5 May 1943, CSS 381.

130 *U.S. views on Pacific strategy:* Joint Planning Staff, "Preparations for the Next U.S.-British Joint Staff Conference," 25 May 1943, JPS 189, CCS 381.

130 *Keeping the British out of Pacific strategy:* Hayes, 458.

130 *Defeating Japan 12 months after Germany:* Ray S. Cline, *Washington Command Post,* 6 fn; also CCS 319/2, "Progress Report to President and Prime Minister . . . ," 21 Aug. 1943.

132 *Different views by different services:* Hayes, 501; Combined Staff Planners 86/2, "The Defeat of Japan within Twelve Months after the Defeat of Germany," 25 Oct. 1943, CCS 381 (National Archives).

132 *King's astonishment:* Hayes, 503; Minutes, JCS 123rd Meeting, 15 Nov. 1943.

133 *"Europe then was the war of choice":* Interview with Harvey Katz. Wounded in the Battle of the Bulge, he received the Bronze Star and the Purple Heart.

133 *Study leading to an assault on Honshu:* Cline, 337; JPS 476, "Operations Against Japan, Subsequent to Formosa," 6 June 1944.

134 *75th in combat:* Russell F. Weigley, *Eisenhower's Lieutenants: The Campaigns of France and Germany 1944–1945,* 776.

135 *Basic Army position:* Cline, 337; Operations Division, War Department General Staff, "Operations in Pacific," 7 Jan. 1943, Strategy Section Papers, SS 282, ABC 381 (National Archives).

135 *Need to prepare for shift to Pacific:* Cline, 341; Memorandum from Brig. Gen. Lincoln for Col. [Frank N.] Roberts, 7 Feb. 1945, 7 [no subject] (National Archives).

135 *Coronet will be the decisive operation:* Cline, 342; Memorandum from Gen. Marshall to Gen. MacArthur, 23 Mar. 1945, file CM-OUT 57902 (MacArthur Archives). The code-name Olympic was changed to Majestic in early August 1945 because of a possible security compromise; for simplicity Olympic is used throughout this book.

136 *MacArthur's command proposals:* Message from Gen. MacArthur to Gen. Marshall, 17 Dec. 1944, WD 890 (MacArthur Archives).

136 *O'Laughlin's criticism of Marshall:* Frazier Hunt, *The Untold Story of Douglas MacArthur,* 375.

137 *Roosevelt on Pacific command selection:* Gen. George C. Kenney, USAF, *Gen. Kenney Reports,* 533.

137 *MacArthur's reaction to Kenney report:* Kenney, 534.

137 *Marshall on MacArthur's appointment:* Message from Gen. Marshall to Gen. MacArthur, 4 Apr. 1945, file WAR 63196, WD 955 (MacArthur Archives); message from War Department to Maj. Gen. Grunert et al., 6 Apr. 1945, file WX63939, WD 959 (MacArthur Archives).

137 *MacArthur's selection:* Message from Joint Chiefs of Staff to MacArthur, Nimitz, and Arnold, 4 Apr. 1945, file WX 62774, WD 957 (MacArthur Archives).

138 *Marshall trying to get MacArthur's cooperation:* Message from Gen. Marshall to Gen. MacArthur, 4 May 1945, file WAR 77081, WD 1008 (MacArthur Archives). The Joint Chiefs of Staff established the 1 Nov. 1945 date for Operation Olympic in "Joint Chiefs of Staff Directive for Operation 'Olympic,' " 25 May 1945, JCS 1331/3 (National Archives).

138 *Nimitz-MacArthur relationship:* E.B. Potter, *Nimitz,* 291.

139 *Five-star rank and insignia:* Potter, 351. In November 1944 the Congress approved eight five-star ranks; the following month President Roosevelt appointed seven, in order of precedence: (1) Fleet Adm. William D. Leahy, Chief of Staff to the President; (2) Gen. of the Army George C. Marshall, Chief of Staff of the Army; (3) Fleet Adm. Ernest J. King, Commander in Chief U.S. Fleet and Chief of Naval Operations; (4) Gen. of the Army Douglas A. MacArthur, Commander in Chief Southwest Pacific Area; (5) Fleet Adm. Chester W. Nimitz, Commander in Chief Pacific Ocean Areas and Pacific Fleet; (6) Gen. of the Army Dwight D. Eisenhower, Supreme Allied Commander Europe; and (7) Gen. of the Army H.H. Arnold, Commanding General Army Air Forces. William F. Halsey was promoted to Fleet Admiral after the war.

139 *Results of MacArthur-Nimitz meetings:* Commander in Chief, Pacific Fleet, Operation Plan No. 10-45, 8 Aug. 1945, Annex B "Coordination of Operations and Command Relations," 6 (Naval Historical Center).

139 *MacArthur tells Marshall problems not settled:* Message from Gen. MacArthur to Gen. Marshall, 21 May 1945 (National Archives). WD 1024 (MacArthur Archives).

139 *Joint Chiefs of Staff direction:* Message from Joint Chiefs of Staff to MacArthur, Nimitz, and Arnold, 26 May 1945, file WX 87938, WD 1028 (MacArthur Archives).

140 *Marshall's proposal for Pacific commanders:* Message from Gen. Marshall to Gen. MacArthur, 6 April 1945, file WAR 64257, WD 964 (MacArthur Archives).

140 *MacArthur's rejection of commanders:* Message from Gen. MacArthur to Gen. Marshall, 7 Apr. 1945, WD 965 (MacArthur Archives).

140 *Marshall continues to propose Bradley:* Message from Gen. Marshall to Gen. MacArthur, 24 Apr. 1945, file W71770, WD 987 (MacArthur Archives).

140 *MacArthur supports Krueger:* Message from Gen. MacArthur to Gen. Marshall, 24 Apr. 1945, WD 989 (MacArthur Archives).

140 *Eisenhower's outrage:* Gen. of the Army Omar N. Bradley, USA, and Clay Blair, *A General's Life: An Autobiography by General of the Army Omar N. Bradley,* 435. In 1950, Bradley became the Chairman of the Joint Chiefs of Staff, making him MacArthur's superior; he was also promoted to five-star rank, the only U.S. officer so promoted after 1945.

141 *Marshall concedes defeat on Bradley:* Message from Gen. Marshall to Gen. Eisenhower, 27 Apr. 1945, Eisenhower papers, vol. IV, 2647–2648 (Eisenhower Library).

141 *Marshall on Stilwell:* Stilwell's Efficiency Report for July 1929–June 1930 in his 201 File, quoted in Barbara W. Tuchman, *Stilwell and the American Experience in China, 1911–45,* 125.

141 *Stilwell seeking a combat command:* Army Ground Forces was one of three commands established on March 9, 1942, under Marshall, to supervise the U.S. military buildup and provide forces to various field commands; the others were the Army Air Forces and Army Service Forces.

141 *Stilwell's views of the invasion of Japan:* Memorandum from Gen. Stilwell to Gen. Marshall [n.d.; no subject] (National Archives).

141 *MacArthur and Stilwell exchange:* Stilwell Diary, 19 June 1945, quoted in Tuchman, 519.

141 *MacArthur rejecting Stilwell:* Message from Gen. MacArthur to Gen. Marshall, 19 June 1945, WD 1059 (MacArthur Archives).

142 *Marshall gives Tenth Army to Stilwell:* Message from Gen. Marshall to Gen. MacArthur, 20 June 1945, file W18901, WD 1061 (MacArthur Archives).

142 *British matériel requirements:* Memorandum by the Representatives of the British Chiefs of Staff, "Scale of British Army Effort in the Pacific After the Defeat of Germany," 15 July 1944, CCS 619; and "Report by the Joint Logistics Committee," enclosure to Joint Logistics Committee, Combined Chiefs of Staff, "Scale of British Army Effort in the Pacific After the Defeat of Germany," 5 Aug. 1944, JLC 151/1 (National Archives).

143 *MacArthur's objection to Indian troops:* Message from Gen. MacArthur to Gen. Marshall, 9 July 1945. The authors have been unable to locate a copy of this message in either the National Archives or the MacArthur Archives. The message is quoted in several Combined Chiefs of Staff memoranda.

143 *British difficulties:* Joint Planning Staff, Chiefs of Staff Committee, "British Participation in the War Against Japan," 29 July 1945, JP(45)179 (British Public Records Office).

144 *Blamey's role:* For most of the 1942–1945 campaigns, MacArthur's naval and air commanders were Americans, Vice Adm. Thomas C. Kinkaid and Lt. Gen. George C. Kenney, respectively.

144 *Confusion among the Australians:* D.M. Horner, *High Command,* 344–349, and various messages quoted in John Robertson and John McCarthy, *Australian War Strategy 1939–1945,* 393–400.

144 *1st Australian Corps:* Memorandum from Lt. Gen. Sir John Northcott to Sir Frederick Shedden [Advisory War Council], "Forces Available to C-in-C S.W.P.A. for Offensive Operations," 15 Nov. 1944.

144 *Australian government desire:* Memorandum from Sir Frederick Shedden to Gen. MacArthur, 15 Feb. 1945 (Australian War Memorial).

145 *American troop movements:* Robert W. Coakley and Richard M. Leighton, *Global Logistics and Strategy 1943–1945,* 563–593; see also Appendix D of this book.

145 *Invasion size:* Commander in Chief, Pacific Fleet, "Operation Plan No. 10-45, Central Pacific Area: Olympic," 8 Aug. 1945 (Naval Historical Center).

146 *Marshall's airborne proposals:* Message from Gen. Marshall to Gen. MacArthur, 7 Apr. 1945, file WX64498, WD 966 (MacArthur Archives). Besides MacArthur's 11th Airborne Division, the Army had four airborne divisions in Europe—the 13th, 17th, 82nd, and 101st.

146 *"It does not . . .":* Message from Gen. MacArthur to Gen. Marshall, 8 Apr. 1945, W64498, WD 968 (MacArthur Archives).

146 *Airborne study:* JCS, Joint War Plans Committee, "Employment of Airborne Units in Operations Against Japan," JWPC 388/1, 13 July 1945 (National Archives).

147 *36,000 hospital beds:* Message from Gen. MacArthur to Gen. Marshall, 20 Apr. 1945, file C14442, WD982 (MacArthur Archives).

147 *Operation Pastel:* See Dr. Thomas M. Huber, *Pastel: Deception in the Invasion of Japan*; Headquarters, U.S. Army Forces Pacific, "Cover Plan PASTEL, Cover and Deception Plan, OLYMPIC Operations," 13 June 1945; "Staff Study, CORONET, Operations in the Kanto Plain of Honshu," 15 Aug. 1945, and "Staff Study, PASTEL TWO, Cover and Deception, OLYMPIC Operations," 30 July 1945 (Center of Military History and Army War College).

148 *Airborne deception:* Huber, 7.

148 *Douglas Fairbanks:* Fairbanks's activities are detailed in his autobiography, *A Hell of a War.*

148 *Broadaxe plan:* Huber, 24–26.

149 *"Experimental" landings:* Interview with Douglas Dies.

150 *Navy turned down Air Forces idea:* Huber, 33.

150 *Diplomatic intercepts:* War Department, "Magic"—Diplomatic Summary, No. 1109, 8 Apr. 1945, SRS 1631 (National Archives).

150 *Guerrilla and insurgent activities:* War Department, "Magic"—Diplomatic Summary, No. 1164, 2 June 1945, SRS 1686 (National Archives).

150 *Derevyanko:* He would sign the Japanese surrender documents on behalf of the Soviet Union on board the battleship *Missouri* in Tokyo Bay on Sept. 2, 1945.

150 *Plans for Hokkaido landing:* Capt. 1st Rank Boris I. Rodionov, Soviet Navy (Ret.), conversation with author.

152 *MacArthur in personal command:* Supreme Allied Commander [Japan], General Staff, *Reports of Gen. MacArthur,* Vol. I, 423.

152 *Eisenhower's divisions:* The divisions assigned to Eisenhower as Supreme Allied Commander in Europe at the end of the war were 68 American, 28 British, 11 French, and 2 Canadian. With support and other combat troops, Eisenhower had just over 3 million U.S. Army personnel, including 458,000 of the Army Air Forces.

CHAPTER 7

154 *Japanese casualties on Hollandia:* "Enemy Casualties by Campaigns," Intelligence Research Project 2112-A, Military Intelligence Service, War Department General Staff (National Archives).

154 *Report on beheadings:* Memorandum for the Commanding General, Army Air Forces, from Brig. Gen. Thomas D. White, assistant chief of Air Staff, Intelligence, 23 May 1944 (National Archives). Further investigation showed the man in the photograph was not an American but an Australian intelligence specialist.

154 *Release of photo:* David McCullough, *Truman,* 439.

154 *Intelligence report on atrocities:* Research Report No. 65 (Supplement No. 1), Allied Translator and Interpreter Section, South West Pacific Area, 29 Mar. 1945 (MacArthur Archives).

155 *Japanese diary quotation:* Research Report No. 65.

155 *Intercepted radio message:* Research Report No. 65.

155 *Execution of Okinawa airmen:* George Feifer, *Tennozan,* 389, 467.

155 *Report on sword-killing contest:* David Bergamini, *Japan's Imperial Conspiracy,* 21, quoting from the account in the *Japan Advertiser,* Dec. 7, 1937.

157 *Killings in Nanking:* Bergamini, 36, based on information about events in Nanking from two sources: (1) Hsu Shu-hsi, *The War Conduct of the Japanese* (Political and Economic Studies No. 3, Council of International Affairs. [Hangkow and Shanghai: Kelley & Walsh Ltd., 1938], eyewitness accounts of Japanese atrocities in China) and (2) testimony and affidavits given by eyewitnesses to the International Military Tribunal for the Far East (IMTFE), better known as the Japanese war-crimes trials.

157 *Rape report, death toll estimate:* Meirion and Susie Harries, *Soldiers of the Sun,* 224, 524; Bergamini, 44.

157 *Death estimates in occupied China:* John W. Dower, *War Without Mercy,* 43.

157 *Army surgeon's confession:* Interview in *Japan Times,* Sept. 19, 1993.

158 *Japan and the Geneva Convention:* Philip E. Ryan, in *Encyclopaedia Britannica, 10 Eventful Years,* Vol. 3, 641; Arnold C. Brackman, *The Other Nuremberg,* 250. Ryan was the director of international activities for the American Red Cross.

158 *Atrocities at Fort Stanley:* Bergamini, 877.

158 *Atrocities in Singapore:* Bergamini, 895–896.

158 *"Breaches of military discipline . . .":* Col. Masanobu Tsuji, *Singapore: The Japanese Version,* 264. Tsuji, sought by Allied officials after the war, according to a footnote in his book (264), "was ordered by the Japanese High Command to disappear and preserve himself for the reconstruction of Japan." He escaped to Thailand, spent some time in China and Indochina, returned to Japan when the Allies restored Japan's sovereignty in 1952, and was elected to Parliament. He later went to Vietnam as a correspondent for a Japanese newspaper and disappeared.

158 *Australian soldier's near-execution:* Brackman, 18–19.

159 *Bataan Death March:* Donald Knox, *Death March,* xxii, xxv, 116, 119, 121.

159 *Report to Roosevelt on prisoners:* "Japanese Atrocities—Reports by Escaped Prisoners," Memorandum from the Chief of Staff, U.S. Army to the Joint Chiefs of Staff, 17 Sept. 1943 (National Archives).

160 *Few Red Cross supplies reached prisoners:* Ryan, 644–645.

160 *Roosevelt and anthropologist:* Dower, 108. Dower's source for the Roosevelt-Hrdlicka correspondence is Christopher Thorne, *Allies of a Kind: The United States, Britain, and the War against Japan, 1941–1945* (London: Oxford University Press, 1978), 158–159, 167–168. See also Michael Schaller, *Douglas MacArthur: The Far Eastern General,* 109.

161 *Arnold suggests annihilation:* Schaller, 109.

161 *"Kill Japs":* Bergamini, 951.

161 *Killing German or Japanese soldier:* Ronald H. Spector, *Eagle Against the Sun,* 409.

161 *"Survival was hard enough . . .":* Eugene B. Sledge, "Peleliu 1944: Why Did We Go There?" U.S. Naval Institute *Proceedings,* Sept. 1994, 74.

161 *Surrender ruses:* Allison B. Gilmore, "In the Wake of Winning Armies: Allied Psychological Warfare Against the Imperial Japanese Army in the Southwest Pacific Area during WWII," Ph.D. dissertation, Ohio State University, 1989, 110–114.

161 *Medical experiments:* At Kyushu Imperial University: Saburo Ienaga, *The Pacific War,* 189–190.
162 *Seawater infection:* Peter Williams and David Wallace, *Unit 731,* 178.
162 *Wake Island killings:* Capt. Earl A. Junghans, U.S. Navy (Ret.), "Wake's POWs," U.S. Naval Institute *Proceedings,* Feb. 1983, 43–50.
162 *Palawan prisoner massacre:* Brackman, 247.
162 *Message to prison camps:* The message is quoted by Bergamini, 1035, from International Prosecution Section Document No. 2697.
162 *Prisoner Payne's recollections:* Author interview.
163 *Percentage of prisoner deaths:* Dower, 48. At the Chang Yi prison camp, filled mostly with British Commonwealth prisoners, the survival rate was only one prisoner in 15. Among those who survived was a British artillery officer, James Clavell, who was only 18 when he was captured. He survived to write *King Rat,* a classic tale of camp life, and later best-selling novels about the Far East, including *Shogun* and *Tai-Pan.*
163 *Korean "comfort girls":* Japanese officials denied for decades that captive women were used as prostitutes for soldiers. Some historians estimate that as many as 200,000 women and teenage girls were forced into prostitution between Japan's invasion of Manchuria in 1932 and the end of the Pacific War. Korean, Chinese, and Filipino women were forced to work in Army-run brothels, including some close to battlefields. Some Dutch women seized in Indonesia also were forced into prostitution. *New York Times,* Aug. 31, 1944.
163 *"Railroad of Death":* Dower, 47, 48; Bergamini, 966–971.
163 *Handbook on interrogation techniques:* "Japanese Knowledge of Allied Activities," Research Report, Allied Translator and Interpreter Service, South West Pacific Area, 29 Mar. 1945 (National Archives).
163 *Hino Ashihei at Bataan:* John W. Dower, *Japan in War & Peace,* 275.
164 *Regulations for civilians:* Ienaga, 112.
164 *Citizen guides:* Harries, 258–259.
164 *Call to the Decisive Battle:* Feifer, 576.
164 *U.S. troops' instructions: Soldier's Guide to the Japanese Army,* Military Intelligence Service, War Department. 15 Nov. 1944 (The Adjutant General's Office Library, Pentagon).
164 *Japanese soldier's booklet:* It was designed so that "anyone could read it lying on his back, on a hot, crowded and uncomfortable ship," wrote Col. Masanobu Tsuji, who helped compile it. The title of the booklet, which is reprinted as an appendix in Tsuji's *Singapore: The Japanese Version,* is sometimes translated as *Read This and the War Is Won.*
165 *Cremation of hand:* Interrogation of Japanese prisoners and U.S. Army photo of remains taken on Feb. 2, 1943, in New Guinea (National Archives).
165 *Japanese soldier's poem:* Dower, *War Without Mercy,* 231.
165 *Yasukuni Shrine:* The shrine, founded by Imperial command in 1869, preserves records of the names, dates, and sites of death in battle of about 2.5 million "spirits now worshipped," according to literature given visitors to the shrine.
166 *Sakurai's order of the day:* Denis and Peggy Warner, with Comdr. Sadao Seno, *The Sacred Warriors: Japan's Suicide Legions,* 62–63.
166 *"Mother," not "Emperor":* Ienaga, 102.
166 *Why Japanese do not surrender:* Interrogations of Japanese Officials on World War II (English Translations), Office of the Chief of Military History. Statement by Lt. Col. Taro Nakamoto, 28 July 1947 (Center of Military History).
166 *Quotation from soldier's manual:* Theodore F. and Haruko Taya Cook, *Japan at War: An Oral History,* 264.
166 *"Please fight well . . .":* Ienaga, 108.
166 *Ogawa Masatsugu quotation:* Cook and Cook, 272.
166 *Killed wounded, blew up tanks:* Cook and Cook, 278–279; Harries, 354.
166 *Marine on Saipan:* Capt. John C. Chapin, USMC (Ret.), "Breaching the Marianas: The Battle for Saipan," Marines in World War II Commemorative Series, 1994, 32–33, 35, 36.
167 *"Our courage . . .":* Cook and Cook, 339. The estimate of 10,000 civilians (Bergamini, 1013) is one of the lower estimates. There are no documented counts of the deaths of civilians on Saipan, Okinawa, or the other islands where great numbers of civilians died.
167 *"Japan's great victory":* Cook and Cook, 339.

167 *Ugaki quotation: Fading Victory,* the diary of Admiral Matome Ugaki, 485.

167 *Suicide aircraft on Okinawa:* Robert Lewin, *The American Magic,* 288.

168 *Special attack weapons:* Ienaga, 183.

168 *"100 million of us":* 100 million was a popular propaganda phrase and an exaggeration. The population of Japan itself was about 70 million, but at the height of its power, the Japanese Empire—stretching from Manchuria and occupied China to the Philippines and New Guinea —had a total population estimated at 438 million (Joseph C. Grew, "Japan and the Pacific," 416).

168 *Intelligence briefing:* Military Intelligence Service, Project 2139-A (National Archives).

168 *Civilian forces on Kyushu: Reports of General MacArthur,* Vol. I, 414–415.

168 *"Born of necessity":* Ienaga, 150.

169 *Report to the Throne:* "Report to the Throne, Report on the Outline of the Operational Plans of the Imperial Army and Navy, January 1945." General Headquarters, Far East Command, Military Intelligence Section, General Staff. Allied Translator and Interpreter Service. Office of the Chief of Military History, Special Staff, U.S. Army Historical Manuscript File. Translation of Japanese Documents, Vol. I (Center of Military History).

169 *Imperial General Staff strategy:* "Military Situation in the Far East," Office of the Chief of Military History, Special Staff, U.S. Army Historical Manuscript File. Translation of Japanese Documents, Vol. I, 3 (Center of Military History).

170 *Strategy of Supreme Council:* Robert J.C. Butow, *Japan's Decision to Surrender,* 81, 95–97, 99; Ienaga, 39: Pacific War Research Society, *The Day Man Lost,* 158.

170 *Japanese analysis of Allied communications:* Memorandum, "Enemy Analysis of Allied Communications," from Lt. Col. Leonard Bickwit to Office of the Chief Signal Officer, Washington, D.C., 15 Dec. 1944 (National Archives).

170 *Masakazu Amano's assessment:* "Statements of Japanese Officials on World War II" (English Translation), Office of the Chief of Military History. Statement by Amano, Masakazu, 2–4 (Center of Military History).

CHAPTER 8

173 *Porter's comments after Tarawa:* Memorandum from Maj. Gen. William N. Porter to Lt. Gen. Joseph McNarney, 17 Dec. 1943; War Department file OPD 385 (Center of Military History).

174 *Evidence kept from war-crimes trials:* Sheldon H. Harris, *Factories of Death,* 203–204.

174 *German gas attack:* The Allies had ample warning of the pending German gas attack from German prisoners and captured documents, while British and Canadian fliers and ground troops observed and even counted the gas cylinders. An earlier German gas attack on October 27, 1914, on the Western Front and another in Poland on January 31, 1915, in Poland were ineffective.

175 *Navy volunteers:* Rexmond C. Cochrane, "Medical Research in Chemical Warfare" (Aberdeen, Md.: Aberdeen Proving Ground, U.S. Army [n.d.; 1946]), Monograph, 163, 167 (Center of Military History).

175 *Naval Research Laboratory tests:* For example, Naval Research Laboratory, "Chamber Tests with Human Subjects, IX. Basic Tests with H Vapor," in Constance M. Pechura and David P. Rall (eds.), *Veterans at Risk,* 361.

176 *Australian test procedures:* Karen Freeman, "The Unfought Chemical War," *The Bulletin of Atomic Scientists* (Dec. 1991), 32.

176 *Chemical munitions inventory:* A detailed breakdown of chemical munitions is provided in Leo P. Brophy et al., *The Chemical Warfare Service: From Laboratory to Field,* 65; this quotes the "Chemical Warfare Service Report of Production, 1 Jan. 1940 through 31 Dec. 1945," CWS 314.7.

176 *Chemical mines and booby traps:* Ben R. Baldwin et al., "Readiness for Gas Warfare in the Theaters of Operations" (manuscript), 449, 454 (Center of Military History).

176 *Diversionary chemical production:* Brophy et al., 70. Lewisite was discovered by Capt. Lee Lewis, USA, working at Northwestern University in World War II as part of the Army's massive research effort into the chemical weapons and defenses.

177 *Roosevelt declaration:* W.H. Lawrence, "U.S. Warns Japan," *New York Times* (June 6, 1942), 1.

177 *Churchill declarations:* Winston S. Churchill, *The Hinge of Fate,* 329–330.

177 *Marshall's views on use of gas:* Assistant Secretary of War John J. McCloy, Memorandum of Conversation with Gen. Marshall, "Objectives towards Japan and Methods of Concluding the War with Minimum Casualties," 29 May 1945 (National Archives).

178 *Army study on reducing casualties with gas:* Memorandum from Gen. Marshall to Adm. King, 14 June 1945, enclosing "Memorandum entitled U.S. Chemical Warfare Policy" (National Archives).

178 *Anti-crop chemicals:* Letters from Chief, Chemical Warfare Service, to Commanding General, Army Service Forces, "Military Requirements for Crop Destruction in Japan," 31 Mar. 1945 and 12 Apr. 1945 (National Archives).

179 *Judge advocate general's opinion:* Memorandum from Judge Advocate General (Army) to the Secretary of War, attention Mr. George Merck, Chairman, U.S. Biological Warfare Committee, "Destruction of Crops by Chemicals," 5 Mar. 1945 (National Archives).

179 *Chemical weapons for Olympic:* Baldwin et al., 469.

179 *Afloat chemical weapons for Olympic:* U.S. Army Forces Pacific, General Headquarters, *Operations Instructions No. 1,* 20 June 1945, Annex 5, 12 (National Archives).

179 *Stilwell's view on the use of gas:* Memorandum from Gen. Stilwell to Gen. Marshall [n.d.; May 1945] (National Archives).

179 Chicago Tribune *editorial: Chicago Tribune,* Mar. 11, 1945.

180 *Formation of Biological Warfare Committee:* Brophy, 47.

180 *Role of Medical Research Division:* Cochrane, 13.

181 *Consent form:* U.S. Army form CD 6-148 L, 13 Nov. 1945; in Cochrane (Center of Military History).

181 *Demand for large-scale production:* Letter from Commanding Officer Camp Detrick to Chief Chemical Warfare Service, 27 Dec. 1943 (Center of Military History).

183 *Leahy on biological weapons:* Fleet Adm. William D. Leahy, USN, *I Was There,* 440.

183 *Reaction of Capt. McVay:* Richard F. Newcomb, *Abandon Ship!,* 35.

184 *Gas canister tactics:* Tanisuga Shizuo, "Gas Soldier," in Theodore F. and Haruko Taya Cook, *Japan at War,* 45.

184 *Using gas canisters:* Shizuo, 45–46.

184 *Ishii's water filter:* Peter Williams and David Wallace, *Unit 731,* 11.

185 *Ishii's men with combat units:* Williams and Wallace, 18.

186 *Material on Japanese biological weapons:* War Department General Staff, Military Intelligence Service, Research Unit, "Japanese Bacterial Bomb," 6 June 1945, Project No. 2244 (National Archives).

187 *Navy order related to biological warfare:* U.S. Army Forces Pacific Ocean Areas, Headquarters, Letter "Bacterial [*sic*] Warfare Intelligence," 28 May 1945; the letter refers to Joint Intelligence Center Pacific Ocean Areas Item No. 16218 (National Archives).

187 *Japanese balloon campaign:* Robert C. Mikesh, *Japan's World War II Balloon Attacks on North America,* 67.

189 *Finding balloons:* Lawrence H. Larsen, "War Balloons Over the Prairie: The Japanese Invasion of South Dakota," *South Dakota History,* Winter 1978, 106, 109.

189 *Research in Nanking:* Sheldon Harris, 101–112.

189 *Plague in China:* John W. Powell, "Japan's Biological Weapons," 44–53.

190 *Knowledge of Ishii's activities:* War Department General Staff, Military Intelligence Service, Research Unit, "Japanese Bacterial Bomb," 6 June 1945, Project No. 2244 (National Archives).

190 *Ishii's prominence:* Ishii was replaced as commander of Unit 731 sometime during the war by Maj. Gen. Masaji Kitano so that Ishii could have a field assignment as medical officer for the First Army to be eligible for promotion to lieutenant general. When Ishii returned to the command Unit 731 in Mar. 1945, Kitano remained as deputy commander. Kitano had a medical background.

190 *Readiness to wage biological warfare:* Williams and Wallace, *Unit 731,* 81.

190 *Troops warned about gas:* Masanobu Tsuji, *Singapore: The Japanese Version,* Appendix

1, *Read This Alone—And the War Can Be Won,* the booklet given to Japanese troops invading Malaya.

CHAPTER 9

193 *Army indoctrination paper:* "Army Talk," Orientation Fact Sheet No. 71, Army Orientation Branch, Information and Education Division, 12 May 1945 (Center of Military History).

193 *Marshall on unconditional surrender:* Memorandum from Marshall to Stimson, June 9, 1945 (National Archives).

193 *Harriman warning:* Len Giovannitti and Fred Freed, *The Decision to Drop the Bomb,* 44.

194 *"Jap war":* Robert H. Ferrell (ed.), *Dear Bess* (New York: Norton, 1983), 520. Truman used the phrase at least twice in letters to his wife, Bess. "Jap" was also used frequently in official communication by General Marshall and other presidential advisers.

194 *Censorship of Magic summaries:* For example, when the summary for July 9 (No. 1201) was declassified by the National Security Agency (NSA) on Nov. 1, 1978, pages 6 to 12 declared "not releasable." The pages appear in the summary released in 1993, which contains a message to Paris from French Ambassador Bonnet on the Big Three conference and a message from the Lebanese foreign minister to his diplomats in Washington, London, and Paris. Information continues about French, Lebanese, and Syrian matters until page 10, which ends about three-quarters down the page. Pages 11 and 12 are blank, with no explanation. Thus, NSA, while admitting finally in 1993 that the United States eavesdropped on Allies, still was sensitive about other wartime intercepts of presumably friendly diplomats.

194 *Magic summaries:* Those quoted in this chapter, intercepted from April to August 1945, were obtained from the National Archives. The postwar repository of the top-secret intercepts was the National Security Agency (NSA), created by secret presidential directive on November 4, 1952. The NSA, which intercepts and decodes communications throughout the world, is probably the most important—and least acknowledged—source of U.S. intelligence. The NSA determines when, if ever, its eavesdropping can be revealed. The NSA began transferring wartime Magic summaries and other intercepts to the National Archives in August 1977. Not all have been transferred. In fact, some Magic summaries obtained by the authors in 1994 had only been released the year before, and a few of those had been censored.

The Magic summaries used in this chapter:

Regarding fall of Germany: No. 1131, 30 April 1945, SRS 1653.
Report from Portuguese diplomat: No. 1131, 30 April 1945, SRS 1653.
Report from Swiss diplomat: No. 1188, 26 June 1945, SRS 1710.
On Japan preparedness: No. 1137, 6 May 1945, SRS 1659.
On stepping up production: No. 1118, 17 April 1945, SRS 1640.
On fighting "a joint war": No. 1088, 18 March 1945, SRS 1610.
Avoid Nazi policy connection: No. 1128, 27 April 1945, SRS 1650.
No German government-in-exile: No. 1139, 8 May 1945, SRS 1661.
Naotake Sato on Soviets as peacemakers: No. 1143, 12 May 1945, SRS 1665.
Separate peace with Chiang Kai-shek: No. 1196, 4 July 1945, SRS 1718.
Kase suggestion on creating Soviet split: No. 1149, 18 May 1945, SRS 1671.
Diplomatic couriers' reports: No. 1226, 3 August 1945, SRS 1748; No. 1159, 28 May 1945, SRS 1681; No. 1185, 23 June 1945, SRS 1707; No. 1226, 3 August 1945, SRS 1748.
Reports of unrest in Manchuria: No. 1137, 6 May 1945, SRS 1659; No. 1121, 20 April 1945, SRS 1643.
Togo message to Manchuria: No. 1136, 5 May 1945, SRS 1658.
Togo-Molotov dialogue: No. 1164, 2 June 1945, SRS 1686.
German naval attaché: No. 1142, 11 May 1945, SRS 1664.
Fujimura cable: No. 1171, 9 June 1945, SRS 1693.
Sell-Ioune incident: No. 1156, 25 May 1945, SRS 1678; No. 1143, 12 May 1945, SRS 1665.

195 *Forming of Suzuki Cabinet:* Robert J.C. Butow, *Japan's Decision to Surrender,* 65, 73, 75.

195 *Shigenori Togo:* David Bergamini, *Japan's Imperial Conspiracy,* 92–93, 946, 1102; Courtney Browne, *Tojo: The Last Banzai,* 106–107.

196 *Soviet maneuvers:* Butow, 58–59.

198 haragei: Butow, 71.

199 *JCS "war weariness" memo:* Memorandum from Joint Chiefs of Staff for the State-War-Navy Coordinating Committee, 8 June 1945 (National Archives).

199 *"Do not live in shame...":* Hiroo Onoda, *No Surrender,* 33, quoting Gen. Hideki Tojo's *Instructions for the Military.* Onoda was a second lieutenant on a small island in the Philippines when the war ended in 1945. He finally emerged from the jungle in 1974 and was hailed as a hero in Japan.

200 *Modification of "unconditional surrender":* Harry S. Truman, *Memoirs by Harry S. Truman,* Vol. 1, 207.

200 *JCS planners report on surrender:* Ray S. Cline, *Washington Command Post: The Operations Division,* 344.

200 *Truman on casualties:* Truman, 265, 270, 314.

200 *Truman sends Hopkins to Moscow:* Truman, 110, 229, 257–259.

200 *Marshall's belief in invasion:* Kent Roberts Greenfield, *American Strategy in World War II: A Reconsideration,* 22.

201 *"Special skills":* John C. Sparrow, *History of Personnel Demobilization in the United States Army,* 311, "Statement by the Secretary of War on War Department Demobilization Plan," War Department Press Release, 10 May 1945 (Center of Military History).

201 *Messages on 93rd Division:* Gen. Marshall to Gen. MacArthur (personal for MacArthur), 1 Mar. 1945, WD 943; Gen. MacArthur to Chief of Staff, War Dept., 4 Mar. 1945, WD 950 (MacArthur Archives). The 93rd did go into combat. Army records credit the 93rd with service in campaigns in New Guinea, the northern Solomons, and the Philippines. But MacArthur limited the 93rd mostly to mopping-up operations. Of the 90 U.S. Army divisions in World War II, only two were not in combat: the 13th Airborne Division in Europe and the 98th Infantry Division in Hawaii.

201 *European casualties:* Charles B. MacDonald, *The Last Offensive, United States Army in World War II,* 478.

201 *"Horses with blinders on...":* Merle Miller, *Plain Speaking,* 205.

203 *Leahy's request for meeting:* Memorandum from Adm. Leahy to the Joint Chiefs of Staff, 14 June 1945. Records of the War Department General and Special Staffs (National Archives).

203 *Hull-Lincoln correspondence:* Memo, Hull to Lincoln, 16 June 1945 (Marshall Library, Lexington, Va.), as cited by John Ray Skates, *The Invasion of Japan,* 80.

203 *Marshall message to MacArthur:* To GHA AFPAC (MacArthur) from Marshall, 16 June 1945, WD 1050 (MacArthur Archives).

204 *MacArthur message to Marshall:* From CINCAFPAC to WARCOS, 17 June 1945, WD 1052 (MacArthur Archives).

204 *Marshall message to MacArthur:* From Gen. Marshall to Gen. MacArthur (Personal), 19 June 1945, WAR 18528, WD 1056 (MacArthur Archives). The June 19 date appears twice on the message, even though the meeting Marshall refers to is June *18.*

204 *MacArthur message to Marshall:* Gen. MacArthur to Gen. Marshall (Personal), C-19848, 19 June 1945, WD 1057 (MacArthur Archives).

209 *Nimitz message to King:* Ronald H. Spector, *Eagle Against the Sun,* 544. The memorandum is dated 28 April 1945.

209 *Interim Committee report:* Martin J. Sherwin, *A World Destroyed,* 304–305.

210 *Attendance at meeting:* Truman Library, President Secretary's Files.

210 *June 18 meeting:* Minutes of meeting held at the White House on Monday, 18 June 1945 at 1530 (National Archives).

214 *McCloy mentions the bomb:* Giovannitti and Freed, 135–137. This is McCloy's account. The official minutes of the meeting do not show any statement from McCloy, but the secrecy surrounding the bomb would have prevented its being mentioned even in such a secret document of extremely limited distribution.

215 *Letter to Bess:* Robert H. Ferrell (ed.), *Dear Bess,* 520.

215 *Hoover memo:* Memorandum on Ending the Japanese War, unsigned, undated, accompa-

nied by memorandum from President Truman to Secretary Stimson, June 9, 1945 (National Archives).

216 *Analysis of Hoover memo:* Memorandum of Comments on "Ending the Japanese War," 14 June 1945 (National Archives). It is unsigned but initialed GAL (presumably Brig. Gen. George A. Lincoln).

216 *End of war 15 November 1946:* Truman, 382.

CHAPTER 10

218 *Tokyo in April 1945:* Richard Rhodes, *The Making of the Atomic Bomb,* 599; Theodore F. and Haruko Taya Cook, *Japan at War: An Oral History,* 340–341.

218 *Decree of Decisive Battle:* Obtained by authors through Japanese sources. Variations on "Honorable Death of a Hundred Million" are mentioned in many sources, including Edward Behr, *Hirohito Behind the Myth,* 293; Cook and Cook, 337, 406.

220 *"Kill all the infirm . . .":* Saburo Ienaga, *The Pacific War,* 182.

221 *Kyushu in myth:* Tracy Dahlby, "Kyushu: Japan's Southern Gateway," *National Geographic,* Jan. 1994, 113.

221 *Report to the Throne:* Quoted in *Reports of General MacArthur,* Vol. 2, part 2, 577.

221 *Eizo Hori:* Alvin D. Coox, "Japanese Military Intelligence in the Pacific Theater: Its Non-Revolutionary Nature," *The Intelligence Revolution,* Proceedings of the 13th Military History Symposium, U.S. Air Force Academy, October 1988.

222 *Ketsu-go: Reports of General MacArthur,* prepared by his general staff, Vol. 1, 403–405.

222 *U.S. intelligence analysis:* General Headquarters, U.S. Army Forces in the Pacific, "G-2 Estimate of the Enemy Situation with Respect to an Operation Against Southern Kyushu in November 1945," 25 Apr. 1945, 2–4, 12 (National Archives).

222 *350,000 troops on Kyushu:* "Estimate Japanese Dispositions 1 November 1945," map prepared 15 June 1945, accompanying JCS briefing for President Truman, 18 June 1945 (National Archives). For estimates of Japanese strength, which accompanied the map, see Appendix A.

222 *Japanese defense plan for Kyushu:* Japanese Monograph No. 17, "Homeland Operations Record" (Center of Military History). The Japanese monographs were adapted from studies prepared under instructions of MacArthur as Supreme Commander for the Allied Powers in Japan. Former officers of the Japanese Army and Navy, supervised by Japanese demobilization officials, wrote the manuscripts which were translated by the Allied Translator-Interpreter Service. Research and editing was done by the Foreign Histories Division of the U.S. Office of Military History in Japan, then distributed by the Office of the Chief of Military History.

223 *U.S. intelligence estimates: Reports of General MacArthur,* Vol. I, 418; from G-2, General Headquarters, U.S. Army Forces Pacific, "Amendment No. 1 to G-2 Estimate of the Enemy Situation with Respect to Kyushu," 29 July 1945.

223 *Marshall message to MacArthur:* Urgent, Marshall to MacArthur (Eyes Only), 7 Aug. 1945, WD 1104 (MacArthur Archives).

223 *MacArthur message to Marshall:* CINCAFPAC to WARCOS, 9 Aug. 1945, WAR 45369, WD 1106 (MacArthur Archives).

224 *MacArthur's disdain for Ultra, OSS:* Ronald Lewin, *The American Magic,* 173, 247. Regarding his attitude toward the OSS, see also G.J.A. O'Toole, *Honorable Treachery* (New York: Atlantic Monthly Press, 1991), 409.

224 *Japanese mobilization: Reports of General MacArthur,* 262, 265, 273.

225 People's Handbook of Resistance Combat: The authors obtained a copy through the courtesy of David Westheimer. Mention of the handbook and home defense units is made in *Reports of General MacArthur,* 266–273.

225 *15-year-old student:* George Feifer, *Tennozan,* 571.

226 *People's spirit:* Interview with Capt. Shin Itonaga, Military History Department, National Institute for Defense Studies.

226 *New Japanese divisions:* "Preliminary Report to Pacific Order of Battle Conference," 15 Aug. 1945, reproduced in Ronald Spector's *Listening to the Enemy,* 254–259.

226 *"Fanatically hostile population":* "Staff Study 'Olympic' Operations in Southern Kyushu," General Headquarters, U.S. Army Forces in the Pacific, 28 May 1945 (National Archives).

226 Kaiten *training:* Interview with Hiroshi Iwai. Still in training when the war ended, he had been told he would be assigned to an invasion-defense station.

227 *Information on submarines:* Dorr Carpenter and Norman Polmar, *Submarines of the Imperial Japanese Navy,* 49–52, 135–136.

227 Fukuryu *units:* Capt. Charles A. Barton, USN (Ret.), "Underwater Guerrillas," U.S. Naval Institute *Proceedings,* Aug. 1983, 47.

227 *Rocket weapons:* General Headquarters, U.S. Army Forces in the Pacific, "G-2 Estimate," 25 Apr. 1945, 5 (National Archives).

228 *Japanese could see them:* Fleet Adm. William F. Halsey and Lt. Comdr. J. Bryan III, USNR, *Admiral Halsey's Story,* 259.

228 *Communist troops in China:* Magic summary No. 1134, 3 May 1945. SRS 1656 (National Archives).

231 *Marines rehearse:* K. Jack Bauer, "Olympic," *Marine Corps Gazette,* Aug. 1965, 39. Bauer, an assistant to Samuel Eliot Morison during the preparation and writing of *History of the United States Naval Operations in World War II,* wrote the U.S. side of the battle in the *Gazette.* The Japanese side of Olympic was written in the same issue by Alan C. Coox, who collaborated with Saburo Hayashi on the English-language edition of a history of the Japanese Army in the Pacific.

231 *Postwar description: Reports of General MacArthur,* Vol. I, 395–427.

231 *Engineers' numbers:* Karl C. Dod, *The Corps of Engineers: The War Against Japan,* 676. *Additional information on engineers:* Annex 7 (Engineer) to Operations Instructions No. 1 General Headquarters U.S. Army Forces, Pacific, 20 June 1945 (National Archives).

232 *B-24 practice:* Correspondence with Major Arlo B. Roth, USAF (Ret.).

232 *Deception plan:* Thomas M. Huber, *Pastel: Deception in the Invasion of Japan.*

233 *Pearl Harbor battleships: Submerged Cultural Resources Study* (report on damage), Daniel J. Lenihan (ed.), Arizona Memorial Museum Association, 1989, 50, 53, 54.

233 *Transportation targets: Reports of General MacArthur,* Vol. I, 407.

233 *Information on Casey:* Dod, 99, 178, 667.

234 *Engineer Intelligence Division:* Correspondence with John A. Wolfe; "Engineer Intelligence Division in the War in the Pacific 1944 to 1945," unpublished manuscript by John A. Wolfe.

234 *Geologic information:* Comparative Terrain Evaluation of Southern Kyushu and Batangas Luzon, P.I., undated. Prepared by Engineer Intelligence Division. Courtesy of John A. Wolfe. Also, Brief Military Geography—Kyushu, 24 July 1945, Research Unit, Military Intelligence Service, Project No. 1886 (National Archives).

234 *Wolfe:* Wolfe, unpublished manuscript.

235 *Winter needs:* "Medical Service in the Asiatic and Pacific Theaters," unpublished manuscript, chapters XV-19, XV-20 (Center of Military History).

235 *Kagoshima to be rebuilt:* Dod, 677–678.

235 *Underground forts:* Dod, 621–622.

236 *Map showing beaches:* Diagram of Beach Designations for Operations Against Kyushu. Appendix (IV) to Annex (A) to COMPHIBPAC of Plan A11-45, 10 Aug. 1945 (Naval Historical Center).

236 *Suicide defenses at sea: Reports of General MacArthur,* Vol. II, 653, 657; Japanese Monograph No. 17, *Homeland Operations Record,* 127. Kamikazes claimed to have sunk 81 ships and damaged 195 in 1,228 one-way missions (out of 2,314 sorties); the U.S. Navy puts the figures at 34 ships sunk (including 2 PT boats) and 288 damaged. See Capt. Rikihei Inoguchi and Comdr. Tadashi Nakajima, with Capt. Roger Pineau, *The Divine Wind,* 256.

237 *Kamikaze rate:* Coox, "Operation Ketsu-go," 40.

237 *10,500 kamikaze aircraft: Homeland Air Operations Record,* Japanese First Demobilization Report, Dec. 1946, cited in *General MacArthur Reports,* Vol. I, 419.

237 *Japanese intentions:* "History of Imperial General Headquarters Army Section (Revised Edition)," Japanese Monograph No. 45, 322 (Center of Military History).

237 *"Die six times":* Interview with Kiyochi Aikawa.

237 *All planes in ten days: Reports of General MacArthur,* Vol. II, 419.

237 *Naval suicidal operations: Reports of General MacArthur,* Vol. I, 419–421; Frank Davis, "Operation Olympic: The Invasion of Japan," *Strategy & Tactics,* July/Aug. 1974, 15.

237 *Fukuryu:* Barton, "Underwater Guerrillas," 47.
238 *Ultra reports 560,000:* Postwar checking of Ultra reports against actual forces showed that, in an amazing intelligence coup, Ultra had correctly identified 13 of the 14 regular divisions and correctly located them. See Edward J. Drea, *MacArthur's ULTRA,* 220.
238 *575,000 home-defense forces:* Spector, 252–253.
238 *About 450,000 defenders:* Bauer, 35.
238 *"Not the recipe for victory":* General Headquarters, U.S. Army Forces in the Pacific, "Amendment No. 1 to G-2 Estimate of the Enemy Situation with Respect to Kyushu (dated 25 April 1945), 29 July 1945, 1, 3 (National Archives).
238 *Yokoyama's defense plan: Homeland Operations Record,* 127–132.
238 *Heavily defended beaches:* Estimates of Japanese forces at the beaches come from Ultra analysis. See Drea, 217–218.

CHAPTER 11

241 *Planning document:* Staff Study Operations "Coronet," undated (MacArthur Archives). An indication of the depth of such studies can be seen in the bibliography for this document: G-2 Estimates of the Enemy Situation, 24 Mar. 1945 and 25 Apr. 1945; Monthly Summary of Enemy Dispositions No. 31, 31 May 1945; Daily Intelligence Summaries; Terrain Studies; Terrain Handbooks on the Tokyo Plain.
241 *Coronet:* Ray S. Cline, *Washington Command Post: The Operations Division,* 342; Memorandum from Gen. Marshall to Gen. MacArthur, 23 Mar. 1945, file CM-OUT 57902.
241 *Redeployment from Europe:* John C. Sparrow, *History of Personnel Demobilization in the United States Army,* Appendix V, "War Department Redeployment Plan" (War Department Press Release, 5 May 1945), 306 (Center of Military History).
243 *Okinawa typhoon:* Action Report, Commander in Chief United States Pacific Fleet and Pacific Ocean Areas, Report of Surrender and Occupation of Japan, August–December 1945, 11 Feb. 1946, Annex A, Typhoon Louise—the 9 Oct. [1945] Storm at Okinawa (Naval Historical Center).
244 *30 to 45 days:* Use of Atomic Bomb on Japan, Memorandum for Chief, Strategic Policy Services. Records of the General Staff, Apr. 30, 1946 (National Archives).
244 *"Amphibious disaster":* Willard Bascom, *Waves and Beaches* (Garden City, N.Y.: Anchor Books, 1964), 196. Bascom was one of several scientists who studied beaches to produce information for planners of U.S. amphibious operations. They particularly studied Leadbetter Spit, on the Washington State shore, because of its similarity to potential Japanese invasion beaches. "After having been in and out through the surf at Leadbetter many times," Bascom wrote, "we reach the conclusion that except in very low surf the attempt to land on Japan [at Katakai] would have been an amphibious disaster."
244 *Description of Kujuri-Hama:* Staff Study Operations "Coronet," I Terrain and Weather, 8 (National Archives). Also, visit of author, who saw the shark warning signs. Local people told him that several of the beaches chosen for the landings are renowned as surfer beaches today.
244 *JCS avoids Coronet:* Grace Person Hayes, *The History of the Joint Chiefs of Staff in World War II: The War Against Japan,* 707. Some planning for the invasion was under way at General MacArthur's headquarters. Preliminary studies of terrain and enemy strength were made, as was GHQ, AFPAC, *Staff Study, "Coronet,"* 15 Aug. 1945. Information from a first draft of this plan, "published as a matter of interest only," appears in *Reports of General MacArthur,* Vol. I, 423–430.
244 *Joint Chiefs briefing document:* Kyushu is described as "the decisive operation" in a Joint War Plans Committee memorandum, Details of the Campaign against Japan, 15 June 1945. The memorandum was prepared by the committee for the use of the JCS and as an aide memoire that President Truman "could examine at his convenience and possible use at the forthcoming tripartite [Potsdam] conference." The memorandum was revised (see page 206, herein) on July 11 and apparently became one of the Potsdam documents. In that revision, the Kyushu invasion is linked to a "Japanese capitulation" (both documents, National Archives).
245 *"Effect an entry":* Occupation of Strategic Areas in Japan Proper in the Event of Collapse or Surrender, Report by the Joint Staff Planners, 8 June 1945 (National Archives).

245 *Nimitz, MacArthur responses:* Memorandum by the Commander in Chief U.S. Fleet, and Chief of Naval Operations, 26 July 1945, quotes the Nimitz plan and recommends it. MacArthur objects in a message to Marshall, CINCAFPAC to Joint Chiefs of Staff, 27 July 1945, WD 1090 (MacArthur Archives).

245 *"Fight to the finish":* Marshall to MacArthur, 31 July 1945, file WAR 40865, WD 1093 (MacArthur Archives).

245 *Northern Honshu invasion:* Dean Marvin Vander Linde, " 'Downfall': The American Plans for the Invasion of Japan in World War II," 102–110. Vander Linde bases his study of this proposed invasion on Joint War Planning Committee 398/1, "Plan for the Invasion of Northern Honshu," 9 Aug. 1945. Records of the Joint Chiefs of Staff, Part I: 1942–1945, the Pacific Theater.

246 *Description of Kanto Plain:* Staff Study Operations "Coronet," I Terrain and Weather, 1–14 (National Archives).

246 *First armored divisions:* These would be the 13th and 20th Armored Divisions, which had fought against the Germans in Central Europe.

246 *MacArthur in "personal command":* Reports of General MacArthur, Vol. I, 423.

246 *Coronet invasion plan:* Vander Linde, 117, based on Joint War Planning Committee 263/4, "An Outline Plan for the invasion of the Kanto (Tokyo) Plain," 5 May 1945.

247 *Information on T-92:* Correspondence, Paul Andrews. He says in his unpublished memoir, "Charlie One, the Last Cannon," that the T-92 he trained on, nicknamed Old Hellfire, was the first—and last—delivered to a tactical battalion before the war ended.

247 *Preinvasion bombing:* Reports of General MacArthur, Vol. I, 431.

248 *Deception planning for the Honshu invasion:* Thomas M. Huber, *Pastel: Deception in the Invasion of Japan,* U.S. Army Command and General Staff College, Fort Leavenworth, Kansas, 1988, 14–22. (Huber bases his information on U.S. Joint Chiefs of Staff, Joint War Plans Committee, "Staff Study: Cover and Deception Plan for 'CORONET,' JWPC 190/16," Washington D.C., 17 July 1945.)

250 *Stalin's plans for Hokkaido:* Capt. 1st Rank Boris I. Rodionov, Soviet Navy (Ret), naval historian, to author.

250 *Japanese had broken some low-level U.S. codes:* Roger Dingham, "The Pacific Theater Comments," *The Intelligence Revolution,* Proceedings of the 13th Military History Symposium, U.S. Air Force Academy, Oct. 1988, 224, 229. Dingham cites J.W. Bennett, W.A. Hobart, and J.B. Spitzer, *Intelligence and Cryptoanalytical Activities of the Japanese During War II: SRH 254, The Japanese Intelligence System, MIS/WDGS* (Laguna Hills, Calif.: Aegean Park Press, reprint ed., 1986), 14, 16, 17, 132.

251 *"Simulate by radio...":* Huber, 21, quoting from U.S. Joint Chiefs of Staff, Joint War Plans Committee, "Staff Study: Cover and Deception Plan for 'CORONET,' JWPC 190/16," 17 July 1945.

251 *Use of other Allied troops:* Reports of General MacArthur, Vol. I, 427.

252 *Yokosuka tunnel complex:* The former Japanese naval base is now a joint U.S.-Japanese naval base. U.S. sailors discovered the caves and have mapped them. The Fact-Finding Mission on Korean Forced Labor found evidence that Korean laborers, using only picks, shovels, and wheelbarrows, dug the caves, starting in 1944. First used as air-raid shelters, the caves evolved into an underground base with aircraft and submarine factories (*Japan Times,* Sept. 13, 1993). Explorers, who estimated that there were 20 miles of caves, found a full-size locomotive, along with living space for 800 people and a hospital big enough for 500 beds (*Seahawk,* the base newspaper, Oct. 20, 1992). See also Tom Tompkins, *Yokosuka: Base of an Empire* (San Francisco: Presido Press, 1981), 37.

252 *Takeshi Maeda:* Correspondence and interview. At the time of the interview he was president of *Unabara-Kai* (Horizon of the Ocean), an organization of about 8,000 World War II naval fliers. "Around August 1945," he wrote in a letter, "all of the Naval Air forces had been distributed for the strategy of the Special Attack Forces without any exception."

252 *Defenses of Kanto Plain:* "Brief Study of Kanto Plain," Research Unit, Military Intelligence Service, WDGS, 4 June 1945 (National Archives).

252 *Estimate of defense forces:* Staff Study Operations "Coronet," Estimate of the Enemy Situation, 15–20 (National Archives).

253 *Coastal-combat troops' strategy:* Reports of General MacArthur, Vol. I, 427. The strategic

analysis ("merging all lines," etc.) was based on statements made by senior Japanese officers interviewed after the war.

253 *Japanese naval units:* Staff Study Operations "Coronet," Estimate of the Enemy Situation, 17 (National Archives).

254 *Underground shelter at Matsushiro:* Translation of "Total View of the Unfinished Matsushiro Headquarters," *Towards the End of the War,* a collection of recollections published in Japan and not available in English. Also, Theodore F. and Haruko Taya Cook, *Japan at War,* 432–435. About 75 percent of the project was completed when the war ended. Today it is the site of the Meteorological Agency Earthquake Observation Station. Many Japanese believe that the Emperor would not have gone to Matsushiro but would have preferred to die in Tokyo. Given the power of the military in Japan's final days, however, the taking of the Emperor to Matsushiro "for his own safety" seems likely. *Reports of General MacArthur,* Vol. I, 430, tells of plans for widespread underground fortifications but does not specifically mention Matsushiro.

254 *MacArthur staff's concern:* In a departure from the usual triumphant style, *Reports of General MacArthur* (Vol. I, 430) says, "Whether or not these desperate but extensive defense measures would have made an invasion prohibitively expensive in American lives is a matter for speculation. It is reasonable to assume, however, that Operation 'Downfall' could have been successfully concluded only after a hard and bitter struggle with no quarter asked or given."

254 *Off-the-record talks:* H.G. Nicholas (ed.), *Washington Despatches 1941–1945,* 527.

254 *Tokyo Rose:* This was the collective name for about 20 women who broadcast English-language propaganda on Japanese radio. After the war, one woman, Iva Ikuko Toguri d'Aquino, a Japanese American born in Los Angeles, was tried for treason and undermining U.S. troop morale. Acquitted of treason, she was sentenced to ten years on the other charge.

254 *Navy's 18-month rotation: Army and Navy Journal,* Jan. 27, 1945.

255 *Men in the Pacific:* Correspondence, Hill, Clark, Logan.

255 *Gallup Poll:* John C. Sparrow, *History of Personnel Demobilization in the United States Army,* 317.

255 *Redeployment problems:* Maj. Bell I. Wiley, USA, "Redeployment Training," Study No. 38, Historical Section—Army Ground Forces, 1946, 5, 10–12 (Center of Military History). In the study a colonel in the headquarters of Army Ground Forces said, "The capitulation of Hirohito on 14 August saved our necks. With things being as they were it would have been absolutely impossible for us to have sent well-trained teams to the Pacific for participation in the scheduled invasion of Japan."

255 *Project Sphinx:* Wiley, "Redeployment Training," 1, 4. The Army Ground Forces prepared a training circular on attacking cave fortifications as part of the Sphinx project.

256 *Japanese defense tactics: Reports of General MacArthur,* Vol. I, 427–428; Staff Study Operations "Coronet," Estimate of the Enemy Situation, 20–21.

256 *Plan for use of gas:* Ben R. Baldwin, Alfred J. Bingham, and Paul W. Pritchard, "History of the Chemical Warfare Service in World War II (1 July 1940–15 Aug. 1945)," Vol. VI, "Readiness for Gas Warfare in Theaters of Operations." Historical Section, Office of the Chief of Chemical Corps, unpublished, 332–333 (National Archives). When the authors read the manuscript at the Army's Center of Military History, top-secret pages had been removed. The MacArthur Foundation archives contain similarly still secret documents regarding offensive use of poison gas in World War II.

257 *Marshall on use of atomic bombs:* Robert J. Donovan, *Conflict and Crisis,* 92.

CHAPTER 12

259 *Use of bomb for blinding:* Comdr. Norris Bradbury, USN, G.B. Kistiakowsky, and M.F. Roy to Capt. W.S. Parsons, "Proposal for a Modified Tactical Use of the Gadget," July 17, 1945, Los Alamos Record, Los Alamos National Laboratory. The memo is cited in Barton J. Bernstein's exhaustive report on thoughts about tactical nuclear weapons, "Eclipsed by Hiroshima and Nagasaki," *International Security* (Spring 1991), 149–173. Parsons would fly as weapons officer on the Hiroshima atomic bomb flight.

259 *Few planners knew:* Of the two senior commanders in the Pacific, Adm. Nimitz learned

of the atomic bomb in early Feb. 1945, from a letter that Adm. King had sent to him via Comdr. Frederick L. Ashworth of the Manhattan Project. (Ashworth would be the weapons officer on the Nagasaki atomic bomb mission.) Nimitz was informed because the B-29s carrying the atomic bombs would fly from Tinian, within his jurisdiction. Gen. MacArthur was not told about the bomb until Aug. 1, 1945, when Lt. Gen. Carl Spaatz informed him.

259 *"Six of these things":* Conolly oral history, 269–270, Columbia University. It is cited in Bernstein's "Eclipsed by Hiroshima and Nagasaki."

259 *Groves on tactical bombs:* Bernstein, 161.

260 *Groves asks Oppenheimer:* J. Robert Oppenheimer to Gen. L.R. Groves, May 7, 1945, Los Alamos Records, Los Alamos National Laboratory, quoted in Bernstein, 91.

260 *"Monitoring teams":* Bernstein, 162.

260 *Marshall on tactical atomic bombs:* Bernstein, 168.

260 *X-ray overexposure: Encyclopaedia Britannica, 10 Eventful Years* (Chicago: University of Chicago Press, 1947), Vol. I, 208.

260 *Death rates soared:* The Committee for the Compilation of Materials on Damage Caused by the Atomic Bombs in Hiroshima and Nagasaki, *Hiroshima and Nagasaki* (New York: Basic Books, 1981), 67–79.

261 *Generalissimo Stalin:* Stalin took the rank of marshal in March 1943, and Generalissimo in June 1945.

261 *"In that two-hour drive":* Harry S. Truman, *Memoirs by Harry S. Truman,* 341.

261 *Test at Alamogordo:* Richard Rhodes, *The Making of the Atomic Bomb,* 654, 665, 670, 685; Maj. Gen. Leslie R. Groves, USA (Ret.), *Now It Can Be Told,* 288–304.

261 *Report on Trinity test:* Memorandum from Maj. Gen. Groves for the Secretary of War, 18 July 1945 (National Archives).

262 *Kido's diary:* Kido gives the date Jan. 6, 1945, as the beginning of Hirohito's serious interest in ending the war. Kido's remarkable diary, which contains extensive quotations from the Emperor, was published in Japan in 1966. A passage written in Dec. 1940 offers an uncanny forecast of Japan's recovery from war. "After this world war," Kido wrote, "the United States and the U.S.S.R. may unquestionably emerge unhurt when all other nations are devastated. I can imagine, therefore, that our country, which is placed between these two giants, may face great hardships. However, there is no need for despair. . . . We will simply have to sleep in the woodshed and eat bitter fruit for a few decades. Then when we have refurbished our manliness inside and out, we may still achieve a favorable result." David Bergamini, *Japan's Imperial Conspiracy,* 733.

262 *Background on Konoye and Kido:* Bergamini, 62, 350, 710.

262 *Formation of Council:* Akira Iriye, *Power and Culture: The Japanese-American War 1941–1945,* 169, 178, 182.

262 *Background on Suzuki:* Courtney Browne, *Tojo: The Last Banzai,* 192–193; Bergamini, 1100; Robert J.C. Butow, *Japan's Decision to Surrender,* 71.

262 *February 1936 mutiny:* Browne, 55–57.

263 *"One hundred million":* Bergamini, 71; Butow, 68.

263 *Togo peace plan:* Butow, 90 *passim.*

263 *Hirota-Malik talks:* Magic summaries No. 1166, 4 June 1945, SRS 1688, and No. 1195, 3 July 1945, SRS 1717 (National Archives). See also "Japanese Surrender Manoeuvers," 274–285; also Ronald H. Spector (ed.), *Listening to the Enemy.*

264 *June 6 meeting:* Butow, 95–97.

264 *"Only one way to win . . .":* Butow, 99.

264 *"Quick Way" pamphlet:* Pacific War Research Society, *The Day Man Lost,* 159. The society, a group of Japanese researchers, produced the book to provide Japanese with a background to the bombing of Hiroshima.

264 *Suzuki's explanation: The Reports of General MacArthur,* Vol. II, Part II, 680.

265 *Togo-Sato messages:* Magic captured these communications and reported them in the following summaries: No. 1201, 9 July 1945, SRS 1723; No. 1202, 10 July 1945, SRS 1724; No. 1204, 12 July 1945, SRS 1726; No. 1205, 13 July 1945, SRS 1727; No. 1206, 14 July 1945, SRS 1728; No. 1207, 15 July 1945, SRS 1729; and No. 1208, 16 July 1945, SRS 1230 (National Archives). Most of these messages were not declassified until Jan. 1993.

266 *Soviets reject Konoye offer:* Various Magic summaries; Butow, 126.

266 *Meeting of July 22:* There is confusion among the Potsdam accounts as to precisely when this meeting was held and who attended. See Margaret Truman, *Harry S. Truman,* 273–274; and *Foreign Relations of the United States: The Conference of Berlin (The Potsdam Conference), 1945,* Vol. II, 243. Churchill joined Truman and his advisers at the end of this meeting (Winston Churchill, *Triumph and Tragedy,* 638).

266 *Truman on casualties:* Truman letter to James Lea Cate, Jan. 12, 1953, reproduced in Craven and Cate, *The Pacific: Matterhorn to Nagasaki,* between pages 712 and 713.

266 *Arnold's views:* Margaret Truman, 273.

267 *Churchill and the bomb:* Churchill had known of the atomic bomb project from its inception, had contributed several scientists to the project, and had garnered from President Roosevelt an agreement that the British would participate in any decision to use the bomb.

267 *Truman tells Stalin about bomb:* Harry S. Truman, 416.

267 *Soviets and the bomb:* Vladimir Chikov, *From Moscow to Los Alamos* (1992), reprinted in *Soyuz* (May 1991), 18; see also David Holloway, *Stalin and the Bomb* (New Haven: Yale University Press, 1994), and Pavel and Anatoli Sudoplatov, *Special Tasks: The Memoirs of an Unwanted Witness—A Soviet Spymaster* (Boston: Little, Brown, 1994).

267 *"Score of bloody Iwo Jimas and Okinawas":* Stimson, Notes for Diary, July 24, 1945, and Stimson Diary, Aug. 10, 1945.

267 *Stimson memo:* Memorandum "Handed to the President by SecWar July 2/45" (National Archives).

267 *Discussions with Forrestal and Grew:* Butow, 139.

268 *Hull on "appeasement":* Butow, 140, quoting Hull *Memoirs,* II, 1593–1594.

268 *Would become the Potsdam Proclamation:* Some of the words in the proclamation would also come, through a bizarre route, from the swashbuckling movie star Douglas Fairbanks, Jr. Then in the Navy's psychological warfare office, Fairbanks had suggested establishing contact with an acquaintance, the Dowager Empress, Hirohito's mother, to serve as an intermediary in peace talks. Through influential friends in Washington, Fairbanks got the support of Grew, who was seeking diplomatic ways to end the war. Although the proposal got nowhere, Fairbanks had enough recognition in high circles to next suggest a proclamation calling on the Japanese to surrender. This was months before the Potsdam Conference. Words he used in his proposal appeared eventually in the preamble of the Potsdam Proclamation. (See Douglas Fairbanks, Jr., *A Hell of a War,* 252–254.)

268 *Potsdam Proclamation:* Herbert Feis, *Japan Subdued,* 91; Butow, 133, 243.

269 *Togo on Potsdam Proclamation:* Magic summaries No. 1224, 1 Aug. 1945, SRS 1746, and No. 1225, 2 Aug. 1945, SRS 1747 (National Archives).

269 *Togo messages to Sato:* Magic summaries No. 1225, 2 Aug. 1945 [no SRS], and No. 1226, 3 Aug. 1945, SRS 1748 (National Archives).

269 Mokusatsu: The authors have drawn from several sources to reconstruct the events of Japan's final days of the war; included were the Pacific War Research Society, *Japan's Longest Day,* for the Japanese viewpoint. This work basically agrees with Western assessments about the elusive meaning of *mokusatsu (Japan's Longest Day,* 17; Butow, 145); also statements that Gen. MacArthur's staff obtained from key Japanese officials after the war along with testimony and affidavits from the war-crimes trials of Japanese.

270 *Stimson on rejection:* Henry L. Stimson, "The Decision to Use the Atomic Bomb," *Harper's,* February 1947, 97–107.

270 *Alternative to invasion:* Stimson, *Harper's.*

270 *Truman release order:* David McCullough, *Truman,* 448.

270 *Cyanide capsules:* James Doolittle, *I Could Never Be So Lucky Again,* 420.

270 *15,000 tons of TNT:* Estimates of the Hiroshima and Nagasaki bomb yields vary considerably; the numbers used here are from the definitive analysis by John Malik of the Los Alamos National Laboratory in his *The Yields of the Hiroshima and Nagasaki Nuclear Explosions* (Los Alamos, N.M.: September 1985). Among the dead at Hiroshima were American prisoners of war. Col. Paul W. Tibbets, pilot of the *Enola Gay,* notes in his book *The Tibbets Story* that the location of prisoner-of-war camps was involved in the selection of target cities. After the war, it was learned that 23 fliers were held captive in Hiroshima when it was destroyed (196).

270 *Truman gets message:* Harry S. Truman, 415. Tokyo was 13 hours ahead of Washington, the latter being on Eastern War Time.

271 *Statement on bomb:* Statement of Aug. 6, 1945, in *Public Papers of the Presidents: Harry S. Truman, 1945* (Washington, D.C.: Government Printing Office, 1961), 199.

271 *Nishina report on bomb:* Butow, 151.

271 *Japan's atomic bomb work:* Deborah Shapley, "Nuclear Weapons History: Japan's Wartime Bomb Projects Revealed," *Science* (Jan. 13, 1978), 152–157; for a description of Japanese atomic bomb efforts (and a critique of the Shapley article), see John W. Dower, *Japan in War and Peace,* 55–100.

271 *U-boat cargo:* Magic summary No. 1134, 3 May 1945, SRS 1656, had reported the sailing of the *U-234* to Japan, carrying a new German air attaché and five other German officers, along with two Japanese naval officers. No mention was made of uranium in the Magic summary.

272 *Genda on atomic bomb:* Statement to author following Genda's appearance at the U.S. Naval Institute, Annapolis, Md., on Mar. 3, 1969; publicly, he had said, "If we had an A-bomb, we might have used that" (John Sherwood, "The Rambler ... Encounters an Old Samurai," *Evening Star,* Mar. 4, 1969, B-1). At the time, Genda was a member of the Japanese Diet.

272 *Soviet invasion:* Japanese Monograph No. 21, *Homeland Operations Record,* Vol. IV, Fifth Area Army, Late 1943–1945; Military Intelligence Service, U.S. Army, "Brief Military Geography—Kurile Islands," Project No. 1886, 18 Sept. 1945 (National Archives).

273 *Propaganda leaflet:* Allison Brooke Gilmore, "In the Wake of Winning Armies," 214.

273 *Order for second A-bomb:* Harry S. Truman, 426.

273 *Lt. McDilda:* Bergamini, 83; Butow, 160.

274 *Anami statement: Japan's Longest Day,* 27.

277 *Halt to city bombing:* Craven and Cate, 732.

277 *Logan recollection:* Author's interview with former Staff Sgt. Logan.

278 *"Sacrifice 20 million":* Butow, 205.

278 *"100,000 people killed":* Ed Cray, *General of the Army,* 540.

278 *Gen. Hull's service:* Biography from Army Center of Military History. Hull continued his interest in atomic bombs. He was in charge of Operation Sandstone, the atomic weapons tests at Eniwetok in the spring of 1948.

278 *Seeman-Hull telephone call:* Transcript of telephone conversation between Lt. Gen. John E. Hull and Col. L.E. Seeman, Aug. 13, 1945 (National Archives). See also Marc Gallicchio, "After Nagasaki," *Prologue* [National Archives journal] (Vol. 23, No. 4), 396–403.

278 *Fat Man bomb:* The Fat Man bomb was a complex "implosion" (plutonium) weapon, which was in series production. The Little Boy was a simpler gun-type (uranium) weapon, but it used a large amount of critical materials. Hence the first bomb, not previously tested, was dropped on Hiroshima. See Groves, *Now It Can Be Told,* and Rhodes, *The Making of the Atomic Bomb.*

278 *Bomb production rate:* Memorandum from George L. Harrison (secretary of Interim Committee) to Secretary of War, Tripartite Conference, Babelsberg, Germany, 24 July 1945 (National Archives).

279 *MacArthur and atomic bombs:* There is good reason to believe that MacArthur would have used atomic bombs in the invasion of Japan. In December 1950, when he was commander of U.S. and United Nations forces in the Korean War, he told the Joint Chiefs of Staff that if the Soviets intervened or Chinese communists increased their intervention, he wanted four atomic bombs to hit enemy invasion troops and 30 more for use against targets in China; see Michael Schaller, *Douglas MacArthur: The Far Eastern General,* 225. MacArthur also proposed laying a belt of radioactive cobalt across North Korea to halt the southward movement of Chinese troops.

279 *15 atomic bombs:* K.D. Nichols, *The Road to Trinity,* 201.

279 *Text of leaflets:* E. Bartlett Kerr, *Flames Over Tokyo,* 290.

279 *Kido reaction to leaflets: Japan's Longest Day,* 77.

280 *Hirohito accepts reply:* Butow, 207; *Japan's Longest Day,* 81. The words come from recollections of participants; there is no known transcript of the meeting.

280 *Joke about war ending:* H.G. Nicholas (ed.), *Washington Despatches 1941–1945,* 606.

283 *Allied prisoners:* In reality, there were about 100,000 U.S., British, Australian, Canadian, and Dutch prisoners held in all areas controlled by the Japanese at this time.

284 *Truman gets surrender news:* Harry S. Truman, 435.

284 *The end of Unit 731:* Peter Williams and David Wallace, *Unit 731,* 84–85; National Committee for the Exhibition of the 731 Unit (Tokyo), "Unit 731" (pamphlet) [n.d.].
285 *Invasion of Hokkaido:* Interview with Capt. 1st Rank Boris Rodionov, Soviet Navy (Ret.), naval historian; also Rear Adm. Ivan Sviatov, Soviet Navy (Ret.), "Ships and People" (unpublished memoirs), chapter "Monsoon Landing Operation." (Sviatov was in command of Soviet cruisers and destroyers in the Pacific at the end of the war.)
286 *Listening to Emperor:* Lester Brooks, *Behind Japan's Surrender,* 356.
286 *Togo on disarming:* Butow, 225.
287 *Post-surrender incidents:* Brooks, 370–379.
287 *Ugaki's last flight:* Vice Adm. Matome Ugaki, *Fading Victory,* 665–666.
288 *Incident in Shanghai:* Ambassador Kichisaburo Nomura, who had been negotiating in Washington on December 7, 1941, lost an eye in the same attack.
288 *Japanese delegates:* Shigemitsu and Umezu were accompanied to the *Missouri* by three officials of the Foreign Ministry, three Army officers, and three Navy officers.
288 *Surrender ceremony:* MacArthur's chief of staff was Lt. Gen. Richard K. Sutherland, USA; details of the ceremony from Fleet Adm. William F. Halsey, USN, and Lt. Comdr. J. Bryan III, USNR, *Admiral Halsey's Story,* 281–283; Rear Adm. Samuel Eliot Morison, USNR, *Victory in the Pacific 1945,* 361–367; and Gen. of the Army Douglas MacArthur, USA, *Reminiscences,* 272–275.
288 *Spruance's absence:* E.B. Potter, *Nimitz,* 394n.

EPILOGUE

291 *Strategic Bombing Survey:* Paul H. Nitze (later U.S. Under Secretary of Defense and presidential adviser) and a few others on the Strategic Bombing Survey had knowledge of Magic-Ultra, but such information was not used in their deliberations; Nitze discussions with author, Nov. 14, 1994, and Feb. 22, 1995.
292 *Intelligence report on Japanese strategy: Reports of General MacArthur,* Vol. I, 418. The interrogated officers were Lt. Gen. Seizo Arisue and Lt. Gen. Torashiro Kawabe, deputy chief, Army General Staff.
292 *Independent estimates of invasion casualties:* "Medical Service in the Asiatic and Pacific Theaters," unpublished manuscript, Chapter XV (Center of Military History). The ordering of Purple Hearts mentioned by Lt. David L. Riley (USN) in *Uncommon Valor . . . Decorations, Badges and Service Medals of the U.S. Navy and Marine Corps* (Hopkinsville, Ky.: Privately printed, 1980), 31. Riley noted that "several hundred thousand" Purple Hearts were manufactured near the end of the war in anticipation of the invasion. It was from this World War II stock that medals were awarded in the Korean, Vietnam, and Persian Gulf wars and in all combat incidents since August 1945. The Air Force Association, a veterans' group, used this information as a gauge for estimating invasion casualties (*Washington Post,* Sept. 26, 1994). The public affairs office at the Defense Personnel Support Center (successor to the Philadelphia Quartermaster Depot) told the authors that records showing the exact size and date of the order could not be found but that the size is such that all Purple Hearts awarded since the end of World War II came from that final order; an unknown number still are in storage. More than 370,000 Purple Hearts have been awarded since 1945.

BIBLIOGRAPHY

The authors relied largely on original documents and interviews, the sources for many of the endnotes, which begin on page 307. Beyond the publications listed below, the authors made extensive use of official records and correspondence held by the National Archives in Washington, D.C., and Suitland, Maryland, and the Douglas MacArthur Memorial Archives and Library in Norfolk, Virginia. Of particular value were the Combined Chiefs of Staff (CSS) files and the unpublished manuscripts of the Army OCMH; these were made available to us at the National Archives and the U.S. Army's Center of Military History.

Also useful were the many interrogations of Japanese officials in the U.S. Strategic Bombing Survey (USSBS) and the Japanese-prepared monographs produced for the U.S. occupation command in Japan. In Tokyo, we were given access to the files of the National Institute for Defense Studies and the Historical Research Institute. Through retired military officers at those institutes we were able to obtain information from pertinent sections of *Series of Military History of World War II,* a 96-volume account of the war published, beginning in 1966, by the Japanese Defense Agency's Defense College. (Information about preparations for defense against the expected invasion is collected in "Section M, Japanese Mainland Region Operations Series," Vols. 19, 51, 57, 85.) In London, we examined documents in the Public Records Office and the Imperial War Museum.

(CMH = Center of Military History, U.S. Army; OCMH = Office of Chief of Military History, U.S. Army; IJA = Imperial Japanese Army; IJN = Imperial Japanese Navy.)

Books

Adamson, Col. Hans Christian, USAF (Ret.), and Capt. George Francis Kosco, USN (Ret.). *Halsey's Typhoons.* New York: Crown, 1967.

Agawa, Hiroyuki. *The Reluctant Admiral: Yamamoto and the Imperial Navy.* Tokyo: Kodansha International, 1979.

Alperovitz, Gar. *Atomic Diplomacy: Hiroshima and Potsdam.* New York: Penguin Books, 1965 and 1985.

Appleman, Roy E., et al. *Okinawa: The Last Battle* in *United States Army in World War II.* Washington, D.C.: OCMH, 1948.

Barker, A.J. *Japanese Army Handbook 1939–1945.* London: Ian Allan, 1979.

Bergamini, David. *Japan's Imperial Conspiracy.* New York: Morrow, 1971. This book has been denounced by many Japanese and some Western historians as an unwarranted attack on Emperor Hirohito, vengefully inspired by the author's boyhood experience as a Japanese prisoner in the Philippines. But the book is well documented and gives an extremely detailed look at a society engaged in a long and costly war.

Berry, William A., with James Edwin Alexander. *Prisoner of the Rising Sun.* Norman: University of Oklahoma Press, 1993.

Blair, Clay, Jr., and Joan Blair. *Return from the River Kwai.* New York: Simon & Schuster, 1979.

Bradley, Gen. of the Army Omar N., USA. *A Soldier's Story.* New York: Henry Holt, 1951.

Bradley, Omar N., and Clay Blair. *A General's Life: An Autobiography by General of the Army Omar N. Bradley.* New York: Simon & Schuster, 1983.

Brooks, Lester. *Behind Japan's Surrender.* New York: McGraw-Hill, 1967.

Brophy, Leo P., and George J.B. Fisher. *The Chemical Warfare Service: Organizing for War* in *United States Army in World War II.* Washington, D.C.: OCMH, 1959.

Brophy, Leo P., Wyndham D. Miles, and Rexmond C. Cochrane. *The Chemical Warfare Service: From Laboratory to Field* in *United States Army in World War II*. Washington, D.C.: OCMH, 1959.

Browne, Courtney. *Tojo: The Last Banzai*. London: Transworld, Corgi Books, 1969.

Buell, Thomas B. *Master of Sea Power: A Biography of Fleet Admiral Ernest J. King*. Boston: Little, Brown, 1980.

Butow, Robert J.C. *Japan's Decision to Surrender*. Stanford: Stanford University Press, 1954.

Carpenter, Dorr, and Norman Polmar. *Submarines of the Imperial Japanese Navy*. Annapolis, Md.: Naval Institute Press, 1986.

Churchill, Winston S. *The Second World War*, 6 vols.

———. *Closing the Ring* in *The Second World War*. Boston, Mass.: Houghton Mifflin, 1951.

———. *The Hinge of Fate*. Boston, Mass.: Houghton Mifflin, 1950.

———. *Their Finest Hour* in *The Second World War*. Boston, Mass.: Houghton Mifflin, 1949.

———. *Triumph and Tragedy* in *The Second World War*. Boston, Mass.: Houghton Mifflin, 1953.

Clemens, Diane Shaver. *Yalta*. New York: Oxford University Press, 1970.

Cline, Ray S. *Washington Command Post: The Operations Division*. Washington, D.C.: OCMH, 1951.

Coakley, Robert W., and Richard M. Leighton. *Global Logistics and Strategy 1943–1945* in *United States Army in World War II*. Washington, D.C.: OCMH, 1968.

Cook, Theodore F., and Haruko Taya Cook. *Japan at War: An Oral History*. New York: New Press, 1992.

Coox, Alvin D. *Japan: The Final Agony*. New York: Ballantine, 1970.

Craig, William. *The Fall of Japan*. New York: Dial Press, 1967.

Craven, Wesley Frank, and James Lea Cate. *Men and Planes*, vol. 6 in *The Army Air Forces in World War II*. Chicago: University of Chicago Press, 1955.

———. *The Pacific: Matterhorn to Nagasaki, June 1944 to August 1945*, vol. 5 in *The Army Air Forces in World War II*. Chicago: University of Chicago Press, 1953.

———. *Plans and Early Operations, January 1939 to August 1942*, vol. 1 in *The Army Air Forces in World War II*. Chicago: University of Chicago Press, 1948.

Cray, Ed. *General of the Army: George C. Marshall, Soldier and Statesman*. New York: Norton, 1990.

Divine, Robert A., ed. *Causes and Consequences of World War II*. Chicago: Quadrangle Books, 1969.

Dod, Karl C. *The Corps of Engineers: The War Against Japan* in *United States Army in World War II*. Washington, D.C.: CMH, 1966.

Donovan, Robert J. *Conflict and Crisis*. New York: Norton, 1977.

Doolittle, Gen. James H., USAAF (Ret.), with Carroll V. Glines. *I Could Never Be So Lucky Again*. New York: Bantam Books, 1992.

Douhet, Gen. Giulio, Italian Army. *Command of the Air*. New York: Coward-McCann, 1942.

Dower, John W. *Japan in War and Peace*. New York: New Press, 1993.

———. *War Without Mercy: Race and Power in the Pacific War*. New York: Pantheon, 1986.

Drea, Edward J. *MacArthur's ULTRA: Codebreaking and the War against Japan, 1942–1945*. Lawrence, Kans.: University of Kansas Press, 1992.

Dyer, Vice Adm. George C., USN (Ret.). *On the Treadmill to Pearl Harbor: The Memoirs of Admiral James O. Richardson, USN (Ret.)*. Washington, D.C.: U.S. Naval History Division, 1973. Richardson was the CinC U.S. Fleet from Jan. 1940 to Feb. 1941.

Edoin, Hoito. *The Night Tokyo Burned*. New York: St. Martin's Press, 1987.

Eichelberger, Gen. Robert L., USA, with Milton Mackaye. *Our Jungle Road to Tokyo*. Nashville, Tenn.: Battery Classics, 1989.

Eliot, George Fielding. *Bombs Bursting in Air*. New York: Harcourt, Brace, 1939.

Eubank, Keith. *Summit at Teheran*. New York: Morrow, 1985.

Fahey, James J. *Pacific War Diary*. Seattle, Wash.: University of Washington Press, 1993. This illustrated edition, edited by Von Hardesty, is an abridged version of Fahey's diary, first published in 1963.

Fairbanks, Douglas, Jr. *A Hell of a War*. New York: St. Martin's Press, 1993.

Feifer, George. *Tennozan*. New York: Ticknor & Fields, 1992. The Okinawa invasion.

Feis, Herbert. *The China Tangle*. Princeton, N.J.: Princeton University Press, 1953. A brilliant account of Chinese-American relations during and after World War II.

————. *Japan Subdued*. Princeton, N.J.: Princeton University Press, 1961. Feis revised the book, and it was republished in 1965 as *The Atomic Bomb and the End of World War II*.

Forty, George. *U.S. Army Handbook 1939–1945*. New York: Charles Scribner's Sons, 1979.

Frank, Benis M., and Henry I. Shaw, Jr. *Victory and Occupation*, vol. V in *History of U.S. Marine Corps Operations in World War II*. Washington, D.C.: Historical Branch, Headquarters, U.S. Marine Corps, 1968.

Gailey, Harry A. *Peleliu, 1944*. Annapolis, Md.: Nautical & Aviation Publishing, 1983.

Giovannitti, Len, and Fred Freed. *The Decision to Drop the Bomb*. New York: Coward-McCann, 1965.

Greenfield, Kent Roberts. *American Strategy in World War II: A Reconsideration*. Baltimore: Johns Hopkins Press, 1963.

Greenfield, Kent Roberts, ed. *Command Decisions*. Washington, D.C.: OCMH, 1960.

Greenfield, Kent Roberts, et al. *The Organization of Ground Combat Troops* in *United States Army in World War II*. Washington, D.C.: OCMH, 1947.

Groves, Maj. Gen. Leslie R., USA. *Now It Can Be Told*. New York: Harper, 1962.

Halsey, Fleet Adm. William F., USN, and Lt. Comdr. J. Bryan III, USNR. *Admiral Halsey's Story*. New York: McGraw-Hill, 1947.

Hansell, Maj. Gen. Haywood S., Jr., USAF. *Strategic Air War Against Japan*. Washington, D.C.: Government Printing Office, 1980.

Hara, Capt. Tameichi, IJN, Fred Saito, and Roger Pineau. *Japanese Destroyer Captain*. New York: Ballantine Books, 1961.

Harries, Meirion, and Susie Harries. *Soldiers of the Sun*. New York: Random House, 1991.

Harriman, W. Averell, and Elie Abel. *Special Envoy to Churchill and Stalin, 1941–1946*. New York: Random House, 1975.

Harris, Robert, and Jeremy Paxman. *A Higher Form of Killing—The Secret Story of Chemical and Biological Warfare*. New York: Hill and Wang, 1982.

Harris, Sheldon H. *Factories of Death*. New York: Routledge, 1994.

Hasegawa, Nyozekan. *The Japanese Character*. Tokyo: Kodansha International, 1966. A collection of essays written between 1935 and 1938, translated by John Bester.

Hattori, Takushiro. *Dai Toa Senso Zenshi* [The Complete History of the Greater East Asia War], 4 vols. Tokyo: Matsu Publishing, 1955.

Hayashi, Saburo. *The Japanese Army in the Pacific War*. Quantico, Va.: Marine Corps Assn., 1959.

Hayes, Grace Person. *The History of the Joint Chiefs of Staff in World War II: The War Against Japan*. Annapolis, Md.: Naval Institute Press, 1982. The official, originally classified JCS history.

Heinl, Col. Robert Debs, Jr., USMC. *Soldiers of the Sea: The U.S. Marine Corps, 1775–1962*. Annapolis, Md.: U.S. Naval Institute, 1962.

Hitchcock, Lt. Col. Walter T., USAF, ed. *The Intelligence Revolution*. Washington, D.C.: Office of Air Force History, 1991. Proceedings of the 13th Military History Symposium, U.S. Air Force Academy, Colorado Springs, Colo., Oct. 12–14, 1988.

Horner, D.M. *High Command: Australia and Allied Strategy 1939–1945*. Sydney: George Allen & Unwin, 1982.

Hough, Lt. Col. Frank O., USMCR, et al. *Pearl Harbor to Guadalcanal: History of U.S. Marine Corps Operations in World War II*, vol. I. Washington, D.C.: Historical Branch, Headquarters, U.S. Marine Corps, 1958.

Huber, Thomas M. *Pastel: Deception in the Invasion of Japan*. Fort Leavenworth, Kans.: Combat Studies Institute, U.S. Army Command and General Staff College, 1988.

Hunt, Frazier. *The Untold Story of Douglas MacArthur*. New York: Devin-Adair Co., 1954.

Ienaga, Saburo. *The Pacific War*. New York: Pantheon Books, 1978. Originally published in Japanese by Iawanami Shoten, 1968.

Inoguchi, Rikihei, and Tadashi Nakajima, with Roger Pineau. *The Divine Wind*. Annapolis, Md.: U.S. Naval Institute, 1958.

Iriye, Akira. *Power and Culture: The Japanese-American War 1941–1945.* Cambridge, Mass.: Harvard University Press, 1981.

Isley, Jeter A., and Philip A. Crowl. *The U.S. Marines and Amphibious War: Its Theory and Its Practice in the Pacific.* Princeton, N.J.: Princeton University Press, 1951.

James, D. Clayton. *The Years of MacArthur,* vol. II: *1941–1945.* Boston: Houghton Mifflin, 1975.

Kenney, Gen. George C., USAF. *Gen. Kenney Reports.* New York: Duell, Sloan, and Pearce, 1949.

Kerr, E. Bartlett. *Flames Over Tokyo.* New York: Donald I. Fine, 1991.

———. *Surrender and Survival.* New York: William Morrow, 1985.

King, Fleet Adm. Ernest J., USN, and Walter Muir Whitehill. *Fleet Admiral King: A Naval Record.* New York: W.W. Norton, 1952.

Kleber, Brooks E., and Dale Birdsell. *The Chemical Warfare Service: Chemicals in Combat* in *United States Army in World War II.* Washington, D.C.: OCMH, 1966.

Knox, Donald. *Death March.* New York: Harcourt Brace Jovanovich, 1981.

Leahy, Fleet Adm. William D., USN. *I Was There: The Personal Story of the Chief of Staff to Presidents Roosevelt and Truman Based on His Notes and Diaries Made at the Time.* New York: Whittlesey House, 1950.

LeMay, Gen. Curtis E., USAF, with MacKinlay Kantor. *Mission with LeMay.* Garden City, N.Y.: Doubleday, 1965.

LeMay, Gen. Curtis E., USAF, and Bill Yenne. *Superfortress: The B-29 and American Air Power.* New York: McGraw-Hill, 1988.

Lewin, Ronald. *The American Magic: Codes, Ciphers and the Defeat of Japan.* New York: Farrar, Straus & Giroux, 1982.

MacArthur, Gen. of the Army Douglas, USA. *Reminiscences.* New York: McGraw-Hill, 1964.

MacDonald, Charles B. *The Last Offensive* in *United States Army in World War II.* Washington, D.C.: OCMH, 1973.

Manchester, William. *American Caesar: Douglas MacArthur, 1880–1964.* Boston: Little, Brown, 1978.

Matloff, Maurice. *Strategic Planning for Coalition Warfare 1943–1944* in *United States Army in World War II.* Washington, D.C.: OCMH, 1959.

Matloff, Maurice, and Edwin M. Snell. *Strategic Planning for Coalition Warfare, 1941–1942* in *United States Army in World War II.* Washington, D.C.: OCMH, 1953.

McCullough, David. *Truman.* New York: Simon & Schuster, 1992.

Mee, Charles L., Jr. *Meeting at Potsdam.* New York: Evans, 1975.

Merrill, James M. *A Sailor's Admiral.* New York: Thomas Y. Crowell, 1976.

Miller, Edward S. *War Plan Orange: The U.S. Strategy to Defeat Japan, 1897–1945.* Annapolis, Md.: Naval Institute Press, 1991.

Miller, Merle. *Plain Speaking: An Oral History of Harry S. Truman.* New York: Berkley, 1974.

Millett, Allan R. *Semper Fidelis: The History of the United States Marine Corps.* New York: Macmillan, 1980.

Mooney, James L., ed. *Dictionary of American Naval Fighting Ships,* vol. VII. Washington, D.C.: Naval History Center, 1981.

Morison, Rear Adm. Samuel Eliot, USNR (Ret.). *Victory in the Pacific 1945,* vol. XIV in *History of United States Naval Operations in World War II.* Boston: Little, Brown, 1960.

Morton, W. Scott. *Japan, Its History and Culture.* New York: McGraw-Hill, 1984.

Newcomb, Richard F. *Abandon Ship! Death of the U.S.S. "Indianapolis."* New York: Henry Holt, 1958.

Nicholas, H.G., ed. *Washington Despatches, 1941–1945.* Chicago: University of Chicago Press, 1981.

Nichols, Maj. Chas. S., Jr., USMC, and Henry I. Shaw, Jr. *Okinawa: Victory in the Pacific.* Washington, D.C.: Historical Branch, Headquarters, U.S. Marine Corps, 1955.

Nichols, Maj. Gen. K.D., USA (Ret.). *The Road to Trinity.* New York: William Morrow, 1987.

Nisbet, Robert. *Roosevelt and Stalin: The Failed Courtship.* Washington: Regnery Gateway, 1988.

Onoda, 2nd Lt. Hiroo, IJA (Ret.). *No Surrender.* Translated by Charles S. Terry. Tokyo: Kodansha International, 1974.

Pacific War Research Society. *The Day Man Lost.* Tokyo and New York: Kodansha International, 1972. An account of U.S. and Japanese atomic bomb research and the dropping of the atomic bomb on Hiroshima, the book was the work of 14 members of the society. The society members are Japanese researchers.

———. *Japan's Longest Day.* Tokyo and New York: Kodansha International, 1968.

Pechura, Constance M., and David P. Rall, eds. *Veterans at Risk: The Health Effects of Mustard Gas and Lewisite.* Washington, D.C.: National Academy Press, 1993.

Pogue, Forrest C. *George C. Marshall: Ordeal and Hope, 1939–1943.* New York: Viking, 1966.

———. *George C. Marshall, Statesman, 1945–1959.* New York: Viking, 1987.

Polmar, Norman, and Thomas B. Allen. *World War II: America at War 1941–1945.* New York: Random House, 1991.

Polmar, Norman, and Peter B. Mersky. *Amphibious Warfare.* London: Blandford/Arms & Armour Press, 1988.

Potter, E.B. *Nimitz.* Annapolis, Md.: Naval Institute Press, 1976.

Pyle, Ernie. *Brave Men.* New York: Henry Holt, 1944.

———. *The Last Chapter.* New York: Henry Holt, 1946.

Reischauer, Edwin O., and Albert M. Craig. *Japan: Tradition and Transformation.* Tokyo: Charles E. Tuttle, 1977.

Rhodes, Richard. *The Making of the Atomic Bomb.* New York: Simon & Schuster, 1986.

Robertson, John, and John McCarthy. *Australian War Strategy 1939–1945: A Documentary History.* Queensland: University of Queensland Press, 1985.

Rogers, Paul D. *The Bitter Years: MacArthur and Sutherland.* New York: Praeger, 1991.

———. *The Good Years: MacArthur and Sutherland.* New York: Praeger, 1991.

Ruppenthal, Roland G. *Logistical Support of the Armies (May 1941–September 1944)* in *United States Army in World War II.* Washington, D.C.: OCMH, 1953.

Schaller, Michael. *Douglas MacArthur: The Far Eastern General.* New York: Oxford University Press, 1989.

Sherrod, Robert. *History of Marine Corps Aviation in World War II.* Washington, D.C.: Combat Forces Press, 1952.

Sherwin, Martin J. *A World Destroyed.* New York: Alfred A. Knopf, 1975.

Shiroyama, Saburo. *War Criminal: The Life and Death of Hirota Koki.* Translated by John Bester. Tokyo: Kodansha International, 1974.

Skates, John Ray. *The Invasion of Japan.* Columbia, S.C.: University of South Carolina Press, 1994.

Smith, Lt. Gen. H.M., USMC, and Percy Finch. *Coral and Brass.* New York: Charles Scribner & Sons, 1949.

Smith, Perry McCoy. *The Air Force Plans for Peace 1943–1945.* Baltimore: Johns Hopkins Press, 1970.

Sparrow, John C. *History of Personnel Demobilization in the United States Army.* Washington, D.C.: Department of the Army, 1952.

Spector, Ronald H. *Eagle Against the Sun.* New York: Free Press, 1985.

Spector, Ronald H., ed. *Listening to the Enemy.* Wilmington, Del.: Scholarly Resources, 1988. A well-organized compilation of U.S. intercepts of Japanese communications, with one section devoted to messages during the last stage of the war.

Spurr, Russell. *A Curious Way to Die: The Kamikaze Mission of the Battleship* Yamato, *April 1945.* New York: New Market Press, 1981.

Stillwell, Paul, ed. *Air Raid: Pearl Harbor!* Annapolis, Md.: Naval Institute Press, 1981.

Thorne, Christopher. *The Far Eastern War.* London: Counterpoint, 1986.

Tibbets, Brig. Gen. Paul W., USAF (Ret.). *The Tibbets Story.* New York: Stein and Day, 1978.

Truman, Harry S. *Year of Decision,* vol. 1 in *Memoirs by Harry S. Truman.* Garden City, N.Y.: Doubleday, 1955.

Truman [Daniel], Margaret. *Harry S. Truman.* New York: William Morrow, 1973.

———. *Where the Buck Stops.* New York: Warner Books, 1989.

Tsuji, Col. Masanobu, IJA. *Singapore: The Japanese Version.* New York: St. Martin's Press, 1960. Originally published in Japanese, it was written to refute Winston Churchill's account of the fall of Singapore in his *Second World War.* The English-language edition was translated by Margaret E. Lake and edited by H.V. Howe.

Tuchman, Barbara W. *Stilwell and the American Experience in China, 1911–45* New York: Macmillan, 1970.

Ugaki, Vice Adm. Matome, IJN *Fading Victory*. Pittsburgh: University of Pittsburgh Press, 1991.

Warner, Denis, and Peggy Warner, with Comdr. Sadao Seno, IJN. *The Sacred Warriors: Japan's Suicide Legions* Melbourne: Van Nostrand Reinhold, 1982

Weigley, Russell F. *Eisenhower's Lieutenants. The Campaigns of France and Germany, 1944– 1945* Bloomington: Indiana University Press, 1981.

Westheimer, David. *Lighter Than a Feather*. Boston: Little, Brown, 1971. This is a fictional account of Olympic, based on considerable research.

Wigmore, Lionel. *The Japanese Thrust,* vol. IV, series 1 (Army): *Australia in the War of 1939– 1945.* Canberra: Australian War Memorial, 1959.

Williams, Peter, and David Wallace. *Unit 731: Japan's Secret Biological Warfare in World War II.* New York: Free Press, 1989.

Willoughby, Maj. Gen. Charles A., USA (Ret.), and John Chamberlain. *MacArthur 1941–1945.* New York: McGraw-Hill, 1954.

Zacharias, Rear Adm. Ellis, USN. *Behind Closed Doors* New York: Putnam, 1950.

ARTICLES

Ballendorf, Dirk Anthony. "Earl Hancock Ellis: A Final Assessment," *Marine Corps Gazette,* Nov. 1990, 78–87.

———. "Earl Hancock Ellis: The Man and His Mission," U.S. Naval Institute *Proceedings,* Nov. 1993, 53–60.

Barton, Capt. Charles A., USN (Ret.). "Underwater Guerrillas," U.S. Naval Institute *Proceedings,* Aug. 1983, 46–47.

Bauer, Dr. K. Jack. "Operation Olympic," *Marine Corps Gazette,* Aug. 1965, 32–44.

Bernstein, Barton J. "The Dropping of the A-Bomb: How Decisions Are Made When a Nation Is at War," *The Center Magazine,* Mar.–Apr. 1983, 7–15.

———. "Eclipsed by Hiroshima and Nagasaki: Early Thinking About Tactical Nuclear Weapons," *International Security,* Spring 1991, 149–173.

———. "The Perils and Politics of Surrender: Ending the War with Japan and Avoiding the Third Atomic Bomb," *Pacific Historical Review,* 1977 46(1): 1–27.

———. "A Postwar Myth: 500,000 U.S. Lives Saved," *Bulletin of the Atomic Scientists,* June/July 1986, 38–40.

Brower, Charles F., IV. "Sophisticated Strategist: General George A. Lincoln and the Defeat of Japan, 1944–45," *Diplomatic History,* 1991, 15(3): 317–337.

Coakley, Robert. "Planning the Last Invasion," *History of the Second World War* (1974), 2487– 2489.

Coox, Alvin D. "Japanese Military Intelligence in the Pacific Theater: Its Non-Revolutionary Nature," *The Intelligence Revolution,* Proceedings of the 13th Military History Symposium, U.S. Air Force Academy, Oct. 1988, 197–201.

———. "Operation Ketsu-go," *Marine Corps Gazette,* Aug. 1965, 33–44.

Davis, Frank. "Operation Olympic: The Invasion of Japan: November 1, 1945," *Strategy & Tactics,* July/Aug. 1974 (45): 4–20.

Doyle, Michael K. "The U.S. Navy and War Plan Orange, 1933–1940: Making Necessity a Virtue," *Naval War College Review,* 1980, 33(3): 49–63.

Falk, Stanley L. "General Kenney, the Indirect Approach, and the B-29s," *Aerospace History,* 1981, 147–155.

Fussell, Paul. "Thank God for the Bomb," *The Guardian,* Jan. 21, 1989.

Gallicchio, Marc. "After Nagasaki: General Marshall's Plan for Tactical Nuclear Weapons in Japan," *Prologue* [National Archives], Winter 1991, 396–404.

Greenwood, John T. "The U.S. Army and Amphibious Warfare During World War II," *Army History* [CMH], Summer 1993, 1–13.

Grew, Joseph C. "Japan and the Pacific," *National Geographic,* April 1944, 385–414.

Inoguchi, Capt. Rikihei, IJN (Ret.). "The Kamikazes," *History of the Second World War* (England, 1974), 2472–2473.

Itani, Dr. Jiro, and Tomoko Rehm-Takahara, with Hans Lengerer. "Japanese Special Attack Weapons," *Warship 1992* (Greenwich, England: Conway Maritime Press, 1993), 170–184.

Junghans, Capt. Earl A., USN (Ret.). "Wake's POWs," U.S. Naval Institute *Proceedings*, Feb. 1983, 43–50.

Kraig, Capt. Walter, USNR (Ret.). "Battleship Banzai!" U.S. Naval Institute *Proceedings*, Oct. 1949, 1151–1158.

Larsen, Lawrence H. "War Balloons Over the Prairie: The Japanese Invasion of South Dakota," *South Dakota History*, 1979, 9(2): 103–115.

Levine, Alan J. "Dropping the A-Bomb in Retrospect," *Asian Profile*, Aug. 1986, 315–325.

Mayo, Marlene J. "An Accounting," *The Diamondback* [University of Maryland], Aug. 8, 1985, 4–5.

Miles, Rufus E., Jr. "Hiroshima: The Strange Myth of Half a Million American Lives Saved," *International Security*, Fall 1985, 121–140.

Miyo, Capt. Kazunari, IJN (Rct.). "Death of a Behemoth" [battleship *Yamato*], *History of the Second World War* (England, 1974), 2476–2479.

Moon, John Ellis van Courtland. "Project Sphinx: The Question of the Use of Gas in the Planned Invasion of Japan," *Journal of Strategic Studies*, Sept. 1989, 303–323.

Niedermair, John C. "As I Recall . . . Designing the LST," U.S. Naval Institute *Proceedings*, Nov. 1982, 58–59.

Pape, Robert A. "Why Japan Surrendered," *International Security*, Fall 1983, 154–201.

Perras, Galen Roger. "Eyes on the Northern Route to Japan: Plans for Canadian Participation in an Invasion of the Kurile Islands—A Study in Coalition Warfare and Civil-Military Relationships," *War & Society*, May 1990, 100–117.

Pineau, Capt. Roger, USN (Ret.). "Okinawa," *History of the Second World War* (England, 1974), 2465–2470.

Powell, John W., Jr. "Japan's Biological Weapons: 1930–1945, A Hidden Chapter in History," *Bulletin of the Atomic Scientists*, Oct. 1981, 44–53.

Reischauer, Edwin O. "Hiroshima Bomb Saved Japan from a Worse Fate," *The Boston Globe*, Aug. 30, 1983, 21.

Sledge, Eugene B. "Peleliu: A Neglected Battle," *Marine Corps Gazette*, Nov. 1979, 88–95; Dec. 1979, 28–41; Jan. 1980, 32–42.

Walker, J. Samuel. "The Decision to Use the Bomb: A Historiographical Update," *Diplomatic History*, 1990, 14(1): 97–114.

Yokoi, Rear Adm. Toshiyuki, IJN. "Kamikazes and the Okinawa Campaign," U.S. Naval Institute *Proceedings*, May 1954, 504–513.

Yoshida, Mitsuru. "The End of the *Yamato*," U.S. Naval Institute *Proceedings*, Feb. 1952, 117–129.

OFFICIAL REPORTS

Allied Translator and Interpreter Service, South West Pacific Area, 29 March 1945. [Intelligence] Research Report No. 65 (Supplement No. 1), (MacArthur Archives).

Chapin, Capt. John C., USMCR (Ret.). "Breaching the Marianas: The Battle for Saipan," Marines in World War II Commemorative Series (Washington, D.C.: History and Museums Division, Headquarters, U.S. Marine Corps, 1944).

Ellis, Earl H. "Advanced Base Operations in Micronesia," Operations Plan 712-H (Marine Corps Schools, Quantico, Va.).

Foreign Relations of the United States, "The Conference of Berlin," 1945, vol. II. Washington: U.S. Government Printing Office, 1960.

General Headquarters, Far East Command, Military Intelligence Section, General Staff. *Report to the Throne, Report on the Outline of the Operational Plans of the Imperial Army and Navy, January 1945*. OCMH, Special Staff, U.S. Army Historical Manuscript File. Translation of Japanese Documents, vol. I, Document Number 47747. Translated by Allied Translator and Interpreter Service (CMH).

General Headquarters (Japanese Imperial General Staff), Army Division. "Decree of Homeland Decisive Battle," Tokyo, April 20, 1945.

———. "The People's Handbook of Resistance Combat," Tokyo, April 1945.

"Japanese Atrocities—Reports by Escaped Prisoners," Memorandum from the Chief of Staff, U.S. Army to the Joint Chiefs of Staff, 17 Sept. 1943 (National Archives).

Military Intelligence Service, War Department General Staff. "Enemy Casualties by Campaigns," Intelligence Research Project 2112-A (National Archives).

Morgan, Lt. Col. Henry G., Jr., USA. *Planning the Defeat of Japan: A Study of Total War Strategy.* Washington, D.C.: OCMH [n.d.].

OCMH, Special Staff, U.S. Army Historical Manuscript File, *Military Situation in the Far East.* Translation of Japanese Documents, vol. I. Historical Manuscript File: Translation of Japanese Documents, vol. I (CMH).

———. Statement by Amano, Masakazu. Statements of Japanese Officials on World War II (English translations) (CMH).

———. Statement by Lt. Col. Taro Nakamoto, 28 July 1947. Interrogations of Japanese Officials on World War II (English translations) (CMH).

Office of the Secretary of War, "Memorandum for the Commanding General, Army Air Forces," from Brig. Gen. Thomas D. White, Assistant Chief of Air Staff, Intelligence, to Secretary, 23 May 1944 (National Archives).

Rosenberg, Max. *The Air Force and the National Guided Missile Program, 1944–1950.* Washington, D.C.: U.S. Air Force, Historical Division Liaison Office, June 1964.

Supreme Allied Commander [Japan], General Staff. *Reports of Gen. MacArthur,* 4 vols. Tokyo, 1950.

U.S. Army Japan/U.S. Army Forces Far East, Headquarters. Japanese Monograph No. 17, "Homeland Operations Record" (includes Nos. 17–20).

———. Japanese Monograph No. 45, "History of the Imperial General Headquarters, Army Section (Revised Edition)."

U.S. Department of Defense. "The Entry of the Soviet Union into the War Against Japan," 1955.

U.S. Department of State. *Foreign Relations of the United States, The Conference of Berlin (The Potsdam Conference) 1945,* 2 vols. Washington, D.C.: Government Printing Office, 1960.

U.S. Strategic Bombing Survey volumes: *Campaigns of the Pacific War, Japan's Struggle to End the War, Summary Report (Pacific War), The Effects of the Atomic Bombs on Hiroshima and Nagasaki.* Washington, D.C.: Government Printing Office, 1946; various other strategic bombing reports and survey volumes.

UNPUBLISHED MANUSCRIPTS

Baldwin, Ben R., Alfred J. Bingham, and Paul W. Pritchard. "History of the Chemical Warfare Service in World War II (1 July 1940–15 Aug. 1945)," vol. VI, "Readiness for Gas Warfare in the Theaters of Operations." Historical Section, Office of the Chief of Chemical Corps (CMH). Top-secret pages removed.

Brophy, Leo P., Wyndham D. Miles, and Rexmond C. Cochrane. "The United States Army in World War II. Technical Services. The Chemical War Service from Laboratory to Field," Department of the Army, 1959.

Gilmore, Allison B. "In the Wake of Winning Armies: Allied Psychological Warfare Against the Imperial Japanese Army in the Southwest Pacific during WWII," Ph.D. dissertation, Ohio State University, 1989.

OCMH. "Medical Service in the Asiatic and Pacific Theaters," chapter XV, "From Olympic to Blacklist" (manuscript in archives of CMH).

Sviatov, Rear Adm. Ivan, Soviet Navy (Ret.). "Ships and People" (unpublished memoirs). Chapter entitled "Monsoon Landing Operation." Sviatov was in command of Soviet cruisers and destroyers in the Pacific at the end of the war.

Truman, Harry S. Handwritten notes on sessions at Yalta, July 25, 1945 (Truman Library).

U.S. Marine Corps. V Amphibious Corps, Headquarters, "Detailed Order of Battle VAC Area," 30 Nov. 1945. [Detailed Japanese order of battle for Sixteenth Army Area.]

Vander Linde, Dean Marvin. "'Downfall': The American Plans for the Invasion of Japan in World War II," M.A. thesis, Michigan State University, 1987.

Wolfe, John A. "Engineer Intelligence Division in the War in the Pacific 1944 to 1945" [n.d.].

ACKNOWLEDGMENTS

The authors are in debt to many individuals, institutions, and organizations for assistance in writing this book. The following individuals gave of their time and knowledge to help us.

We wish to express special thanks for the help from men on both sides who would probably have participated in the invasion of Japan: Kiyochi Aikawa; Paul I. Andrews; Wade P. Bettis; William T. Clark; James Martin Davis; Douglas Dies; Robert A. Fleming; the late Gen. Minoru Genda, Japanese Air Self-Defense Force (Ret.); Whitmal W. Hill; Brig. Gen. J.D. Hittle, U.S. Marine Corps (Ret.); Harvey Katz; William Leasure; Paul J. Limm; Raymond E. Logan; Rudy Malkin; James M. Morley; Grayford C. Payne; Arlo B. Roth; Sadao Seno; William Troy; Jackson S. Wallace; Lyndolph Ward; John A. Wolfe; Jiro Yoshida; and Ted Zahn.

We received a great deal of assistance from the dedicated men and women of the National Archives in Washington, D.C. We wish to particularly thank John Taylor, the fount of all knowledge about World War II and a living American treasure, Edward Reese, Sandy Smith, Victoria Washington, and Wilbert Mahoney. At the Douglas MacArthur Memorial Archives and Library in Norfolk, Virginia, we received courteous and knowledgeable assistance from archivist Edward J. Boone and his most helpful assistant, James W. Zobel.

Our thanks also go to Guy Aceto, art director, *Air Force Magazine;* Dr. Dean Allard, director of U.S. Naval History; Dennis Bilger of the Harry S. Truman Library; Amy Cantin, archivist, Marine Corps Historical Center (MCHC); Dr. Don Carter, Center of Military History (CMH); Bernard F. Cavalcante, Naval History Center (NHC); John Correll, editor in chief, *Air Force Magazine;* Robert Cowley, editor of *Military History Quarterly;* Penny Daly, finder of hard-to-find books; James David of the Advisory Committee on Human Radiation Experiments; Lee Davidson, chief Washington correspondent for the *Deseret News,* Utah; Pearlie M. Draughn, librarian, Air Force Association; Dr. Edward J. Drea, chief of research and analysis division, CMH; Kensuke Ebata, Japanese journalist; Russell Egnor, head of still photography, U.S. Navy Office of Information; Kate Farris, Russian translator; Benis M. Frank, chief historian, MCHC; Col. John Greenwood, USMC (Ret.), editor,

Marine Corps Gazette; Dr. Richard P. Hallion, Chief of Air Force History; Dr. Sheldon H. Harris, historian; Grace Person Hayes, historian; Dr. John E. Haynes, Library of Congress; Joyce Hudson, archivist, MCHC; Hiroshi Iwai, veteran of the Imperial Japanese Navy; Paul Kemp, Imperial War Museum, London; and the late Capt. Roger Pineau, U.S. Navy (Ret.).

Also, Kathy Lloyd, NHC; Professor Robert Love, History Department, U.S. Naval Academy; Helen MacDonald of the Nimitz Museum; Sidney S. McMath, former governor of Arkansas and retired Marine Corps general; Peter M. Mersky, naval aviation historian; Ella Nargele, NHC; Col. Brooke Nihart, USMC (Ret.), former director, Marine Corps Museums; Ambassador Paul Nitze, a director of the U.S. Strategic Bombing Survey and author of the USSBS report *The Effects of the Atomic Bombs on Hiroshima and Nagasaki;* Ivar Oswalt, specialist on battle simulation; Dr. Diane T. Putney, of Air Force History; Capt. 1st Rank Boris I. Rodionov (Ret.), Russian naval historian; Dr. Frank N. Schubert, historian, Office of the Joint Chiefs of Staff; James P. Stevenson, aviation historian; Mary Beth Straight, U.S. Naval Institute; Capt. 1st Rank George I. Sviatov (Ret.), Russian naval historian; David Westheimer, novelist and potential Operation Olympic warrior; and Mrs. Stanley T. Wray, who provided information about her late husband's bomber command.

Thanks also to Eric Wertheim, our senior researcher; to researchers Annie Harris, Joseph Rhinewine, Miya Rhinewine, and Constance Allen Witte; and to our translators, Kanuobu Horiuchi and Rumiko Sakai.

In Japan, we wish to express our thanks to those who helped at the National Institute for Defense Studies in Tokyo: Capt. Teruaki Kawano (Japanese Maritime Self-Defense Force, Ret.) and Capt. Shin Itonaga, JMSDF (Ret.). At the Historical Research Institute in Tokyo, we wish to thank Todaka Kazushige, Rear Adm. Tadashi Tajiri, JMSDF (Ret.), and Masaharu Yamamoto. In both Tokyo and on Kyushu, members of the Zero Fighter Pilots Association provided help and interviews, especially Jiro Yoshida. Translations and invaluable research assistance was provided by Miwa Munehiro and Kunio Kadowaki. At the joint U.S. Navy–JMSDF base at Yokosuka, help was given by Capt. K. Greg Kouta, JMSDF chief liaison officer, and Curtis D. Carey, U.S. Navy public affairs officer.

As always, we are in debt to Roger MacBride Allen for periodic editorial guidance and computer doctoring and to Michael Polmar for demonstrating his computer expertise when needed.

Finally, we wish to acknowledge the labors of our editors, Fred Hills and Burton Beals. They helped us greatly, Fred by his suggestions on the structure and thrust of the book, Burton for providing his editorial skills and good sense, paragraph by paragraph—and often sentence by sentence. Fred's assistants, Laureen Connelly Rowland and Hilary Black, kept our efforts on track and were always helpful.

INDEX

[Ranks indicated are the highest used in the text]

Picture Credits

Page